# THE FRENCH WARS OF RELIGION

## DOCUMENTS IN HISTORY SERIES

General Editor: Jeremy Black

*Published titles*

DOCUMENTS ON EUROPEAN UNION
Edited and translated by A. G. Harryvan and J. van der Harst

DOCUMENTS ON THE LATER CRUSADES, 1274–1580
Edited and translated by Norman Housley

THE OCCULT IN EARLY MODERN EUROPE:
A DOCUMENTARY HISTORY
Edited and translated by P. G. Maxwell-Stuart

DOCUMENTS ON THE CONTINENTAL REFORMATION
Edited and translated by William G. Naphy

THE FRENCH WARS OF RELIGION: SELECTED DOCUMENTS
Edited and translated by David Potter

DOCUMENTS ON THE FRENCH REVOLUTION OF 1848
Edited by Roger Price

---

**Documents in History**

**Series Standing Order**
**ISBN 0–333–71698–1 hardcover**
**ISBN 0–333–69340–X paperback**
(outside North America only)

You can receive future titles in this series as they are published by placing a standing order. Please contact your bookseller or, in the case of difficulty, write to us at the address below with your name and address, the title of the series and the ISBN quoted above.

Customer Services Department, Macmillan Distribution Ltd
Houndmills, Basingstoke, Hampshire RG21 6XS, England

---

# The French Wars of Religion

**Selected Documents**

Edited and translated by David Potter

First published 1997 by
MACMILLAN PRESS LTD
Houndmills, Basingstoke, Hampshire RG21 6XS
and London
Companies and representatives
throughout the world

ISBN-13:978-0-333-64799-8 paperback
ISBN-10:0-333-64799-8 paperback
ISBN-13:978-0-333-64798-1 hardback
ISBN-10:0-333-64798-X hardback

A catalogue record for this book is available
from the British Library.

This book is printed on paper suitable for recycling and
made from fully managed and sustained forest sources.
Logging, pulping and manufacturing processes are
expected to conform to the environmental regulations
of the country of origin.

Printed and bound in Great Britain by
CPI Antony Rowe, Chippenham and Eastbourne

Published in the United States of America 1997 by
ST. MARTIN'S PRESS, INC.
Scholarly and Reference Division
175 Fifth Avenue, New York, N.Y. 10010

ISBN 0-312-17545-0

# Contents

## Chapter Five: The Era of the Saint Bartholomew Massacre          122

# List of Maps

# Notes on the Text

**Money**

Coins in circulation, like the *écu* and the *teston*, were given a face value in 'money of account' called the *livre tournois* (*lt.*), divided into 20 *sols*, each *sol* divided into 12 *deniers*. The pattern is like the old sterling pound, shillings and pence except that the French 'pound' or *livre* was worth about 2/2d sterling (in 1568). The main gold coin, the *écu d'or soleil*, was fixed at 60 *sols* or 3 *livres* in 1574. From 1578 to 1602, the *livre tournois* (*lt.*) was replaced as money of account by the *écu*.

**Dates**

From 1567, the old 'paschal year' that began on Easter Sunday was replaced by the 'Roman year' that began on 1 January. The Gregorian Calendar was introduced into France in 1582, so that 9 December was followed by 20th in that year.

**Translation and usages**

Certain usages such as *ledit* for 'the said' have been cut. Titles have been translated to their English equivalent ('duke of') but offices are rendered with their French particle ('Constable de'). *Monsieur* is rendered in a number of ways. As a title, for instance *Monsieur l'Amiral*, it becomes 'my Lord Admiral'. As a term of address it becomes 'Sir', and as part of a name, just 'M. de. . .'. The term *la Religion Prétendue Réformée* is often shortened to RPR and this is retained. *La Religion Catholique Apostolique et Romaine* is simply rendered 'Catholic'. All translations are my own, except in a small number of cases, for example some royal edicts or princely declarations, when I have reproduced a contemporary English printed translation. I must acknowledge the help of Dr Peter Laven in dealing with some of the more tortuous Italian texts.

**Notes on persons**

Brief biographical details on individuals mentioned in the text will be found in the Index.

# List of Abbreviations

| | |
|---|---|
| *AC* | *Archives curieuses de l'histoire de France*, ed. L. Cimber and F. Danjou, 30 vols (Paris, 1834–49) |
| AD | Archives départementales |
| *ADE* | *Archivo Documental Español: Negociaciones con Francia*, 9 vols (Madrid: Real Academia de Historia, 1950–4) |
| AM | Archives municipales |
| AN | Archives nationales, Paris |
| AGS | Archivo General, Simancas, Series Estado, incl. K 1493–1567, Spanish ambassadors in France (microfilm in AN) |
| *ANG* | *Acta Nuntiaturae Gallicae: Correspondance des nonces en France* (Univ. Pontificale and École française de Rome), 14 vols (1961– ) |
| Aubigné | Agrippa d'Aubigné, *Histoire universelle*, ed. A. de Ruble, 10 vols (Paris, 1886–1909) |
| Aumale | Henri d'Orléans, duc d'Aumale, *Histoire des princes de Condé*, 8 vols (Paris, 1863–96) |
| Baguenault | G. Baguenault de Puchesse, *Jean de Morvillier, évêque d'Orléans et garde des sceaux de France* (Paris, 1870) |
| Bernard | A. Bernard (ed.), *Procès-verbaux des états généraux de 1593* (Paris: CDI, 1842) |
| *Biron* | *Letters and Documents of Armand de Gontaut, Baron de Biron, Marshal of France, 1524–92*, ed. S. H. Ehrman and J. W. Thompson, 2 vols (Berkeley, CA, 1936) |
| BL | British Library |
| BM | Bibliothèque municipale |
| BN | Bibliothèque Nationale, Paris |

| | |
|---|---|
| Brantôme | Pierre de Bourdeilles de Brantôme, *Oeuvres complètes*, ed. L. Lalanne, 12 vols (Paris: SHF, 1864–96) |
| *Breunot* | *Journal de Gabriel Breunot, conseiller au Parlement de Dijon*, ed. J. Garnier, Analecta Divionensia, vols 1–3 (Dijon, 1866) |
| *BSHPF* | *Bulletin de la Société de l'Histoire du Protestantisme Français.* |
| Buchon | J. A. C. Buchon, *Choix de chroniques et mémoires sur l'histoire de France, Panthéon littéraire. Littérature française. Histoire*, 20 vols (Paris, 1836–40) |
| Burel | *Mémoires de Jean Burel. Journal d'un bourgeois du Puy à l'époque des guerres de religion*, ed. A. Chassaing, new edn (Saint-Vidal, 1983) |
| Cabié, *Ambassade* | E. Cabié (ed.), *Ambassade en Espagne de Jean Ebrard de Saint-Sulpice, 1562–1565* (Albi, 1903) |
| Cabié, *Guerres* | E. Cabié, (ed.), *Les Guerres de religion dans le sud-ouest de la France et principalement dans le Quercy, d'après les papiers des seigneurs de Saint-Sulpice, de 1561 à 1590* (Paris and Albi, 1906) |
| Callières | J. de Callières, *Histoire du maréchal de Matignon* (Paris, 1661) |
| *Carorguy* | *Mémoires de Jacques Carorguy, greffier de Bar-sur-Seine (1582–1595)*, ed. E. Bruwaert (Paris, 1880) |
| *Castelnau* | *Les mémoires de Messire Michel de Castelnau* (1621), M&P, 1st series, vol. 9 (Paris, 1836); see also Le Laboureur |
| CDI | Collection de documents inédits sur l'histoire de France |
| Combes | F. Combes, *L'Entrevue de Bayonne de 1565* (Paris, 1882) |
| Croze | J. de Croze, *Les Guises, les Valois et Philippe II*, 2 vols (Paris, 1866) |
| Desjardins | A. Desjardins (ed.), *Négociations diplomatiques de la France avec la Toscane*, 6 vols (Paris, 1859–86) |
| Devyver | A. Devyver, *Le Sang épuré. Les Préjugés de race chez les gentilshommes français de l'Ancien Régime (1560–1720)* (Brussels, 1973) |
| Digges | Sir Dudley Digges, *The Compleat Ambassador* (London, 1655) |

| | |
|---|---|
| Douais, *Fourquevaux* | C. Douais (ed.), *Les Guerres de religion en Languedoc d'après les papiers du baron de Fourquevaux, Annales du Midi, IV & V* (Toulouse, 1892–3) |
| Dumont | Jean Dumont, *Corps universel diplomatique du droit des gens*, 8 vols (The Hague, 1726–31) |
| *Fénelon* | *Correspondance diplomatique de Bertrand de Salignac de La Mothe Fénelon, ambassadeur de France en Angleterre*, ed. C. P. Cooper and A. Teulet, 7 vols (Paris and London, 1838–40) |
| Franklin, *Journal* | J. Franklin, *Journal du siège de Paris en 1590* (repr. 1977) |
| Fontanon | A. Fontanon, *Les Edicts et ordonnances des Rois de France*, 4 vols (Paris, 1611) |
| Gaches, *Mémoires* | Jacques Gaches, *Mémoires sur les guerres de religion à Castres et dans le Languedoc, 1555–1610*, ed. C. Pradel (Paris, 1879) |
| Garnier, *Dijon* | J. Garnier (ed.), *Correspondance de la Mairie de Dijon extraite des archives de cette ville*, 3 vols (Dijon, 1868–70) |
| *Gouberville* | *Le Journal du Sire de Gouberville*, ed. A. de Blangy, abbé Tollemer and E. Robillard de Beaurepaire, centenary reprint of original edition, in 4 vols (Bricqueboscq, 1993–4) |
| Goulart, *Charles IX* | S. Goulart, *Mémoires de l'estat de France sous Charles IX*, 3 vols (Middleburg, 1577) |
| Goulart, *Ligue* | [S. Goulart], *Mémoires de la Ligue, contenant les événements les plus remarquables depuis 1576 jusqu'à la paix . . . en 1598*, new edn, 6 vols (Amsterdam, 1758) |
| Griffiths | G. Griffiths, *Representative Government in Western Europe in the Sixteenth Century* (Oxford, 1968) |
| Guise | François de Lorraine, duc de Guise, *Mémoires–journaux*, ed. M&P, 1st series, vol. 6 (Paris, 1850), pp. 1–539 |
| Haton | Claude Haton, *Mémoires contenant le récit des événements accomplis de 1553 à 1587*, ed. F. Bourquelot, 2 vols (Paris, 1857) |
| *HE* | *Histoire ecclésiastique des églises réformées du royaume de France* (T. de Bèze), ed. G. Baum and E. Cunitz, 3 vols (Paris, 1883–9) |

| | |
|---|---|
| *Histoire Auvergne* | *L'Histoire vue de l'Auvergne*, ed. A. G. Manry, R. Sève and M. Chaulanges, 3 vols (Clermont-Ferrand, 1955–59) |
| Hotman, *Tigre* | François Hotman, *Le Tigre de 1560*, ed. C. Read (Paris, 1875; repr. Geneva, 1970) |
| *IS* | *Inventaire sommaire* [of departmental or communal archives] |
| Isambert | F. A. Isambert, *Recueil général des anciennes lois françaises*, 29 vols (Paris, 1822–33) |
| Julien Blauf | Julien Blauf, *Histoire*, ed. A. Serre, as *Issoire pendant les Guerres de Religion. Chronique des temps d'épouvante* (Clermont-Ferrand, 1977) |
| La Ferrière, *Les Valois* | H. de La Ferrière-Percy, *Le XVIe siècle et les Valois d'après les documents inédits du British Museum* (Paris, 1879) |
| La Fosse | Jean de La Fosse, *Journal d'un curé ligueur de Paris sous les trois derniers Valois, suivi du Journal du secrétaire Philippe du Bec, archévêque de Reims, de 1588 à 1605*, ed. E. de Barthélemy (Paris, 1866) |
| Lalourcé and Duval | C. Lalourcé and Duval, *Recueil de pièces originales . . . concernant la tenue des Etats-généraux*, 4 vols (Paris, 1789) |
| La Place | P. de La Place, *Commentaires de l'estat de la religion et république* (1565), ed. J. A. C. Buchon, vol. 16 |
| La Planche | Regnier de La Planche, *Histoire de l'estat de France . . . sous le règne de François II* (1576), ed. J. A. C. Buchon, vol. 16 |
| La Popelinière | Lancelot du Voisin, sieur de La Popelinière, *Histoire de France, enrichie des plus notables occurances survenues ez Provinces de l'Europe & pays voisins*, 2 vols (La Rochelle, 1581) |
| *LCM* | *Lettres de Catherine de Médicis*, ed. H. de La Ferrière-Percy, J. Baguenault de Puchesse, and A. Lesort, 11 vols (Paris: CDI, 1880–1943) |
| Le Laboureur | *Mémoires de Michel de Castelnau, seigneur de La Mauvissière, illustrez et augmentez de plusieurs commentaires et manuscrits*, ed. J. Le Laboureur, 3 vols (Paris, 1731) |
| L'Estoile | Pierre de L'Estoile, *Journal pour le règne de Henri III (1574–1589)*, ed. L. R. Lefèvre (Paris, 1943) |

| | |
|---|---|
| *LH3* | *Lettres de Henri III roi de France*, ed. P. Champion, M. François and H. Zuber, 4 vols (Paris, 1959–84) |
| L'Hospital | Michel de l'Hospital, *Discours pour la majorité de Charles IX et trois autres discours*, ed. R. Descimon (Paris, 1993) |
| *LMH4* | *Receuil de lettres missives de Henri IV*, ed. Berger de Xivrey and J. Guadet, 9 vols (Paris: CDI, 1843–76) |
| Loutchitsky | Jean Loutchitsky, *Documents inédits pour servir à l'histoire de la Réforme et de la Ligue* (Kiev, 1875) |
| Lublinskaya | A. D. Lublinskaya, *Documents pour servir à l'histoire des guerres civiles en France (1561–63)* (Moscow, 1962) |
| Lucinge, *Ligue* | R. de Lucinge, *Lettres sur les débuts de la Ligue (1585)*, ed. A. Dufour (Paris, Geneva, 1964) |
| Lucinge, *Cour* | R. de Lucinge, *Lettres sur la cour de Henri III en 1586*, ed. A. Dufour (Geneva, 1966) |
| Lucinge, *1587* | R. de Lucinge, *Lettres de 1587. L'année des reîtres*, ed. J. J. Supple (Paris, Geneva, 1994) |
| Lucinge, *Miroir* | R. de Lucinge, *Le Miroir des princes ou grands de France*, ed. A. Dufour, *Annuaire-bulletin de la Société de l'Histoire de France*, 1954–5, pp. 95–186 |
| Martin | W. Martin, *La Saint-Barthélemy devant le Sénat de Venise. Relation des ambassadeurs Giovanni Michiel et Sigismondo Cavalli* (Paris, 1872) |
| Mayer | C. J. Mayer (ed.), *Des États Généraux et autres assemblées nationales*, 18 vols (The Hague, 1788–9) |
| *MC* | *Mémoires de Condé ou Recueil pour servir à l'histoire de France*, ed. D. F. Secousse, 6 vols (London: The Hague, 1743) |
| *MC*, M&P | *Mémoires de Louis de Bourbon, prince de Condé. Recueil des choses mémorables faites et passées pour le faict de la religion et estat de ce royaume depuis la mort du roy Henri II jusqu'en l'année 1564* (basic text), ed. M&P, 1st series, vol. 6 (Paris, 1850), pp. 545–711 |
| *Millau* | *Mémoires d'un Calviniste de Millau, publiés d'après le manuscrit original*, ed. J.-L. Rigal, *Archives historiques du Rouergue*, II (Rodez, 1911) |

| | |
|---|---|
| Monluc | Blaise de Monluc, *Commentaires et lettres*, ed. A. de Ruble, 5 vols (Paris: SHF, 1864–72) |
| *Mornay* | *Mémoires et correspondance de Duplessis Mornay*, 12 vols (Paris, 1824–5) |
| M&P | J. F. Michaud and J. J. F. Poujoulat, *Nouvelle collection de mémoires pour servir à l'histoire de France*, 32 vols (Paris, Lyon, 1836–9) |
| Nevers | Louis de Gonzague, duc de Nevers, *Mémoires de M. le duc de Nevers*, ed. J. Cusson, 2 pts (Paris, 1665) |
| Noailles | E. H. V. de Noailles, *Henri de Valois et la Pologne en 1572*, 3 vols (Paris, 1867) |
| Palma Cayet | *Chronologie novenaire*, ed. Buchon, vols 21–2 |
| Paris, *Négociations* | L. Paris (ed.), *Négociations, lettres et pièces diverses relatives au règne de François II. Tirées du portefeuille de Sébastien de l'Aubespine, évêque de Limoges* (Paris: CDI, 1841) |
| Paschal | Pierre de Paschal, *Journal de ce qui s'est passé en France durant l'année 1562*, ed. M. François (Paris: SHF, 1950) |
| Pasquier, *Lettres hist.* | Estienne Pasquier, *Lettres historiques pour les années 1556–1594*, ed. D. Thickett (Geneva, 1966) |
| Pasquier, *Recherches* | Estienne Pasquier, *Les Recherches de France*, in *Œuvres*, 2 vols (Amsterdam, 1723) |
| Prarond | E. Prarond, *La Ligue à Abbeville, 1576–94*, 3 vols (Mémoires de la Société d'Émulation d'Abbeville, 1868, 1873) |
| *Registres, Paris* | *Histoire générale de Paris. Collection de documents. Registres des délibérations du bureau de la ville de Paris*, ed. A. Tuety, F. Bonnardot and P. Guérin, 18 vols (Paris, 1883–1953) |
| *RH* | *Revue historique* |
| Sassetti | J. Tedeschi, 'Tomasso Sassetti's Account of the St Bartholomew's Day Massacre', in A. Soman (ed.), *The Massacre of Saint Bartholomew, Reappraisals and Documents* (The Hague, 1974), pp. 99–152 |
| SHF | Société de l'Histoire de France (publications of) |
| SP | Public Record Office, London, State Paper series |

| | |
|---|---|
| *STC* | *A Short-Title Catalogue of Books Printed in England, Scotland and Ireland and of English Books Printed Abroad, 1475–1640*, ed. A. Pollard and G. Redgrave, 2nd edn, revised (London, 1986–91) |
| Stegman | A. Stegman, *Les Édits des guerres de religion* (Paris, 1979) |
| Sully | Maximilien de Béthune, marquis de Rosny, duc de Sully, *Les Œconomies royales*, ed. D. Buisseret, B. Barbiche, 2 vols (Paris: SHF, 1970–88) |
| *Tavannes* | Jean de Saulx, *Mémoires de très-noble et très illustre Gaspard de Saulx, seigneur de Tavannes*, ed. Buchon, vol. 14, pp. 1–491 [partly apocryphal, first pub. 1620] |
| Thierry | A. Thierry, *Recueil des monuments inédits de l'histoire du Tiers-État. Ière série, région du Nord*, 4 vols (Paris: CDI, 1856–70) |
| De Thou | J. A. de Thou, *Histoire universelle*, trans. P. du Ryer, 3 vols (Paris, 1659); 16 vols (London, 1734) |
| Tommaseo | N. Tommaseo (ed.), *Relations des ambassadeurs vénitiens sur les affaires de France au XVIe siècle*, 2 vols (Paris: CDI, 1838) |
| Vaissette | Dom J. Vaissette and Dom C. Devic, *Histoire générale de Languedoc, avec des notes et les pièces justificatives*, 15 vols (Toulouse, 1872–93) |
| Valois | C. Valois (ed.), *Histoire de la Ligue* (Paris: SHF, 1914) |
| Villeroy | Nicolas de Neufville, sr. de Villeroy, *Mémoires d'estat*, 4 vols (Paris, 1622–6); M&P, vol. 11 |
| Weiss | C. Weiss (ed.), *Papiers d'état du cardinal de Granvelle, d'après les manuscrits de la Bibliothèque de Besançon*, 9 vols (Paris: CDI, 1841–52) |

# Possible claimants to the throne, 1589

## House of Valois-Angoulême

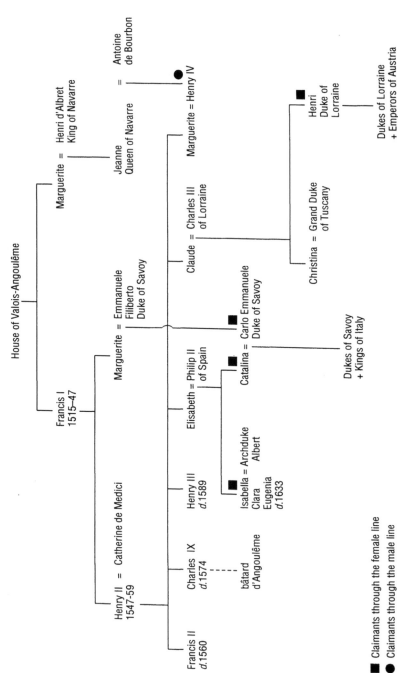

Claimants through the female line

● Claimants through the male line

# THE BOURBONS: Senior princes of the blood from 1527

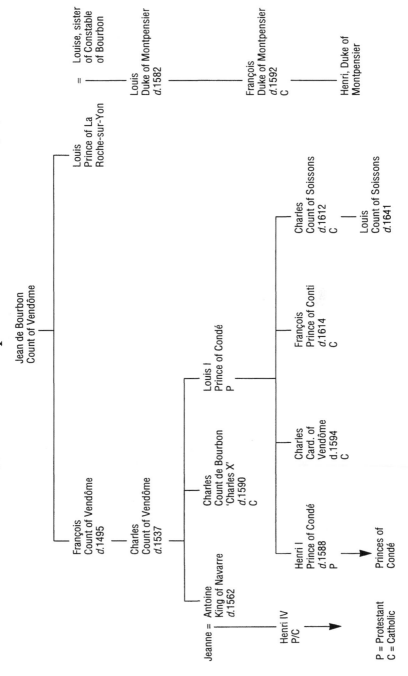

Jean de Bourbon
Count of Vendôme

François
Count of Vendôme
*d.*1495

Charles
Count of Vendôme
*d.*1537

Louis
Prince of La
Roche-sur-Yon

= Louise, sister
of Constable
of Bourbon

Louis
Duke of Montpensier
*d.*1582

François
Duke of Montpensier
*d.*1592
C

Henri, Duke of
Montpensier

Antoine
King of Navarre
*d.*1562

Jeanne =

Charles
Count de Bourbon
'Charles X'
*d.*1590
C

Louis I
Prince of Condé
P

Henri I
Prince of Condé
*d.*1588
P

Charles
Card. of
Vendôme
*d.*1594
C

François
Prince of Conti
*d.*1614
C

Charles
Count of Soissons
*d.*1612
C

Henri IV
P/C

Princes of
Condé

Louis
Count of Soissons
*d.*1641

P = Protestant
C = Catholic

# Claims to descent from the Carolingian House

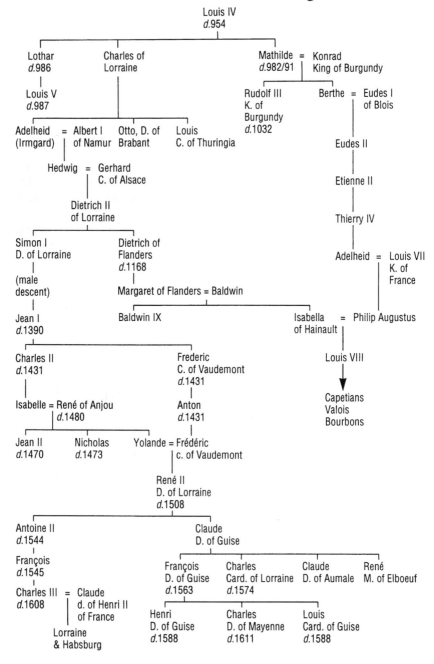

# Introduction

This body of translated documents represents roughly half the volume of texts originally assembled for study of the subject. It is therefore the result of some rigorous selection in which the criteria of general importance, centrality and usefulness to students have been decisive. Inevitably some important topics including a chapter on Henry III's reforms (1577–83) had to be set aside, though it is hoped without too much damage.

One of the objectives has been to make a range of documents accessible for study to students whose knowledge of French would not otherwise enable them to read them with confidence. A word is perhaps in order about the general range of primary sources on the French Wars of Religion available in English and with which I have tried to avoid overlap. The English were profoundly influenced by the course of the Civil Wars in France, which, according to taste, they saw as a great battle between the forces of good and evil or a severe threat to the security of their country. It is unsurprising, therefore, that there was a market for books and pamphlets about contemporary French events, including translations of newsletters, accounts of major events such as the Massacre of Saint Bartholomew and, perhaps more surprisingly, translations of key legal and constitutional documents which had some bearing on the conflict.[1] These in themselves form an interesting corpus in the history of translation and have been used here where appropriate.

The English government was naturally seriously concerned by events across the Channel, and the reports of its ambassadors and agents have long been considered a prime source by historians. The bulk of this material in the Public Records Office is available to readers in variable summary form down to 1589 in the *Calendar of State Papers, Foreign*.[2] Documents used here are transcribed from the originals. It should also be remembered that the equally important material in the British Library (Harleian, Lansdowne, Cotton collections) should be consulted in MS. In addition to this, some bodies of reports have been published separately – notably: many of the despatches of Nicholas Throckmorton and Henry Killigrew for 1559–63, published by Forbes;[3] Walsingham's reports from France in 1570–2 in Digges;[4] those of Henry Unton, 1591–2, and Thomas Edmondes, 1592–9, both published by the Roxburghe Club.[5] Together, these form a valuable source of easily accessible evidence on events in France in that period.

As for other ambassadors of the period, in France, the most accessible materials in English are those summarised in the *Calendars of State Papers, Venetian* and *Spanish*,[6] which often contain documents emanating from the embassies in France. The despatches of Michele Suriano and Marc'Antonio Barbaro for 1561–2 were translated by Layard.[7] Some of the Relations of Venetian ambassadors in France have also been translated into English.[8]

Other collections of sources available in English include important or influential memoirs. Among the most useful are excerpts from the Parisian journal of Pierre de L'Estoile, edited by N. L. Roelker.[9] This is, though, only a very small portion of the whole and the translations used here avoid duplication of Roelker's work. The important memoirs or autobiographical works available in English are those of Blaise de Monluc, available in a modern selection by I. Roy for the 1560s. A fuller English translation by Cotton was made in the Seventeenth century.[10] The memoir by Madame du Plessis Mornay of her husband's life has been translated,[11] as well as the short memoir by Agrippa d'Aubigné for his children.[12] The largely apocryphal though not uninteresting Memoirs of Marguerite de Valois – la reine Margot – have been translated.[13] Some documents on the Massacre of Saint Bartholomew, notably accounts of German soldiers who participated in it, are available in the English translation of Erlanger's work.[14]

For those interested in systematic political theory, of the major French works on political theory for the sixteenth century, English readers are now well served, from Claude de Seyssel's *La Monarchie de France* of 1516,[15] to Bodin's *Six Books of the Commonwealth*, first translated into English in 1606 but available in a modern version,[16] as well as his *Methodus* and Charles Loyseau's *Traité des ordres* of 1610.[17]

Of the controversialist literature of the monarchomach era, we have La Boétie's *Contr'un*, an attack on tyranny written about 1560 though published later,[18] and Hotman's *Franco-Gallia*.[19] Hotman's other works of the period were also translated at the time. Thus, there are sixteenth-century English versions of the *De Furoribus Gallicis*.[20] Hotman's biography of Coligny[21] and Jean de Serres's *Commentaries* were quickly translated into English and became widely read.[22] Henri Estienne's savage attack on Catherine de Medici appeared in English in 1575.[23] In a later period, the *politique Satire Ménipée* of 1594 appeared in English in 1595.[24]

Finally, the only modern compilation of documents in English is that of R. J. Knecht, which contains 18 documents, mostly not repeated here, including the text of the Edict of Nantes.[25]

## Notes

[1] A. G. Dickens, 'The Elizabethans and St. Bartholomew', in A. Soman (ed.), *The Massacre of St. Bartholomew: Reappraisals and Documents* (The Hague, 1974), pp. 52–70. For what should be

classified as public acts translated from French into English from 1562 to 1598, see *STC* 5042, 11263, 5035, 5036, 5037, 5039, 11266, 11311, 13091, 13091.5, 13092, 13093, 13096, 13098, 13098.2, 13098.5, 13098.3, 13112, 13113, 13113.5, 13114, 13116, 13116.5, 13117, 13118, 13119, 13120.

[2] *Calendar of State Papers, Foreign Series, of the Reign of Elizabeth, Preserved in the Public Record Office*, 23 vols (London, 1863–1950).

[3] P. Forbes, *A Full View of the Transactions in the Reign of Queen Elizabeth*, 2 vols (London, 1740–1).

[4] Dudley Digges, *The Compleat Ambassador* (London, 1655), translated into French as *Mémoires et instructions pour les ambassadeurs ou lettres et négociations de Walsingham* (Amsterdam, 1700).

[5] J. Stevenson (ed.), *Correspondence of Sir Henry Unton*, Roxburghe Club, 65 (London, 1847); G. Butler (ed.), *The Edmondes Papers*, Roxburghe Club, 164 (London, 1913).

[6] *Calendar of Letters and State Papers relating to English Affairs of the Reign of Queen Elizabeth, Preserved . . . in the Archives of Simancas*, 4 vols (London, 1892–9); *Calendar of State Papers and Manuscripts relating to English Affairs in the Archives and Collections of Venice*, vols 7–9 (London, 1890–7).

[7] H. Layard (ed.), *Despatches of Michele Suriano and Marc'Antonio Barbaro . . . 1560–63*, Proceedings of the Huguenot Society of London (1891).

[8] J. C. Davis (ed.), *Pursuit of Power: Venetian Ambassadors' Reports on Turkey, France and Spain in the Reign of Philip II, 1560–1600* (New York, 1970); and J. B. Ross and M. McLaughlin, *The Portable Renaissance Reader* (London, 1977), pp. 305–27.

[9] N. L. Roelker, *The Paris of Henry of Navarre, as seen by Pierre de L'Estoile* (Cambridge, MA, 1958).

[10] I. Roy (ed.), *The Habsburg–Valois Wars and the French Wars of Religion. Blaise de Monluc* (London, 1971); C. Cotton (trans.), *The Commentaries of Messire Blaize de Monluc* (London, 1674).

[11] L. Crump, *A Huguenot Family in the XVI Century: The Memoirs of Philippe de Mornay, sieur du Plessis Marly, Written by his Wife* (London: Routledge, n.d.).

[12] J. Nothnagle (ed.), *Théodore-Agrippa d'Aubigné, His Life to his Children* (Lincoln, NE, 1984).

[13] *Memoirs of Margaret de Valois, Queen of Navarre*, Court Memoirs Series (London: H. S. Nichols, 1895), based on the 1813 translation. The first English translation appeared in 1658.

[14] P. Erlanger, *Saint Bartholomew's Night: The Massacre of Saint Bartholomew* (Westport, CT: 1975)

[15] Modern text: C. de Seyssel, *La Monarchie de France*, ed. J. Poujol (Paris, 1961), trans. J. H. Hexter, *The Monarchy of France* (New Haven, CT, 1981).

[16] J. Bodin, *Les Six livres de la République* (1576), trans. R. Knolles, *The Six Bookes of a Commonweale* (London, 1606); abridged version ed. M. J. Tooley (Oxford, 1955).

[17] C. Loyseau, *A Treatise of Orders and Plain Dignities*, ed. H. A. Lloyd (Cambridge, 1994).

[18] *Anti-Dictator: The Discours sur la servitude volontaire of Étienne de La Boétie*, trans. H. Kurz (New York, 1942); first trans. into in English for T. Smith (London, 1735).

[19] First published Geneva, 1573. R. E. Giesey and J. H. Salmon (eds), *Franco-Gallia* (Cambridge, 1972).

[20] E. Varamundus [François Hotman], *De furoribus Gallicis* (Edinburgh/Basel: Guérin, 1573), translated as *A true and plaine report of the furious outrages of Fraunce* (Stirling/London: Bynneman, 1574) and reprinted in *The Harleian Miscellany*, 12 vols (London, 1808–11), vol. I, pp. 431–83.

[21] *Gasparis Colinii Castellonii, magni quondam Franciae amiralii* (Geneva: Vignon, 1575), translated as *The lyfe of the most godly, valeant and noble capteine . . . Iasper Colignie Shatilion* (London: Vautrollier, 1576), *STC* 22248.

[22] *Commentariorum de statu religionis et republicae* (1572–5), translated by Thomas Tymme as *The Three Partes of the Commentaries* (London: H. Middleton, 1574) with the *Fourth Parte* added (London: Binneman, 1576).

[23] *Discours merveilleux de la vie . . . de Catherine de Médicis, Royne mere* (Geneva: Rivery, 1575), translated as *A mervaylous discourse upon the lyfe, deedes and behaviours of Katherine de Medicis, Queen Mother* (Heidelberg/London: Middleton, 1575), *STC* 10550.

[24] *A Pleasant Satyre or Poesie, wherein is discovered the Catholicon of Spayne and the chief leaders of the League* (*STC* 15489).

[25] R. J. Knecht, *The French Wars of Religion, 1559–98* (London: 1989; rev. edn, 1995). All the parts of the Edict of Nantes are published in R. Mousnier, *The Assassination of Henry IV*, trans. J. Spencer (London, 1973), pp. 316–63.

# 1 France on the Eve of War

rance in the first half of the sixteenth century had experienced a period of growth, political expansion and stability. Beneath the surface, however, by 1560 the kingdom was becoming dangerously divided and unstable. The long period of warfare between 1551 and 1559 had seriously undermined the finances of the state. The burdens of war were all the more disruptive for an incipient economic and social malaise. In addition to this, from the 1540s the difficulties stemming from religious division and the advent of Calvinism had gradually become insoluble (see Chapter 2). The accidental death of Henry II in July 1559 precipitated a crisis in which all these problems became intertwined.

How did contemporaries try to understand the problems? Catherine de Medici, writing a letter of advice for her sons some time after the wars had begun, looked back with approval to the way Henry II and Francis I had ruled and managed their courts. For them, she claimed, due order, respect and the accessibility of the sovereign were crucial and these had been forgotten (see Document 3). As a manual of how to run the court of France, her analysis is lucid and convincing. However, one of Catherine's contemporaries, the diplomat Jean de Fraisse, provided a very different picture of the court and politics that prevailed under Henry II, arguing, in a way that has shaped the views of historians over the centuries, that the seeds of conflict were sown by the faction disputes that grew up in the 1540s and that Henry II was a weak king who let others rule for him (see Document 6). The idea that selfish politicians were latching onto a religious dispute for their own ends is an ancient one and was to be repeated constantly from the start to the end of the Wars. Ambitious and selfish grandees had grasped at religion to prosecute their objectives, the authoritarian measures of Francis II's government had been cut off by his death and things had gone to pieces. It was commonplace to take the view that a conjunction of political and religious division would have disastrous consequences.

There were many other problems in France which were converging around the year 1560 that provide the context for the power struggles resulting from royal weakness. The state during the Renaissance had been consolidated on the basis of a consensus between the crown and the nobility which allowed the latter a wide degree of autonomy while ensuring an adequate financial base for

5

the crown in its primary function: the waging of war. This in effect continued the absorption of the nobility into the pursuit of interest within the rebuilt monarchical system of the late fifteenth century. The maintenance of harmony always depended on the effective flow of patronage from the crown to the nobility and the latter's willingness to serve in war. It also crucially depended on the benign workings of the world of patronage and clientage that, with kindred and family, naturally constituted the social articulation of France from the later middle ages onward. Noble service to the crown depended heavily on an effective flow of patronage that was already coming under strain by 1560. To some extent, power was mobilised through family bonds but, though such ties were important in early modern society, they were by no means exclusive; families both high and low were divided. Linked to faction, religion or ideology, clientage could become extremely disruptive, though its exact definition was always hazy and has remained a matter of historical debate. That contemporaries were aware of the import of clientage in shaping factions and power groups is clear. From 1560, there was also an increasingly widespread debate about the basis of aristocratic privilege, the claims of blood lineage, merit, achievement and education. By its nature, clientage encompassed fierce ties of loyalty or opportunistic arrangements. Though links between nobles in the world of patronage were expressed in a discourse of honour, as the conflict developed it became clearer that necessity dictated that the search for patrons and clients would be more ruthless and self-interested.

In terms of political ideology, the aristocratic constitutionalism that was to be voiced more and more openly as the wars went on was not fully developed in 1560. Instead, the norm was the idea that the nobility of France had a central and proper place in the kingdom and owed its service to the King in return for all the bounty it received. This was a question of its honour. The theme of an ideal harmony lies behind the picture of the monarchical order on the eve of the Wars in 1561, when the count of Rochefort published his celebrated speech in the 1560 Estates-General (see Document 4). Yet another treatise responded to the threats posed by 'evil humours' that had entered society during the excessive Habsburg–Valois Wars (see Document 5).

The problem was that the ideal of harmony remained partly a fiction. The increasing propensity of the crown to act in a regulatory and authoritarian manner had, during the reign of Francis I, led to some major confrontations between the monarchy and its quintessential servants, the Parlements, which more than any other institutions had worked to impose an order of royal justice throughout the realm in the aftermath of the Hundred Years War. These conflicts were only partially assuaged by Francis I's decisive action in 1526 and were to surface again at the end of the 1550s. The thinking behind such opposition is exemplified by La Boétie's thesis on tyranny (see Document 1).

There were two main immediate reasons for discontent by 1560. One was obviously the state of religion; uniformity had not been imposed despite all the efforts over twenty years to create a system of effective control. Failure brought the authority of the crown into disrepute. The most immediate calamity, though, was the catastrophic indebtedness of the crown that resulted from the maintenance of a war-finance regime throughout the 1550s (see Document 2). Taxes had been increased, particularly on the clergy, under Henry II, which bore comparison only with the notorious later years of Louis XI. Discontent on these two themes emerges amply from any examination of the grievances voiced by the local estates that met all over France in 1560. Each region had its own preoccupations but the prevalence of disquiet over the state of the Church and discontent over taxation are the common threads.

The rapid spread of Protestantism in France at the end of the 1550s coincided with a crisis of authority in the state when Henri II died, as a result of wounds in a jousting accident, on 10 July 1559. His successor, Francis II, was 15 and had therefore attained his majority. This view of the king's majority was only seriously challenged by Protestants (some of whom even argued that a king had to be 25 to rule with full authority) but the King's majority was generally recognised and cogently advanced by the lawyer Jean du Tillet. However, it did transpire that Francis was in practice too young to rule for himself. The consequence was that there was no regency, but that power effectively passed into the hands of his wife's, Mary Stuart's, uncles, the duke of Guise and the cardinal of Lorraine. Guise and Lorraine had exercised wide power in the year between the Constable de Montmorency's defeat at Saint-Quentin in 1557 and his return from captivity in the following year. They could therefore build on the position of influence they had already acquired. The position was unwelcome to Catherine de Medici, the King's mother, but she had to accept reality.

The eighteen-month reign of Francis II saw a growing sense of physical insecurity. Most ominously, there was an intersection of aristocratic faction and the religious divide. The princes of the blood who felt they had most claim to authority, Antoine, King of Navarre, and his brother the prince of Condé, were attracted towards the reformed religion, while their Coligny cousins, nephews to the Constable, were already seriously involved in the new faith. It has become one of the enduring clichés of French history that the aristocratic world was dominated by three great factions: the Guises, the Bourbons and the Montmorencys. In one sense this stems from the way contemporaries spoke of them in a sort of shorthand (see Document 6). In reality, the Lorraines, Bourbons and Colignys should be seen as part of a widely interrelated aristocratic kindred that was rapidly being divided over political and religious policy. However, there was never any exclusively noble religious faction. The

Guises had clients who were Protestant; the Bourbons were a family deeply divided over religion, which included several Catholic branches (notably the Montpensiers) as well as the main branch that itself was divided (Cardinal Charles, the brother of Antoine de Bourbon, remained Catholic, while the children of the first prince of Condé by his second marriage were Catholic). The Constable de Montmorency was fiercely Catholic, his Coligny nephews, of course, Calvinist and his sons Catholic but always willing to work with Protestants. This did not make the religious dimension of faction unimportant – religion constantly fuelled political conflict – but it made it more complicated.

In 1559–60, the first prince of the blood, Antoine de Bourbon, nominal King of Navarre, was more interested in making good his claims to his Pyrenean kingdom with Philip II. His wife Jeanne d'Albret, heiress to the Pyrenean lands and niece of Francis I, was perhaps the most genuine and energetic aristocratic leader of French Protestantism. Antoine, who was perhaps toying with Protestantism, withdrew to his south-western domains and left the field open for the Guises. It was his brother Louis, prince of Condé, who took up the cause of the family and of the reformed religion seriously and sought to challenge the prevailing regime. The Constable de Montmorency, the leading figure of the old regime, seemed to have been pushed out and his adherents were threatened with losses. The anger behind this was fuelled by the fact that, facing as it did such an enormous crisis in state finance, the Guise-dominated regime had to embark on retrenchment of expenditure (resumption of the domain, limitation of pensions and reduction in the military establishment) that easily looked as though they were feathering their own nest and favouring their friends.

The consequence was in effect an attempted coup d'état in March 1560 in which a Protestant gentleman, Godefroy du Barry sieur de La Renaudie, organised several hundred troops to seize the royal family at Amboise (see Document 8). Part large-scale lobbying enterprise for freedom of conscience and part military coup directed at the Guises, the plot seems to have leaked out very early; arrests started at Tours on 11 March and La Renaudie himself died in a skirmish on the 19th. Many more were captured and several hundred executed in particularly gruesome ways. Though the prince of Condé was careful to distance himself from the plot at the time, it seems that the Guises were under no illusions about him.

The Protestant leaders saw the brutal, if understandable, repression of the conspirators as an act of tyranny and it was to become a focal point of the burgeoning propaganda war that developed and made 1560 the point of departure for a new kind of politics, involving a frenetic outburst of publications on all subjects in public life. One of the most symptomatic was the venomous *Tigre de France*, launched at the cardinal of Lorraine and almost certainly written by the Protestant lawyer Hotman in full tabloid mode (see Document 7). The regime, which had been seriously alarmed at the vast ramifications of the plot, lost no time in spreading the idea that Huguenotism – a name then newly in vogue – was just a cover for individual ambition and sedition.

In the aftermath of these events, in May, the Edict of Romorantin transferred much of the cognisance of heresy to the church courts. This could be viewed in two ways. For Catholics, it might have been a way of short-circuiting the sluggishness of the civil courts in prosecuting heresy. For reformers, it may have been seen as a way round the draconian penalties of the civil courts (see Document 9). It was at best a holding operation and was bound to be opposed by the Parlements. Catherine, the Chancellor and Coligny also proposed a meeting of the princes, knights of the order and 'men of authority', what is usually called an Assembly of Notables. Some Protestants argued that the Guises were only too willing for this to go ahead and that they saw it as a way of trapping their enemies, since they would have the majority of voices. The Assembly agreed on the idea of Estates-General and a National Council of the Church. Though it seems likely that the ruling group had its own ideas on how to use these meetings, there was a consensus that they were needed. However, the autumn of 1560 saw an accelerating slide towards anarchy in the provinces, with plots and assemblies of soldiers reported all over the south and west and the government hurriedly assembling men. It looked as though the problem was to be solved by extreme action when Condé was arrested on suspicion of involvement in the Amboise plot and plans for his trial for treason were made. Even Navarre was brought under suspicion.

The death of Francis II at Orléans on 5 December 1560 before the Estates could meet overturned all expectations. Condé was released and Catherine was installed as Regent in all but name on 6 December 1560 having agreed on an essential division of authority with Navarre. For the moment the Lorraines left the court and it looked as though the Catholic cause had been damaged (see Document 10). Catherine's broad approach was to appease the ominous religious and factional conflict by relaxing persecution and seeking compromise. Anxious to maintain the independence of the crown as far as possible, she brought figures like Coligny and Condé back into the Council (15 March 1561) though Navarre did not formally become Lieutenant-General of the kingdom until 8 April 1561. Her position depended crucially on the maintenance of the loyalty of a large and strong central group of grandees, Catholic and Protestant, nominally led by Navarre. To this end, she sought to effect 'reconciliations'. In the light of the hatreds which already existed, this proved impossible, while the relaxation of persecution gave the Catholic aristocrats a ready-made weapon. In the background, disorder had gradually spread through the provinces in the wake of the Conspiracy of Amboise and had not been suppressed.

The first business of the new reign was to hold the Estates-General, which had already been summoned, and which opened on 13 December. The discussion of reform of the realm was extensive and detailed and legislation was proposed for the financial overhaul of the state. On the controversial matter of religion, though, it was simply decided to grant a general pardon for all offences without demands for recantation. Proposals for the reform of the clergy were also advanced. In February 1561, the Estates were prorogued until May–June at Pontoise to give time for further local discussions of the religious problems. When the Estates reassembled, business centred on attacks on the clergy and proposals for them to make their wealth available for the restoration of state finance.

By the spring of 1561, a pattern of general and accelerating disorder was apparent. The sessions of the Estates revealed serious and widening faction rifts, which Catherine had the utmost difficulty in dealing with. It is difficult not to link Navarre's appointment as Lieutenant-General with the emergence, probably on 6 April, of the alliance later known as the Triumvirate, formed by Guise, Montmorency and Saint-André. It also included others, such as the cardinal of Lorraine, and had the patronage of Philip II through his agent Manrique. The Guises may have been edged out of power but they were undefeated and eager for revenge, while Navarre's Lieutenancy in some senses limited Montmorency's authority as Constable. The association was formed to oppose the spread of religous toleration. The so-called 'treaty' of the Triumvirate is a highly controversial document, actually included in the justificatory compilation known as the Guise memoirs (which was not printed until the nineteenth century and also contains other contemporary libels of the Guise) (see Document 13). It was also included in the similar compilation for Condé, who probably published it in April 1562. It is not itself dated (though the editor has given the date 1561), but it certainly refers to the issues prevalent when the Triumvirate was formed. At the most, it is likely only partly to be based on a genuine document. Otherwise, it is expanded as a virulent and bloodthirsty scheme for the universal extirpation of all Protestantism in Europe, Lutheran and Calvinist. As a Protestant device for undermining the duke of Guise's negotiations with the Lutheran duke of Württemberg in 1561 it makes some sense. It is included here as an example of a document which contributed heavily to the 'black legend' of the Guises.

The year 1561 was dominated, of course, by attempts on the part of Catherine and her close advisers to find a compromise solution to the religious problems. On 7 January 1561, the Edict of Romorantin was confirmed, and on 28 January the 'lettres de cachet' ordered a cessation of arrests and allowed

Protestants to return from exile (see Document 11). An edict in April added further prohibitions on mutual insults and on unlawful entry into the houses of heresy suspects. The Parlement of Paris was already exercised about the provisions of the Edict of Romorantin and entered opposition to it while taking steps itself to root out conventicles in Paris. The crown acceded partially to its concerns in the July Edict by forbidding conventicles but limiting to banishment the penalties that could be imposed by royal courts on those delivered to the secular arm under the Edict of Romorantin. It also transferred cognisance of sedition to the Presidial courts (see Document 12). At Easter 1561, the distinctly eirenic bishop of Valence, Jean de Monluc, preached at court. This was one of the reasons that provoked Montmorency to join what was later to be the Triumvirate. All this led to a dangerous confrontation in the political elite, for, with religious accommodation in the air and the promulgation of relaxations in the laws relating to heresy, the leaders of Catholic opinion began to regroup. The young King's illness early in October led to rumours that the Guises were about to spirit the heir away to Lorraine. With Calvinism increasingly viewed as fashionable at court, the house of Guise withdrew in October to concentrate on protecting its flank by links with the Lutheran duke of Württemberg. This was seen by the Calvinist Bèze as the point when the Triumvirate became visible and active.

These developments took place during the period of the Colloquy of Poissy. Even under Francis II, the idea of a General Council under the form of the Council of Trent was looked on with suspicion in France and the Guise regime had declared its intention of summoning a National Council of the French Church, though probably intending it to seal the proscription of the heretics. Catherine's preferred option was such a National Council Church and this was summoned to Poissy to meet in July at the same time as the Estates-General at Pontoise. That this would include Protestants only became apparent at the last moment. In fact, the Protestant churches presented a request to the King for toleration and for their own places of worship on 11 June 1561. The Privy Council deferred a decision until the meeting of the clergy at Poissy but in the meantime agreed the new Edict modifying that of Romorantin (see Document 12).

The Colloquy started on 9 September, after preliminary meetings between the cardinal of Lorraine and Bèze, the Calvinist theologian. Though it failure is obvious, there has been much debate on its meaning. That Catherine hoped for a compromise that would head off the looming conflict seems reasonably clear. A constant theme in Protestant political action in the period was to stress loyalty to the crown and the orthodoxy of its beliefs in comparison with the wilder sects such as Anabaptists. At Poissy, Bèze, while stressing there was no contradiction between its faith and its loyalty to the crown, was also concerned to keep the French Protestant community together. In doing this, he had to make a fairly uncompromising statement of doctrine. As for Lorraine, it is debated whether he seriously hoped for an agreement or was just using the meeting as part of a general objective to split the French Calvinists from the Lutherans in Germany. Lorraine, who was later to be viewed widely by Protestants as the soul of religious reaction, seems to have held vaguely liberal theological views at the time of Poissy. The most important point to draw from the Colloquy though, is that it reveals, as Nugent put it, that there was 'no psychological readiness' for agreement on either side.

The manifest failure of a national solution to an international problem forced Catherine towards the high-risk policy of a more general toleration for Protestants that was bound to lead to a collision with the Catholic aristocratic leadership and popular Catholic opinion. In the second half of 1561, Protestants were already beginning to seize churches for their own use (see Chapter 2), though Catherine took steps to limit this. Requested for an enumeration of their resources in view of threats to the crown, the Protestants, who quickly reported that they had more than 2,100 churches, actively petitioned for their own places of worship as the only way to avoid conflict (see Document 15). The apparently growing numbers of armed Protestants led the crown further to relax restrictions on heresy so long as Protestants remained peaceful. The dimensions of the problem were ably mapped out in a pamphlet which was published ostensibly as a petition of the King to the Pope but was, according to the Spanish ambassador, written by Jean de Monluc. It gave a very high figure for Protestants and argued that they were too powerful to be crushed by force (see Document 14).

The Edict of Saint-Germain, often called the Edict of January (1562), was the first formal recognition of Protestant rights to worship, and though its provisions were narrow (worship was prohibited in towns and at night) it provided a legal basis for Protestant worship elsewhere, especially on noble estates (see Document 16). Not surprisingly, Catholic leaders were furious and even the crown swiftly began to row back on it by an interpretative declaration on 14 February that it intended no permanent toleration (see Document 17). The Parlement of Paris remonstrated against the edict and it took two royal *lettres de jussion* to force them to register it on 6 March. Only a few days before, though, the massacre at Vassy (see Chapter 2) signalled the opening of the first civil war.

---

## 1 A parlementaire critique of monarchical authority, *c.*1561

It is not necessary to fight or to defend oneself against this sole tyrant; he is of himself defeated as long as the country refuses to accept its servitude. Nothing need be taken from him if nothing is given to him. The country need not act for itself, just not go to the trouble of acting against itself. Peoples allow themselves to be eaten up, but when they cease to serve they are free. It is the people who submit to slavery, who cut their own throats; who, having the choice of being subjects or free men, quit freedom and choose the yoke . . . just as a spark becomes a flame and burns stronger the more tinder it finds, it will burn itself out without water if no more wood is put on it, and will cease to be a fire. Likewise, tyrants, the more they pillage and demand, the more they ruin and destroy, the more they are given and are served, so they fortify themselves and become stronger and more capable of destroying everything. If they are given nothing, are not obeyed, but without violence, they will remain naked and undone, no longer anything . . . Be resolved to serve no more and, there you are, free. . . .

Consider the Venetians, a handful of people living so freely that the most wicked among them would not wish to be king, all brought up to know no other ambition than that which conduces to their liberty; so brought up from their cradles, they would not accept all the happiness of the world in return for the smallest fraction of their liberty. He who has seen them and then travels on to the lands of him whom we call the Grand Seigneur, seeing there men who are born only for servitude and who, to maintain it, give up their lives, would he not think . . . that he had moved from a city of men to an animals' cage? . . .

It is a pity to hear about the things tyrants used in past times to reinforce their tyranny, how many little things they used. . . . Ours scattered in France I don't know many such excrescences: fleurs de lys, the holy ampulla, the oriflamme. I for my part do not want to disbelieve in them since our ancestors had no reason to disbelieve. They always had kings who were good in peace and valiant in war, who, though born to kingship, seem to have been rather chosen by almighty God for the government of this kingdom. Even were that not the case, I would not enter the lists to debate the truth of our histories, or pick over, even in private, this fine state that our French poetry fences over. . . . I would do it great wrong, I say, to deprive it of those lovely stories of King Clovis, in which our Ronsard in his Franciade takes such pleasure. . . .

SOURCE: Etienne de La Boétie, *De la servitude volontaire*, in Goulart, *Charles IX* (1577), pp. 163–6, 171–4, 181–3.

## 2  The deficit in the royal budget, 1561

|  | livres | | sols | | deniers |
|---|---|---|---|---|---|
| Sum of expenditure | 6,346,111 | . | 12 | | |
| and the receipt equals | 8,646,875 | . | 17 | . | 10 |
| Thus, the surplus is | 2,300,763 | . | 5 | . | 10 |

Which sum will be employed as follows:

|  | livres | | sols | | deniers |
|---|---|---|---|---|---|
| Still to be paid from 1560 | 1,992,412 | . | 18 | . | 1 |
| Second payment for the marriages | 908,332 | . | 6 | . | 8 |
| Assignation of Georges Obreth | 519,000 | | | | |
| Assignation of Albisse d'Elbène | 252,000 | | | | |
| Sum total | 3,671,746 | . | 4 | | 9 |
| Thus there is a deficit of | 1,370,981 | . | 18 | | 11 |

Summary of the debts and items to be paid:

|  | livres | | sols | | deniers |
|---|---|---|---|---|---|
| Debts with interest | 15,926,555 | . | 12 | . | 8 |
| Other debts without interest | 2,012,610 | . | 17 | . | 6 |
| Arrears from 1559 and other yrs | 5,514,592 | . | 8 | . | 11 |
| Marriages/ debts of Ferrara | 14,961,787 | . | 15 | . | 8 |
| Alienations of domain/gabelles | 1,564,787 | . | 2 | . | 12 |
| Arrears for 1560 | 427,626 | . | 15 | . | 3 |
| Sum total | 43,483,939 | . | 9 | . | 6 |
| The surplus for this yr | 2,300,763 | . | 5 | . | 10 |
| Therefore remains due | 41,183,175 | . | 3 | . | 8 |

Source: Copy, AD, Puy-de-Dôme, 5C, Aa, 3i(2).

---

## 3  The Court and Government: Catherine de Medici's advice to her son, 1563

[*Catherine writes advice to her son on how to re-establish order by good example and restore the court to good order, as it was under his predecessors.*]

And so that this should be known to all, I would wish that you appoint a certain time for your *lever* and, to content your nobility, do as the late king your father did; for when he took his shirt and the accoutrements were brought in, all the princes, lords, captains, knights of the order, gentlemen of the chamber, masters of the household and serving gentlemen then entered and he spoke to them, saw them and gave them much content.

That done, he went to his [*Council of*] affairs and everyone went out except those who were [*members*] of it and the four secretaries. If you do the same, that would much content them since it has long been the custom under your father and grandfather. After that, give an hour or two to hear the despatches which cannot be sent without your presence. Then no later than ten go to Mass, as did your father and grandfather, accompanied by the princes and lords and not, as I see you doing, just accompanied by the archers [*of the guard*]. After Mass, dine if the time is late or, if not, go for a healthy walk and dine at the latest at eleven. Then, after dinner, at least twice a week give audience, which will greatly please your subjects, and then visit me or the Queen, so that the fashion of the court be known, a thing that greatly pleases the French because they are accustomed to it. After an hour or two in public, you may withdraw to your study or privy apartments as you choose. At three o'clock in the afternoon, you may go to walk or ride so as to show yourself to and content the nobility, or pass some time with them in some gentlemanly sport, if not every day at least two or three times a week. That will please them greatly since it was the custom of the king your father, whom they loved utterly. After that, there will be supper with your family and after supper, twice a week, hold a ball, for I have heard the king your grandfather say that two things were necessary to live in peace with the French: to keep them merry and to occupy them with some exercise. For this purpose, combats on foot or horseback and jousting with the lance were necessary; the king your father also did this with gentlemanly exercises in which he occupied them, for the French have always been used to either war or exercises; if they are not given them, they will get involved in more dangerous matters. . . .

To return to the government of the court in the time of the king your grandfather, there was no man so bold he dared offer injury to another in his court, for if he had been so reported he was brought before the provost of the household. The captains of the guards usually patrolled the halls and the courtyard. When the king had withdrawn to his chamber or to the apartments of the ladies in the afternoon, the archers were stationed in the halls and the staircases and courtyard to stop the pages and lackeys playing and gaming as they do usually in the castle where you are residing, with execrable blasphemies and oaths. You should renew the ancient ordinances and your own, in making exemplary punishment so that they all refrain from this. Also the Swiss usually patrolled the courtyard as well as the provost of the household with his archers in the outer yard and the inns and public places, to see what was going on and stop wickedness and punish wrongdoers. . . . Every night, the Grand Master ordered the masters of the household to have the torches lit in all the halls and passages, at the four corners of the yard and the staircases. The gates of the castle were never opened until the king rose and no man came in or out, whoever he was. So also in the evening, once the king was in bed, the gates were closed and the keys placed at his bedside; and in the morning, when the table was being set for dinner or supper, the gentleman carver went to ask him for the place setting and carried the salt-cellar and the knives for carving; and before him went the usher of the hall and after him the officers for the table. So also, when the meat was brought, the master of the household went in person with the pantler, followed by the children of honour and pages, without valets and with no one else but the squire of the kitchen. After dinner or supper, when the king asked for his beverage, a serving gentleman brought the cup in his hand followed by the pantlers and cup-bearers. Also, no one entered the chamber when the king's bed was being made; if the great chamberlain or first gentleman of the chamber were not there, one of the principal gentlemen of the chamber was present. In the evening, the king disrobed in the presence of those who were there in the morning when his clothes were brought in.

I wanted to tell you about the way the kings your father and grandfather did things, both because I saw them so loved and honoured by their subjects, who were well content with them, as also since I wanted to see you similarly regarded, thinking I could give you no better advice than to govern yourself like them.

Monsieur my son, having spoken to you of the order of the court and what is necessary for you to establish all orders in your kingdom, it seems to me that one of the most necessary things to make yourself loved by your subjects is that they should know that in all matters you have a care for them, as much for those of your entourage as those who are further away. I say this because you have seen how malign persons, in their wickedness, have spread the idea generally that you do not care for their preservation and you do not wish to see them. That has proceeded from the bad offices and lies of those who, to make you hated, have thought to increase their power; and that because of the press of business and negligence of those to whom you give the orders, very often the necessary despatches, instead of being diligently replied to, have not been sent but rather have been left for a month or six weeks, so that those messengers sent by the men you have appointed in the provinces, not being able to get a reply, have returned without them. Because of this, seeing such negligence, they thought that what the ill-disposed had said was true. All this makes me beseech you that, from now on, you allow no day to pass without, at a time of your choosing, seeing all the despatches from wherever they come, and that you take pains to hear those who are sent to you; and if there are things that the Council can help you with, to send them to it and command the Chancellor that in all matters concerning the affairs of your State, before the masters of requests enter the Council chamber, he set aside an hour to deal with them and only then let them into the Council for Suits (*Conseil pour Parties*). This is the form that, during the reign of the kings your father and grandfather, my lord Constable observed and those who were present in the Council. As for other matters that depend on your will alone, after having heard them, as has been said, you should command the despatches and replies according to your will, to the secretaries; and the next day, before seeing anything new, you will have them read and command that they be sent off without delay. In doing this, difficulties in your affairs will be avoided and your subjects will know the care you take of them and that you wish to be well and promptly obeyed; that will make them more diligent and careful and they will further know how you wish to preserve your State as well as the care you take over your affairs. When people from the provinces are sent, either by your servants or by others, take pains to speak to them, ask them their duties and, if they have none, where they come from so they know you wish to know what is happening in your kingdom. Make them good cheer and do not speak to them just once but when you see them in your chamber or elsewhere always say a word to them.

This is how I saw the kings your father and grandfather act, to the point of asking them, when they had no other means of entertaining them, about their homes, so as to speak to them and let them know that it was agreeable to meet them. In doing this, the lying inventions that have been made to distort you to your subjects will be known to all and you will be loved and honoured, for, on returning to their countries, they will spread the truth so that those who have tried to destroy you will be known for the wicked men they are.

SOURCE: Letter to the King [8 Sept. 1563?], *LCM*, vol. II, pp. 90–5.

## 4 The nobility calls for the return of the golden age, 1560

The nobles were ordained by God for loyalty and obedience to their kings and the defence of their subjects. . . . If kings disagree with their nobles, this can only give rise to discord and rebellion. When they maintain them, they defend them and are their first recourse. It is commonly said that good blood runs straight to the wound. For this reason, the nobles in all commonwealths were for ever privileged by arms and accoutrements that the rest dared not bear. . . . The kings your predecessors have long continued, through their laws, to maintain these, so that the gentlemen have been known and honoured by them. Several other estates wanted to follow this on the pretext that two great philosophers divided the nobility into four: that of birth, that of the men of power and great administrators, that of military prowess . . . and the last, of those who have discovered great arts or knowledge. But those of the last three parts, in abusing this, have caused great disorder and a wretched admixture among the people, as well as great losses to the King in his revenues, since every man wanted to obtain enfranchisement as if he were a gentleman. Another ill has struck the estate of the nobility . . . this is that the nobles have given so much to the church that they have ruined and wasted their patrimonies. Most take advantage of this, so that the gentleman is so persecuted and cheated that, having used up his substance, he is in debt and has no means, as he would wish, quickly to come at your summons to serve you as he should. [*The clergy should confine themselves to their proper functions. The King should appoint as judges only virtuous and capable men. The number of officials should be reduced.*]

The commonwealth can only be harmed by having so many magistrates who live at the expense of the public and who, through delayed justice, destroy us and give rise to endless disputes. We would live in greater calm and France in greater peace and you, Sire, would take pleasure, if you were to give gentlemen the means of employment in that respect. That was the will of the great and admirable King Francis your grandfather, inasmuch as the nobles hold honour dearer than their lives. [*The writer wishes there be fewer cases before the municipal courts*] and that so many plaintiffs, writings and law court vermin were punished under the law. Then the fair Astraea would return us to the age of gold and the good old times would come back to France. . . .

Sire, you must maintain the nobility in its privileges, freedoms and liberties that are as old as the institution of monarchy and which cannot reasonably be severed from its estate and condition without the prince damaging himself and weakening his own grandeur and majesty, of which the nobility is the principal support.

SOURCE: J. de Silly, sr de Rochefort, *La Harangue de par la noblesse de toute la France au Roy* (Paris: Perier, 1561).

---

## 5   The nobility's obligation to serve the King, 1568

This kingdom is one of, or rather the, most well founded and established in Christendom and in which kings have until now been willingly obeyed by their faithful subjects. In this, our nation has been especially blessed above all others. However, it cannot be doubted that the long continuance of our foreign wars under the late kings of happy memory Francis I and Henry II have bred a great abundance of evil humours which have little by little accustomed the body of this state to accept change and mutability, from which since then, as now, it is still grievously tormented and afflicted in all its members. For war is the mother and nurse of all licence [*and rebels take advantage of the King's youth . . .*].

First, if it is the case, as it is, that the nobility has more reason than any other people to thank a benign and almighty God for the grace and favour it receives, it is most reasonable that it strive to maintain the honour due to Him by not permitting that it be challenged by new and false errors that a heap of fantastical and mutable minds strive to sow among us to deceive and pervert the integrity of our consciences. Since we are divided over religion, the best way we can behave and the surest method is not to meddle in matters we do not understand, nor rely on our own opinions, but rather, by controlling them, conform to the majority and to the faith and belief of our ancestors, which is still at present, by the grace of God, inviolably observed by the King and the greater number of his subjects.

Furthermore, in matters of fighting for the country or in the extension of our territory, or to prevent the least of our villages from being overrun, they [*the nobles*] have never refused to risk and expend their persons and the substance of their families. . . .

Finally, as this kingdom is the first in Christendom, so its subjects are reputed the more loving and affectionate towards their prince and in particular the lords and gentlemen who, in return for the liberties, authority and rewards that they receive, have long dedicated themselves to observing [*the King's*] will and good pleasure. Foreigners say that our kings have as much power to command over their nobility as they wish to exercise and that the nobility is so subservient and obsequious that they summon them from their estates whenever they like. But we can reply that, besides the duty by which all vassals are obliged, by the nature of their fiefs, to serve their sovereign lord, our kings give us so many benefits that we could not do otherwise, much less disobey them, without contravening and departing from our oaths and the honour which we should cherish above all things in this world. It is not without burdens that gentlemen have been by the ordinance and authority of kings marked off from the people to live in liberty and immunity from all servile conditions, to have the right to hunt, superiority and pre-eminence over the subjects and jurisdiction over them, the power to exact rents and dues, labour service and other impositions. It is not, then, without corresponding duties they have this grant and the right to carry a sword. It is so that they understand that kings have selected them as those they considered most noble, and for this reason, have not wished to subject them to financial or manual work so that, in devoting themselves entirely to the exercise of arms, they might act as their shield and rampart in the course of affairs and, in the event of war, resist the endeavours of their enemies. Thus, the nobility, as the creation of sovereigns, holding from them their liberties and privileges, derive their being and sustenance from the advantage, profit and maintenance of their head.

To return to the generality, I dare say that, if fiefs oblige the nobility to every duty, affection and loyalty to our kings, great benefits further bind us in such a way that there is no excuse, however well founded we might think it, that could divorce us from it. And on that matter, when one considers that all the wealth and opulence of this realm, all the grandeur and commodities flow back to the gentlemen and that all the King's revenue is employed in the maintenance and payment of the great appointments and pensions of officers of the crown, marshals, governors, captains, lieutenants, men-at-arms; that valuable benefices are given to their relatives; in short, when we consider the resources of the King and his people, that the fruits and revenues of both are distributed to and shared out among them, such is their obligation to the care and defence of both, it seems that, should it be forgotten, such infidelity and ingratitude could not be detested enough.

But it is also certain, and can be clearly proved from our history, that the

nobility, have always recognised that their good and advancement, through the
liberality of our kings, and their preservation were so interlinked that the head
could not suffer the members to be disadvantaged, and have behaved in their
service with such perfect devotion and will that until our times it has served as a
glass and example to other nations of Christendom . . . [*examples of this from
history*].

. . . since our King's accession to the crown, the gentlemen have given such proof
of their fidelity and affection that they have surpassed the virtue and glory of their
ancestors. For, as for seven years this kingdom has been constantly tormented by
troubles [*the King had to be protected. In the last troubles, at the battle of Saint Denis,
the King besieged by rebels in Paris aiming to destroy the church, nobility and
Parlements*], who was it if not the gentlemen of His Majesty's party who set out to
reach the place to which they were summoned? Some, half retired from arms
because of age, set their armour on their backs again. Some had been forced to
retire to their estates to save money and pay off their debts but once again
mortgaged their farms and mills to buy horses; others came from the farthest
frontiers of France to rescue their King with the best equipage they could muster.
Now we have returned for the third time to this fever, I have no doubt that,
summoned by His Majesty, they will do the same. . . .

For it is certain that the outcome of this war will be either the punishment of the
rebels and the establishment of the Monarchy or, if the King's army loses, the
usurpation of the crown. . . .

SOURCE: J. du Tillet?, *Advertisement à la noblesse de France tant du party du Roy que des rebelles coniurez* (1568, 1574 edn, sig. Aij-Cij).

## FACTION

### 6   Jean de Fraisse, on faction under Henry II (written *c*.1570s)

Francis, the First of that name, King of France, having died, Henry his son, also
Second of that name, succeeded to this crown. During this reign, which lasted
thirteen years, and was cut off, and indeed from its very start, the seeds of our civil
wars were sown among those who held first place in the public administration.
With time they took such deep root that they have brought the finest and most
flourishing state in the world to the brink of ruin and collapse, from which it has
been preserved not by human prudence but by the special favour and grace of
God. . . .

This prince was in truth, very well formed both in body and mind; of the best
and well-finished figure and proportions, robust, strong and eager for work, to
which he was much given, and of a disposition that was to be desired. He had an

affable and humane manner by which, from the first, he won the heart and devotion of all. He always cherished and loved his subjects in his lifetime and was regretted after his death. The Latin couplet written after the battle of Saint-Quentin bears this out:

The people excuses Henry, curses Montmorency,
Hates Diane and above all also those of the Guise.

Montmorency, Constable of France, was the one who introduced him to war in that army the King his father assembled at Avignon to oppose the Emperor Charles V who had invaded Provence. That, we may suppose, along with this person's many other considerable qualities, ensured that he would always be loved and honoured and that [*the King*] would recall him on his accession after he had been relegated to his estates six years before for having assured the King of the Emperor's promises on his journey through France, in which both master and minister had been deceived.

Before he came to the throne, this prince had conceived a great priviness with Diane de Poitiers. . . . This woman acquired such authority and power over this prince that, though she was much older than him, she always entirely governed him by her will. Just as the Sun and the Moon rule the sky, so Montmorency and Diane had entire and absolute power in this realm; the first over the crown, the other over the person.

The brothers François de Lorraine, duke of Guise, and Charles, cardinal of Lorraine were very close to this prince when he was but Dauphin, though not so securely that they could not be shaken. So, to secure themselves, they at first joined the party of this woman, particularly the cardinal, who was one of the most adept of courtiers. As a result, for two years, having no table of his own [*at court*], he dined at her table; thus was she also called by the Queen herself. Also, by his dealings and favour he acquired all the great benefices of his uncle the cardinal of Lorraine after his death, which, joined to his own, brought him in 300,000 *lt.* a year. He also took his uncle's effects, which were precious, and left all his debts, which were immense, to his creditors, succeeding to them under bankruptcy.

Jacques d'Albon, sr de Saint-André, one of the most sharp and subtle courtiers of his time, as first gentleman of the chamber, also had great influence over [*the King*]. He had a lively understanding, agreeable tact, great substance, adroitness in arms and was sharp and subtle in affairs. His good qualities were counterbalanced by all sorts of lasciviousness and profusion, for which divine justice caused him to do penitence later because of a carnal appetite that travailed him in his private parts all his life.

These five were chosen for the conduct and direction of affairs. It will be found strange that a woman was included, considering her sex and the general custom of all nations, but it happened in truth. For, by what followed, it will be seen that she made peace and war, particularly in two treaties, namely that with the Theatine Pope [*Paul IV*], called the Holy League, the archetype and mould of our last League, and that of Cateau-Cambrésis, and deposed and created Chancellors of France at her will. Who should then find our civil wars strange? – for government by women in this France of ours, unhappy and fatal at all times, as experience shows, could not escape her malign influence. . . .

[*The order of the new King's Council; Francis I's recommendation not to call the Guises to it 'because they would not fail to reduce him and his children to their doublets and their people to their shirts'.*]

There is no law so universal and complete that it does not have some fault, as the following will show; for the Constable de Montmorency, having absolute power over military affairs, as this prince wished, and he, by nature grave and imperious, keeping all to himself not only in army matters but also affairs in council, left the brothers Guise with their hands full of the wind and an authority in name only. Here was the fallow field in which the seeds of our civil wars were sown. The cardinal, very clever and careful to tend and water them, never ceased to intrigue abroad, prevented from doing so at home, for his brother, as he did in that unhappy Theatine treaty, under which and at public expense he had reserved for him the crowns of Sicily and Naples as heritage of his house and the papal tiara for himself. . . .

Whatever the change that happened in this state, at first it was happy and as was desired, for the fires of our ambitions not yet lit, all was still only a question of the public good and who would do best. But, as Pope Julius was the end of the Emperor's prosperity and the start of his misfortune, so the Theatine Pope and his friends were the authors of our ruin; the course of affairs bears this out only too well.

Would that this woman and the cardinal had never been, for these two alone were the kindling of our misfortunes, as everyone has always known. The duke of Guise was a great war leader and a captain capable of serving his country, had not the ambition of his brother poisoned him. As he said himself: in the end these men will be our ruin. And as for Saint-André, he was always worthy of his command. . . .

We should add, in the year 1548, the great quarrel between the late prince of La Roche-sur-Yon and Monsieur d'Andelot as preamble and the first trial run for our civil wars. . . .

SOURCE: *Histoire particulière de la court du Roy Henry II*, AC, ser. I, vol. 3, pp. 273–306.

## 7   The Conspiracy of Amboise: propaganda

Fiendish tiger! Poisonous snake! Sepulcre of abomination! Spectacle of wretchedness! How long will you abuse the youth of our King? Will you never make an end of your unbridled ambition, your pretences and thefts? Know you not that the whole world sees and understands them? Who do you think does not know your detestable intent or does not read in your face the misfortune of all our days, the ruin of this realm and the death of our King? . . . How do you reply when . . . I say to you that, to break the power of justice in France and set up corrupt judges like unto you, you introduced the semester chamber in the Court of Parlement? When I tell you that you used the late king as minister in your wickedness and impiety? When I tell you that the shortfalls in the revenues of France stem from your robberies? . . . If I say further that you have seized the government of France and stripped this honour from the princes of the blood in order to set the crown of France in your house? What can you reply?

SOURCE: Hotman, *Tigre*, pp. 37, 42–3.

---

## 8  La Planche on the Conspiracy of Amboise

Louis de Bourbon, prince of Condé, a truly noble prince among all the princes of the blood, asked to see to these affairs and prevent the ruin of the King and the whole state, having long and carefully weighed the matter, as its importance warranted, commissioned certain prudent persons to enquire secretly and exactly into the charges laid against the Guises. . . . The enquiry made, it was found by reliable, notable and qualified witnesses that they were charged with several treasons and a mass of peculations and corruptions not only in the King's finances but against his subjects. . . .

These enquiries, viewed and reported to the prince's Council, and the King's youth preventing him from taking cognisance of the wrongs done him and all France, let alone take order for them surrounded as he was by his enemies, it was discussed how best to seize the persons of François, duke of Guise, and Charles cardinal of Lorraine, his brother, to bring them to trial before the Estates. But there was a difficulty in deciding who would sound the charge, since all wise persons thought it highly risky considering their grandeur and authority. Thus none of them, though they were courageous, wished to undertake it since in the case of failure loss of life and property would be inevitable. Finally, after various discussions, a baron of Périgord, a gentleman of old family, named Godefroy de Barry, seigneur de La Renaudie, called La Forest, volunteered. . . . The company judged him suitable to handle the affair under the authority of the said lord prince, who, founding himself on his duty to his country, His Majesty and his lineage, seeing this person well disposed to the same, empowered him to appear in his name where appropriate to take counsel on what was necessary. And the prince promised him to be present when the said arrest took place, to favour it as far as he could, provided that nothing was said or done in any way against God, the King, his brothers, the princes or the state. . . .

Thus authorised, La Renaudie lost no time and on 1 February assembled at Nantes a good number of the nobility and third estate from all the provinces of France. . . .

In this assembly, after invoking the name of God, La Renaudie outlined at length the state of the kingdom, not only concerning individual consciences but above all on the management of the state, which he said was in the hands of foreigners who had got themselves the place by their own manoeuvres without any authorisation in the old laws, remonstrating the danger to come since the Guises had plotted the ruin of the King, my lords of his blood and all the lords of the kingdom not of their party. In short . . . he asked them to declare their view on what to do in the event that a prince of the blood, or a gentleman duly authorised by him, were to be ready, whether they would help to seize these tyrants so as to assemble the Estates-General to try them and appoint a Council for the King in his youth in the accustomed way. . . .

[*Opinions were taken and the decision to swear an oath not to act against the King or the princes. . . .*]

La Renaudie, having taken the oath of everyone and in turn given his own, declared [the name of] the prince on behalf of whom he was acting and showed his commission, having seen which, they appointed him councillors from all the provinces. . . .

SOURCE: La Planche, vol. II, pp. 238–9, based partly on an original relation.

---

## 9  The Edict of Romorantin, May 1560

[*Preamble deploring the spread of heresy and noting that the King's predecessors had taken in hand the prosecution and execution of heretics.*]

However, we, with the advice of our most honoured lady and mother, the princes of our blood and men of our Council, have since decided to restore matters to their old form and state in the hope that, by this means, just as God in olden times brought an end to sects and diversity of opinion in His Church and restored it to a good union, so will He do now and give us His peace and grace and all His Christian people will live in general concord.

1  We commit the entire cognisance of the crime of heresy to the prelates of our kingdom, as the natural judges of that crime, and as they had it of old time. In this we admonish and exhort them to reside in their dioceses and work for the order of the Holy Church, the extirpation of heresy by the example of a good and moral life, prayers, sermons and persuasion, so as to return those who are in error to the way of truth. . . . We forbid our courts of Parlement, baillis,

seneschals and other judges to undertake any cognisance of the crime of heresy and in no wise meddle in it unless invited by ecclesiastical judges to help them in the execution of their judgments. [*Royal judges to inform the King of any absentee prelates.*]

2 Since it has happened recently (a thing we never thought could happen) that some of our subjects, on pretext of religion, took arms and rose up to trouble the state and peace of us and our subjects, thinking to plant their new opinions in religion by force of arms; of whom some were bold enough to approach our residence with such damnable intent that, if the result had followed their intentions, the subversion and desolation of our state would infallibly have followed . . . we have prohibited and forbidden, prohibit and forbid all illicit assemblies and public armed gatherings, declaring those who have held them or will attend them, our enemies and rebels, subject to the penalties for treason [*measures for investigation and prosecution*].

3 We also declare all preachers not empowered by the prelates or others with authority to do so, makers of placards, flysheets or defamatory libels which can only tend to raise the people to sedition, printers, sellers of the same, enemies of us and the public peace and traitors and subject to the same penalties as for sedition. . . .

SOURCE: Isambert, vol. XIV, i, pp. 31–3.

## 10 Consequences of the death of Francis II

The lords of Guise and all the Catholics of France were cast down because of the miseries and ruin that the kingdom fell into through this change of the state. . . . The cards, so well shaken over the previous years in France, were this time so reshuffled and the best players so far from getting back into the game, that they left them and set themselves to play quite another game, as will be seen from what follows.

The moment the late king Francis was dead, my lords of Bourbon were freed and, released from prison, the prince of Condé swaggered round Orléans with the lords of his faction. Instantly, there was a new Council, though including the Constable, which ordered that the King of Navarre and the Queen Mother would be governors of the young King and the kingdom. They signified to M. de Guise that he should no longer meddle in any matter concerning the affairs of the kingdom but should go and watch over the body of the late king. On this, the lord of Guise, having set his affairs in order, withdrew from Orléans with a well-armed entourage for his security, in case my lords of Bourbon should attack him, which seemed likely. There left Orléans with the lord of Guise more than 500 mounted gentlemen of his following, ready to take arms in his defence if need be. The said lord was followed by more people and gentlemen than the young King and his governors. The lords of Bourbon, the King of Navarre and the Queen Mother were very dismayed at this and on the advice of the Constable, sent after him not to abandon the King and to return to court. What astonished the princes of Bourbon most about this withdrawal of the lord of Guise from court was that, besides the gentlemen of his own entourage, he was then followed by nearly all the ordonnance companies, both horse and foot, that the late king had summoned to Orléans for the security of his person and of the Estates. These companies offered their services to the lord of Guise to the last drop of their blood and to die at his feet if need be. The lord of Aumale, the marquis of Elboeuf, the grand prior of France and the cardinals of Lorraine and Guise, all brothers, also left court and abandoned the King to follow their brother with all their train and the men they could assemble. So there were left with the King only the Queen Mother, the King of Navarre, the prince of Condé and the Constable, who had fewer men than the Guises, whose leader, through the princes and lords who followed him and the men of his party, could, if he had wanted, have made himself King of France.

[*Military weakness of Condé.*] The King of Navarre made as if he could think of nothing but attending to the affairs of the King, the kingdom and the Estates. . . . The Constable seemed to wish not to espouse the cause of one or the other . . . but worked for the pacification of the troubles he saw beginning between the princes of Bourbon and Guise. . . . The Queen Mother, dissimulating with the Constable, wanted vengeance on the Guises and secretly provoked the King of Navarre and the prince of Condé to be their mortal enemies, telling them that the moves against them by the late king had been made only on the advice of Guise. . . . On the other hand, to play the tragedy to the full, she sent messages and sometimes in person told Guise of the ill will towards them of the princes of Bourbon. . . . By such means she sowed such discord between these two houses of Bourbon and Guise that they never dared trust each other but maintained a suspicion of each other until death. The said lady did this in order to govern France, being of the opinion that, had my lords the princes of France been united and of one accord together, she would have been sent back to Italy. . . .

SOURCE: Haton, vol. I, pp. 116–19.

---

## ATTEMPTS TO PROVIDE A LEGAL FRAMEWORK FOR RELIGIOUS DISSENT

### 11   The *lettres de cachet*, 28 January 1561

By the King. Trusty and well beloved, considering the affairs of our realm, chiefly those matters most necessary for the maintenance of public peace [*the King, by the advice of his mother, the King of Navarre, the princes and men of his Privy Council, has been reminded of the clemency of his father and brother*]. Considering that, by their example, and as a thing most decent and fitting in our youth, we could do no better at this our accession to the crown than to extend this to our subjects who find themselves travailed and imprisoned for the sake of religion, in the hope we have for the good that may result, having taken the advice of our said lady and mother, of our uncle, the princes and men of our Council . . . we will, command and ordain you most expressly to cease and desist from all prosecutions and pursuits . . . of all persons, of whatever quality, for the sake of religion, though they may have been present at meetings in arms for their security or have furnished money or otherwise. Likewise that you set at full liberty . . . all those who for this reason may be under arrest, admonishing them to live hereafter catholicly and without any scandalous or seditious act [*though excluding those who have borne arms against the crown. Order for the implementation of the Edict of Romorantin*].

SOUCE: *MC*, vol. II, pp. 268–9.

## 12 The Edict of Saint-Germain, 11 July 1561

3 We have attributed final cognisance of cases of sedition to the judges, councillors and magistrates in our presidial courts . . . without their being able to judge definitively or with torture unless they be at least ten in number. . . .

4 We have forbidden and forbid, on pain of arrest and confiscation of property, all conventicles, public assemblies, with or without arms, as well as private ones where there are sermons and the administration of sacraments in any form other than the usage received in the Catholic Church . . .

5 As for simple heresy, we ordain and are pleased that the Edict of Romorantin issued by the late King Francis our dearest lord and brother in May 1560, be observed and kept. . . .

6 In cases where those accused of that crime are delivered by church judges to the secular arm, we will and intend and are pleased that our secular judges proceed against them without imposing any greater penalty than exile from our lands and territories only; all provisionally and until the decision of a General Council or the assembly of the prelates of our realm, following what has been done by us since our accession.

7. Continuing our same clemency and mercy, we have issued and do issue grace, pardon and abolition to all persons of whatsoever quality they be, none excepted, for all faults past proceeding from the matter of religion and sedition caused by it since the death of the late king our most honoured lord and father. All cases against them and judgments given against them are annulled and they are enjoined to live henceforth peaceably, catholicly, according to the observances in the times of our predecessors.

8  [*Prohibition on the molestation of the King's subjects by judges and punishment for false accusations.*]
9  [*Prohibition on the bearing of arms, especially firearms, except those authorised.*]
10  [*Prohibition on daggers and swords except for gentlemen.*]

SOURCE: Isambert, vol. XIV, i, pp. 109–11.

## 13  The so-called 'treaty' of the Triumvirate, 1561

First, so the matter may be more authoritatively handled, it is agreed to give supervision of the affair to the Catholic King, Philip, as the leader of the whole enterprise. They have thought good to proceed thus: that King Philip tackle the King of Navarre with complaints and disputes because, contrary to his predecessors' way, and to the great danger of the young King, whom he has charge of, he is encouraging a new religion. If he prove difficult, the Catholic King will, with fair promises, try to divert him from his wicked and unhappy policies with hope of recovering his kingdom of Navarre or some other great endowment in compensation for that kingdom. He will sweeten and manipulate him to win him to our side and join against the authors of this pernicious sect. If this works, any future military action will be easier and quicker. If he remains obstinate, King Philip will, with the authority of the Holy Council and as a neighbour whom the matter concerns, admonish him with gentle and gracious letters to do his duty, mixing threats with his promises. Meanwhile, as secretly as possible, a levy of crack troops can be made during the winter in Spain. Then, with his forces ready, he will declare himself; and the King of Navarre, without troops and taken by surprise, will be tied down, even though he might try to resist with hastily gathered forces to stop the enemy entering his territory.

Now, if he yields he will be easily expelled from his kingdom with his wife and children. If he holds out with some volunteer troops (for some of the conspirators of the sect may move to delay the victory) then the duke of Guise will declare himself chief of the Catholic confession, will assemble valiant men-at-arms and his entourage, and on his side will press the Navarrese king so that, caught between the two, he will be at their mercy. Certainly, such a king cannot resist two chiefs and two such powerful armies.

The Emperor and the other German Catholic princes will close the crossings into France for fear of the Protestant princes sending some force to help the King of Navarre. To prevent the Swiss sending aid, the Catholic cantons must attack the others and the Pope send what forces he can to help the cantons of his religion and secretly send money and other necessaries for war.

Meanwhile, the Catholic King will send part of his army to the duke of Savoy, who will levy as many men as he can in his lands. The Pope and the other Italian princes will declare the duke of Ferrara their chief and will come to join the duke of

Savoy, and, to increase their forces, the Emperor Ferdinand will give order for some German infantry and cavalry.

The duke of Savoy will thus, during the war, trouble France and the Swiss with all his forces and will unexpectedly attack Geneva on lake Lausanne and will take it by storm or siege, putting to the sword everyone within, of both sexes as an example to all that divine punishment has made up for its delay by the greatness of the execution and as a memorable example to the children of their parents' wickedness. . . .

In France, for various good and just reasons, it is better to follow another way and spare the lives of none who have once made profession of this sect. The commission to extirpate all those of the new religion will be given to the duke of Guise, who will have the charge to wipe out entirely the name, family and lineage of the Bourbons for fear that one should arise from them to pursue vengeance for these things or revive the new religion.

Thus, with matters ordered in France and restored to their old and pristine state, with men assembled from all sides, Germany must be invaded, and with the help of the Emperor and the bishops, brought back to the Holy Apostolic See. If this war is longer and harder than expected, the duke of Guise, to avoid the war being conducted more slowly for lack of money, will lend the Emperor and the other German princes and ecclesiastical lords all the money he will have gathered by confiscation from the rich nobles and bourgeois who will have been killed in France because of their new religion, which will be a great sum. The duke will get a guarantee that, after the waging of this war, he will be repaid out of the spoilation of the Lutherans and others killed for their religion in Germany. . . .

With France and Germany by these means chastised and abased before the Roman church, the Fathers do not doubt that the times will be propitious for the other neighbouring kingdoms to be brought back into the fold under an apostolic governor and pastor, if it please God to aid and favour the present pious and holy designs.

SOURCE: Guise, pp. 464–5.

---

## 14   The state of religious confrontation, late 1561

[*An invitation to the Pope to come to France. There*] he would on the one hand see in France a great many souls lost for want of knowing the true path they should take for their salvation and would be so distressed at such a miserable situation that he would, if necessary, risk his own life to remedy it. On the other hand, he could understand that a quarter of this kingdom has left the communion of the church, which quarter is made up of gentlemen, men of letters, the chief bourgeois of the cities and the lesser people, all of whom know the world and are trained in arms. Thus these separated people have no lack of military resources, including in their number a great many gentlemen and some old soldiers experienced in war. They have no lack of good counsel, having with them more than three-quarters of the men of letters; they lack no money to support their affairs, for they have among them a good proportion of the great cities and powerful families, both of the nobility and of the third estate. Furthermore, there is such unity among them and such resolve to support each other, that there is no hope of dividing them and still less of bringing them back by force without putting this kingdom in danger of becoming prey to foreign conquest, or so weakening it that it would not return to its former state for fifty years. During that time, the kings would be at the mercy of their neighbours. Since this crown has always been the surest refuge and recourse of the Holy Apostolic See . . . it is certain that our Holy Father . . . would wish to use all his means to remedy this. . . . [*The Queen seeks the Pope's help in keeping the people together and is advised this is easier in France*] thanks be to God, since there are no Anabaptists or heretics who deny the twelve articles or the decretals of the six General Councils. [*The remainder is an argument for the orthodoxy of French Protestants and a list of their complaints about ceremonies and church government, and their need for vernacular services.*]

SOURCE: 'Remonstrance to Pope Pius IV on the part of Charles IX', late 1561, probably by Jean de Monluc, bishop of Valence, *MC*, vol. II, pp. 562–75.

## 15   The Protestant petition for temples, late 1561

[*The deputies of 2,150 Reformed churches, following their petition of 11 June 1561, ask the King that he be pleased to allow them*], who in their consciences cannot and will not, if it cost a thousand lives, participate in the ceremonies of the Roman Church, to make public profession of all the articles contained in their Confession. To this end they ask you to assign them, through your magistrates, temples suitable for the number of the faithful in each town and village of your kingdom. For, Sire, since the lord God planted his word in this realm, it has taken root so deeply in the hearts of so many people of both sexes, all ages and qualities, that private houses are inadequate. Moreover, experience of private assemblies has shown well enough how much slander they are exposed to, as well as being subject to villainous and execrable crimes on the part of the enemies of the Gospel, who seek only to render your petitioners odious and obscure their innocence. [*They ask for the use of disused churches.*] This is the way, Sire, to prevent tumults and rebellions that are daily multiplying and spreading in your kingdom . . . in addition, the gate will be shut on all libertines, Anabaptists and other pernicious sects who might enter the church of God. To prevent lawless people, on pretext of the previous edicts, attacking your petitioners [*they ask for the Edict of July 1561[see Document 12] to be revoked pending the outcome of the Colloquy of Poissy*].

SOURCE: *MC*, vol. II, pp. 575–8.

## 16   The Edict of Saint-Germain, 17 January 1562

Charles, by the grace of God King of France. To all those to whom these present letters appertain, greetings. It is well enough known what troubles and seditions are now in hand and are daily instigated and increased in our kingdom by the malice of the times and the diversity of opinions which reign in religion. . . . [*In view of the provisionality of the Edict of July 1561, the King has assembled his uncle the King of Navarre, the princes, privy councillors and chief counsellors of the sovereign courts on a new edict to deal with religious diversity*]:

All those of the new religion or others who have taken over temples, will on the publication of these letters vacate them, as well as the houses, property and revenues belonging to the clergy wherever they are situated. . . .

They will return the reliquaries and ornaments they have taken from the said temples and churches. Nor will those of the new religion be able to take other temples nor build any within or without towns, nor give any trouble now or in the future to the clergy in the enjoyment and collection of their tithes, revenues and other rights and goods . . . nor smash or demolish crosses or images, and do other scandalous and seditious acts, on pain of death, without hope of grace or remission.

Likewise, they will not gather in the towns to hear sermons or preaching either in public or in private, by day or night.

Nevertheless, to keep our subjects in peace and concord, while awaiting for God to do us the grace to be able to reunite and restore them to the same sheep-fold, which is our entire desire and chief intention:

We have provisionally, and awaiting determination by a General Council or until we decide otherwise, suspended, superseded, suspend and supersede the prohibitions and punishments contained in the Edict of July and previous edicts concerning assemblies made in daylight outside the said towns for preaching, prayers and other practices of their religion.

We forbid on the said penalties all judges, magistrates and other persons of whatever quality, when those of the new Religion go to and return from and gather outside the towns for their religion, to impede, disquiet, molest or overrun them in whatever way it might be.

But where some would attack them, we command our magistrates and officers that, to avoid trouble and sedition, they prevent them; and have all troublemakers of whatever religion summarily and severely punished according to the content of our previous edicts, especially concerning those troublemakers and for the bearing of arms, that we will and intend in all other matters to be carried out entirely and remain in force and virtue.

Enjoining anew. . . all our subjects, of whatever religion, estate, quality and condition they be, that they make no assembly in arms, nor injure, reproach or provoke each other for the sake of religion, nor cause, move, favour or procure any sedition; but live and behave to each other gently and graciously, bearing no pistol, pistolet, arquebus or other arms, either at the said assemblies or elsewhere; except the gentlemen for daggers and swords, which are the arms they normally bear.

We forbid, furthermore, the ministers of the new religion to receive in their assemblies any person without first enquiring well into their lives, morals and conditions, so that, should they by pursued in justice or condemned by default or contempt of a crime meriting punishment, they may hand them over to our officers for punishment.

Whenever our officers want to attend these assemblies to be present at their sermons to see what doctrine is being declared, that they receive and respect them according to the dignity of their charges. . . .

That they hold no synod or consistory without leave or in the presence of our officers, nor any creation of magistrates, laws, statutes or ordinances among them, since these are matters for us alone. . . .

Those of the new Religion will be held to keep our politic laws; even those received in the Catholic Church in the matters of festivals and non-work days; and on marriage, for the degrees of consanguinity and affinity; so as to avoid disputes and cases that could stem from them, to the ruin of the greater part of the good families of our kingdom and the dissolution of the ties of amity which are acquired by marriage and alliance between our subjects.

The ministers will be held to appear before our officers in those places to swear, by their hands, to observe the present [*Edict*] and to promise not to preach any doctrine contrary to pure word of God, as is defined in the Nicene Creed and in the canonical books of the Old and New Testaments, so as not to fill our subjects with new heresies.

Forbidding them most expressly, and on the same penalties as above, to form their sermons as attacks on the Mass and the ceremonies received and kept in our Catholic Church; nor to go from one place to another, from village to village, to preach by force against the will of the lords, curés, vicars and churchwardens of the parishes. . . .

*Registered by the Parlement of Paris, 6 March,* 'due to the pressing urgency of circumstances, obeying the royal will; but without approbation of the new Religion; and everything is to be provisional, until it be otherwise ordained by the said lord King'.

SOURCE: Stegman, pp. 8–12; *MC,* vol. III, p. 17.

## 17 Royal interpretative declaration, 14 February 1562

. . . not that by our ordinance and present declaration we intended or intend to approve two religions in our kingdom, but rather one only, which is that of our Holy Church, in which the kings our predecessors have ever lived.

SOURCE: Fontanon (1611) vol. IV, p. 270.

# 2   Religious Violence in the Early Years of Conflict

The Wars of Religion would not have taken the course they did without fundamental and catastrophic religious hatred. This rather simple fact has tended to be obscured by the readiness of contemporaries to view religion as a 'veil' for political objectives and the unwillingness of historians from the eighteenth century onwards to accept the motivating power of religious hatred for its own sake. More recently, an urge to set religious 'choice' in a social context has led to inconclusive arguments over whether Protestants should be viewed as groups who adopted a 'new' religion as a function of their social and economic role. The very concept of 'choice', though, is anachronistic. Religion was not a 'lifestyle' option so much as a given framework for eternal salvation or damnation. The risks of departing from the age-old majority practices were enormous.

The years from 1560 to 1572 saw communal religious confrontation at its height in France, since the lines of division between the religious communities were still blurred. It is sometimes forgotten that the first years of conflict, 1561–2, and then the killings of the summer of 1568, after the 'peace' of Longjumeau, saw some of the worst massacres of the Wars of Religion, rivalling and in some ways surpassing those of the era of Saint Bartholomew in 1572. As the Parisian observer Pierre de Paschal put it in June of 1562: 'Around that time great murders were carried out all over France by both sides. At Saint-Cales, an abbey near Le Mans, the Papists filled up the wells with Huguenots but they were soon paid back in the same coin.' Paschal, historiographer royal, was trying to be commendably even-handed but it should be noted that the predominance of the Catholics in numbers meant that they were responsible for far more extensive massacres than the Protestants. For many of them, there was the incentive of a physical purging of the world of the 'filth' or 'plague' of heresy, which Natalie Davis has so amply discussed. In their turn, the Protestants were enthusiastic iconoclasts, understanding the power of symbols for traditional belief.

It need hardly be stressed that such violence did not come out of thin air. It was from the 1540s, and more sharply from around 1550, that an anxiety about the end of the world, linked to what seemed to be a periodically half-hearted tolerance of heresy on the part of authority, was becoming widely disseminated in France (see Documents 1–3). For their part, Protestants in France around 1560–2 were at the height of their self-confidence and optimism (see Documents 4–6). There were elements of fatalism but they shared the Catholics' messianic conviction of righteousness and had good reason to think that their increasing numbers were a sign of God's approval.

In Paris, the elements of confrontation were already clear during the discovery of Protestant conventicles in 1561 (see Document 7), which culminated in the riots of the Saint-Médard affair at the end of the year (see Documents 8–9). They were immeasurably exacerbated by the partial toleration edicts of 1561 and then the Edict of January 1562 (see Chapter 1), which allowed open Protestant worship just outside the walls. All sources converge on the exceptional violence of anti-Protestant mass action there during the following months, when the presence of the three Protestant meeting-houses in the suburbs of Saint-Antoine, Saint-Marcel and Saint-Jacques proved so disruptive that they created constant tension and eventually both political and mob action (see Documents 20–1).

The most famous outbreak of such violence in 1562, though, was the Massacre of Vassy. Opinions have always been divided on the responsibility for this. The Protestants were quite sure it was a premeditated act of persecution by Guise (see Document 18), who was certainly not slow elsewhere to order the execution of ministers (see Document 27). The cult was exercised at Vassy under the terms of the Edict of January, though technically within the walls. Some claimed that to establish a temple here, so near the duke's domain, even though the town was a royal one, was an act of provocation. The duke claimed he had only intended to admonish the Protestants since the site of the temple was on property that formed part of the dower of his niece, Mary Stuart (see Document 19). The Protestants could hardly be blamed for fearing the worst when his armed men appeared, or afterwards, for thinking it had all been planned. His own account is testimony enough to his aristocratic contempt for any rabble who dared to defy him, and his detestation of the sectaries is clear. If premeditation is not so obvious, the long-term importance of the Massacre is clear. As with so many spectacular acts involving the house of Guise, it completely overturned the existing direction of public policy. It solidified the reputation of the duke of Guise among Protestants as a cruel tyrant and the idea that the Massacre had been premeditated became an article of faith to the extent that even those Protestants, such as La Popelinière, who later questioned the facts were severely censured. On the other side, Guise's action firmly established him as the Catholic paladin. Vassy formed the centre-piece, in effect, of a vast outbreak of communal religious violence all over France. The Massacre of Sens followed on 12 April (see Documents 22–3).

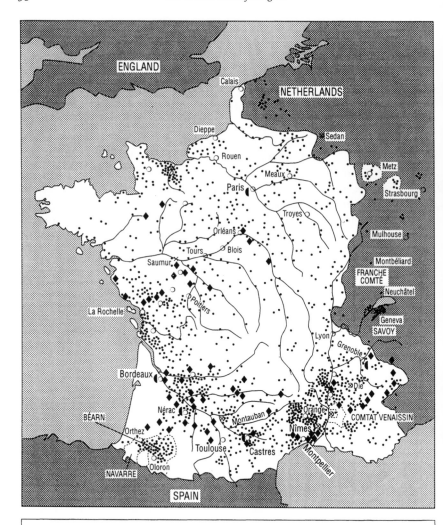

- · Established church (greater or lesser period)
- ○ Church with more than one pastor
- × Protestant Academy
- ❨ Bi-partisan Chamber in a Parlement
- ◆ Place de Sûrete

**Map I** The reformed churches of sixteenth-century France

Source: *Histoire du Christianisme*, vol. 8: *Le temps des confessions (1530–1620)* (Paris: Desclée, 1992), map 8

Religious confrontation was not, of course, confined to the capital. Throughout 1560 and 1561, as government and the courts gave out contradictory messages (see Chapter 1), the presence of Protestantism was more openly felt throughout the south and especially in Languedoc (see Documents 15–17). Both before and after the Edict of January, outbreaks of communal violence were acute in towns where Protestants were numerous enough to present a threat but not strong enough to seize control (see Documents 10–11 and 14). Elsewhere, Protestants in small minorities were brought under extreme pressure (see Documents 12–13). Attempts to seize control by well-placed Protestant minorities were sometimes successful (Rouen, Lyon) sometimes went disastrously wrong, with consequent purges, as at Toulouse (see Documents 24–5). Here again, the killings were seen as a time of tribulation by Protestants, though, viewed by the crown, they were measures of policing and security. The formal fighting is impossible to disentangle from a vast array of attacks, slaughters and sackings that went on across France in April–June. In Paris, where Protestants were in a precarious position, there was no less a tendency to massacre, which was in some ways comparable to the more famous massacre of 1572 (see Documents 20–1). In May, Protestants were formally expelled from the capital and their persons and property given over to systematic looting.

The documents in this chapter illustrate some of the rituals of religious conflict and the characteristic attacks mounted by both sides. Ministers were regarded as straightforward rebels and hanged when caught (see Documents 27). As Natalie Davis has made clear, religious violence was meant both to restore the divine order and to allay divine anger. This is why Catholics were so concerned to purify society of heretic pollution through fire and water. The bonfire was an age-old device for dealing with deviation, in this period particularly in evidence in book-burning (see Documents 36). By 1562, the Parlement of Paris, purged of sympathisers, was determined to rein in heresy and took active steps to eliminate office-holders who were covert Protestants, ordering banishments and executions. However, because so much of the killing was done extra-judicially, by mob seizures (see Documents 39–40), from the earliest religious violence of the Wars French Protestants were also cast, dead or alive, into rivers (see Documents 44). Indeed, it is hard to avoid the conclusion that, for the pious Catholic, the rivers of France were a vast sewage disposal system for heresy. The anguish about the end of the world that has been so amply documented by Denis Crouzet was the main fuel for this dementia. Victims were first dehumanised by degradation and then disposed of (see Documents 29–31). The natural savagery of children and youths was mobilised by Catholic enthusiasts to take a leading part in the violence (see Documents 41–3). For Protestants, the need to reinforce their faith and a righteous anger fuelled their attacks on the physical adjuncts of Catholic worship – essentially iconoclasm but also destruction of the instruments of the Mass (see Documents 32–4, 45). Confrontations commonly took place at set times, when Protestants were on their way to their meetings or during Catholic processions (see Documents 22, 35 and 38). By the middle of the 1560s, it is no exaggeration to say that two distinct views of the relations between man and God had generated two incompatible religious communities and that, without this collision, the Wars of Religion would not have proceeded in the way they did.

A further development of the 1560s made this collision more destructive. A major response of the Catholic community to the threat of heresy was the genesis of small local Catholic leagues. The first of these was probably the association formed to frustrate Protestant designs on Bordeaux in 1560. The years 1562–3 saw more of them emerge, notably at Agen and Toulouse, but they gained momentum particularly as a result of the second civil war and the peace of Longjumeau. In July 1567 the well-known Confraternity of the Holy Spirit was formed at Dijon; the foundations of mass Catholic action had been laid.

---

## MOBILIZATION OF CATHOLIC FEARS

### 1   Catholic invective (i)

Since God created the world, never was seen so strange a time in which famine, war and pestilence reigned, the avaricious rich, the more they had the less they were content. Could we see a more horrible time, sons opposing their fathers in false argument, daughters denying the holy sacrament to their mothers, false preachers preaching a thousand open abuses. Is it possible to envisage a worse time, God's blood flowing in the street in such floods it is terrible to see and stones cast at the cross?

SOURCE: Désiré, *Le miroir des francs taupins autrement dits Antéchrists* (1550), sig. Ciii.

---

### 2   Catholic invective (ii)

Now heresy is the sign of the end of this mortal world. Daniel, on whom I rest, is our witness for he says that the false, filthy people will overthrow through their malice the pure Host and the daily sacrifice. He says, too, that in the holy Temple there will be such great abomination that heresy will prevail until the end of things and that when the Church ceases to offer its oblation, everything on earth will be consumed by fire from heaven.

SOURCE: Desiré, *La complainte de la cité chrestienne* (n.d.), p. 61.

## 3   Claude Haton on the preacher Pierre Dyvolé at Provins, 1561

And furthermore he predicted the evil to come which would shortly be wrought by them in France; how they would rise in arms and rebellion against the King, his state and the public peace, laying waste towns, sacking churches and temples, ill-treating priests, trying to abolish all true religion, all divine, politic and civil laws, all sacraments and divine service; how by their pride they would take up arms to exterminate the King and his state as well as all the Catholic people. . . . And to conclude, he prophesied the ruin and coming desolation of France and called it several times in his sermons 'miserable, desolate and cursed of God', basing his argument on holy scripture, where it is said and cried aloud: 'Woe to thee, o land, when thy king is a child! Cursed be the kingdom whose princes are disloyal and consorts of thieves, judging them not', and other arguments from holy writ.

SOURCE: Haton, vol. 1, pp. 137–8.

## 4   The start of a national Protestant organisation, 1559

Whatever problems confronted the poor believers on every side, they were far from being daunted. On the contrary, it was at this time that God, through his special grace, inspired all the Christian churches set up in France to meet together to agree on a common doctrine and discipline in conformity with the word of God. Thus, on 26 May 1559, deputies from all the churches established by then in France met at Paris and there, by general agreement, the 'Confession of Faith' and 'Church discipline' were written down, as near as possible to those of the Apostles, in so far as the circumstances of the age allowed. This was truly done through the intervention of God's spirit to preserve unity, which has lasted since. The occasion of the assembly was that, at the end of the previous year, 1558, when Antoine de Chandieu was sent by the church of Paris to that of Poitiers . . . the time came for the Lord's Supper to be celebrated in that church. Thus, there was a large assembly not only of the people but of ministers from the region. After the celebration of the Supper, the ministers met to discuss both doctrine and the discipline oberved among them. In the course of this they began to understand how useful it would be if it should please God that all the churches of France should set up by agreement a confession of faith and church discipline. . . . When report of this was made to the church of Paris, after many difficulties had been surmounted and the churches asked by letter about the National Synod for their advice, it was agreed that the Synod should be held at Paris to begin with, this not to attribute special status to it but because it was the most convenient city in which to assemble a large number of ministers and elders secretly.

SOURCE: *HE*, vol. I, pp. 199–200.

## 5   The Calvinist of Millau on the Protestant self-image, 1560

In this present year 1560, the Gospel started to be revealed everywhere in this kingdom; for it had been hidden almost since the time of the Apostles until now, resulting in the tyrannies and cruelties that had been exercised throughout Christendom by princes, kings and great lords, fed by lies, and by false prophets against God, who had weakened the Church. The Pope had participated, calling himself the church and God on earth, which antichrist had himself worshipped throughout the world and, by idolatry, had wood, stone and the Mass god worshipped. Thus he had seduced the people and did not allow them to understand divine scripture. But, despite this, the Lord showed himself in this kingdom this year, during King Henry's life, in several places including Paris, Auvergne, Gévaudan, Velay, Dauphiné, Vivarais, Lyon, Languedoc, Provence and all or most of Guyenne. The result was that those who supported the Pope, including the King, brought great persecution on those of the Religion, who then started to be called Huguenots, through disdain and injury, conveying the idea that they were traitors (as was, once, Hugues Capet traitor to France) and thus gave this name to all those of the Religion: Huguenots. Then they unleashed great persecutions, murders and cruelties against those of the Religion, such that it was pitiful to see and hear.

SOURCE: Millau, pp. 5–6.

## THE EMERGENCE OF COMMUNAL DISPUTES

### 6   A Catholic view of toleration, early 1561

In all the towns of France where there were Huguenots, either openly or secretly, the edict was well received, and chiefly in those where there were Huguenot judges, who, with unspeakable arrogance, took pains to publish and enforce it to the profit of the Huguenots. The Catholics were instantly held in such scorn that some, weak in their faith and devotion, left the Roman and Apostolic Church to join the Huguenot church. In all gatherings and public places, the Huguenots had the upper hand, using threats and detracting from the Catholic church and its sacraments, especially the sacrament of the altar and the Mass. Though by the edict all were forbidden to insult each other, they never stopped insulting the Catholics as

'Papists', 'idolaters', 'poor fools', 'burning brands of the Pope's purgatory', and sought only sedition and to provoke Catholics against them so they could be put in prison. . . .

SOURCE: Haton, vol. I, p. 122.

## CONFRONTATION AT PARIS, 1561

### 7  Pierre Bruslart on riots in Paris, 1561

In the month of April, many conventicles were held in Paris without any action being taken. On 27th of this month, a great crowd of common people went to a house where one Longemeau was lodged, where it was suspected that illicit conventicles and preachings were held against the Christian religion. This house was in the Pré aux Clercs. Longemeau got his defences ready with more than 300 men armed with pistols, and several of the commons were killed. In this company was one Ruzé, advocate in the Court, who, because he was Longemeau's lawyer, was present armed in this assembly for the defence of the new religion, dressed in a violet gown, wielding his sword against the poor commons with a will. . . .

On the 1st and 2nd of November, various great assemblies and conventicles were held in the city of Paris involving 2,000–3,000 people in different places. This was to cause no small trouble to the Christian community. What is worse, though the prince of La Roche-sur-Yon was the King's Lieutenant at Paris, he gave no order despite this, saying he had command to appease and prevent sedition but that he had no powers to prevent preachings and conventicles and had no force to do it, so he said.

SOURCE: Bruslart, *MC*, vol. I, pp. 26, 59.

### 8  The Saint-Médard riots, Christmas 1561, a Protestant view

On the Saturday after Christmas, 27 December, the faithful had gathered publicly, as they were permitted, in the Saint-Marceau suburb in a place called le Patriarche. . . . After a quarter of an hour of the sermon, those of the Saint-Médard parish in that suburb started, out of deliberate malice (and after their vespers), to ring all their bells at once with such violence that since there is only a little street between the two places, the sound rang so loud in le Patriarche that it was impossible to hear the sermon. As a result, two people were sent, unarmed, to pray them to desist so that the company should not be prevented from hearing the word of God. On this humble request, the priests and some other rioters all said of one accord that they would go on ringing despite them. . . . They closed the great door, trapping one of the two; the other escaped quickly and fled to his own people. Though he had only a little knife on him, they killed him with seven blows, either of swords or halberds, all of them mortal. Also, the doors opening onto the street adjoining le Patriarche were shut and they started throwing stones and shooting arrows, of which they had good store. The shouts of those in need of help alarmed the whole gathering, whose last thought was of such an uproar. What heightened this was the tocsin ringing and the battery of stones and arrows that started so suddenly that it is to be supposed that it was premeditated. However, good order was given so rapidly, in these desperate circumstances, by the evangelicals that, having drawn up those in that company ready for defence – very few indeed out of such a large gathering, not less (in my opinion) than 12,000 or 13,000 people – they so reassured the rest that after the singing of a psalm the sermon continued. [*However, the battery of stones and ringing of bells continued, the provost-marshal of the governor was repelled and the Protestants decided to go over to the attack, breaking into the church and driving the priests into the tower.*] I cannot pass over in silence the prodigious fury of certain priests who were so inflamed by rage that, as their store of stones gave out, they got up on the altars and started breaking the images that beforehand they had so reverently worshipped and used pieces of them to throw at their enemies. But this is less remarkable than it seems, for this fury revealed their true nature. It would be difficult to know whether they were more insane when they thus irreligiously smashed the things they so honoured or when they worshipped things so foolish.

SOURCE: *Histoire véritable de la mutinerie, tumulte et sedition, AC*, vol. IV, pp. 51–62.

## 9   The Saint-Médard riots, a Catholic view

[*The Protestants*] indignant that this bell-ringing stopped their preacher from being heard, went in great numbers to the church of Saint-Médard, which they pillaged, mortally wounding several parishioners and smashing the images of the church. It happened that a poor baker of the parish, father of twelve children, seeing the massacre in the church, took the ciborium with the reserved sacrament, saying to them: 'My masters, do not touch this, for the honour of he who reposes within.' But a wicked man ran him through with a halberd, killing him next to the high altar and said to him: 'Is this your pastry God who now delivers you from the torments of death?' And they crushed under foot the precious body of Our Lord and smashed the ciborium into a thousand pieces. The poor people, in fear of attack, retreated to the tower and rang the alarm bell but were not rescued since their enemies were 3,000 or 4,000 in number and held the surrounding streets. Two others were killed and several others wounded, and yet these were led to prison tied by thick cables as though condemned to the galleys. The people of Paris were very aroused, especially as the watch had helped the Huguenots, along with a lieutenant of the short gown called Desjardins.

SOURCE: Bruslart, *MC*, vol. I, pp. 68–9.

## 10 Protestants and Catholics in Picardy, 1561 (i)

For three or four days now, certain little children of 8 to 14 have joined in bands of 100 or 200 and gone out every night to make processions through the streets of this town, some carrying crosses, others lead sacraments and other things; notably, they stopped before certain doors and sang certain salutations. At this time, only divisions and seditions can result from this, especially as some of them are followed by adults and yesterday there was seen a man with a sword under his arm saying to them: 'Sing, sing, my children, sing despite the Huguenots.' [*It is agreed that the mayor and échevins should go to the bishop to get him to bring a halt to the processions by gentle means.*]

SOURCE: Amiens, deliberation of 22 June 1561, Thierry, vol. II, pp. 687.

## 11 Protestants and Catholics in Picardy, 1561 (ii)

The 7th and 8th of December last, certain unruly people, provoked to sedition by the sermons of last Advent by the Jacobin, Carmelite, Augustinian and Cordelier preachers brought in by my lord the bishop of Amiens, the old enemy of the corporation of this town, engaged in various insolences, beatings, excesses, disobedience, rebellion and scandals to the disturbance of the public peace. When the tocsin was sounded at the church of Saint-Firmin and in the great church of Our Lady, to the full knowledge of the bishop, dean, provost and others, the mayor and provost of Amiens were grievously outraged in their persons and the dignity and reverence due to their magistracy was not enough to protect them from being outraged and wounded with the others. . . . [*Appeal for impartial judges in the town's collective case before the bailliage and accusation that a Catholic faction including Lequien, lieutenant particular, and a number of councillors of the bailliage were involved*] because they so hate those who profess the gospel and who say they follow the Reformed Church, among whom are those outraged, that they do their best to attack first before the case is brought against them; so that, in particular, Castelet, Picquet and Cousin, councillors, in giving their opinion at the assembly of Estates of the town about the King's demand for aid, dared to say publicly that those who attended assemblies to pray to God must be burned as rebels and their goods confiscated for the King's help . . . thus everyone knows they will make no trouble in acquitting the said seditious. . . .

SOURCE: Remonstrance of the échevinage of Amiens to the bailliage, 5 January 1562, Thierry, vol. II, pp. 700–3.

## 12 Protestants in Brittany, 1561

Madame, those of the Religion, seeing that their assemblies were not welcome and that I have said publicly that, if I hear for any reason that thirty persons have assembled, I would punish them so firmly that they would be an example, have presented a summary they have agreed on their manner of life, awaiting the King's and your pleasure on the matter; requesting that, to remove all cause of suspicion, someone be sent to be present and see what is done. I replied to those who talked to me that I thought the intention of Your Majesties was that nothing should be done. They said that, without it, great difficulties would result, as you could see from their request, which, in view of the present circumstances and the assembly of the Estates of this country being so near, and of our need to avoid causing discontent, I did not wish to refuse, admonishing them ever to live in patience and give no cause of scandal. . . . Madame, since the writing of this letter those of the Rennes district came to me with the same message and, considering the stubbornness of both sides, there cannot fail to be disorder if provision is not taken soon. . . .

SOURCE: Duke of Étampes, gov. of Brittany, to Catherine, Nantes, 3 March 1560/61, Lublinskaya, no. 5.

## 13   Request of the Catholics of Nantes

They remonstrate that they have been informed that certain persons, both of the town and of the district, have petitioned you to permit them to have temples in this town to preach and have the sacraments in the forbidden way, the consequence of which is so great and pernicious to the honour of God, the King's authority and the public peace that it has been, by good and holy cause, forbidden by the holy decrees, edicts and ordinances of the King. They also remonstrate that heretofore a certain person of the said opinion has put himself forward as procurator for the said inhabitants and, as such, has petitioned the King to allow a temple at Nantes to hold their assemblies in, even though this is contrary to their wish and rather they have ever desired to live as Catholics according to the Roman Church. . . . Most of those who want such temples are outsiders, vagabonds, working men and artisans who have only recently arrived and have no houses or property whatever in the town or environs; and against those of this new opinion there will be found ten thousand more men of substance, serving God and obeying the King and his laws, who will disavow this false procurator if need be. . . .

For this reason, my lord, they humbly beg you not to allow any other temples than those in which it has been accustomed to say Mass and divine service, and to prohibit all other illicit assemblies of whatever number; and that henceforth they be not allowed to commit such execrable faults as to undertake baptisms and celebrate weddings and other sacraments on their own authority against the ordinances of the Church and the King, so that his loyal subjects and faithful servants may live in peace under their accustomed law, which is good, holy and approved by Holy Councils and under which so many praiseworthy kings and princes since Clovis have lived, as does the present King. . . .

SOURCE: Requête des catholiques de Nantes au vicomte de Martigues, ? July 1561, Lublinskaya, no. 11

## 14　Petition of the magistrates and inhabitants of Dijon to the duke of Aumale, 1561

1. On the feast days ordered in the Catholic church, the so-called Reformed open and work publicly in their shops, contrary to the King's edicts.
2. Booksellers put scandalous books on sale publicly.
3. In front of the palace and in public places throughout this town defamatory booklets and pictures are sold deriding the holy sacrament of the mass.
4. Several of their opinion have daily put out blasphemies and scandalous and unworthy opinions about the holy sacrament and the mass, daring shamelessly to call it Jean Le Blanc.
5. Hoteliers, tavern-keepers and cooks provide meat indiscriminately on prohibited days, to the scandal of good and true Catholics.
6. They celebrate their weddings and baptisms on days and at times prohibited by the church.
7. They make assemblies in the town.
8. Contrary to the King's will, they assemble at cemetaries designated for Catholics.
9. They have a common chest and pay much money into it, by which they attract various poor and miserable persons on pretext of such false and pretensed alms and charitable gifts.

SOURCE: AM, Dijon, D 63.

## 15　Protestants and Catholics in Languedoc, 1561 (i)

I can only report the continuation of the disorders in your government and especially in the town of Nîmes where things are now so out of order that the justices who are devoted to the King's service have no other course than to leave the city and, having left, could find no other place of refuge in the whole of Languedoc than in my house . . . for they, or those judges under arrest in the town, are threatened with death by this scum. . . . I am awaiting the arrival of M. de Villars with some troops in order to punish these rebels. The more force the King can send us the better we can punish the main promoters of these assemblies and those who have abetted them. I know who they are and that the poor people are well-disposed towards their King. But these malefactors work on them with such promises and lies that they are quickly seduced. I am aware of the mistake of not having punished those I arrested last Easter. . . . A registrar of the town called Ranchon, who is at court . . . is the one who, all last Winter, had a Genevan minister preach publicly in his house, where there were large assemblies. I must warn you also, my lord, that two weeks ago more than 1,200 soldiers, raised in this country, passed through in small parties to the mountains of Gévaudan and Velay. . . . I believe they are on their way to Lyon . . . and of the suspicion I have had for about four months of the town of Aigues Mortes, as I am aware that it has been badly infected by this sect. I still fear this scum will take over as we have seen happen elsewhere in Provence and in the papal territories. . . .

SOURCE: Joyeuse to Montmorency, 8 September 1560, Vaissette, pp. 570–1.

## 16    Protestants and Catholics in Languedoc, 1561 (ii)

[*Report on his suppression of Protestant moves at Béziers.*] I can assure you, my lord, that this scum is so out of control that we have to take arms hourly. At Montpellier they have seized the great church of Our Lady in the middle of the city. I could not stop them or resist such a number for, as the consuls and the royal judges I summoned told me, there were more than 3,000 of them. I only have 30 arquebusiers and a quarter of the count of Roussillon's company. You can imagine, my lord, how effective they are for dealing with assemblies in a hundred places of your government, widely separated. Of the three companies which were to come, I have had no word. In the Toulouse area, they hold the country and attack the towns, having taken Lavaur, Réaulmont, Rabastens, Revel, Castres and some other places.

SOURCE: Joyeuse to Montmorency, Béziers, 30 September 1561, Vaissette, pp. 585–6.

## 17    Protestants and Catholics in Languedoc, 1561 (iii)

In this month of October, those of the Religion set themselves to take the temple of Saint-Pierre at Montpellier for their preaching. They were resisted, for within it there were canons, well provided with food and weapons as well as soldiers. The canons, seeing the temple virtually lost, came to parley, but, at the moment of agreement, a family called the Rogons, who were inside, the father with three or four of his children, killed two of the *Religionnaires*. The latter, seeing themselves attacked under cover of parley, broke in and gained control of the temple and cloister, killing the father and two of the children. . . . But once inside, they of the Religion killed 15 men in all, of the Papists. They were now in control and expelled the canons, all the priests, monks and nuns of the town. Thus, at Montpellier no one now dare avow themselves Papists.

SOURCE: *Millau*, p. 25.

# RESPONSES TO THE EDICT OF JANUARY

## The Massacre of Vassy

### 18    The Massacre of Vassy, the Protestant view

On Saturday, last day of February 1561(2), Monsieur de Guise left Joinville and went to spend the night at Dommartin-le-franc, two leagues away. Next day, 1 March, he left Dommartin and went to Vassy, a little town, about 8 in the morning, accompanied by many gentlemen to the number of more than 200, mostly armed with pistols and arquebuses. Passing via Bronzeval, a village half a league from Vassy, they heard a bell ringing and asked some of the company: 'Is that the sermon of the Huguenots?' and were told it was. Then they said: 'God's death, we will huguenot them by and by in another fashion' and some of the servants and lackeys said, swearing and blaspheming: 'Will they not give us the spoil?'

Arrived at Vassy, the duke of Guise stopped in front of the monastery with the cardinal his brother and several other of the gentlemen. [*There then arrived a crowd of officers and men of the duke's company, who were already in the town.*] They went straight to a barn, which those of the Reformed Religion had earlier taken for this purpose, where there were about 1,200 people assembled to hear the word of God preached, about an arquebus-shot from the monastery. The duke of Guise followed. . . . Arriving at the door of the temple at which the minister of Vassy, Léonard Morel, was preaching, La Brosse entered with five or six of his men. Some of the assembly said to them: 'My masters, if it please you, take a seat.' To which they replied: 'God's death, let us kill them all.' Those of the assembly who were near the door, hearing this, and seeing the duke of Guise approach with a great number of gentlemen, pages and lackeys, tried to close the door on them but could not because they were prevented by La Brosse and the others, who started to attack those who were closing the doors and fire into the assembly with their pistols. Then the duke of Guise entered with his suite and started likewise to lay about with swords, arquebuses and pistols, so they killed and wounded a great number. Seeing this, many in the assembly, to avoid this fury, broke open the roof of the barn to flee but the men outside fired on them with their long arquebuses, some of which were brought from the prior of Vassy's house by a brother and servants; they made a great many fall, some dead, some wounded. The rest, who could not get up to the roof, seeing themselves attacked . . . were forced to pass between two rows of the gentlemen outside the temple, who beat them with their swords and staves so that some did not get far before they were killed. . . . This affair lasted a whole hour and, once done, the retreat was sounded by trumpet. . . . There are presently 40 dead and buried, men and women, and 25 likely to die and more then 100 wounded.

SOURCE: Report sent to the duke of Württemberg (printed in *BSHPF*, 24 (1875), pp. 218–21) forming the basis for the standard account printed in various forms in *Histoire des martyres, MC*, vol. III, pp. 111–24, and *Mémoires de Guise*, pp. 471–3; in English as *The Destruction and sacke cruelly committed by the Duke of Guyse . . . in the towne of Vassy* (Edward Sutton, 1562).

## 19   The Massacre of Vassy: the duke of Guise's view

I must, however, inform you of an accident that happened to me on route as I was hastening my journey. Leaving my estate of Joinville to go to another of my houses called Esclaron, taking the road through a little town between them belonging to the King, called Vassy, there happened something I had never thought of and which I would never have expected from such near neighbours, most of them my subjects who know me well. It is true that, knowing for a long time that most of them were scandalous, arrogant and bold Calvinists professing the religion they call Reformed, I did not want to take my dinner there and so ordered it served in another village half a league away, expressly to avoid what happened as a result of my following. . . . But passing through, on a Sunday, the 1st of March, to hear Mass (as is my custom), it was reported to me while I was in the church and the divine service had started, that not far from there in a barn which in part belonged to me, a sermon was in progress in the presence of more than 500 people. Complaints had already been made to me that, on the persuasion of some ministers from Geneva, the people were very cool in their obedience to the King. So, as the town was part of the dower of the Queen of Scotland my niece, and in view of the orders I had given as her general administrator and because most of those present were my subjects, it seemed to me that they were too near, there being no more than a street in between, for me not to make the remonstrances I thought suitable, so they should know how much they were lacking in the duty they owed and in respect for the King, and because of the rebellions and insolences they had shown shortly before to certain prelates of this kingdom. I wished to meddle no further with religious matters, except in so far as it was contrary to the King's ordinances and commands. Moved by these considerations, thinking to make them a gracious and honest remonstrance and not knowing they were armed, as was subsequently found, with arquebuses and pistols contrary to His Majesty's edicts, I sent two or three of my gentlemen to indicate my desire to speak to them, and followed myself. No sooner were they at the door, which was half open, than suddenly those without impetuously sought to shut it and to repel those I had sent, with stones they had ready on scaffolding in front of the barn. Thus, throwing down these stones and firing arquebuses and pistols on me and my company of about thirty persons, we having only our swords with us, they did all they could to harm us, and me in particular, so that 15 or 16 of my gentlemen were wounded. I myself received three blows, which were (thank God) superficial. . . . They just failed to reach an adjoining house where there was a table loaded with weapons all ready and windows for firing from, about which I had not heard. However, their attempt was not good enough to stop me gaining control of the door, but this was not (much to my regret) without the killing of 25 or 30 people. . . . All this would not have happened without the attack from those of the town, and most of the killing was done by certain valets of the entourage, who arrived to find their masters wounded and the sound of pistols firing. In the midst of this insolence, and seeing myself still being attacked, I did not fail to restore order as quickly as possible and to stop what was happening. Without that, much worse would have happened.

SOURCE: To the duke of Württemberg, 17 March [1562], full version in *BSHPF*, 24 (1875), pp. 212–17; reprinted from a pamphlet, *Guise*, pp. 473–6, and *MC*, vol. III, pp. 119–22.

---

Confrontation at Paris:

## 20   Pierre Paschal on confrontations at Paris, March–April 1562

On 19th [*March*], the ministers took the oath before the lieutenant civil of the Châtelet, according to the Edict. President Baillet went to the prince of Condé on behalf of the Parlement to tell him to ensure that the ministers did not preach where they were doing, because the lord of the fief there had complained; and it was stated in the Edict that there could be no preaching without the permission of the immediate lord. He replied that, whatever the court had ordered, since it pleased the King that the ministers preach, they would preach there.

[*On Palm Sunday*] in the morning M. Bèze preached at the assembly and there were baptisms in the old and new traditions. After dinner there were more sermons where there were large numbers. M. Bèze preached in the garden and M. La Rivière from a window for those who were in the moat [*near the Saint-Jacques gate*]. It should be noted that on that day, the two sides were clearly marked, for the Papists carried palms in their hands in the old custom while the Huguenots did not and many mocked those who did. It was clear on this day that the number of Catholics was greater by far than that of the Huguenots. . . . .

[*On 23 March, after Condé's departure*], the preaching was continued but there were very few people there compared with the days before. It was easy to see that the prince of Condé had left. . . .

On Good Friday, the Huguenots held their sermon in their accustomed place near the Saint-Jacques gate, where there were many people. Because the town had mounted some artillery pieces on the gate, they placed, as a joke, some butter tubs and mortars mounted like artillery pieces on the window ledges of the house where the assembly was held. . . .

[*Easter Monday*], this day the address was at Popincourt, outside the Saint-Antoine gate, and also the absolution; the Papists and the Huguenots came and went together, the former to the absolution and the latter to their sermon, looking at each other without a word. They all came in and went out via the wicket because the gates were shut and the drawbridges up. . . .

Monday, 1 April, the boatmen came to the rue Saint-Antoine, where people were on their way to the address at Popincourt, determined to kill Malot the minister, who had been preaching that day. He escaped in the crowd but a merchant who looked very like him was killed, as well as a young lady and a woman. M. de Termes, who had the gout, had himself borne there to quell the tumult but one of his men, who was in advance of him, was killed, as well as one of his valets. Seven or eight were left for dead there. . . .

On Saturday, 4 April, Low Sunday eve, the Constable came from the court at Melun and, with many men, went to the preaching-house in the Saint-Jacques suburb and seized all the arms there and gave them as booty to his soldiers. . . . He had the pulpit, the benches and everything of wood burned. From there he went to Popincourt and did the same. He had the minister, La Rivière, imprisoned and sought out Malot, but he escaped. He also had Ruzé, advocate in the Parlement, and several others arrested.

Low Sunday, 5 April, great crowds went to Popincourt and demolished the house, tore out all the wood and beams and took them to the Town Hall where they were burned, shouting: 'God has not forgotten the people of Paris.' If anyone grumbled, he was beaten or killed on the spot. . . .

On 9 April it was publicly proclaimed that no man was to attack another, either for religion or otherwise. Because those of the old religion were sacking some houses of the Huguenots, it was proclaimed on pain of death that none should do this, on the pretext of religion or anything else that could be claimed. . . .

Sunday, 12 April, it was decided at the King's inner Council in the morning that the Edict of religion would be confirmed, except that ministers would not preach at Paris, in its suburbs or in the bailliage and viscounty.

SOURCE: Paschal, pp. 9–24 passim.

---

## 21    Throckmorton from Paris, 23 July 1562

The daily despites, injuries and threatenings put towards me and mine by the insolent raging people of this town doth so assure me of mine own destruction as I am not ashamed to declare unto Your Majesty that I am afeared and amazed, and by so much the more as I do see that neither the authority of the King, the Queen his mother nor other person can be sanctuary either for me or such as these furious people do malice . . . the prince's commandment is daily despiteously contemned and broken, not forbearing to kill daily, yet almost hourly both men, women and children, notwithstanding any edict or defence to the contrary.

SOURCE: Throckmorton to Elizabeth I, Paris, 23 July 1562, SP 70/39, no. 251, fo. 130r.

## 22   Claude Haton on the Massacre at Sens

After the publication of the Edict of January in all the towns and bailliages of France except in the Parlement and jurisdiction of Toulouse, preachings were started everywhere where there were enough Huguenots to sustain ministers and preachers. There was a great crush to get to them and for every Huguenot in France six more appeared, both for the liberty of conscience the preachers taught as well as for the welcome that was made to them. Even gentlemen and judges, though they were dressed richly, took their places alongside artisans and men of all trades, and, be they pigmen or cowherds, invited them to sit alongside them . . . and, to encourage them to come back, offered them drinks in silver cups and the best viands they had brought to the preachings, which usually took place at mid-day and after eating. This nibbling and warm welcome attracted many; others, when they saw who was involved, left and did not come back.

Those of Provins had no means of setting up sermons or maintaining a preacher in their town because of their small numbers and their fear of M. de Guise; but they went instead to the preaching in the houses of such gentlemen as the sieurs de Saint-Simon, Chantalous, Éternay, La Motte-Tilly-les-Nogent, as did those of the towns of Bray, Nogent and Pons-sur-Seine. Those of Provins met sometimes in the evening or daytime in private houses but not publicly for fear of being sacked.

The Huguenots of Sens and nearby set up a pulpit in the suburbs to practise their religion and obtained letters of safeguard for their attendance. For their greater security they brought to Sens a Gascon captain with some men to guard them while they were at the sermon. There were a great number of Huguenots at Sens, both of the town and from nearby villages, who were trying to gain control of the town of Sens to seize it and pillage it when the time was right, because of the rich treasures in the great church and the monasteries. They were waiting only for the watchword of their protectors and chiefs. Now it happened one day in this year . . . that the Catholics of the town made a general procession one Sunday to the church of Saint-Savinien to pray, hear God's holy word that was being preached by a Catholic preacher, Cordelier or Jacobin, and also to hear Mass sung, all in good devotion. Because of all this, the Huguenots of the town were indignant and, to dispute with and provoke the Catholics to riot, decided to go to their sermon at the same time, agreeing to go through the middle of the Catholic procession, insulting them, as was their custom, with words like 'Papists', 'firebrands of the Pope's purgatory', 'idolaters' and 'poor blind men sorely abused by the caffar priests'. To all this, the Catholics at first did not react, but seeing this, the Huguenots, continuing their insults and passing some Catholics in the streets, shouldered them so roughly that some fell down. This bold enterprise was the reason the Catholics there were provoked, with rough words, to attack the Huguenots and give them insult for insult. At that point the riot began.

However, at the start the Catholics offered no violence since they had only their books of hours in their hands while the Huguenots had pistols ready to draw. . . . That day there were certain men and women from the villages who had come on pilgrimage to pray in the churches there. They, seeing the audacity of the Huguenots and indignant at it, asked only to attack them and wipe them out. Once the Catholic procession had arrived at Saint-Savinien, and the Huguenot heretics at their sermon not far away, the Catholic sermon was made by their doctor and the sermon made to the heretics by their preacher and minister. This preacher, as was reported by some observers who were still Catholics, strongly incited his hearers to riot against the Catholics, to the point of saying that to exterminate this papal vermin would be a great sacrifice to God, and cursing all the church ceremonies and processions of the Catholics, calling them Papists.

The Catholic preacher said no less to his hearers than the Huguenot minister, though not inciting them to attack the heretics, but rather, while forbidding them to riot, exhorting them to patience in the defence of the Catholic Church of Jesus Christ in the manner of St Savinien and his confrères when they first brought it to Sens. . . . However, he warned his hearers to be vigilant and make sure they were not surprised and sacked by the Huguenots, reminding them of the riots that had already happened in certain places and towns of the kingdom, notably in Paris, capital of all France, and the sack of the church of Saint-Médard there. So he exhorted them in their procession and assembly to pray God for the maintenance of the universal church, bride of Jesus Christ, of the little king and the kingdom, which were all in imminent danger of being pillaged, destroyed and ruined if God did not take more pity on them than their rulers.

[*While this sermon and that of the minister went on*], all of a sudden and unexpectedly, [the Huguenots] were assaulted at the sermon by unknown men from the villages and suburbs, who attacked them so hotly with sticks and stones, hedge stakes and crow-bars that the Huguenots had no time to lay hands on their pistols and arquebuses. Being without their Gascon captain and guards that day, the preacher and his bold Huguenots were at such a disadvantage that in the fight a fairly large number were quickly killed and their place of assembly was demolished and totally ruined in less than half an hour, without a single beam left above ground. This was done while the Catholics were at their sermon and Mass for their procession, who, when they were returning, saw the riot in their town, the streets full of angry men attacking each other. The Huguenots who had escaped from the sermon, now able to make use of their firearms, started firing on the Catholics in the streets, some of whom were wounded. This made the riot worse, since the Catholics, seeing themselves attacked, set to in their defence and the rest of the day was so violent that not one Huguenot remained except those who managed to hide themselves. Any Mr Huguenot who was lucky enough to reach the house of a priest friend to escape was fortunate. The slaughter of the Huguenots was so great that only those who could not be found were spared, without distinction of man, woman, priest monk or clerk. But no ill was done to the little children, save to one, who was killed in the arms of a lawyer named Master Jean Haton, killed by a blow aimed at his father. The death of the child saved the father, who escaped the riot and was not killed, by means of his Catholic friends and relatives, who hid him in their houses until after the riot had stopped.

[*The Gascon captain returned in the evening and tried with his men to avenge the attack on his people but he was overwhelmed*] and he, the Gascon, half dead, was dragged through the streets by the children of Sens by a rope from one of his feet, from crossroad to crossroad, raising the hue and cry: 'Guard your pigs, here we have the pigman' and at each crossroad they burned his body with oven spits. The called the captain the pigman and the Huguenots of Sens the pigs because their preaching place was in the pig market. The children, having dragged the captain through the streets, went and threw him, with his other pigs, into the river Yonne. By this time night had fallen and imposed a silence on the fury, and the morrow there was no man so bold as to appear in the streets of Sens and declare himself a Huguenot.

SOURCE: Haton, vol. I, pp. 189–94.

## 23 Paschal on the Massacre of Sens

[*On 17 April, during musters held by the Constable near Paris*], while the troops were crossing the river Seine, there floated past dead bodies, being those recently killed by the Papists and thrown into the river at Sens.

SOURCE: Paschal, p. 29.

## The upheaval at Toulouse:

## 24 Toulouse, May 1562, a Catholic view

[*After the Edict of January, the heretic magistrates [Capitouls], elected in November 1561, received ministers in the city*], to whom the Parlement provisionally allocated a site just outside the town moat near the Villeneuve gate. Though by the Edict it was prohibited that those of the pretensed Religion should bear arms at their sermons and conventicles, the magistrates nevertheless allowed 100–120 armed with armour and firearms to attend. So as the more easily to carry out their bold enterprise, the magistrates ordered, on the pretext of avoiding popular disturbances, that all the arms of the inhabitants be deposited at the Town Hall, aiming thus to disarm the Catholics. Furthermore, three months before the sedition happened, they had brought in certain outsider heretics. . . . On 11 May 1562 they seized the colleges of Saint-Martial, Sainte-Catherine and Périgord and on that day nearly all the *capitouls* withdrew to the Town Hall . . . and the next day, Tuesday 12th, at about 8 in the morning, they began to show openly their cruel intentions, sending their soldiers out into the streets of the town. . . .

The court [of Parlement], seeing the treachery of the capitouls openly revealed, and the bodies and souls of the Catholics in the town in imminent danger, immediately elected eight new capitouls, notable persons, and suddenly the common people and the better part of the grandees of all estates, seeing themselves unexpectedly assailed, opened their hearts to God and by his grace and mercy decided to sustain his honour. . . . The Wednesday and Thursday following, there came to the support of the Catholics the companies of foot of Captains Bezordan, Clermont and Blanhac and on the Thursday the cavalry companies of MM. de Termes, Terride and Fourquevaux entered the town and prevented heretics from Castres and Montauban coming to the aid of their accomplices. The rebels, seeing the Catholics resisting them unexpectedly, attacked along the streets and especially the church of Saint-Sernin, seeking to enter and enrich themselves with the precious reliquaries of the saints. But the captain, with a good number of soldiers, repelled them. . . . The Huguenots went on until Thursday pillaging the churches in their control, pulling down and burning the holy images. . . . But the Catholics repelled them so stoutly that they were forced to retreat towards their redoubt at the Town Hall. These functionaries, knowing themselves balked of their bold enterprise, asked for a truce on Saturday afternoon, the eve of Pentecost, so as to escape by night. This was agreed by the Catholics, who were expecting the arrival of the cavalry company of M. de Monluc, which was approaching rapidly. The same day, the 16th, the Huguenots started to escape from the town hall by the Villeneuve gate, where part of their forces were stationed. . . . Because this was not expected, it was not immediately detected. But, having heard of it, the cavalry went out and defeated some of them while the country people dealt with some others. Thus, most of their troop withdrew to Montauban and Castres.

Thus, on Pentecost, 17 May, the Catholics entered the Town Hall . . . and, of the traitor *capitouls*, found only one, who was degraded and then beheaded. The viguier, Captain Saulz, some lawyers, burgesses and others of the faction were also executed and the seven fugitive *capitouls* hanged in effigy. . . .

SOURCE: 'Briefve narration de la sédition advenue en Tholose, 1562, en may par les hérétiques', Vaissette, pp. 617–22.

## 25 Toulouse, a Protestant view

All of a sudden, then, these madmen started scouring the streets, killing as many suspects as they could, many of those of the Religion having stayed with their families, either unaware of the hasty decision to seize the Town Hall or not approving of it. Many were unable to bear arms and others were caught by fear.

Thus, there were not a few houses to pillage and people to kill. The least crazy took those whom they met to prison, though these had to bear on their way many punches and blows with daggers or stones. If they could get to prison, there they were subjected to a thousand outrages, some having their beards torn out, others being prodded with halberds until cast into the dungeons in chains by two gaolers, Léonard Robin and his son Nicolas, two of the wickedest men in France, convicted of all sorts of crimes. The prison was so quickly filled that they were turned away and many were slaughtered at the gates. For the rest, with the fury constantly growing across the town, those found inside or outside their houses were stripped to the shirt, killed, dragged along and thrown in the river. . . . Poor servant-maids going for water were thrown in the river, men women and children were thrown out of windows into the river. If, by chance, they got to the bank they were shot or stoned to death.

. . . During these disorders, there were heard only the terrible screams and lamentations of the innocent. Some took refuge with friends or neighbours, who often handed them over to their enemies. Others strove to get to the Town Hall as they could not leave the town, those of the Religion controlling only one gate. . . . In the evening, seeing a poor dressmaker coming out of one of the entrances to the town sewers near the old bridge, hoping to escape, they seized him and forced him to reveal that there were 24 others who had escaped into the sewers. Instead of having pity on them, they flushed great quantities of water down the sewer entrances, which forced out those poor people covered with excrement. So they were stripped to their shirts and all drowned in the river.

SOURCE: *HE*, vol. III, pp. 17–19.

## 26   Protestants at Castres, Languedoc

[*After the Edict of January*] they of Castres, having asked the magistrates for temples in consequence of this edict, and being refused, went to preach on the Albinque ravelin under some sheets and then, because of the inconvenience, moved to the old school, and because they were cramped there, expanded into some private houses. . . . The Catholics were impatient about this growth in those of the Religion and, not knowing how to stop it, had their monks preach against them with all sorts of insults, inciting people to attack them. This provoked the trouble and the magistrates had much ado to stop it. Those of the Religion, being in constant fear and seeing the Catholics continuing to try to ruin them, were compelled to summon some neighbours secretly, both of the town and some gentlemen . . . who only awaited the order from the prince [of Condé]'s lieutenant Crussol, by the deputy they had sent to the prince. The latter came with the order to seize the town and arrest the Catholics as hostages for those of the Religion in their hands. The consuls got everything ready and warned the neighbours and friends of the town so secretly that the Catholics were taken unawares.

SOURCE: Gaches, *Mémoires*, pp. 13–14.

## PATTERNS OF COMMUNAL RELIGIOUS CONFRONTATION IN THE 1560S

### 27   The pursuit of ministers, Poitou and Dauphiné, 1562

You should execute the minister you have had arrested at Thouars as a rebel and disturber of the public peace, either by hanging him or by throwing him into the river in a sack. As for the rest, you are to remove all arms from the Huguenots and give the Catholics back theirs.

SOURCE: Montmorency to La Trémoille, Blois, 23 July 1562, AN, 1AP 29, no. 5.

You must trap the preachers when they are poorly accompanied or in other places as you find suitable and, as quickly as possible, have them hanged, placard dangling, as rebels and infringers of the King's edicts. Some of my neighbours and subjects, some of them merchants, wanted to defy me three days ago and wounded a dozen of my gentlemen. So much for their fine gospels!

SOURCE: Guise to La Mothe-Gondrin, lieut. in Dauphiné, 28 February 1562, *HE*, vol. III, p. 250.

### 28   A religious riot at Vire, Normandy, 1562

[*Montgomery, as Condé's lieutenant at Vire, had allowed the Protestants to break into the house of the Cordeliers on the pretext that there were arms inside. Soon after, Montgomery had the relics broken open for exposure as frauds.*] Soon after Montgomery's departure, those of the Roman Religion, greatly irritated by this, decided on vengeance. Two days afterwards, the last day of July, they gathered as a mob at the end of the sermon in the great church so that the minister, Fugeras, had great difficulty in escaping to an out-of-the-way barn, while his servant was cruelly killed. Among others, a poor mercer named Louis Pinette, not knowing of the riot and thinking they were after a wolf – their cry was 'le loup' – was seized and drowned in a little stream. Though he prayed for those who were stoning him, he could not move the crowd of women who were forcing him under with their hail of stones.

SOURCE: *HE*, vol. II, p. 846.

## 29   Gouberville on the desecration of corpses at Valognes (Normandy)

7 June . . . [*Symonnet returned from Valognes*] after sunset and told me that when they were at Beaumont on their return they heard the tocsin ringing at Valognes and Alleaume.

. . . 8 June . . . today in the afternoon I was told that yesterday evening, about 5 o'clock, there was such a great commotion of the people at Valognes that the sieurs de Hoesville, de Cosqueville, master Gilles Mychault, doctor, Gilles Louvet, tailor, Robert de Verdun and Jean Giffart, alias Pont-l'Évesque, were killed, several wounded; the houses of Cosqueville were looted and destroyed, and that the bodies of the dead were still in the street today after mid-day, with the women of Valognes coming to attack the corpses with stones and staves. It was also said that the house of master Étienne Lesney, sieur de Haultgars and élu of Valognes, was also looted and destroyed. Charlot left at 2 for Valognes to verify this and returned after sunset to tell me that all the above was true and that the people of Valognes were in a great rage.

SOURCE: *Gouberville*, vol. III, p. 789.

## 30   Bruslart on the desecration of corpses at Paris

Two men had been condemned to be hanged by the provost of Paris for having cut down a man executed judicially, dragged the body through the streets and thrown it in the river. That day, as they were being led to execution, they were rescued by the common people from the hands of justice. In the process, a notary's clerk, a young man present at the riot, was shot.

SOURCE: Bruslart, 28 June 1563, *MC*, vol. I, p. 130.

## 31   Paschal on the desecration of corpses at Paris

On Sunday, 15 March, a Huguenot was buried in the new manner at the Innocents, but the Papists quickly came to disinter it and flung the dead body into the mud in the Grande Rue [*Saint-Denis*]. The Huguenots wanted to rebury it and the Papists immediately flung it out. There were some wounded and one man killed on the spot.

SOURCE: Paschal, p. 7.

## Iconoclasm, late 1561

## 32   Protestant iconoclasm at Mont-de Marsan

It happened at this time that certain people from various places assembled to roam about breaking images. Having heard this, the people of Mont-de-Marsan, foreseeing that their enemies would be aware of this, warned the magistrates to take measures, advising them to lock up the images and ornaments in the great church, so that the troops of image-breakers could be told their work had already been done. But the magistrates, not agreeing, allowed these people into the town, where everything was smashed as elsewhere. But the gold and silver ornaments were handed over to the mayor for inventory.

SOURCE: *HE*, vol. II, pp. 963–4.

## 33   Iconoclasm at Millau

[*At Millau, Rouergue, in late November, the great church was seized and*] all the wooden idols in the temples were taken, even those of certain papists who had hidden them in their houses thinking to put them back afterwards. All those that could be found were taken; there were many wooden Gods and Virgin Marys, as well as saints of wood and stone. Those of wood were burned, those of stone smashed, without any opposition, on St Anthony's day, 17 January 1562. [*After the Edict of January, the Protestants refused to return the church to the Catholics.*] The town, by common consent, handed the reliquaries of gold and silver, the relics within them and all the instruments of idolatry for inventory to Master Pierre Pascalis, doctor of Millau and consul, to answer for them when required.

SOURCE: *Millau*, pp. 28–9.

## 34   Iconoclasm and riot at Issoire, Auvergne, 1562

. . . Morange, the minister . . . went to preach in the lower court of the house of Antoine Vialle; and from an upper gallery that served him for a pulpit, preached to the crowd in the lower court. There, he exhorted the people to embrace the truth of religion and turn from the true religion and, above all hold in detestation images, crosses and other things preached by Papist abuses. Consequently, he forbad them to go to the priests and monks who might make them falter and slip back into their original errors. His words had such an effect on those of the Religion that shortly afterwards, without fear of or respect for the King or justice, at night, they smashed all the crosses both within and without the town, not leaving a single one standing. When this was reported to the minister, he praised them highly in his next sermon saying they had done a notable thing for the honour of God, instead of admonishing them for this public scandal. Another night they brought down all the images of the Virgin Mary, both those in the market place, where their pedestals are still seen, as well as those outside the town, as at Our Lady in the Fields, which they pulled down after breaking up the iron grills, which they took away. They rejoiced at all these evils, while the Catholics wept to see these insolences, approved by the minister. They went to ask him to put a stop to acts so pernicious and of such evil example, which presaged some misfortune for the public weal of Issoire; added to which, the governor, Monsieur de Saint-Herem, would not tolerate them. Moranges, mockingly, replied to their remonstrances: 'It seems, Messieurs, that you are sorry to see the coming of the reign of Christ.' With this bold reply, he sent them away perplexed. Those of the Religion, told of this, decided to do even worse, so that a few days later, during the night, they went to smash all the windows of the priests in the town, threatening them that if they did not get out or change their religion they would be killed. Things had come to such a point that monks and priests in the street were jeered at so they could not go out: 'Look at the fox, the sneak, the Papist!' Furthermore, they beat on their shutters with stones, hammers and staves so that they drowned out the noise of everything else, adding horrible yowls that redoubled the din, so that the clergy could only go into the streets with fear. The minister approved all this and lauded the humanity of their faith in his sermons as if they had done something for the honour of God. This made them so bold that they wanted a captain at their door during the exercise of their religion, to command with all authority, without respect for the King or Monsieur de Saint-Herem, the governor. Having decided this, they sent for the Sieur de Chavaignac as their chief. He came to Issoire and those of the Religion, as a sign of welcome, gave him a white satin cap with a white plume. It was hoped that his coming would calm the popular fury and bring an end to these evils. But the contrary happened; for Chavaignac, to win their approval, gave them more licence than the minister. Everything thus being permitted to them, they went on Sunday to the Cordwainers to pray to God, so they said. Then, entering the town to the number of two or three hundred, they followed the same route as the Holy Sacrament procession, singing the psalms of David as they went, so that the sound was more like thunder than praise of God. As they passed the houses of Catholics, they went to the doors and shouted: 'Papists, sneaks!' Once they had brought Chavaignac in, they wanted to increase the number of their ministers, so they summoned cellarer Le Court, his wife and children, another named Dufaux and another called Messire Georges Laurent, so, as they said, that the gospel should flourish despite the papists. The respect they bore these ministers was so great that when they returned from their sermons to their houses, they were accompanied by two or three hundred men to honour them, often with the sieur de Chavaignac, with his white plume. Their intention was to exterminate the Mass and other church ceremonies. To accomplish this, they assembled some little children in the market place in various different bands that they drew up, like savage beasts, crying to each other: 'Haw, haw, the mass is done for. One hundred priests for three blancs.'

SOURCE: Julien Blauf, pp. 39–42, revised from AD, Puy-de-Dôme, J353, pp. 58–60.

## 35  Incitement to riot by scripture-reading, Gien, 1562

At this very time, the people of Ozay-sur-Trézée, a walled town three leagues from Gien, of which it is a dependency, inhabited by vineyard workers, labourers and other manual workers long of evil repute, started, on pretext of guarding (as they said) their religion and images, to rob and despoil travellers and even pillage the farms of the people of Gien, to whom most of them were in debt. And even though remedy was attempted, they continued in this fashion and committed great evils. That was the reason why the Reformed, whereas they had always preached outside the town of Gien (despite the tumults), after the Edict of January started (for fear of attack) to preach in the churches despite the protests of the priests that it was against the law. At this time another opportunity arose to enter the churches, though against the wishes of the townspeople. This was on 3 May, just as the ordinary scripture-reading was going on and before the time of the Catechism, at the moment of the reading of the 12th chapter of Deuteronomy, where mention is made of the destruction of altars and images. This was not long after the arrival of news about the destruction of images at Orléans. Some soldiers of Captain de La Borde, who had earlier behaved wisely, entered the town (unknown to people at the sermon) and set themselves to destroy the churches and altars, not forgetting all the appurtenances of the Mass, which from that time ceased completely, even though the priests were unharmed. This might have caused great scandal, had not de La Borde and his men returned to Orléans on the orders of the prince of Condé, who sent Captain Noisy in his place. This captain was without conscience, though he pretended otherwise, and his men were disposed only to plunder the church under the pretext of religion, of which they had no understanding. . . .

SOURCE: *HE*, vol. II, pp. 537–8.

## 36  Catholic book-burning at Paris, 1562

On 8 June a great number of books, such as Bibles, commentaries on the Bible, books by Calvin, Bèze and Mornay and other ministers, were burned at the end of the Notre-Dame bridge, opposite Saint-Denis-de-la-Châtre. In the rue Saint-Jacques so many were burned in one pyre that the fire lasted from an hour after mid-day until four in the evening. . . .

On 14 June, the burning of books was continued and a great many were burned in the place Maubert.

SOURCE: Paschal, pp. 49 and 52.

## 37  Riot during religious meetings, Rouen, 1562

On the 17th of the month, the Edict of January was published at Rouen and following it the Reformed service was set up in the suburbs and with such effect that, even though it was usual in the town for many outrages and mascarades to take place in the week before Lent by a group called *Les Conards*, all that was stopped by the common consent of the people, who condemned such follies and evil doing. Some, more offended at this than others, tried to do something but were opposed by the lesser people even with stones. This state of affairs continued until 8 March, when some images at the portals of certain churches were smashed. This was blamed on priests trying to incite a riot after having heard of certain changes at court, and as they were incited to do by a most seditious Cordelier, Hugonis, who was preaching at the cathedral, notwithstanding his condemnation in the Parlement of Paris under Henry II for lewdness with the abbess of Montmartre-lès-Paris, and having since made a serving girl pregnant in one of the good houses of Paris where he used to go after preaching. On that occasion, to save the honour of his order, he had the effrontery to remark that people might have had reason to be shocked if he had been made pregnant by the girl. Such had long been the life of this pillar of the Church, on whom it now depended whether the town of Rouen would fall into horrendous riot. Seeing this, the Reformed, hearing of the massacre of Vassy, started to go armed to their sermons.

SOURCE: *HE*, vol. II, p. 713.

## 38   Killing during Catholic processions, Paris, 1562

[*At Paris during the procession on Holy Innocents' day 1562*] it happened near the Innocents' that there was a poor man who ill-advisedly, as the procession passed, said out loud: 'Ha! If I had six more here of my courage, we would kill or put to flight all these idolaters.' He had no sooner uttered these words than he was slaughtered by those around him. The same day several houses were attacked because they had not put out displays like the others.

SOURCE: Paschal, p. 43.

## 39   Crowds seizing prisoners and carrying out sentences (i)

[*After the fall of Rouen to the Catholics, Raoullin de Longpaon (one of the councillors of the Parlement)*] pretended to calm down the people, who were shouting whatever was put into their mouths, mainly that they would not allow royal letters of pardon to be accepted and that certain men named by them had to die; among others, a clerk of the Parlement named Gaurelet, not generally known but personally hated by Bigot and Péricart, whose injustices and iniquities he had often declared in open Parlement. Longpaon told them that what they wanted would be done and slowly the mob dispersed without further violence. But five or six days afterwards, this poor man, judged by his enemies of a certain crime, was followed to the gallows by a great number of rioters in arms singing: 'Tant vous allés doux Guillemette' and was hanged at this fine ceremony. . . .

Five or six days later, the seigneur de Bosroger, whose death was demanded by the rioters though he had not openly professed the faith, but for the same cause as Gaurelet, was caught while leaving the town. He managed to get to safety on a galley moored in the river but, after his enemies had sworn he would come to no harm, he was handed over, saying these words (since faithfully reported): 'Gentlemen, I am charged with no crime and there is no accusation against me. In all these tumults, I have done nothing for which I fear justice by any judge but I have offended God in being backward in his service and having followed the opinions of those who did not love God.' Once in their hands, he was taken to the gate and battered with halberd blows and pistol shots. His corpse lay 28 hours on the pavement.

SOURCE: *HE*, vol. II, pp. 791–3.

## 40    Crowds seizing prisoners and carrying out sentences (ii)

A painter who had been imprisoned as a Huguenot by the abbot of Saint-Germain-des-Prés, was released by the abbot's officers. The people cried out at this and rebelled, taking him to the river. As he was able to swim, he tried to escape by jumping in. But the banks were quickly full of people ready to slaughter him as soon as he got to land. The boatmen in the river would not rescue him, so that tormented and exhausted, with nowhere to go, he was drowned; this was a piteous sight. The same was being done every day; there was no justice to be had.

SOURCE: Paschal, p. 79.

## 41    The savagery of children, Paris, 1562 (i)

On 23 July, the lieutenant of the bailli of Pontoise was executed in the place de Grève, convicted of having tried to hand that town over to the Huguenots. The executioner had no sooner done his work than the children took the dead body from him and dragged it through the mud, tore it into several pieces and then threw it into the river. They tore down the gallows, smashed it up and burned it.

SOURCE: Paschal, pp. 80–1.

## 42    The savagery of children, Paris, 1562 (ii)

On Lady Day, August, as a Huguenot bookseller was being taken to prison, there passed the holy sacrament that was being taken to a sick-bed. As he resisted being made to kneel like everyone else, the children seized him from those who were in charge of him, killing and tearing him to pieces, and took the body to be burned at the refuse dump near the pig market.

SOURCE: Paschal, p. 89.

## 43   Thomas Smith on the same, 1563

They of Paris do still murder one or other for Huguenots, which is the most cruel and barbarous disorder that ever was seen in any commonwealth. For it is enough for a boy of 13 or 14 years old or younger, when he seeth a man in the street, to cry: 'Voilà un Huguenot' and straight the idle vagabonds and such as go about to cry things to sell, and crocheteurs set upon him with stones and such things as they have ready, and then cometh out the handicraftsmen and idle apprentices and with swords and such other weapons as they have, every man that may, and then they spoil him of his clothes and the boys and that canaille trail him down with ropes to the river, and so casteth him into the water. If he be a town dweller, after that they have killed him they enter in his house, spoileth and carieth away all that he hath; and if his wife and children be not the sooner carried away, they kill them likewise.

SOURCE: T. Smith to Cecil, 4 February 1563, SP70/50, no. 221.

## 44   Corpses cast into rivers

[*On the day an edict declaring as traitors Huguenots who had sacked churches was issued, 27 June 1562*], several people were killed at Paris, among whom was the clerk of M. de La Haye, master of requests, who, taken by the mob and questioned as to his faith, said he was a Huguenot and would remain one. So, he was quickly done to death by the people and then thrown into the river. The same was done, in the same street, to the servant and chamber-maid of a jeweller. A woman was brought from the Saint-Victor suburb to the drinking-trough in the place Maubert and was accused of not going to Mass for ten years. Having been thoroughly battered, she was thrown into the river, where, when she surfaced, the boatmen finished her off with oars and staves. It was a shame to see people taken in this way, and often those who were not suspected of anything. . . .

On 13 July, two men accused of coming from Orléans were cruelly murdered and thrown into the river. One was taken at the Saint-Marceau gate and led to prison by 15 or 20 well-armed men. But the mob took him from them, led him to the place Maubert, killed him and threw him into the river. The same happened in the Saint-Marceau suburb, except that the man was not taken from a guard but seized in his own house, killed, torn to pieces, dragged throught the streets and from there to the river. The children carried the murdered man's blood-soaked doublet aloft on a staff in front of the body shouting: 'Look at the wicked Huguenot heretic!' . . .

On 14 and 15 July poor Huguenots were thrown into the river and many books were burned in Paris.

SOURCE: Paschal, pp. 61–2 and 72.

## 45    Protestant sacrilege, 1563

An unhappy deed was done in the church of Ste Geneviève. A wretched Huguenot, just as the priest was holding up the precious body of Christ to show it to the people, grabbed it from his hands and crushed it under his feet, holding a dagger to kill the priest. He was instantly taken and quickly condemned by the lieutenant criminal. The same day he was executed and burned in the place Maubert. By the King's command, M. de Montmorency and his company were present at the execution.

SOURCE: Bruslart, 22 November 1563, *MC*, vol. I, p. 139.

# 3 The First War of Religion and the Pacification, 1562-6

As the crisis over the registration of the Edict of January mounted, Navarre dramatically reversed his position and in February invited Guise to Paris, announcing that he wished to live in friendship with him; Navarre's office of Lieutenant-General was ample cover for opposition to the Edict of January. It was in the course of Guise's journey to Paris that the Massacre of Vassy took place on 1 March (see Chapter 2). The immediate political effect of the Massacre was finally to crystallise the political divisions and plunge the country into full civil war. As the political elite fell to fighting, there was, in effect, a vast urban insurrection led by Protestants all over France that brought Calvinist leadership to some of the most important cities of the country, including Rouen and Lyon, which was seized by the turbulent baron des Adrets (see Document 6). Small towns all over Languedoc and Guyenne fell, though the key position of Toulouse was seized by royal forces (see Document 7). Most of the towns of the Loire region, including Tours, Blois, Orléans and Bourges – the old centre of royal power – and in the west, Le Mans, Poitiers, Angoulême and Angers also fell. When towns came into Protestant hands, there was inevitably much iconoclasm and tomb smashing.

Paris was the crucial exception. On 15 March, the Triumvirs arrived in Paris to general rejoicing. Condé, who had been at court, arrived the same day on his way to Picardy but found his position impossible and withdrew from the city on 23 March (see Document 1). Catherine was now increasingly under pressure from the Triumvirate, now linked to the King of Navarre (see Document 4). Her plan to withdraw the King to Blois was stopped and she was compelled to take him to Fontainebleau.

The prince of Condé, who had gone to Meaux, arrived before the gates of Paris with Coligny and Andelot on 29 March, and failing in his purpose to gain control of the royal family (they had been moved to Melun by the Triumvirate on 27 March), he entered Orléans on 2 April 1562 (see Document 2). He quickly began a furious publicity campaign to justify his position. In a letter to the Reformed Churches, of 7 April, he declared he was defending true religion and called for military support. On the 8th he issued the first of his manifestos, in which he argued that the crown was in effect captive in the hands of the Triumvirate, and Guise especially, yet appealed to Catherine to escape Guise control. He demanded that the Triumvirs withdraw (see Document 3). Catherine, for her part, in ever greater fear of the Huguenot rebellion, had to accommodate the policies of the Triumvirate, though she affected to believe that Condé was a prisoner of his party (see Document 4). Condé's case was a lengthy one and replied to by an even more lengthy rebuttal. On 11 April, Condé published a 'Treaty of Association' for the maintenance of God's honour, the public peace and the King's liberty, in effect an instrument of government, and formally assumed command of the Huguenot forces. This was followed by a Second Declaration on 25 April, sent to the Parlement of Paris. He also entered into a direct public communication with Catherine in May but by this stage was wasting his opportunity of striking a decisive blow.

At this time, the cry was heard repeatedly that the prince of Condé and his party were using religion as a cloak for their political aims. Catherine said this in April (see Document 4) and the duke of Guise and the Spanish ambassador both made the same point (see Document 5). This is an opinion which has been influential with historians but should be treated with caution for the simple fact that politics and the religious dilemma were inseparable.

The Triumvirs, in their demands to Catherine of 4 May, for their part ostentatiously covered themselves in the Lieutenancy of Navarre and offered to disarm if Condé's forces did the same, as well to let him re-enter the council. Though the Edict of January was confirmed, with the exception of Paris, the Triumvirs were calling early in May for the complete predominance of the Catholic religion. Catherine was forced to agree that she could not allow the Triumvirs to withdraw. Access to the recruiting grounds of foreign mercenaries now became crucial for the two sides, both short of men and money. The crown (Triumvirs) aimed to draw troops not only from Spain but also from Catholic Germany and Switzerland. Condé's regime at Orléans depended no less on supplies of men from Lutheran Germany and the Swiss, and in April appealed to Elizabeth I for help. Any Protestant hope of success had depended on rapid triumph. Instead, Condé, no doubt conscious of his weaknesses, put off the confrontation. The royal and Protestant armies approached each other around Orléans early in June but, though the truce expired on 21 June, no major battle followed as the two sides manoeuvred around each other. Last-minute peace talks brokered by Catherine seemed to outsiders to promise well on 24 July but were just devices to gain time and had collapsed by the end of the month. There was a certain reluctance to fight and the conditions for both sides were foul in the summer of 1562 (see Document 8). However, every week that passed sapped Huguenot strength. Blois, Tours, Poitiers and Angoulême were lost one by one. The main operations began with the siege of Bourges on 19 August and its surrender on gracious terms on 31

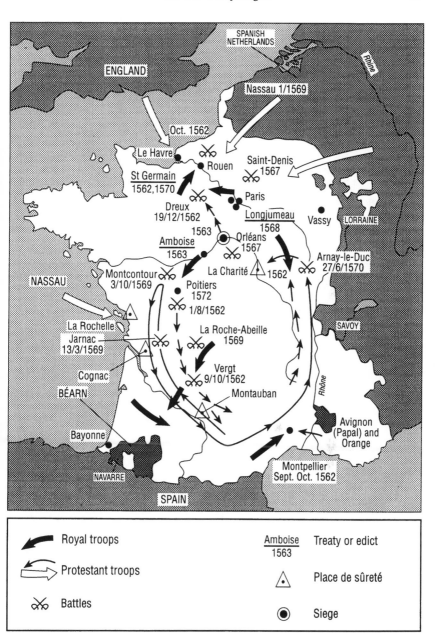

**Map 2**  The first wars, 1560–72

Source: Based on Michel Pèronnet, *Le XVIᵉ siècle, 1492–1620* (Paris: Hachette, 1995), map 9

August. Troops being brought from Germany by Andelot were too late to stop this but he was able to outwit Aumale and get through to join Condé.

Elsewhere, the old Captain Blaise de Monluc, commissioned in January to regain control of Guyenne, effectively blocked a Protestant triumph in the south and west by operating from Bordeaux and Toulouse, where Protestant moves had been crushed ruthlessly in the early stages, to chip away at Huguenot positions, using calculated cruelty to intimidate his enemies. Tavannes consolidated the hold of the crown and Catholicism in Burgundy, and in Picardy Amiens was secured for the crown by a decisive remodelling of the city council. In Languedoc, however, the position of royal representatives was weaker. Gradually, Jacques de Crussol emerged as the military chief of a Huguenot network that claimed to represent the Estates (see Document 11). In Auvergne, as the estates complained later in the year, law and order were breaking down (see Document 10).

After the taking of Bourges, the royal army was unable to attack Orléans and the focus of the war moved to the siege of Rouen. Condé was more than ever in need of English help and negotiations throughout August conducted by his agent the vidame de Chartres resulted in the Treaty of Hampton Court on 10 September. The terms were the handing over of Le Havre, then in Protestant hands, in return for 140,000 crowns to be employed in the defence of Rouen. Le Havre was to be returned to France on the restoration of Calais. The English landed there on 4 October. By then, however, fort Saint-Catherine had been taken at Rouen and the city was beleaguered. Only a small English relief party got in and negotiations broke down. On 26 October, the city was taken by storm, the day Navarre died of wounds received some weeks before.

The royal position had much improved. Only Orléans and Lyon held out among the major cities. In fact, peace-feelers had been put out to Condé even during the siege of Rouen. Navarre's death enabled him to assume the Lieutenant-Generalship of the Realm by the decrees of the Estates-General, but the Triumvirs and Catherine refused to recognise this, installing instead the manipulable cardinal of Bourbon, his brother. Condé's position seemed to improve early in December, when he was able to bring an army of around 10,000 up to Paris while the royal forces were unprepared. Catherine parleyed while troops were brought up and it was in these talks that the first outlines of the regime of toleration, to be clarified in successive edicts, was mapped out. However, for Condé the delay was a disaster. His army began to melt to 7,000 men, now faced by a royal army of 15,000. Unable to reach English allies and short of supplies, he was compelled on 19 December to give battle at Dreux to Guise and the royal army, in extremely unfavourable circumstances, fortified only by the psalms of the ministers (see Document 12). The defeat was predictable, though it established a pattern for the rest of the Wars. The

Protestants lost, but not badly enough to be crushed and with assets enough to recover their position. Condé, not a great general but personally brave, was captured in the charge. The old Constable de Montmorency was also captured and whisked off to Orléans in short order. Marshal de Saint-André was killed. Thus, though the Protestants' losses were greater, the astute tactics of Admiral Coligny enabled them to withdraw and regroup, even though heavily outnumbered and cut off from their allies. Coligny reinforced the garrison at Orléans and then moved into Normandy to join Montgomery.

The position of the Protestant lords was grim. On the other hand, the move toward peace was helped by a number of factors. Firstly, Guise's determination to press on against Orléans was foiled by the conditions of the country; secondly, Montmorency, in captivity there, was eager to negotiate a peace; thirdly, Catherine was eager to turn royal forces against the English at Le Havre in case they became too ensconced there. Guise began the siege of Orléans on 4 February but conditions were difficult on both sides. Then, an assassin managed to wound him on the night of 18 February; he died the next day. The disappearance of Guise left only Montmorency alive of the original Triumvirs. It also proved to be the removal of a road-block on the way to peace, though it had other long-term consequences: it enabled the Guises to nourish among themselves the conviction that the Admiral and Condé had planned the assassination and thus justify a campaign of revenge that was to culminate in 1572. The continuation of Huguenot rebellions in Guyenne, Poitou and Languedoc proved an extra spur to peace.

Negotiations followed rapidly under the Queen's aegis. Condé and Montmorency were released and met on 8 March. It was agreed that Condé should succeed as Lieutenant-General (a promise unfulfilled) and that his army should be paid off. The Edict based on the negotiations was issued on 19 March and represented to some extent an advantage for aristocratic Protestantism: though toleration of private consciences was enshrined in it, only nobles with high justice obtained extensive rights of the cult. Elsewhere, only one town per bailliage was to have a place of public preaching (the places were not specified and this caused problems later) (see Document 13). The Parlements, dominated now by Catholics, were generally reluctant to register the Edict and had to be forced to do so. However, it soon became apparent that the Edict was to be interpreted very strictly; the crown sought to ensure that towns of lesser importance were designated for worship and the interpretative edict of December 1563 further limited its freedoms (see Document 14). Moreover, the prohibition of the Protestant cult at court (see Document 15) rendered it difficult for figures like Coligny to take an active part in government, though he was restored to his office as Admiral (temporarily held by his cousin Damville).

The summer of 1563 was occupied with the campaign in Normandy to oust

the English from Le Havre and the implementation of the Pacification Edict. The
condition of the country was parlous and the task of getting the German
mercenaries hired by both sides out of the country extremely difficult. Some of
the worst damage took place over the summer and autumn of 1563.

The court came to Rouen after the fall of Le Havre (30 July). There, the
ceremony for the declaration of the royal majority was held on 15 August in
the Great Hall of the Parlement. The occasion was controversial in that
Charles IX was just entering his 14th year rather than 14 years old. Chancellor
L'Hospital made a memorable speech on the royal prerogatives (see Document
21); the points were echoed by the King himself in his later insistence to the
Parlement of Paris that Parlements should simply act as law-courts and cease
their political activities now he had come of age (see Document 22). The
Rouen session also saw the declaration of the definitive English forfeiture of
Calais. The following day war was belatedly declared against England, though
the ambassador, Throckmorton, continued negotiations while in detention
which were to culminate in the signature of the Treaty of Troyes on 12 April
1564.

By that stage, the court, after a brilliant stay at Fontainebleau (31 January–
13 March 1564), which is as good an illustration as any of the principle that it
was necessary to keep up appearances in order to maintain credit, had set off
on its long tour of pacification round the country. It had rapidly become
apparent after the Edict of Amboise that neither side was willing to abide by
the terms. Catholics refused Protestant rights to worship, Protestants refused,
in areas they dominated, to re-admit the clergy and elsewhere to conform to
Catholic ceremonies in public (see Document 16). Despite the stringent
attitude of the crown to designating them, there was general trouble in
agreeing the places of concession for public worship in each bailliage (see
Document 17–19). These were the problems Catherine set out to deal with in
the tour (see Document 23).

The measures employed by Catherine in this nearly two-year perambulation
around the kingdom were designed to ensure that the Edict of Pacification
worked, and this meant settling a vast number of local disputes and hatreds.
Sometimes, as in the Protestant towns of Languedoc, the experience was highly
uncomfortable. At Nîmes, where a large crowd pressed in calling 'justice,
justice!', the court stayed only one day. At Montpellier, still strongly Protestant,
the compulsory holding of a general Christmas procession was highly
disturbing. One advantage, at least, was that Crussol had returned to
obedience and welcomed the court. Elsewhere, as at Lyon, the visit was crucial
in the re-establishment of royal control. Catherine's policy was reinforcement
of royal authority. She was accused by her enemies of a cynical balancing act
between Protestants and Catholics (see Document 27). It is certainly true that

she needed Coligny and Condé but she governed effectively through Catholic generals such as Tavannes and Vieilleville, members of well-established courtier families like Lansac, and new favourites like Albert de Gondi, count of Retz. For Catholics, the tour was crucial in re-establishing the Catholic credentials of the court in the provinces (see Document 25–6). Another facet was the continuing work of law reform carried on by Chancellor L'Hospital, symbolised by the assembly at Moulins in February 1566 towards the end of the great tour (see Document 24).

The most widely noted event, of course, was Catherine's meeting with her daughter, the Queen of Spain, and the duke of Alva at Bayonne (15 June–2 July 1565). A great deal of ink has been spilt in arguments over whether it was at this meeting that Catherine committed herself to a policy of elimination of the Protestant leadership. There is no doubt that Philip II wanted to pressure her into suppressing Protestant freedom of worship and implementing the Council of Trent. On the other hand, the documentation about what exactly Catherine committed herself to is highly ambiguous and, in one celebrated case, subject to severe mistranslation (see Document 28). Given the general trend of her policy to damp down hostilities, it seems highly unlikely that she would willingly have gone along with such a policy. This is reflected in her correspondence with the ambassador in Spain, Saint-Sulpice. However, she had a weak hand to play and had to offer something. Alva wanted her to undertake to expel Protestant ministers, and it is possible that she gave a vague undertaking along these lines, as well as to submit the decrees of the Council to a discussion of their political implications in France. The Spanish envoys to the meeting, taking the view that she was devious, were themselves extremely cagey and sought to draw her out. That she undertook to rescind religious toleration or to cut down the Protestant leadership seems unlikely. It is true that there were Catholic grandees who may have supported such a policy in discussions with Alva, partly for religious reasons, partly out of personal vendetta. The most lasting consequence of the meeting, though, was to instill in the Protestant leadership an attitude of suspicion and foreboding that led directly to the renewal of the civil war two years later.

---

## DECLARATIONS OF HOSTILITY

### 1   Pasquier on the seizure of arms

All is chaos and confusion [*in Paris*]. Men of both parties assemble in the town with their leaders. Pistol and cannon shots mark the hours. . . . Some time after, it was agreed among these lords that the prince of Condé would leave the town first to avoid conflict, followed the next day by the King of Navarre and his adherents. . . . If I were permitted to judge these events, I would say that it is the start of a tragedy which will be played out among us at our expense; may God will that only our purses are hit. . . . The prince [*of Condé*] has committed in all this certain mistakes. I will not mention his change of religion, still less his taking arms, which are indeed grave faults. But since it happened that he crossed the Rubicon, he should not have quitted Paris and the King's presence; for whoever has possession of both will have great advantages over his enemy. [*Condé's seizure of Orléans.*] This has to some extent surprised the Catholic princes and lords. This is why they resolved to bring the King, then at Melun, to Paris. The Constable arrived first, quietly, and the day after, 4 April 1562, mustered the citizens with great pomp to the joy of all, *dulce bellum inexpertis.* . . . Nothing but war is now spoken of. Every man now polishes his weapons. The Chancellor grieves while the rest take pleasure. When he came to speak, the Constable told him that it was no business of men of the long robe to discuss war. But he replied that, though such men could not command armies, they might judge when to fight. This reply does not seem to me less true for being bold, for there is nothing so much to be feared in a commonwealth than a civil war and most of all a civil war fought under the cloak of religion, especially while a King, because of his youth, has not the power to command absolutely.

SOURCE: Pasquier, *Lettres hist.*, pp. 98–100.

## 2  The prince of Condé at Orléans

All through these days [*of March*] gentlemen and soldiers of both sides, some for the prince and Huguenots, others for Guise and Papists, flocked in [*to Paris*]. On the 18th and 19th the prince did not go to the assembly as he had done the previous days but stayed in his house well accompanied. . . .

The 20th, with MM. de Condé and Guise at Paris and many men coming in to support one side or the other, the cardinal of Bourbon arranged that they both withdraw the next day. I do not know why this was not carried out. The whole town was in almighty fear of some great disorder . . . through the whole town, firing could be heard as though Paris were a frontier town. . . .

[*On 23 March*] the prince of Condé left Paris to go to one of his houses, though he had said he would never leave unless M. de Guise did so. . . .

[*In Early April*] the prince of Condé was sending men to Orléans, who arrived like travellers, but they stopped there, making as little fuss as possible. Meanwhile, he made his way there as best he could with his troops. On his arrival, the gates were locked and entry denied on the King's orders, but those who were already inside came to the gates in arms and opened them, so he entered with his company and seized the town. . . . From every side great men flocked to Orléans, some for fear of justice, others to carry out the commands of the prince of Condé, who had seized the artillery munitions of Tours, Orléans and other places on the river Loire.

SOURCE: Paschal, pp. 10–20 passim.

## 3 Condé's manifesto

[*The Edict of January had given great hope of settling the troubles of the kingdom, though the delay in its registration and various manoeuvres gave rise to suspicions that it would not last long.*] However, that did not move the lord prince or others of the Reformed churches to say or do anything to trouble the public peace of this kingdom. . . . Meanwhile, news was brought of the cruel and horrible carnage wrought at Vassy, in the presence of M. de Guise, where many of the King's subjects were inhumanly slaughtered, men women and children, while assembled without arms in their usual way to hear the sermon and pray to God according to the religion and pure word of God, which the lord prince maintains along with them, and hopes to do so until his death, by all lawful means.

[*While Condé went to remonstrate with the King and Queen Mother at Monceaux, Guise, Montmorency and Saint-André ignored the court and made a triumphal entry into Paris. There*] they daily held council, summoning the King's officers, presidents, councillors, and town officers, giving out that this was the King's true council, considering it was held by the chief officers of the kingdom. [*Such a Council was only the continuation of a long-hatched plot and Condé could expect no good from it. It also showed Guise's continued lack of respect for the King and Queen Mother.*]

Besides all this, the lord of Guise, from his arrival in Paris, used all his friends and influence to retain the Queen at Fontainebleau for fear that she would go to Orléans. [*His intention in this was to control both the court and Paris. Condé then withdrew to La Ferté. Then*] the duke of Guise went to the King and Queen Mother in arms, as during war and against his greatest enemies, an unaccustomed and unacceptable thing in view of the King's youth and that the Queen, though she is endowed with singular virtue and constancy, could not help being intimidated at being thus surrounded by forces against her will and express command. Ample proof of this is afforded by our King's tears, which he wept when forced to go to Melun a few days ago, which those present may be pleased to remember. Thus, such a coming of the lord of Guise, the Constable and Saint-André, in open arms, seizing the persons of the King, the Queen-Mother and M. d'Orléans . . . cannot but be viewed as their captivity, the most damaging, miserable and shameful that ever happened in this kingdom. . . . And because the lord of Guise, as Grand Master and Great Chamberlain, with the Constable and Marshal Saint-André, shield themselves behind the estates and charges they hold in this kingdom, saying

that it is for them to take arms whenever they think fit; added to which, they abuse
the authority of the King of Navarre . . . the lord prince declares that the above
could not have better shown how far they are from their duty of maintaining the
King's authority. . . .

Protestation

First, he protests that he is moved by no private concern, but that solely his duty to
God, the particular duty he owes to the crown of France, the Queen's government
and finally his love of this kingdom, compel him to seek all lawful means before
God and men and according to the rank and degree he holds in this kingdom to
restore the King's person, the Queen and my lords her children to full liberty and
to maintain the observation of the edicts and ordinances of His Majesty, especially
the last edict promulgated for the matter of religion with the advice of the princes
of the blood, lords of the Council, presidents and councillors of the Parlements of
this kingdom; praying affectionately all good and loyal subjects of his Majesty to
weigh carefully the abovesaid matters, so as to lend him all aid, favour and
assistance in such a good, just and holy defence.

And in so far as the King, at his accession to the crown, found himself burdened
with a mass of debts, with few means of contenting the least part of his creditors,
and that his good and loyal subjects have willingly accorded him a great deal of
money, both for paying them and for repurchasing his domain, and that those who
start this war with light hearts will not scruple to lay hands on it and employ it for
other purposes than for which it was intended; the poor people will have just cause
to complain, losing the hope that the Queen and the King of Navarre offered them
of using all these taxes, and other money that could be spared, for paying what is
due and recovering alienations, so as to relieve the kingdom and restore it to the
state it was in the reign of King Louis XII. For these reasons, the lord prince
protests against those who will dare lay hands on any moneys of the King's, which
they must produce and account for. For his part, he and his company intend to
spend only his own, without burdening anyone, nor committing oppressions and
violence. He also protests that the clamour of the poor people, when oppressed, be
brought before God against those who are its cause and who refuse all reasonable
conditions, forcing so many men of honour to this last resort.

And also, because it is known that the King and Queen are surrounded by armed
persons who control their wills, and that most of the Council are intimidated, so
that there is no one who dares contradict those who think only of their vengeance
and carrying out their long-laid plans; the said lord prince protests and declares
from this moment that, though he will give ground to no man living in the
obedience he owes to His Majesty and the Queen his mother, neither will he allow
a foot to be placed on his throat on pretext of some mandates, letters patent or
other despatches of the above, under the name and seal of His Majesty, until the

said King and Queen and his lawful Council be in such place and freedom as belongs to a King and Queen, revered, honoured and uniquely loved by all their subjects.

Furthermore, the lord prince protests, concerning the King of Navarre his brother, that with the obligation of fraternal love and the particular respect he owes and wants to give him, he intends recognising him according to his rank and degree in this kingdom, with all obedience after the King and Queen; as also he is sure the said lord King, considering the above, will have such regard as reason and the present necessity will require, about which the said lord prince beseaches him humbly and most urgently.

Finally, the lord prince, with a great and honourable company of lords, Knights of the Order, captains, gentlemen, men of war and various good persons of all estates, wisdom, property and virtue, to show that they speak in truth and that they hold nothing so dear, after the honour of God, as the tranquillity and grandeur of the King, most humbly require the Queen that, for fear of those who surround her in arms, quite otherwise than has ever been seen in this kingdom, she should judge freely, according to her view, of which of the two Parties is in the wrong. For this reason, may she go to whatever town in this kingdom she pleases, from that place to issue the command, by the least of her household if she chooses, to both parties to lay down their arms and render the obedience due from subjects to their King and sovereign lord, requiring both to render account of their claims, according to reason and the order of justice. The lord prince promises that, for his part, he will obey everything she commands, provided the above show him the way. For, should they do otherwise, he will venture his life and those of 50,000 men of the same opinion to support the authority of the King and Queen. And if the Queen does not wish to leave the place where she is, the said lord prince and others of his party beseach her most humbly that it please her at least to send home all those who have come to her in arms, which they have taken up on their own authority; that is to say: the said lord of Guise and his brothers, with the Constable and Marshal Saint-André. And though the said lord prince is not of the rank to be sent back to his house (in so far as he has the honour to belong to the King and be a prince of his blood), nevertheless he offers to retire voluntarily and make all the company with him disarm, on the above conditions; also that the King's Council be not henceforth intimidated either by threats or by force and that the King's edicts, specifically that of January on the matter of religion, be inviolably kept and maintained until the King be of age to judge for himself and punish all those who have abused his authority. And should these conditions be unacceptable and if they refuse to restore the King and Queen to their accustomed liberty with their Council, and continue to abuse their name and oppress their subjects, the said lord prince protests that, for his part, he neither can nor will endure it and that, for all the ills, miseries and calamities that will stem from this, the blame can never be imputed to him but rather to those who are the authors and sole cause of it.

SOURCE: Stegman, pp. 25–8.

## 4 Catherine de Medici and the crisis

I have always waited to see if Our Lord would bring some improvement and whether this fire, that began so long ago, as you know, may be put out or at least kept down . . . and thus sought all the expedients and remedies I thought, on advice, might serve. I acted in this as a woman and the mother of a King in his minority, who thought gentleness more suitable for this malady than any other remedy . . . but in the end it has not pleased Our Lord that this should work. For, on the contrary, the evil has got worse, so that those who wanted this fire, seeing my plans to be other than theirs, have torn off their mask, and, claiming a feigned mistrust that they had of being attacked, and on this pretext covering themselves in the cloak of religion, have taken arms and assembled many of their opinion and all sorts of men to seize the town of Orléans, which they hold by force. Not content with that, they have taken the town and castle of Blois, Tours and Le Mans. . . . As for myself, I feel so deeply offended . . . that, for two reasons, I have never, other than by the great loss I have already suffered, been so touched to the heart. The first is that I see the honour of God taken as a pretext and cover for one of the most pernicious and unhappy enterprises ever undertaken in this kingdom, which is that of the children God gave me the grace to bear, in which I have received such honour that I would spend a thousand lives to preserve it. The second is that I see my name and what I hold dearer than life brought into dispute, so that I am participant in this pitiable enterprise that is led by such dangerous leaders. I must believe that they hold my cousin the prince of Condé in Orléans against his will to give greater authority to their acts. I have tried all the means I could to disarm and disband them and sought all means to get them to change their plans. But they are hard, and I see such venom in them that I have decided (to my great regret) to use all means to make them understand that all my life I have never shared their views. The gentleness I have used hitherto has been to try to overcome the malady by gracious remedies. . . . I have found my brother the King of Navarre and all the princes and lords here well disposed to serve the King my son and support my good intentions and I am far from doubting their good will towards me.

SOURCE: Catherine to S. de Laubespine, bp. of Limoges, 11 April 1562, *LCM*, vol. i, pp. 293–6.

## 5 Chantonnay, Spanish envoy, on the crisis

[*Catherine and Navarre accept Philip II's offer of 30,000 foot and 6,000 horse but think that 3,000 horse and 10,000 foot will be enough.*] In truth it can now be clearly understood that what we see now is more a matter of rebellion than of religion, as I made the Queen admit; and the actions of the enemy are very different from what in their Associations they say they have sworn to God and His angels to do, which is to maintain the Edict of January and not to sack, pillage or usurp the churches or smash images. This is what they have done at Orléans, Lyon and Rouen and all the other cities where they have been. . . .

SOURCE: Chantonnay to Margaret of Parma, 7 May 1562, *MC*, vol. II, pp. 38–9.

## 6   The seizure of Lyon, April 1562

Captain Moreau was sent in diligence to Orléans by the churches of the Comtat Venaissin, Languedoc, Dauphiné and Lyon to hear from the Prince what were his orders for the King's service and the peace of the kingdom against the breakers of the Edict of January. The prince sent him straight back . . . praying those of the Religion, especially at Lyon, to send him men and to take control of the town for the King under the command of the sieur de Sault as its governor. . . . Following this decision . . . on the last day of April and 2 after midnight, those of the Religion went out and attacked the guard at [*the church of*] Saint-Nizier and the Town Hall, the most important places. . . . Thus they gained control of both. At the same time they broke into the churches of the Cordeliers and of Confort, seizing the towers that commanded the squares in front of them. . . .

[*On 2 April there arrived the baron des Adrets, who*] before that had been colonel of legionnaires . . . a most vigilant, bold and fortunate commander and truly gifted with some qualities necessary in a great captain but, for all that, cruel and extremely ambitious. . . . As soon as he heard what had happened in Lyon, he lost no time in getting there. Though he had been given no appointment, unless he considered his election as chief in Dauphiné covered Lyon, and without any opposition, in view of his being thought decisive and likely to leave again for Dauphiné once he had given his advice, he seized all authority, ordering everything as he pleased.

SOURCE: *HE*, vol. III, pp. 254–63.

## 7   Monluc on the recapture of Toulouse

[*Blaise de Monluc, having dealt with the Protestants of Guyenne, was summoned to Toulouse by the first president of the Parlement. He was joined by forces under Terride and Charry.*] The enemy, having heard we would be at the gates by sunrise, panicked during the night . . . they left at nightfall by the gates they held and were followed by a troop of gentlemen who cut to pieces three or four hundred. The rest escaped, though not all, for the peasants pursued them and killed more. They had four ensigns at Montauban who arrived there the day before their defeat, and were coming to their relief, but having heard that the companies of Terride and Charry were on the way, they retreated to Montauban. The next day they came to Lavaur, where they looted all those of your religion and made welcome those who had escaped the defeat in this city. There are now 1,500–2,000 of them at Lavaur, Rabastens and Castres. You can be sure, Sire, that the great diligence shown in the relief of the city was the reason it was saved. . . .

I humbly beg your pardon for writing the truth frankly, as you will learn that you have only three companies here which do not consist largely of the new religion: those of the Marshal de Termes, of Terride, and mine. Some gentlemen of the marshal's company, who were all his relatives or officers, having learned that you had divided it between Escars and Martigues are resolved to depart and most declare they will never again bear arms. . . .

SOURCE: Monluc to Charles IX, Toulouse, 22 May 1562, Monluc, vol. IV, pp. 136–7.

## 8   The conditions of fighting, Summer 1562

In this time, the mortality of the plague was great, particularly in the city of Paris and most of the cities of the kingdom.

SOURCE: Bruslart, August 1562, *MC*, vol. I, p. 95.

The weather was so vile, with endless rain, that the poor people could not gather their corn, which was already ripe and sprouting in the ear. This was a great pity and no one knew whether it was winter or summer, except for the length of the days, for the sky was always cloudy and the roads deep in mud, just as in mid-winter. All this raised the price of food. Plague, which had been in Paris for some time, got worse because of the adverse conditions. Thus, France was afflicted heavily with the three scourges of God: plague, famine and civil war.

SOURCE: Paschal, p. 71.

On 13 July it was decided in the Privy Council that those at Orléans or of the other side, having taken arms against the King, should be declared rebels and enemies of the crown of France and their property confiscated and annexed to the crown if, within a certain time, they did not return to the King.

SOURCE: Paschal, pp. 72–3.

## 9   Gouberville observes the troubles in the Cotentin

7 April . . . the abbot of Cherbourg brought all his movables into Cherbourg because of a rumour this morning that the forest was full of Huguenots come to

take the abbey. For this foolish rumour and other reasons, the sieur de Magneville and the captain forced all the judges and lawyers out of the town and the people of the town were in commotion. I left with Pinchon at mid-day. Cantepye went home. I spoke for a long time to M. de St Naser in the shelter of a boat. It was raining hard.

14 May . . . [*At Vire on business*] where we arrived after sunset. Those of the town assembled at the lieutenant's to find out who we were. They thought we had hackbutts and pistols. We went to talk to the lieutenant, while there were 200 people gathered in the street to shackle my horses.

17 May, Pentecost, before 7 o'clock we went to the sermon of the sieur de Villiez, minister, at the temple of Saint-Malo, then we came back to dine at Russy.

Thursday 18 June, I stayed at home. I was warned three times from Cherbourg to be on my guard and that M. de Matignon would pass here and sack my house. Because I thought I was in no wise at fault, I did not worry, also because more news is false than true. . . .

19 June . . . I was alerted again this morning that the sieur de Matignon was very angry with me, so I spent all day hiding my coffers and other movables, had my horses saddled and led to the woods. . . .

21 June . . . I was ill all day from the pain, anxiety and anger I had felt since Thursday.

1 July . . . All day, cannon shots were heard constantly afar off and very loud. No one knew what it was. . . .

2 July . . . all day the noise of heavy artillery was heard up the coast. It was said it was at Le Havre. The noise started on Monday and no one knew what it was; some said it was coming from the direction of the Channel Isles. Everyone was dismayed at what it could be.

20 July . . . we arrived at Russy [near Bayeux] about 10 at night. St. Samson, who had to leave next day to go to the Cotentin, told me I should bring in my livestock, fodder and the rest of my property because it was said that M. d'Aumale was to come to lay siege to Caen and sack all the villages in this country of Bessin, both papists and huguenots and wipe the country clean of all the inhabitants he found there, as he had done in the pays de Caux.

3 August . . . On my return I found contrôleur Noël and Jehan France walking in the fields. We talked until we came to the rue d'Argouges. While we were talking about religion and the great divisions and controversies of opinions there are these days between men, France said: 'If I had my way, a new God would be made who was neither Papist nor Huguenot so that it could no longer be said that so-and-so is a Papist and so-and-so a heretic or Huguenot. To which I said 'Unus est Deus ab eterno et eternus. We cannot make Gods since we are just men.' It seemed to me that Noël was very offended at France's words.

30 August . . . Today, after supper, we strolled in front of the great abbey [*of*

*Caen*] for an hour, the sieur du Fort, Lescures, Rampan and several others from Bayeux whom I knew not, talking of the troubles and misfortune there is at present between the rulers of this kingdom and the subjects.

1 October . . . After I had entered the court at Valognes and listened to the reading of my lord of Matignon's letters, lieutenant Bastard, from the bench, asked me: 'Monsieur de Gouberville, do you swear to live in obedience to the King and according to his laws, statutes and ordinances as did the other gentlemen of this viscounty yesterday and to bring no aid or comfort to the rebels contrary to his will?' To which I replied: 'Yes, Sir. That is why I am here.' [*Afterwards at dinner*] the lieutenant asked me if I had sworn like the others. To which I replied: 'yes', as I had done this morning, and that I would live in the law and faith of Our Lord Jesus Christ and according to the laws of the Holy Catholic, Apostolic and Roman Church. Then I took my leave.

Source: *Gouberville*, vol. III, pp. 774, 782, 783, 792–3, 802, 805–6, 812–13, 823–4.

---

## 10  Remonstrances of the Third Estate of Auvergne on disorder, September 1562

. . . Two or three months ago, in several places, almost everywhere in this country, on the main roads and in other places, there were many men in large or small bands which thieved from any people they found in their way. It is common to hear complaints of this and everyone knows about the evils that happen daily to carters, merchants and other men on their travels, from whom gold, silver, goods, horses, pack animals and other things they have to transport are stolen. As a result, people can only leave the towns with great danger and the King's subjects cannot trade or transport goods from one place to another as their business requires. . . .

Moreover, companies of soldiers in great numbers pass through this country, and are to be found in the small towns, who claim and vaunt to have powers against all those of the new religion, to arrest their persons and property. On this pretext . . . by force and violence, and without distinction, they lay hands on the property of good loyal subjects of the said lord [*King*], especially those they know to be the richest, whom they put to ransom for as much as they can, though these subjects are known to be of good life and conversation, good Catholics and in no way suspect for the new religion or any act of rebellion. Nor does it pertain to the said soldiers to take cognisance of this, but it is rather for you [*the governor, Saint-Herem*] to deal with it through justice and for royal justices and officers to take order.

The said soldiers live at their discretion throughout the country without paying anything, taking as well from the poor people everything they please, so that some of the best villages of the country are stripped and ruined; as well as the fact, moreover, that besides the *tailles* levied by the King's command, the people of the third and common estate have paid large sums of money for the payment and upkeep of these soldiers.

SOURCE: *Histoire Auvergne*, vol. I, pp. 270–1.

## 11   The beginning of autonomy in Languedoc

As for the affairs of this country, there is trouble and cruel civil war between the libertines and us. The third brother of M. de Crussol has made himself chief of the libertines and calls himself King's Lieutenant in Languedoc, elected by the communities and commanding in all things as if he really were so. Thus, he assesses and demands moneys like His Majesty, he issues charges and commissions and commands entirely in the places under their control as if he were the King himself. Now, M. de Joyeuse is in the process of dealing with this by force and has retaken the town of Limouz by assault. . . . Likewise, MM. de Sommerive and de Suze have gathered 7,000–8,000 men in Provence against the libertines and have reduced it to the same obedience by force. This has cost at the city of Orange the lives of all the men, for the libertines there, expecting a siege, killed all the Catholics, and our men, after entering the place, massacred all the libertines or Huguenots as they are called. . . . Returning to this country, I would wish His Catholic Majesty had aided their Majesties with 4 or 6 ensigns of foot under M. de Joyeuse in the reconquest of this country and 300 or 400 horse, for the soldiers of the country prefer pillage to fighting and there is no captain who can make himself obeyed, so that every man is plunged into doing evil.

SOURCE: Fourquevaux to Saint-Sulpice, 17 June 1562, in Cabié, *Guerres*, cols 5–6.

## 12   The battle of Dreux, 19 December 1562

Six things should be pointed out about this battle: that the fight was without preliminary skirmishing, the extreme bravery of the Swiss, the patience of the duke of Guise, the length of the combat, the capture of the two generals (Montmorency and Condé) and the retreat of both armies. I would add the Admiral's furious charges, his rallying the men in confusion, his manoeuvring of the artillery, his having brought the fight to his profit in the last stages and his retreat to the enemy's relief. The losses on this day were estimated at 8,000 men, though some say 6,000. It is certain that when the Admiral reviewed his forces the following day, his losses were found to to be 2,250 foot and 140 horse, including the 400 or 500 lansquenets that the duke of Guise was content to disarm and send back to their country. What made the losses so great on the Catholic side was mainly the great defeat of the Swiss. The notable dead on the Catholic side were Montbrun [*the Constable's son*], Marshal d'Annebault, Givry and his whole company, the count of Rochefort, Beauvais, La Brosse, the duke's lieutenant . . . La Brosse the younger,

Marshal de Saint-André who, having brought his troops to rescue the Constable, was taken and killed by Baubigny [*as a result of a personal feud*]. The other main losses included the duke of Nevers [*killed by his own man des Bordes*]. The main dead among the Reformed were Arpajon, the count of Sault, Chandieu, Liancourt, Carrelière, tied to a tree and shot, some said on the orders of the duke of Guise because he received him roughly, saying: 'Here's one of my chevaliers of Amboise.' But this act of inhumanity is not in tune with that prince's other acts of courtesy. . . . As for the prince of Condé, he was received by the duke with all courtesy and, because his baggage, bedding and plate had been taken away by his own lansquenets, these two generals were content to share a bed. So, the fortunes of war envelopped smarting regrets, thoughts of vengeance by the vanquished, as well as the restrained joy, high hopes and wise courtesies of the victors beneath the same bedclothes.

SOURCE: Aubigné, vol. III, pp. 114–18.

## 13   The Edict of Amboise, 19 March 1563

Charles, by the Grace of God, King of France, to all those who see these present letters, greetings. [*Preamble, on the growth of divergent ideas in religion, the promulgation of edicts that have not prevented the seizure of arms and the consequent tumults. Seeing how the war was so damaging to the kingdom he has, with the grace of God, found the means to pacify the troubles. This edict issued with the advice of the Queen, cardinal of Bourbon, prince of Condé, duke of Montpensier, prince of La Roche-sur-Yon for the princes of the blood, the dukes of Guise, Aumale, Montmorency, Étampes; the Marshals Brissac and Bourdillon; lords of Andelot, Sansac, Sipierre and others of the Privy Council.*]

1   Henceforth, all gentlemen who are barons, castellans, high-justiciars holding hauberk fiefs, each and every one of them, can have liberty of conscience in the houses where they live and the practice of the religion they call Reformed, along with their family and subjects who wish to attend, freely and without constraint.

2   And other gentlemen holding fiefs, also in their houses, for them and their families only, provided they do not live in towns, townships or villages of lords of high justice other than us; in which cases they may only practise the said religion in those places with the permission and leave of their lords and not otherwise.

3   In each bailliage, seneschalcy and government with the seat of a bailliage, such as Péronne, Montdidier and Roye, and La Rochelle, and others of like nature, in the direct jurisdiction and appeal of our courts of Parlement, we will and ordain, at the request of those of the Religion, one town in the suburbs of

which the exercise of the said Religion may be held for all those who wish to go; and not otherwise and not elsewhere.

4 Nevertheless, everyone may live and dwell in his home everywhere without being pursued or molested, forced or constrained for matters of conscience.

5 In all towns in which the said Religion was practised until 7 March, other than those towns which will be, as is said above, specified in each bailliage and seneschalcy, the same practice will continue in one or two places within the said town, as shall be by us ordained; without those of the Religion being able to take or retain any temple or church from the clergy, whom we intend henceforth to be restored to their churches, houses, goods, possessions and revenues, to enjoy and use as they did before the troubles, in whatsoever place in our kingdom it be. . . .

6 We also intend that the city and jurisdiction of the provostship and viscounty of Paris be and remain exempt from all exercise of the Religion. Nevertheless, those who have their houses and revenues within the said city and jurisdiction may return to them and enjoy their property peaceably without being constrained, pursued or disturbed in their consciences, for things past or to come. . . .

10 We also ordain, will, and it pleases us that our cousin the prince of Condé remain discharged, and by these presents signed by our hand, we discharge him of all moneys that have been, by him or by his command and ordinance, taken and levied from our receivers of finance, for whatever sum to which this might amount.

11 Likewise, that he be discharged for those sums that have been, as has been said, taken by his ordinance and levied on the communities, towns, treasuries, rents and revenues of the churches and others, and by him employed on account of the present war; without his being in any way pursued for the present or in the future, or his followers commissioned for the levy of the said moneys (who, and likewise those who have paid them, will be discharged); nor also for the striking of coins, founding of artillery, making of powder and saltpetre, fortifications of towns and demolitions for them, all by the command of our same cousin the prince of Condé, in all towns of this our kingdom and lands of our obedience, of which the corporations and inhabitants will remain also discharged and we discharge them by these presents.

12 All prisoners, of war or for religion, will be set at liberty in their persons and goods without payment of ransom; in this not included thieves, brigands, robbers and murderers, who are not comprised in these presents.

13 And in so far as we desire singularly that all occasions for these troubles, tumults and seditions should cease, and to reconcile and unite the wills of our subjects towards each other and from this union the more easily maintain the

obedience that all of them owe to us, we have ordained and ordain, intend, will, and it pleases us:

14 that all injuries and offences that the iniquity of the time and the events that have happened have bred between our subjects, and all other things past and caused in these present tumults, should remain extinguished, as if dead and buried and as if they had not happened; forbidding most strictly on pain of death all our subjects, of whatever estate or quality, to attack, injure or provoke each other by reproaches for things past, to dispute, quarrel or contest together over religion, offend or outrage by word or deed; but rather live peacefully together like brothers, friends and fellow citizens; on pain that those who contravene and will be the cause and movers of any injury or offence that follows, will be summarily and without other form of trial punished according to the rigour of this present ordinance.

In consideration of which, and of the above, and to remove all doubt, our subjects will leave and desist from all Associations they have within or without the kingdom and will henceforth make no levy of money, enrolment of men, congregations or assemblies other than the above-mentioned, and not in arms. This we prohibit and forbid also on pain of being punished rigorously and as being in contempt and infraction of our commands and ordinances.

SOURCE: Isambert, vol. XIV, i, pp. 135–40; Stegman, pp. 32–36, abridged text.

---

## 14   Interpretative declaration on the Edict of Amboise, 22 December 1563

1 [*On noble privileges of worship:*] We did not intend, nor do we now, that this liberty of exercise of religion should extend to those high justices and hauberk fiefs that have been bought from church property. [*On claims that these privileges only applied to principal residences:*] When those gentlemen move to their other houses where they have high justice . . . they can, while residing there, have the exercise of the said Religion.

2 [*On the nomination of places of worship in each bailliage, governors are to accept royal lists, but where the crown had not named a place:*] our will is that the governors and commissaires together, or the governors acting alone in their absence, should proceed to the nomination, accommodating one with another gently and amiably. . . .

3 [*On the provision for exercise of the Religion in 'all the towns' where it was exercised up to 7 March 1563, this means only:*] those which were held by force during the troubles.

4 The inhabitants of our good city of Paris and the jurisdiction of the provostship and viscounty thereof, who are of the RPR, may not travel to neighbouring

bailliages to attend services of that religion held there. They may live within their houses in liberty of conscience without being sought out . . . [*If they have scruples of conscience, they may move to other bailliages.*]

5 [*On baptisms and burials:*] For baptisms, we permit relatives and godparents of children born in all places, without exception, where there is no exercise of Religion, to take children for baptism, in the company of no more than four or five, at the nearest place where there is exercise of the Religion [*though declaring for registration, which is to be kept separately from others*].

As for burials, we permit them likewise to buy by mutual agreement a place for burial outside the cities, towns and villages where they live. Cortèges may not consist of more than 25 or 30 people. [*However, in Paris, the official is*] to take care that there be no scandal and go to collect the corpse at night, carrying it for interment at the parish graveyard without any company in attendance.

SOURCE: *Déclaration et interprétation du Roy sur l'Édict de la Pacification* (Paris, 1563).

## 15  Declaration forbidding the Reformed religion at court, 24 July 1564

. . . In so far as, among other points put forth [*in the Edict of Amboise*], it was agreed that whatever freedom, granted by that Edict of declaration, to preach and exercise the Religion in certain cities, suburbs and villages of our kingdom, nevertheless in all places of our residence the said exercise would cease during the period of our stay. In fact, shortly afterwards, by an ordinance issued at bois de Vincennes and published in Parlement, our intention was made very clear on this and has been observed in all the places of our kingdom that we have visited. We have found our subjects most obedient in this. However, so the matter should not remain in any uncertainty because it was not included in the Edict of Pacification or that it may not be claimed that, by the Interpretative Declaration we made in December last, our intention had altered, and without intending any alteration or innovation in our Edict of Pacification, we have, by the advice of our Lady and Mother the Queen, the princes of our blood and our councillors, declared and do declare:

1 . . . that in our retinue there be no [*exercise of the RPR*], while, in the places we travel through, the said exercise should cease during our residence . . . but those who profess it should remain modestly in their houses, where we intend they may live freely with their families without any manner of inquiry. . . .

2 [*Baptisms and marriages during that period may be carried out in the nearest places permitted.*]

SOURCE: Isambert, vol. XIV, i, pp. 171–4.

## 16  Royal attempts to maintain the Edict, 1564

The King, seeing that bitterness was growing, now admixed with the ambitions of grandees who fostered the evil, ordered the provincial governors, mayors and town échevins to say nothing to Huguenots who were singing psalms elsewhere than in their assemblies; that they be not forced to reverence the holy bread or to put out displays at their doors and windows on Corpus Christi or to contribute to church funds for the poor and to the Confraternities. It was ordered that, in those places where there were Huguenots who would not put out displays, the commissaires and captains of the quarters and other officers would do it for them.

SOURCE: *Castelnau*, M&P, 1564, p. 505.

## 17  Implementation in Picardy

I know for certain that there are many people of the Reformed Religion at Roye, le Plessier, Guermigny, Crapaumesnil and other neighbouring places who wish in all quietness to live in the practice of that Religion. However, they fear that you might be lobbied by various people of contrary views to prevent them. For this reason they have come to me both to know my intention in the matter and to pray me to write to you. Considering that it would be pernicious and harmful to the consciences of so many people to live without religion I have for this reason permitted that, on the lands belonging to me around Roye and its suburbs, they may, in all honest freedom, exercise the ministry of the Religion without impediment and also go to Cany, if they wish, on condition that they behave with such decorum that no tumults occur.

SOURCE: Condé to Humières, La Fère, 15 April 1564, Aumale , vol. I, p. 509.

## 18  Implementation in Normandy

Those of the Reformed Church in Alençon have come to me here to report the difficulty they find themselves in as a result of the suspension of the exercise of their religion, conceded by our lord the King, as they had it before you had forbidden Master Pierre Merlin, their minister, on pretext that he had been accused of preaching in an orchard in the suburbs of the town, of having received at communion persons not of the bailliage and of having taken a nun to wife. . . . Knowing, on the other hand, that His Majesty has granted them letters patent both for the reinstatement of Merlin in his ministry and to let him live peacefully with his lawful wife, which, as I am informed, you retain in your hands, I wished to write you this letter to tell you that, since these poor people have in no way contravened His Majesty's laws and wishes, it is not reasonable that they be deprived of the enjoyment of their religion, which, I assure you, is the strongest bond there could be to maintain the people in obedience to their prince. . . .

SOURCE: Condé to Matignon, Vendôme, 10 November 1565, Aumale, vol. I, pp. 511–12.

## 19   Implementation in Languedoc (i)

In all the towns of this quarter, the Edict of Peace has been received and published and, I hope, will be maintained. But as for the towns and regions where those of the new religion have, for 14 or 15 months, had more power than me and command absolutely, the sieur de Caylus went himself to make known Your Majesty's will. Before he could have any reply, M. de Crussol called an assembly at Montpellier of those of the new religion, which they call the assembly of the Three Estates of Languedoc as if it had been summoned by your command. After lengthy discussions by minor persons of no quality, M. de Caylus could obtain no reply except that the sieur de Crussol and those of the Religion would in no way restore the towns they occupied to me. . . . Sire, I received by Your Majesty's last despatch the command to disarm completely and stand down all the companies and soldiers who are here. Having seen the refusal of the sieur de Crussol and that he reinforces himself daily, I have still retained some troops so that your subjects should not despair. . . .

SOURCE: Joyeuse to Charles IX, Narbonne, 21 May 1563, Vaissette, pp. 669–71.

## 20   Implementation in Languedoc (ii)

By the Edict of Peace it was stipulated, among other articles, that the towns of the Religion would receive garrisons and that the inhabitants would be disarmed. In consequence, M. de Joyeuse sent a company in garrison to Castres commanded by a Catholic, Captain Sonnerie, quartered on the inhabitants who were of the Religion . . . to whom they acted with great cruelty. . . . [*On Damville's appointment as governor, he deputed a Catholic, d'Ambres, as his lieutenant at Castres, who entered on 17 October with the bishop*] followed by a large number of religious people carrying the cross, who formed a procession and entered through the New Gate insulting and threatening all those whom they met. They were accompanied by many soldiers and valets armed with swords and staves, with which they insolently beat those whom they encountered, saying: 'Huguenot scum, you made us go to the preaching, now we will make you go to Mass at the point of the sword.' This was borne for the moment with impatience and disdain and, were it not for the affliction [*of the plague*] they were suffering, they would have repelled these injuries.

SOURCE: Gaches, *Mémoires*, pp. 38–40.

## THE CROWN AND REFORM OF THE REALM

### 21 Michel de L'Hospital on the declaration of the King's majority, Rouen 15 August 1563

May God, of his grace, give the King to reign well, with the good counsel of the Queen his mother and of the princes and lords. The King, now of age, wanted to make his entry to the city and to declare briefly the form of the law which he intends to maintain during his reign, as did the ancient praetors at the start of their magistrature; to make law not for his own profit but as a good shepherd for his sheep. He wishes his edicts and ordinances to be observed, notably the Edict for Pacification of the troubles, which he did not draw up alone but with the advice and counsel of his mother the Queen and of the princes and lords of his Council. . . . I am unhappy about the disorder in justice. It is well said that the Church is in need of reform but justice has as much need of reform as the Church. I will not speak of precepts for teaching how to judge well. You have books enough for that. I simply admonish you to bear yourselves in your judgments blamelessly, holding to the straight and narrow, without diverging to right or to left. You swear when you take office to keep the laws and you take an oath to that effect when you enter into your duties. Do you keep them well? Most are ill kept and you treat them like wax, to be moulded to your will. What is worse, you say you are above the ordinances and are not obliged to obey them unless you are pleased to do so. Gentlemen, act as though the law was above you. You say you are sovereign. An ordinance is the King's command and you are not above the King. All, be they princes or others, must obey the King's laws. So, the oath you take to keep them is a vain one. . . . Take care not to bring enmity, favour or prejudice to your judgments. I see many judges who seek to judge in the cases of their friends or enemies. Daily, I see men who are involved as enemies or friends of persons, sects or factions, judging for or against without considering the equity of the case. You are judges of acts, not of lives, morals or religion. You think it good to award the case to the one you think the worthy man, the better Christian, as though it were a question between parties of which was the better poet, orator, painter, worker – in the end a master of art, doctrine, valour or whatever other quality – not of the matter that has caused the case. . . . Good men also complain about the length and multiplication of cases. . . . The judge's true law is to cut down the number of cases and avoid cases if possible; just as those laws that prevent crimes from happening are better than those that punish them. . . . You complain of revelations to the King of the court's secrets by men you describe as wicked and treacherous. I do not think such tale-tellers good men if they act out of ambition to gain the good graces of the King or the lords. But he who acts justly fears not that his acts be known and seen, as though in a theatre, and will hold such revelations of little account. The eye of justice sees all, the King sees all, time reveals all. Do nothing that you would not wish to be known. . . . It is His Majesty's right to know how his justice is administered and whether his judges are doing their duty. It is too arrogant for judges to maintain that they can do no wrong. . . .

SOURCE: L'Hospital, pp. 99–111.

## 22  Charles IX's speech on his majority

You have heard my will and that I made this ordinance not of my own opinion only, nor that of the Queen my mother, though I have no need to be accountable to you, both as your King and because others have never done so. But on this occasion I wished to do so in order that you cease to act as you did during my minority, meddling with what does not concern you. Now I am in my majority, I wish you only to concern yourselves with good and speedy justice for my subjects, for the kings my predecessors placed you in your positions only for that purpose . . . and not to make yourselves either my tutors or the protectors of the realm, nor conservators of the city of Paris. You have given to understand hitherto that you were all those things. I wish to leave you in no error but command you that, as in the time of my late father and grandfather, you concern yourselves only with matters of justice. When I command you to do something, if there is any difficulty in meaning, I shall always allow you to make remonstrances as you did to the kings my predecessors, but not as governors. After you have made them, having heard my will without further reply, you are to obey. . . .

(These words came from the repertoire of my lord Chancellor and not from the King, as was the common rumour, since the King's age made it impossible for him to formulate them.)

SOURCE: The King's reply to the remonstrance of the Parlement of Paris, Bruslart, *MC,* vol. I, pp. 135–6.

## 23  Catherine's objectives in the tour of France

[*Having received from Coligny a list of Protestant grievances*] I wish to assure you that there is no one in this kingdom who desires more than I do the observation of the edicts and ordinances of my lord and son the King or who is more sorry to see those who violate them go unpunished. . . . This has not resulted from the failure of myself or the King to write frequently and expressly to justices, who, to tell the truth, have not hitherto done their duty very well in many places. This is one of the main reasons that have led the King my son to undertake this journey, so that he may more clearly make his will known in the places he visits and no one may henceforth use pretexts for contravening the edicts. Speaking of this, I must tell you that I am most unhappy about the suspicion you tell me those of the Religion have conceived, because of a false rumour that they are soon to be dealt with and that this will be done at Lyon. For, if they base this mistrust on fear that my lord the King and I wished to have the Edict of Pacification broken, it seems to me that the public and private declarations he and I have made to the contary . . . should suffice to remove such a false suspicion from their minds. . . . Were there to be any who tried to persuade us to do so, rest assured that I understand all too clearly the danger of such an enterprise. . . .

SOURCE: Catherine to Coligny, 17 April 1564, *LCM*, vol II, p. 177.

## The Assembly of Moulins, February 1566

### 24    Michel de L'Hospital's speech at the Assembly of Moulins, February 1566

The King has travelled round his kingdom and heard many complaints about his officers of justice. You should not find it strange, then, if he calls a spade a spade without concealment – a brigand a brigand, a thief a thief – in noting the faults he has found. . . .

. . . Some say there are too many laws and there is no need of more, rather that many should be removed and thus that this assembly is pointless. . . . [*Argues that natural justice was more powerful in the past and better administered; also that litigation has increased.*]

So that everything should be restored to the good old ways of justice, all means should be sought to remove avarice, ambition, theft and malice. Since, in this respect, it is well known that the proliferation of judges is the cause of law cases expanding, it will be well to remove the presidial judges or cut down their numbers. If they remain, their perquisites should be removed in favour of proper salaries. Shoemakers would go out of business if we all took to going barefoot. So judges would be sorry if there were no more cases. Justice is for the King, not for private persons; those who say that offices are inherited and wish to make them their own property are wrong. . . . In this monarchy, the interpretation of the law belongs to the King and no other.

Resignations of office are another abuse in this kingdom. For, though it is very reasonable that a councillor or other should be rewarded for long service and that, in all decency, he should be permitted to resign his post to his son, son-in-law or nephew, it thus happens that the King does not have the choice, and instead of a wise, prudent and experienced man, the King is presented with a young man who, though he may be learned and capable, is not as experienced as the King and the people require. For prudence only comes with age and experience and it is clear that the people are not served as they should be by those who acquire posts by resignation.

There is another abuse in nominations which, though they are permitted by ordinance, it is well known how they are done and how many conspiracies there are to place a relative or friend of some councillors or presidents. . . .

As for perquisites, they are certainly allowed by usage. However, abuses are evident in them and they must be dealt with. If the King's finances could stand it, it would be better to give them proper salaries as is done in Italy and remove perquisites, but that cannot be done at the moment.

I find another greater abuse in the fact that the judges and magistrates of this kingdom never give account of themselves. . . . I can say, Sire, that I have never seen a case against a judge carried through. While he is irremovable, there is no one, neither witness nor sergeant, who dare attack him or who would not be intimidated, imprisoned or mistreated either by the judge or by his friends. . . .

The abuse of giving offices as rewards is very great. Though a good servant may have served his prince for a long time, either in war, in the courts or otherwise . . . and merits reward, this is no reason to give him an office he does not know how to exercise. . . .

The ambition of judges is also a great plague. An advocate is never content with his lot until he becomes a councillor; the councillor, the moment he is apppointed, tries to fly higher so as to become a president; the president wants to be Chancellor; as for me, if there were anything higher, I would aspire to it, either as cardinal or even as Pope. Meanwhile, no one does his duty, with his heart consumed by ambition. Ambition is fed by the lords and princes and there are many presidents and councillors who are more devoted to the princes and lords than to the King himself, so that they fear not to condemn the King in order to serve whom they please. . . .

. . . Evocations must be dealt with so that subjects are not so easily transferred from their jurisdictions. There have been certain general evocations to the Great Council, because of the troubles, for certain princes and great lords whom it was inexpedient to touch for the moment, considering those to whom they have been given. But there are others that must be dealt with. . . .

[*Attacks the misuse of letters of committimus, church benefice cases, the expansion of cases involving quarrels among the nobility, abuse of power by municipal judges, the abuse of local justice, abuses in obtaining chancellery letters and brevets.*]

Above all, let the King's authority be obeyed. This is not to say that remonstrances will not be received, but they must be made summarily and quickly without error. The King will be glad to be informed.

His Majesty must be petitioned not to give so many letters of grace for crimes. . .

SOURCE: L'Hospital, pp. 121–30.

## 25    A Catholic view of the tour from the provinces

[1564] In February of this year after Candlemas, the King left Paris to undertake the journey to visit his kingdom. He stayed at Fontainebleau and from there passed by Sens. He stopped at the city of Troyes in Champagne where he stayed eight days and left at the start of March. He had sent an order to the towns which were seats of bailliages that the legal officers and the gentlemen of the bailliages of Champagne and Brie should attend him on a certain day in the city of Troyes to hear his will and what he had to tell them concerning the regulation of justice and the observation of the Edicts of Pacification under the peace of Orléans, and, following the Edicts, they should ensure that everyone lived in peace until his return. . . .

The Huguenots of Provins and its bailliage, both nobles and artisans, had petitioned the King through the bailli, while he was at Troyes, for the establishment of a preaching-place at Provins under the peace of Orléans. His Majesty accorded this and ordered the president of the town to allot them a suitable place for the preaching and protect them during their attendance against fears of the Catholics' attacking them. These letters and orders were dismissed again by the president and he sent them away. Thus this year passed without any preaching at Provins. . . .

[1565] The visit of the King to the lands of Dauphiné, Languedoc and Provence, and elsewhere suited the Catholics very well and intimidated the Huguenot heretics. The Catholics were maintained in their Apostolic and Roman religion, seeing the King as a Catholic going to Mass each day, as also his brother, the Queen their mother, the Constable and other lords of his entourage, whom they thought to be all Huguenots. For the Huguenots, or at least some, His Majesty's visit served to withdraw them from their error and make them simulate true religion. For seeing him as a Catholic going to Mass so devoutly, they left off their heresy and were Catholics, or at least made a show of being. The religion of the prince, be it good or ill, induces the subject to observe it.

Source: Haton, vol. I, pp. 376–80.

## 26    Blaise de Monluc's analysis, June 1565

[*Argues that in view of the widespread belief that the court sympathised with Protestantism, the purpose of the tour was firstly*] that everyone should see clearly to what religion the King, she and all her children held. In all the great cities, on the least feast day, the King had solemn processions made with the order that all should be present, in which the Queen, Monsieur and Madame were always present and likewise heard solemn Masses with great devotion, so that all should know that they had no wish to change the religion of their predecessors. . . . Meanwhile, the King was growing in stature and strength day by day so that it seemed to all who saw him that his growth in power, grandeur, mind and speech was miraculous. The journey also had the benefit that all those of our religion who see him are so attached in love and devotion that, if he demanded it, we would place our lives and goods at his disposal. . . .

The other benefit of the journey is that the Queen wanted to get control of the rebel towns and see that they remained under the King's control, as at Lyon chiefly, for she had been advised that there was an intention to make it like a Swiss canton. For this reason, she had a citadel built and so disrupted their plans. She is now going from here to La Rochelle, a rebel town, and plans to erect another citadel, and from there to Xaintonge, where all the nobility is tainted with that Religion. She will not, I am sure, remedy all in matters religious but will at least render the King the stronger party; for to smash their religion and build up the King's forces at the same time would only be to rekindle the sedition. I firmly believe she will dissimulate in matters religious. . . . She has told me her objectives, which I can reveal, or at least assure myself about without telling anyone, for she forbad me to. Once their Majesties are back in Paris and the King has visited all the provinces of his realm he will have made known that he is a man who can bear arms and that people have to deal not with a woman but with an adult King; and shown everyone what religion he holds and wishes his subjects to hold. Then, for certain, the Queen's aim is to issue an edict that whoever will not live under the King's religion should leave the kingdom within a month, with permission to sell his property. . . . [*Goes on to assert that the intentions of the Huguenots are to limit the powers of the crown and reduce taxes should they control the King.*]

The objectives of the Queen are good and holy. However, I fear that the prolongation of the matter will bring us great misfortunes because of the favour and help that those of the new religion have from the Chancellor and all his house. They wax daily and we wane. . . . To remedy all matters, it seems to me that His Majesty the King of Spain should offer our King, by all assurances possible, fraternal friendship. . . . [*Advice to Alva for the meeting at Bayonne.*]

The Queen of Spain will privately pray and require my lords the cardinals, the duke of Montpensier, the prince of La Roche-sur-Yon, the Constable and Marshal de Bourdillon, the count of Villars, Damville and Sipierre to work always for the support of the Catholics in the Council, all interests apart, and maintain the amity between the King of Spain and our King, as I am sure she will also do with the Queen her mother and the King her brother. She should tell them that God has put them in this world as monarchs and they are supported as such by the religion we hold, for the other religion can only reduce their monarchy to a republic. The grandees who support that religion do it only to increase their power, through a republic, above that which they have under a monarchy.

SOURCE: Memoir for Philip II, Monluc, vol. V, pp. 23–35.

## 27    Spanish views of the Bayonne meeting, July–August 1565 (i)

[*The Queen Mother*] has promised to do marvels, though with the proviso that she would avoid anything that could cause the renewal of hostilities. Now, she would not have recourse to arms if she employed means suitable for the situation. But I believe her so thoroughly persuaded by the idea that, in entertaining these two parties, she has found the means of consolidating her authority in that kingdom, that I believe she will follow this course. From this will surely result the ruin of religion and her son's authority. Thus, I am persuaded she will do nothing that is any good and I have all too many reasons to fear great misfortunes.

SOURCE: Granvelle to del Canto, 20 August 1565, Weiss, vol. IX, pp. 476–81.

## 28    Spanish views of the Bayonne meeting, July–August 1565 (ii)

The duke of Alva will make known to the King and your lordship the resolutions he has agreed with this Queen. If they come to fruition, this will be a great service for God and for the King our lord. I am troubled because I foresee that these heretics, and others who are not openly heretics, may attack her. Your lordship may consider in your great prudence whether these propositions before God and His Majesty may be pursued. The main consideration is His Majesty's contentment in the carrying out of this negotiation.

SOURCE: Alava to Eraso, 4 July 1565, AGS, Est. 147, fo. 13, Combes, pp. 37–8, defective trans.

# 4 The Second and Third Wars, 1567–70

The attempts of the middle 1560s to pacify the country and reform the government were running out of time since the basic problems had not been solved: how to restore a stable and vigorous monarchy that could hold the rival factions in check and calm the continuing communal strife between the religions. Only in that way could a regime of toleration be made to work. Yet, paradoxically, the effective revival of monarchical power would spell doom for Protestant hopes of expansion. In Languedoc, low-level disturbances had hardly ceased, despite the royal visit. In national politics, rising taxes and the continued influence of 'foreigners' and hangers-on at court provided plenty of arguments for discontented Protestant aristocrats to play on (see Document 1). By 1567, the most controversial aspect was the growing dominance of the cardinal of Lorraine in the royal Council, making it increasingly difficult for Protestant leaders to attend. In the country, Catholics widely feared royal attempts at compromise.

In the summer of 1567 internal and external crises began to intertwine. The Protestant leaders were in the royal Council when counter-measures to the transfer of Spanish troops to the Low Countries under Alva were discussed. But a projected war against Spain, if it had ever been seriously considered, would have been difficult to fund and led by a divided nobility. No doubt Catherine, as in 1572, understood this, but the change of policy was inevitably blamed on her Machiavellian scheming with Alva at Bayonne. When further moves were made to restrict the freedoms allowed under the Edict of Amboise, a Protestant synod met at Valléry which could not be controlled by the Admiral and Condé; the leadership met at the Admiral's house at Châtillon to plan a coup d'état (see Document 2). The programme of the leaders was both religious and political; Condé, in his new declaration justifying the uprising, called both for the maintenance of religious liberty and for the settlement of the ills of the kingdom through the Estates-General (see Document 3).

That the coup so nearly succeeded was probably the result of rapid action rather than organisation. Time did not allow word to get out. The second civil war effectively began when news reached the court at Meaux on the evening of 24 September that Condé's troops were massing. Faced with the choice of staying put or flight to Paris under cover of the newly recruited Swiss troops,

Charles IX opted for the latter and left with his retinue at 4 the following morning.

The second War of Religion was no more than an affair of the autumn and winter of 1567–8. The first phase of the war involved the gradual investment of Paris by Condé's then superior army, the Queen Mother's usual delaying negotiations until the assembly of a sufficient royal army, and finally the Battle of Saint-Denis on 10 November. The effect was a draw; Condé's army was forced to give up the siege of Paris but the old Constable was mortally wounded (see Document 4). Condé was able to move off towards Lorraine in order to join forces with a new levy of reiters under John Casimir of the Palatinate.

The royal army was able to do no more than shadow Condé's forces; funds were seriously short and there was a general lack of enthusiasm for the prosecution of the war in court circles (see Document 5). Even in Catholic Paris, from which all Protestants had been driven, the populace was sick of paying for war and of the depredations of the royal mercenaries. The Queen Mother was blamed for engineering the war for her own ends. Peace terms were intermittently discussed throughout December and January until delegates were appointed by the crown on 28 February 1568 to go to Longjumeau to treat with Condé.

The Edict or 'peace' of Longjumeau (26 March 1568), which brought the Second War to an end, was drawn up as a confirmation of the Edict of Amboise, removing all subsequent caveats and thus reintroducing all the uncertainties of that Edict (see Document 6). Any possible opposition from the Parlements was sidestepped by sending it directly to the governors for publication, and the Edict was now specifically applied in Provence, which had not been the case before. However, Condé's demands for 'places de sureté' were refused and he did not insist.

The peace was the most short-lived of the Wars of Religion and highly unwelcome in Catholic Paris (see Document 7). On 29 March, the Guises may have held a secret meeting at which the renewal of war, after the disarmament of the Protestants, was discussed. Whatever their leaders expected, the Protestants were never convinced that the peace was a genuine one. They were convinced of the culpability of Lorraine for the breakdown of the peace and mounted a coherent publicity campaign in the summer of 1568 to make this clear. The cardinal of Châtillon, in England, argued that Lorraine had never been prepared to accept peace, had striven to invite Alva's intervention and had deliberately engineered the renewal of war (see Document 8). Châtillon believed that Lorraine did attempt to use the Council to mount his own coup against Condé and Coligny (like theirs, it failed). In fact, though Protestant sources agree on Guise culpability for the renewal of war, this is not certain.

The Protestant leaders fled to La Rochelle on 23 August, taking up their position in a pre-prepared redoubt. War was made certain by the revocation of toleration by the declaration of Saint-Maur (see Document 10). The Third War of Religion was to be the most destructive so far, involving more German and Swiss mercenaries and a search for foreign support for both sides as well as a higher degree of indirect and direct mass participation on both sides.

The renewal of war brought a fresh manifesto from Condé (La Rochelle, 8 September) (see Document 9) as well as the royal revocation of toleration (see Document 10). Control by the ultras over royal policy was strengthened by the clash between Lorraine and Chancellor L'Hospital in the Council over the terms of church taxation conceded by the Papacy in return for the end of toleration (see Document 11). L'Hospital lost the great seal on 28 September and it was given to Birague, later to become Chancellor. Anjou's position as Lieutenant-General of the realm was renewed. As in the previous war, much depended on access to the German and Swiss mercenaries by both sides, as well as on the co-operation between the prince of Orange and duke Wolfgang-Wilhelm of Zweibrücken on behalf of the Protestants. Zweibrücken had offered 8,000 reiters and 40 ensigns of foot, which were to be paid for by England.

The centre of the fighting was in the south-west, either for control of the lower Loire or along the Charente, and this was a problem for the crown, which, as in the previous conflict, found it difficult to concentrate its numerically superior forces. Royal forces were nominally commanded by Anjou but in reality by the veteran marshal, Tavannes. Nevertheless, the encounter at Jarnac on 13 March 1569, a fierce if brief battle, was a severe blow for the Protestants since Condé, hitherto their supreme commander, was shamefully and deliberately killed after his capture (see Documents 12–13). However, widespread Catholic gloating was premature. Coligny took effective command in the name of the young Protestant princes and withdrew his army south-westward, falling back on his strongholds along the Charente. Meanwhile, Anjou was unable to take Angoulême. The Protestant high command took urgent steps to reassure their allies that the defeat had been marginal, despite their regret at the loss of Condé. The Admiral's strategy was to await the arrival of Zweibrücken's men, who had left the Rhineland early in February and, shadowed by Aumale's troops, marched through Burgundy and the Auxerrois to cross the Loire and take La Charité on 20 May. From there, they moved through the Bourbonnais, crossed the Cher and reached the Limousin. All this was done while the royal army under Anjou remained to the west, doing nothing to prevent the juncture of the forces opposed to them until the arrival of the Queen Mother and Lorraine for a council of war. Seriously depleted by exhaustion and illness, it too was a multi-national force, composed, as well as of French, of Walloons, Provençals, Swiss and reiters under the young Rhinegraves; the Germans in particular were unenthusiastic. For some weeks, the royal army could only hover and watch its enemies manoeuvre, and not until early June could it take an initiative with 8,000 horse and 15,000 foot. Zweibrücken pushed forward his forces with energy; they entered Limousin avoiding the royal army and causing much devastation. But on the day of his arrival at Nexon for his meeting with the Admiral (11 June) the duke suddenly died, probably of a heart attack brought on by long and hard drinking. He was succeeded by another veteran, count Volradt of Mansfeld.

Catherine stayed at Limoges until 19 June trying to energise a disorderly royal army constantly short of supplies. It was this desperation as much as anything else that prompted them to give battle at La Roche-l'Abeille on 25 June and concede to Coligny one of the rare Protestant victories of the war, in which Marshal Strozzi was taken prisoner. The royal army was reduced to a rabble but Coligny was unable to take advantage of this, not least because his German troops were discontented. However, from 25 July to 7 September he managed to besiege Poitiers and the outcome of the campaign hung in the balance (see Document 14). Coligny, though, made the mistake of going to the relief of Châtellerault, besieged by Anjou's army to draw him off, and the opportunity was lost. Pitched battle was now more likely, even though Coligny wanted to avoid it, especially since the German troops on both sides were clamouring for battle. The matter was settled at Moncontour on 3 October with another disaster for the Protestants (see Document 15). Their only comfort was in being able to withdraw southwards in order to regroup with Mansfeld's reiters and the gentry of the region – the vicomtes – under Coligny's command.

It was now time for the royal army to clinch the campaign but Anjou made the disastrous decision to sit down and besiege M. de Pilles in Saint-Jean d'Angély. In the course of the winter siege (the town surrendered on 2 December), his army slowly but surely disintegrated for lack of money and supplies. Marshal Tavannes's son and biographer, Jean de Saulx, was later to remark pertinently that 'revolts in France are most dangerous during the winter'. The nobility were difficult to retain at the colours, as were the troops who followed them. Rebels were hardened over the winter and could fortify themselves, while sieges were more difficult. This was exactly the situation over the winter of 1569–70. In addition, the Catholic cause was severely damaged by the constant hostility between the local governors, Monluc in Guyenne and Damville in Languedoc. Monluc, originally a Guise client but fiercely loyal to the crown, had earned a reputation for savagery in his maintenance of royal authority in Guyenne which left him open to attack at court by his enemies. His inability to work with Damville led to his resignation in November, though he quickly changed his mind. However, he was increasingly out of sympathy with the direction of affairs.

Voices in the Council calling for peace began to predominate and talks were opened in December. Jeanne d'Albret handled the talks for the Protestants, which got down to details at the start of February 1570. The main lines of negotiation had been apparent since the first Protestant demands in 1568: unrestricted freedom of worship and a limited cult even at court and in the area around Paris, the concession of 'places de sureté', the restoration of all confiscated offices granted out during the war, and the crown's part payment of the Protestants' mercenaries (see Document 17). The negotiations stalled over most issues. The unwillingness of the crown to restore non-noble Protestant office-holders was seen as an attempt to drive a wedge between nobility and commons on the Protestant side, a point over which the leaders were particularly sensitive.

The terms still lay on the table when fighting began again in the spring. Coligny had used the winter ably to regroup his forces in the south in conjunction with Montgomery (see Document 16) and the vicomtes, who had scored the brilliant success during the previous autumn of rescuing Béarn from Catholic occupation. This campaign was vital in reorienting the Protestant military system. However, abandoning any idea of concentrating on a Huguenot redoubt in the south-west, Coligny struck first at Toulouse, unsuccessfully (22 January–20 February), and then further into the north. He was able to move onto the attack, taking his forces from Auvergne to the Loire in order to guard La Charité, a place of vital importance as the only major Protestant crossing of the Loire. On 25–6 June 1570, he gave battle to Cossé at Arnay-le-Duc, vastly outnumbered but using innovative cavalry tactics. The outcome, in allowing Coligny to get to La Charité, was a severe reverse for the royal army.

Peace negotiations through Catherine and Jeanne d'Albret had not ceased and it is clear that the King himself realised in February that the game was up (see Document 18). New proposals were submitted by the Protestants after Arnay-le-Duc and, after some last-minute horse-trading, the court came to terms. A truce was agreed and peace terms were finalised. The cardinal of Lorraine was for the moment disgraced, Guise out of favour, Monluc dismissed as governor of Guyenne (see Document 19). The conclusion of peace was followed by the issue of the new Edict of Pacification, that of Saint-Germain (8 August 1570), the first formally to be qualified as 'perpetual and irrevocable'. The text registered the regained strength of the Protestants (see Document 20). Although the numbers of places of Protestant worship were limited to the suburbs of two towns per government (rather than one per bailliage), the places were actually spelled out to avoid dispute; those towns held by the Protestants on 1 August were allowed to maintain their worship and in these places open worship within them was conceded for the first time. The vexed question of confiscated offices was to be solved by reinstatement or compensation. Other new features were the concession of 'places de sureté' to the Protestants for a limited period and the first tentative measures to regulate mixed law cases. So-called 'secret articles' regulated the crown's obligations to pay off the Protestant mercenaries.

The Frst and Second Wars starkly illustrate the futility of trying to settle the religious chasm within French society through pitched battle. No matter how many brilliant victories were won, the crown was still forced to concede a form, and this time an extensive form, of religious toleration to the Protestant minority. The implications of this will be examined in the next chapter.

---

## 1    The grievances of the malcontent nobility, 1567

[*After an attack on the Guise seizure of power and the treatment of the conspirators of Amboise, argues that this is an attack on true nobility, those who strive follow the course of virtue.*] For to linger in the shade during summer or by the fire during winter, to be a retailer of gossip, liar, pimp, fornicator, noted thief, drunkard and denier of God are these days the qualities most welcome at court and common to the vilest men in the world. But to fight to maintain the honour of God, the peace of the realm, and extend the King's power over his enemies, and for this not to fear the cold or the heat but bravely risk one's life, that is true virtue. From this, the nobility has derived its dignity and privileges. . . . [*Those in charge of the state feel themselves unworthy and employ men of base condition.*] Thus, they thought they must cast down some and raise up others, to make a gentleman a villein and a villein a gentleman, surely a transubstantiation of contrary honours. [*The governors of the realm gave away the conquests of king Henry and put out his servants from power.*] And to bastardise further the heart of the nobility, when some companies of gens d'armes fell vacant, instead of gratifying those who had served so well in the tough wars against the Emperor Charles or compensating those who had been improperly deprived of their posts, they granted them to the sons of presidents of Paris and others to men who had never set foot outside the brothels of Paris, or others who had never commanded any but their valets, gentlemen like them, or at least their tailors, shoemakers, painters, embroiderers and other tradesmen of the wardrobe; others were reputed gentlemen of lineage but so little experienced in war that the most skilled could do little to acquit himself as a soldier. . . . [*The nobility as a whole*]. will remain utterly oppressed and without honour if it is stripped of the insignia which mark it off from the common people. The ornaments of nobility are the marks of honour that gentlemen acquire by their merits and fine deeds. . . .

Thus, when the gentlemen of France have been stripped of their honours . . . to transfer them to villeins who never did anything worthy of them . . . is this not completely to ruin the nobility? . . .

There is another thing worse which I cannot describe without blushing with shame. They have put matters in such disorder that, in their desire to bastardise the nobility, they have so shamed the King, in surrounding him with villeins, that it could be argued that the King, as yet unaware of his ancestors' grandeur, gives places about himself to the lowest creatures of his kingdom. I ask you, what would foreigners, who have always held the French nobility in such high esteem, think . . . when they hear that the first gentleman of the King's chamber is the son of a thrice bankrupt banker and a mother who was a courtisan at Lyons . . . or that the son of one who was originally a broquette seller at Avignon is a gentleman of the King's chamber and among his most intimate attendants? What do they say when they see the King, the Queen and his brothers served as maîtres d'hôtel by merchants who used to be shopkeepers at Lyon and elsewhere and others bank clerks at Venice and Rome or valets de chambre to cardinals and other lords? . . . What do foreigners say in seeing secretary de Laubespine do practically what he likes, through the authority he holds, depriving the worthiest lords of the Council of cognisance of the most important affairs, especially that virtuous old man the Chancellor? What do kings and princes say when they have sent to them the children of this new King of Bourges . . . where they used to see gentlemen of honour? . . .

All these things considered, what will the nobility hope for? What will it do? What will it demand? Will it serve villeins? No, for that would be too disgraceful. Will it go in search of a new land? . . . No, but it will take good advice to approach the King and re-emblazon the ancient virtue of our ancestors . . . that this villainy will melt away like snow in the sun.

[*To all this damage is added that in the pocket.*] To attain their goal, they use certain names more sweet-sounding than *tailles*, tributes or servitudes, such as subventions, aids and other admittedly gracious terms, whose effects are no less cruel and rigorous. I should like to know if it is not making a gentleman pay *taille* when you make him buy justice that the King owes us and swears to administer to us and our subjects when he is anointed. I pray you, who has more need of the law, the gentleman or the peasant? If, as is commonly said, he who owns land has to fight for it, he who has more land is in greater danger of legal process. . . . I should also like to be told, who will pay most of these 6*d*. per *livre* that are levied on hoteliers; the gentleman with great equipage, the peasant on foot or the merchant with one horse? Meanwhile, the noble is forced, under this name of subvention, to pay the *taille* like the villein; the name makes the thing no more honourable since the effect is the same. Conclusion: we are all made villeins or at least are treated as such. I say nothing of the other estates of the realm, for most have what they want and only the gentlemen and their subjects are oppressed. Lower magistrates bind us by the feet, the head and the hands; the Parlements are at our throat with their daggers drawn to spill our blood; the Italian salt-tax men and farmers of new subsidies and others from the most malignant ranks of the people, are prepared to receive it. It would still be some consolation if the money produced by these exactions were employed for the reason given, to pay off the King's debts. But it is all spent in building these fine Tuileries, or on the assignation of the lady du Perron, journeys to Bayonne to see the King of Spain, which have consumed a million in gold for the desire of seeing him and yet he was not there. . . .

SOURCE: *Lettre missive d'un gentilhomme*, 1567, Devyver, pp. 472–7.

## 2   Claude Haton on the conspiracy of Meaux, 28–9 September 1567

The rebel lords . . . assembled a council to which all the main leaders, lords and captains of their faction and pretensed Religion were called, at the Admiral's castle at Châtillon, on pretext of a banquet. . . . A number of ministers and preachers were at this Council, which met on 12 July and lasted for a whole week before they arrived at their decision. This was: that on a certain Sunday at the preachings, all Huguenots in France would be summoned in their bailliages and seneschalcies by the deacons and superintendants of their pretensed Religion to take communion and hear the decision of the Council; that they would provide money according to their means, for which they would be assessed, to pay for the necessary costs of the reiters, foreigners and Germans that the count palatine of the Rhine had raised for them; that Frenchmen of the Religion, and others who could be persuaded, would be enrolled, which enrolment would be done of all the young men and journeymen of the Religion who could bear arms. . . . Those of the bailliage of Provins assembled on 1 August to hear the rebel communication and only the most able were called to this assembly to hear these secret words. . . .

[*The Protestants*] . . . gathered all the leaders of their conspiracy at the castle of Vallery-lès-Sens, with about 1,500 well-armed horse and some thousands of foot. These, before moving, sent to warn the enrolled Huguenots of the churches of Troyes in Champagne, Sézanne, Provins, Sens and Montargis to be ready to take the field the day after Saint Michael's day, last of September. The assembly of Vallery started to gather from 10 and 12 September, with the King near Meaux. . . . With all these affairs of the Huguenots under way, a large force left the village of Vallery to undertake what had been decided. They took the road to Montereau-fault-Yonne. . . .

SOURCE: Haton, vol. I, pp. 424–32.

## 3   Condé's justification, October 1567

Sire, after we received certain news, through many witnesses and evident proofs, of the determination to abolish the exercise of the Reformed Religion and exterminate and drive out of your kingdom all those who profess it, as well as of the preparation of forces against us for this purpose, we were reduced to the extreme of being forced against our will to assemble and, with great regret, decide, according to the laws and duties of nature, to defend and preserve our lives, goods and liberty of conscience. We were thus armed for our security against our enemies, who surround you and who otherwise would not have allowed us access to Your Majesty, and we approached you with no other purpose than of dispelling the calumnies and falsehoods of our enemies and remonstrating the ills, ruin and desolation that such cruel and pernicious counsel could bring. We know this cannot proceed from your own age and disposition and that it is far removed from Your Majesty's accustomed mercy and goodness. We pray you above all . . . to allow us to worship and invoke God publicly according to the purity of His Gospel, without distinction of place or persons, removing the interpretations and restrictions added to your Edict of Pacification, which the malignity and passion of our enemies have used to cast us again into these present troubles. . . . Sire, in so far as we are your subjects and thus obliged to strive as far as we can for the preservation and sure establishment of your state, seeing the discontent of many, especially of the people, because of the great burdens and new levies which are raised without their being of any profit to you; considering also that the good will of your subjects is the prop and support of your crown, we have for this reason prayed Your Majesty, Sire, but only as advice and remonstrance, to cast your eyes in pity on your poor people in order to relieve them. So that Your Majesty should understand whence comes this ill, may it please you, if you think fit, to summon the Estates of your kingdom, which is a means and remedy which the kings your predecessors, being then of full age, used and with less reason, both to content their subjects and to establish their state. . . . For the rest, Sire, we protest both before God and his angels that we never thought to attempt anything against your person or your state.

SOURCE: *La requeste du prince de Condé et gentilshommes de France*, c. October 1567, SP70/95, fos. 96–7.

## 4   The battle of Saint-Denis, 10 November 1567

Many have debated who won the battle. Some would have it that the loss of the field and possession of the bodies for a time are sufficient for the honour to go to the Catholics. Others allege that the loss of the chief general, and [*the Protestants*] offering of battle the next day by skirmishes into the camp, are marks of victory for the Reformed. . . . As for the Constable, he died of six wounds the following day (12th), old in years, honourable in his place. He was a great captain, a good servant but a bad friend, who used the discoveries, efforts and losses of others and acted by subterfuge but, when this was not enough, acted with valour. . . . He was mourned deeply by the old councillors of state who, under his shadow and authority, dared to maintain middling opinions and now no longer expected any assurance of freedom for their views.

SOURCE: Aubigné, vol. II, pp. 248–50.

## 5  The cost of the royal army in January 1568

(in *livres tournois*, converted to sterling)

Pistoliers/reiters:

| | |
|---|---:|
| 2,500 in 8 cornets under duke Johan Wilhelm of Saxony, costs of levy, one month's pay, duke's pension and retainer for 3,500 others . . . | 204,000 |
| 3,300 in 11 cornets under the young Rhinegrave, Bassompierre and baron de Saint-Amant | 110,000 |
| 2,700 in 9 cornets under Reiffenberg, the young Landgrave, Adam Ways | 90,000 |

Swiss:

| | |
|---|---:|
| 4,000 from 2 January | 50,000 |
| 6,000 from 21 January | 74,500 |

Light horse:

| | |
|---|---:|
| 14 cornets of mounted arquebusiers | 30,000 |
| 25 cornets of mounted arquebusiers | 25,000 |

Infantry:

| | |
|---|---:|
| 25 ensigns of Strozzi's regiment | 50,000 |
| 45 ensigns under Brissac | 90,000 |
| 9 French ensigns and 20 Italian from Piedmont | 40,000 |
| Bands levied by Aumale, Guise and Tavannes | 40,000 |
| 5 companies of the baron de Semy | 10,000 |
| 6 ensigns + 200 mounted arquebusiers under Foisy | 14,000 |
| 22 Gascon ensigns under Monluc and Tillades | 24,000 |
| 7 ensigns under Martinengo | 14,000 |
| 5 under Capts Verrard, Chailly, La Roche & Angu | 8,854 |
| 9 Breton bands | 18,000 |
| 3 bands under baron de Blaignac | 6,000 |
| Garrisons in and around Paris | 2,198 |

Camp, unexpected expenses, costs of transport, commissaires
and money: 60,000

Sum total: 987,052
= 388,821 crowns
= £116,646 . 9s st.
Of which the treasurer had received 266,053 *lt.*

SOURCE: Account of treasurer Faget, SP70/96, fos. 148–9, copy annotated by W. Cecil for conversion into English money.

---

## 6 The Peace of Longjumeau, 23 March 1568

*[Preamble in which, to pacify the troubles, the King, on the advice of his mother, of Anjou, Lieutenant-General, Alençon and members of the Privy Council, ordains:]*

1 That all those of the RPR will benefit from the Edict of Pacification [*of Amboise, 1563*] purely and simply and that it be implemented in all points and articles in its original terms, removing all restrictions, modifications, declarations and interpretations that have been added since its date until this publication.

2 As for the gentlemen and lords having the status to hold preachings in their houses under the Edict of Pacification, having assured us that, on pretext of these, they are doing nothing contrary to or abusing our service, we remove all restrictions on those who may attend them.

3 Furthermore, gentlemen of Provence holding that status will enjoy the benefit of the Edict and may conduct preaching in their houses, as do those of other provinces of that status. Nevertheless, as for the county and seneschalcy of Provence, only that of Mérindol is concerned.

4 *[Restoration of all offices and property to Protestants.]*

5 *[Restoration of Condé to the King's favour.]*

6 *[Amnesty for all Condé's actions in raising money, troops etc.]*

7 None of our subjects may dispute or start litigation over revenues, arrears, rents, money and other property that they claim has been taken or levied from them, or over any other damage done to them since the start of these troubles until the publication of this present in the two armies. This will be taken to be: for the Parlement of Paris, three days after the date of this present and for the other Parlements, eight days after. Within that time our governors and Lieutenants-General will be notified urgently to publish it immediately throughout their governments and to ensure its observation, without waiting for publication in the courts [*of Parlement*], so that none may claim ignorance and that all acts of hostility, seizures and demolitions on both sides cease. . . .

8 *[Order to the Parlements to publish.]*

9 We intend further that the town and jurisdiction of the provostship and viscounty of Paris shall remain exempt from all exercise of the Religion, following the provisions of the Edict of Pacification, which remains in full force.

10 We likewise will that, after publication of these letters in the Parlement of Paris and the two armies, those of the Religion disarm promptly and disband their forces to withdraw and that the towns and fortresses occupied by them be promptly returned to their original state and commerce, with all artillery and supplies. Also all private houses occupied on both sides will be returned to their owners and all prisoners, both of war and for religion, set at liberty without ransom.

11 [*Act of oblivion for all offences, private and public, so that there should be reconciliation.*]

12 To end all scruple and doubt, our subjects will abandon all Associations they have both within and without this kingdom, and will henceforth make no levies of money, enrolments of men or any assemblies except those permitted by this present Edict, and not in arms, on pain of punishment as breakers of our commands and ordinances.

13 [*Restoration of the clergy to all their revenues and buildings.*]

SOURCE: Stegman, pp. 53–8. Registered by the Parlement of Paris, 27 March 1568.

---

## 7 Catholic resistance to the peace

The Parisians, having heard that the King was inclining to conclude a peace, came to His Majesty to remonstrate that he should not grant the peace on the basis of the Huguenot articles. He, to excuse himself, said he could do no other, or at least that his kingdom was going to ruin for lack of money to sustain the war, in which scarcely any would serve him. . . .

The preachers and doctors in their Lenten sermons in the city of Paris cried out in their sermons against the King and his Council and said out loud that God would be revenged on His Majesty and the Council and that the King in this life would endure punishment and adversity in his soul and body, his life would be brief and his death hastened by the Huguenots, who would never rest until they had destroyed him, no matter what peace he made with them. They accused the King, his mother and his Council of being, by this peace, the cause of the ruin of the true Catholic religion. . . . It happened that these preachers appeared before the King at the Louvre, whether summoned by His Majesty or of their own accord I do not know. Once there, they had audience of His Majesty and with Master d'Ivollé as spokesman. . . . His Majesty listened impatiently, being aggrieved that they had accused him covertly of heresy because of the agreement made with the Huguenots

by the peace he had made or wished to conclude. Ivollé replied that they had made
no open or covert accusation. . . .

SOURCE: Haton, vol. II, pp. 526–9

## THE RENEWAL OF THE WARS

### 8 Cardinal de Châtillon's treatise on the renewal of the wars

In order to lay bare the sources of our ills and calamities, I shall start with what is
well enough known to all those who have some means to understand what has been
happening in France. From the moment it pleased the King to pacify the troubles
of his kingdom by the peace agreed at Longjumeau, instead of observing it sincerely
as was necessary in this poor kingdom already drowned in blood, cruelty, affliction
and deformity, the hearts of certain Catholics around His Majesty, particularly the
cardinal of Lorraine, were so poisoned with hatred for the good and repose of the
kingdom that, to the great contempt of the truth of the King's word and bond,
they swore and resolved in a council held before the publication of the peace at the
Louvre in the cabinet of one of the greatest in the land, not to observe it and
covertly to do away with all prominent men of the Religion whom they could trap
and to carry out under cover of the peace what they had been unable to do through
war: namely, to liquidate the Religion and all those who profess it in France and
then afterwards, joining forces with those of their league, to do the same to those
princes and foreign nations holding that Religion. This is proved by the letter the
cardinal and the lord of Aumale his brother wrote to Madame de Guise their
mother, by which they informed her that, since they had been unable to prevent
the peace, they would take such steps that the Huguenots would find it worse than
war and that it would only be a short truce. It can thus be seen what spirit prompts
the cardinal and the Catholics who manage the affairs of France and what care they
have for the preservation of the kingdom and the public peace.

As for the prince of Condé, the gentlemen and others of the Religion who
adhered to him since they were forced last year to take arms as a final recourse for
their preservation and security, all their actions show that they have no other hope
or aim but the maintenance of the Religion and the defence of their honour, life
and goods. This may be shown by the fact that from the start they had required
only their freedom of religion and enjoyment of the Edict of Orléans without
modification or restriction. As soon as His Majesty's deputies agreed this at
Longjumeau, though the lord prince and those of the Religion had the advantage
of force on their side, they were satisfied. . . .

[*The Protestant leaders carried out the peace faithfully and delivered their children to
court to reassure the King. They also disarmed. On their side, the Catholics delayed*

*implementation, carried out atrocities against the Protestants and prevented Condé from entering his government of Picardy.*]

As for the court, which should be a refuge and place of safety, the Protestants have had no sure access there since the peace. Rather, in the very presence of the King, who owes his subjects justice and protection, those who risked going there to make requests were forced to flee from threats and quarrels; as was captain Poyet, sent to Their Majesties by the Admiral, by the baron de Neubourg; and captain Chat, one of Mgr de Montmorency's men, by one of the royal guards. Some were imprisoned without charge or any form of justice while others were advised to hide or flee quickly. There were some killed, including Captain Toloni of Provence, sent by the late sieur de Sipierres to his mother the countess of Tende, who was murdered 200 yards from the King's lodging by four soldiers of his guard. These are just examples of many such acts.

In the city of Paris, while the King was there, 14 or 15 inhabitants were looted, robbed or killed both in the rue saint Antoine and in other places. A poor woman of the Religion, who found her husband's headless body in the river, demanded justice with tears and pitiful cries while the King was at the château de Madrid. Seeing that those who owed her justice just laughed, she went to the Chancellor, who gave her access to the Parlement, but he was immediately told to leave the case and that the King was reserving it to his own judgment.

[*There follows an account of all the massacres and murders of Protestants over the previous summer throughout France.*]

The lord prince, wishing after the peace to go to his government, came to his house at Muret, which he was forced to leave straight away because infantry companies were sent to be stationed nearby at Soissons, Laon and La Fère. He came to another of his houses at Condé, but having heard of the plan against him and the names of the plotters, and thinking his house insecure, he was forced to leave and take his wife and children, some in swaddling-clothes and others in his arms, to an estate of his called Noyers, further from the frontier and all cause of suspicion. But there was no sure refuge for him as was seen later when he surprised two or three spies testing the depth of the moat and the height of the walls. . . . Finally, when the time agreed to surprise him was approaching, the Spanish ambassador took to Their Majesties a forged despatch from the duke of Alva, by which he said the prince of Orange was ready to enter Franche-Comté and he did not know what his intention was. This was spread around at court and in Paris to give a pretext to send all the troops into Burgundy near the house of my lord the prince and hasten them on to entrap him. . . . But the prince, warned in time by a captain who was in on the plot . . . decided with the Admiral to escape the danger and get to La Rochelle and the house of his brother-in-law the count of La Rochefoucauld, as the only place where he could take refuge in this kingdom once he had fled from so many houses. On leaving, he wrote to the King asking him not to take his departure in bad part since it was only to save his life and not to renew the troubles, throwing the blame for all the ills of France on the cardinal of Lorraine.

The moment this news was received it became clear how much they regretted that their prey had escaped them, and there was no more talk of the prince of Orange, but rather of turning the troops towards the road to Orléans and La Rochelle. The cardinal's power was such that the moment the news of the prince's departure was received, without any discussion with the marshals of France of such a momentous decision as the declaration of war, it was quickly resolved, without any justification other than their grievance that the prince had not allowed his throat to be cut.

Such, then, was the remarkable treatment of a prince of the blood since the peace, which should move all the princes of Christendom to pity and compassion. . . .

Meanwhile, certain subtle practisers and barefaced liers put it about that the prince and the Admiral began the troubles only out of envy and spite that they could not exercise their offices and that they were not employed in the direction of state affairs. It is easy to show this to be slander by all the letters and envoys the lords sent to Their Majesties, in which it will be found that they never made any mention of their private interests, nor of the property, offices and pensions they had never received, but wished only to protest at the violence done against those of the Religion, the infringements of the Edict and the breaking of the public peace and trust.

[*There follows a detailed refutation of the accusations of rebellion, especially for La Rochelle, Castres and Montauban in refusing to admit garrisons, and a catalogue of Catholic brutalities at Auxerre, Soissons and in Languedoc. Even Catholic rulers have criticised these.*]

[*The persuaders try to argue that the King has no ill will against the Protestants and treats well those who serve him.*] It would be difficult to give an example of this except for the sieur de Piennes, who is held to be sympathetic to the advancement of God's honour and service, as his actions amply show. During the first troubles he was at Orléans for some months, where he led such a dissolute life that, seeing he could no longer be tolerated, he withdrew with his mistress and her daughter. He feigns to be of the Religion and close to the grandees so as to encourage others to follow his example, and to lower the guard of those amongst us who are prone to self-deception and do not realise that, if the cause were ruined, no better deal would be made with them than with the rest.

[*As for the King's desire for their obedience, they never went home more determined to observe the edicts, but the Catholics continued their accustomed violence.*] Were we to change our religion, which is founded on the consent of all the Estates of France, authorised and established by several royal edicts, so that we hold and practise it lawfully, non-violent and lawful methods would be needed, having equal authority and solemnity, avoiding the paths of injustice, cruelty, murder and abominable perfidy before God and men. Vengeance cannot fail but fall, through the just judgment of God, on those who are the authors, abettors and counsellors of this. It is to be feared that God in his anger will discharge his arrows against this poor kingdom until they are bathed in our blood. May He by His grace look upon us with pity, turn away his anger and incline the heart of our King to follow the path of His commandments.

SOURCE: SP70/102 no. 1977, fos. 2–6; sent by Châtillon to Cecil from Sheen, 27 November 1568.

## 9  The Protestation of Condé, La Rochelle, 9 September 1568

We Louis de Bourbon, prince of Condé . . . protest before God and his angels and in the presence of this holy assembly that, as declared in the remonstrances sent by us to our lord the King, we have no intention of taking arms to attempt anything to the prejudice of His Majesty or his state. Rather, we recognise him as our King and sovereign lord ordained by God and declare that what we do is only for the preservation of our liberty of conscience and the exercise of the Reformed Religion, to guarantee our lives, honour and goods from the tyranny and oppression that the cardinal of Lorraine, and other enemies and disturbers of the good and the public peace of this realm, have constantly exercised against those of the Religion, contrary to the will of His Majesty declared both by his edicts and by various express declarations and despatches made to us. To this end and to preserve the lives, honour and liberty of conscience both of us and of the lords, gentlemen and other subjects of this realm who profess the Reformed Religion, we declare ourselves ready to employ our person, life and all other means that it may please God to give us.

[*Followed by an oath to follow the prince and obey his orders, and then an ordinance on military discipline.*]

SOURCE: *Déclaration et protestation de Monseigneur le prince de Condé des causes qui l'ont contraint de prendre les armes, imprimé nouvellement,* 1568, SP70/102 fos. 59–67.

## 10  The Ordinances of Saint-Maur, September 1568

[*Long history of the Edicts of Pacification from 1561 down to that of 1567. The failure of the Protestants to return La Rochelle, Montauban and Castres under the terms of the treaty of Longjumeau (art. 10).*]

Wherein we, seeing them so oft and so many times to abuse our clemency and favour, that we can no more doubt of their wicked and damnable [*intent*], which is to establish and set up in this said realm some other sovereign and supreme government, to the overthrowing of ours, ordained and set up by God, and by such practices to pluck from us our good subjects, by the means of the permission and toleration of the said exercise of their religion and of the assemblies which they do make under colour of their preachings and communions, at the which they make gatherings of money, billing of men, oaths, confederacies, practices and devices, as well within as without our said realm, they trouble and disquiet it. Yea, and having their weapons in their hands, they deal with us as fellows and companions, not as our obedient subjects . . . [*they seek to overthrow the King's religion*] and remain the only lords and masters by means of the said exercise permitted unto them during our minority and somewhat after continued for the love of peace and quiet, and to avoid thereby a worse inconvenience, directly against our own will and mind. We have at all times fast settled in our heart the true Religion as Most Christian Kings ought to have and who be fully resolved to live and die therein. . . .

For these causes and other great and weighty considerations moving us hereunto, having had hereupon the advice of our most excellent Lady and Mother, of our said dear and best beloved brethren, of other princes of our blood and of other men of honour, the lords and the honourable of our Privy Council, we have by Edict and Ordinance perpetual and irrevocable inhibited and forbidden, we do inhibit and forbid upon pain of confiscation of body and goods, to all persons of what dignity, condition or quality soever they be, within our said realm and land of our obedience, all manner exercise of any religion than only of the Catholic and Roman . . . and to this effect we ordain that all ministers of the said Religion pretended reformed be bound within xv days after the publication of these presents, to avoid and depart our said realm. . . .

This notwithstanding, we mean not, nor will not, that those of the said Religion pretended reformed be by any means examined upon their consciences, so that they refrain from the exercise of all other religion than of the said Catholic and Roman: hoping that hereafter, by the inspiration of God and by the great diligence we purpose to use, to see that all bishops and pastors of the church of our said realm do their endeavour and duty also, hoping, I say, that our said subjects of the said pretended Religion will return and join again with us and with our subjects in the unity of the holy Catholic Church. [*Enjoins all those in arms to lay them down within 20 days in return for which they will be pardoned and received into protection. Towns are to be returned. All private quarrels to cease.*]

SOURCE: *An Edict or ordinance of the French King, conteining a Prohibition and Interdiction of all Preaching, assembling or exercise of anie other Religion than the Catholicke* (1568); Stegman, p. 59.

## 11   The quarrel between Lorraine and L'Hospital

[*The Chancellor had refused to seal the King's promulgation of a papal bull authorising the alienation of church property to finance the war, on condition that the Edict of Longjumeau was rescinded.*] Whereupon, he was called to come to the Council. The

Cardinal of Lorraine being there, forthwith he asked him for what cause he refused to seal it, saying further that it was his ordinary [custom] to make the like difficulty when it pleased him. The Chancellor alleged diverse reasons in that behalf and, amongst others, that to break the Edict of Pacification was the next way to cause open wars and to draw the Almains into his realm, in doing quite contrary to that was accorded. The Cardinal, being herewith much stirred (besides of long time there hath been suspect between them) began to injure him, reproaching him to be but an hypocrite and that his wife and daughter were Calvinists and that this was not the first time that he had of his race, which had deserved evil of the King, meaning his father, physician to the duke of Bourbon, who departed this realm with him towards the Emperor, not leaving him until his death. To this the Chancellor replied that he had as honest of his race as he. The Cardinal asked if he meant to make comparison with him of races. He answered no, but he spake of the honesty of his. Whereupon, the Cardinal gave him the lie and, rising incontinently out of his chair to take him by the beard, the marshal Montmorency stepped between them. After, the Cardinal in great colour turning towards the Queen said: 'Madam, this is only he that is the cause of the troubles chanced in this realm and if he were in the hands of the Parlement, his head should not tarry upon his shoulders xxiiij hours.' The Chancellor answered that if the Cardinal's actions were examined by justice, that he should find more to do than he and, whatsoever he had done in his office, he was ready to render account; but, contrariwise, that the Cardinal had been the original cause of all the mischiefs and disorders chanced as well in France within these viij years as to the rest of Christendom. And hereof he reported him to the common bruit, yea unto them that most favour him, as to the people of Paris, upon whom he reposeth his greatest affiance, who condemn him without any other figure of process. Notwithstanding all this debate, the King's letters patent were sealed and the next day sent unto the Parlement of Paris with the bulls, which were there published in the same instant. Afterwards, the Queen did essay to appease the matter and caused them to speak together, excusing the one towards the other, but friendship (in this court), being once suspected, is of small assurance and that [which] is new reconciled, of all others is most feeble. . . .

SOURCE: Norris to Cecil, 25 September 1568, SP70/102 no. 2033.

---

## 12   The battle of Jarnac, report by Norris

A little before the rencounter, the Admiral defeated near unto Jarnac between 700 and 800 horses, putting to flight Martigues, Brissac and others and recovered from them the town and castle of Jarnac by composition, which captain La Rivière had taken before. Whereupon, the 11th of this same month the duke of Anjou would have encamped near unto Cognac but seeing the other army ready to rencounter, he returned to Châteauneuf. At the last, having caused to be made two or three bridges upon the river of Charente and been advertised that the Prince would fight with him, he caused at midnight by little and little all his vanguard and the most part of his horsemen to pass over the bridge before the Prince's army was informed thereof, which was the cause that the next day, being the 13th of this month, the Admiral came to assail them and overthrew part of them. But, seeing the strength of the Duke's army coming upon him, he sent forthwith unto the Prince (who had undertaken with seven or eight hundred horsemen to keep the passage of the bridges) that he should retire himself towards him, both to succour him and also that he should not endanger himself among his enemies. And so, by little and little, the said Admiral retired himself near unto a village called Bassac between Châteauneuf and Jarnac, where the Prince followed with such a fury and so strangely that he broke the whole vanguard of the Duke but the same being renforced by eight cornets of the reiters, the Prince's men were constrained to retire. As touching the Prince being so hot in the fight as he would not retire himself, his horse was first killed under him and he hurt and taken prisoner by the sieur d'Argence. And it is said that he was killed after he was taken, which was done by Martigues and others who were expressly sent with him for that purpose by the duke of Anjou, and so was his body mangled after he was dead. Stuart the Scottish man was also slain after he was taken and his head carried upon a pike's point about the army. Mons. de Losses was forthwith sent hither to Paris with the news, where he arrived the 18th of this month. It is certain that without the reiters the army of the Duke of Anjou had been wholly defeated, minding nothing else but to fly. But the reiters, being a great company and hard to be broken, pursued somewhat the Prince's men and yet the Admiral and generally all the chiefs except the Prince retired themselves safely and sound to Cognac, where they have in the space of two days assembled all their forces again.

SOURCE: Report of the battle sent by Norris, SP70/106 no. 144.

## 13  The Battle of Jarnac, Navarre's bulletin, 18 April 1569

The late Prince of Condé had his horse killed under him in a charge and, having been taken prisoner by the srs d'Argences and Saint-Jean he was deliberately, cruelly and inhumanly killed by the sr de Montesquiou, captain of the Swiss guard of Monsieur, the King's brother, with several other men. It is certain that the enemy lost more than 200 men . . . and we lost only 50 or 60, of whom 35 or 40 are prisoners. . . . [*News had been received*] that on the 30th last our reiters crossed over and were to have been Thursday or yesterday at the Loire where they have decided to besiege Nemps or La Charité to assure their crossing. The Duke of Zweibrücken has 10,000 reiters and 8,000 lansquenets besides 2,500 horse, 5,000 or 6,000 French arquebusiers, 20 cannons, 50 milliers of powder, shot and other munitions. The prince of Orange and his brother Duke Ludovic of Nassau have joined the said Duke with fine troops and they expect more.

SOURCE: Bulletin of Navarre and the other leaders from Saintes, 18 April 1569, SP70/107 no. 223; Aumale, vol. II, pp. 403–7.

## 14    Norris on the siege of Poitiers, summer–autumn 1569

It is strange that the wisest men here are now persuaded the importance of the war to depend chiefly upon the success of Poitiers. For, if the Admiral take this place, he hath in his hands the chief branches of the house of Guise, the duke and the marquess his brother, besides great riches, ransoms of noblemen, Frenchmen and strangers, the flower of the King's army, which thing should give him the means either to make capitulations with his great advantage or else, speedily pursuing his fortune, possess himself of all other towns as be upon the river of Loire, which are but weakly garnished in respect of this, and by their example will doubt their own forces. On the other part, if the Admiral abandon it without taking the same, the loss of time, men, munition and such other necessaries will be no small hindrance, besides the encouraging of the enemy, the payment of his strangers and wearying of his camp. And, since natural causes are to be approved by reason and sounded by judgment, I must finally consent that the event hereof shall either bring, in taking the town, some notable hap to the army of the Religion, or else the departing from this attempt must needs be accompanied with some disaster if the same in time be not prudently foreseen and sustained by some extraordinary means.

SOURCE: Norris to Elizabeth I, Amboise, 28 August 1569, SP70/108 no. 343.

## 15    Norris on the Battle of Moncontour

[*Report of the Battle of Moncontour.*] All men doth agree that of long time there hath not been a more cruel and bloody battle. And at my being with the King, I said unto him that, since it pleased God to give him the victory, he could do nothing more acceptable to God nor more worthy of himself than to take compassion of his poor subjects. Whereunto the King said that such as were willing to return to their due obedience, they should find him a merciful prince. Marry, the obstinate he meant to pursue with all rigour and extremity. And since Your Majesty may perceive the loss of this battle to be of great consequence and long ago understanding the determination of the Catholic princes against the Protestants if they can bring their designs to their desired effect, I shall not need to make any tedious rehearsal. . . .

SOURCE: Norris to Elizabeth I, Tours, 5 October 1569, SP70/108 no. 382.

## 16   The recovery of the Protestant forces, winter 1569–70

My lord Admiral writes on 1 January that the army of my lords the princes is in
very good spirits and healthier than it has been for a year. He considers that the
change of air has been one of the ways God has brought an end to the illnesses that
reigned until then. The army was at the port of Sainte-Marie three leagues from
Agen and holds all the bank of the river Garonne from the gates of Agen to beyond
Marmande and along the river Lot up to Neufville, where the towns are small but
rich and abundant in all necessities for an army and from which money can be
raised.

The count of Montgomery holds the other bank of the river Garonne and all the
country up to Béarn and the upper reaches of the river up to Hautvillier and on his
part gathers as much money as he can. . . .

Monsieur Pilles and those who were within Saint-Jean have arrived in the camp
healthy and in good spirits, having sustained the siege as long as their powder held
out and wrought as warlike and magnanimous acts as have ever been done in our
age during a siege.

A boat bridge had been thrown across the river Garonne over which men, horses,
carts and artillery have passed for a week. . . .

Monsieur de Lavauguyon came to the land between the rivers Dordogne and Lot
with twenty cornets of cavalry to hold the crossings of those rivers . . . but that has
not stopped Pilles crossing the Lot. . . .

The reiters of the lords Princes have been paid and are more satisfied, content
and obedient a nation as has been seen. They left the river with the count of
Montgomery without difficulty. . . .

My lord count of Mansfeld does many good offices every day and shows, in this,
great zeal for the cause . . . and it cannot be doubted that God sent him to do a
great good, as he did count Ludovic of Nassau, a most Christian and very wise
prince. . . .

SOURCE: Digest of letters from La Rochelle, January 1570, SP70/110 no. 533.

---

# PEACE NEGOTIATIONS, NOVEMBER 1569

## 17   Protestant peace terms, November 1569

That the Reformed Religion may be exercised in all towns, villages, castles and
other places in this kingdom without exception where any of the inhabitants wish it
in general or private and all persons may attend without distinction, subjects or
non-subjects, native or foreign. For this exercise, the evangelicals may be able to
build for their use temples and other places as they need without restriction of

numbers. Town dwellers will be able to worship in the towns without having to confine themselves to suburbs.

That all ministers, natives or foreign, may exercise their ministry in this kingdom.

That, for the exercise of that Religion and the observation of church discipline, synods, colloquies and consistories may be permitted them in places and at times that they think fit, at which the governors of provinces and towns, or their lieutenants, and the royal judges may be present so as to ensure that nothing is done contrary to the King's service. The ministers may issue the censures necessary and usual in the Reformed Church.

That, to avoid both the multiplicity of religions and impiety and atheism, all natives shall be required to declare themselves of one of the two religions: that is, the Reformed, according to the confession approved in it, or the Roman, also according to its confession, without liberty to chose a third or declare neutrality. Nor shall this article remove the liberty of those who have so declared themselves afterwards to join the other or attend preaching or other practice. Also, ministers and prelates shall not be prevented from the use of ecclesiastical censures against recalcitrants. . . .

Council and justice:

It will please His Majesty to appoint to his Privy Council a certain number of councillors of the long robe, learned and virtuous and professing the Reformed Religion, besides those at present members, who may see that there be no enterprise contrary to surety of the pacification it will please His Majesty to concede his subjects and to advise His Majesty thereof.

. . . In all judgments of cases between those of different religions, both civil and criminal, both in the court of Parlement and in other sovereign or inferior courts, the judges will be of equal numbers of the two religions. Otherwise, sentences and judgments will be void unless the parties renounce this regulation by express public renunciation registered by notary and recorded in the proceedings read publicly at the hearing. . . .

Means for the security of the public pacification:

[*Several demands for equal representation in all town magistracies.*]
And to provide against all the lack of faith that has been used against the evangelicals to the prejudice of the previous edicts of pacification contrary to the King's will witnessed by his oaths, His Majesty may be pleased to accord that the princes of Navarre and Condé and their associates may hold for their security the towns of La Rochelle, Angoulême, Cognac, Blaye, Saint-Jean d'Angély, Taillebourg, Castres, Montauban, Aurillac, La Charité and Sancerre until the Edict of Pacification be published in all courts of Parlement and towns of the kingdom

and that all foreign troops be withdrawn and garrisons removed from the towns and that there be effective means for the foreigners to withdraw to their homes. . . .

That the duke of Zweibrücken, the prince of Orange, his brothers and the count of Mansfeld be comprehended in this present pacification.

SOURCE: SP70/109 no. 462.

## 18  Charles IX to Fourquevaux, February 1570, on the necessity of peace

Seeing the great difficulty of making an end by force of arms, especially since at the moment they are supported on all sides, and that they have such contacts with foreign nations from whom they await reinforcements; and that pursuing such a course after such fine and great victories would be to risk the outcome of this war on a chancy and dangerous event, a good pacification would be much more easy and gentle. On the other hand there is such licence among my subjects on both sides that they do not obey me as they should, having forgotten all fear or love of God and their prince. There is no control or military discipline among the gentlemen and soldiers, who, in making leagues among themselves, seek only to defend themselves against each other from the dangers and difficulties of this war without serving me in my need. [*Churches and monasteries are so ruined or occupied that the King fears for the Catholic faith.*] Furthermore, the houses of most lords and gentlemen of my realm are ruined or burned, while they still hold a certain number of towns and fortresses which, even though I had disposed of the army they have in the field, it would be impossible for me to recover except with great delay, loss of men, ruin and great expense. Then, I am informed by a great prince that there is an army in Germany ready to invade my realm unless I send my forces to the frontier to prevent the entry of the foreigners who come to the aid of the princes. All means of war fail me, my finances are exhausted by the expenditure I have made, besides the great sums I owe to the foreigners who have served me and so many debts owed which I could never repay, as I must, if the wars continue. These are the reasons why, with the advice of the chiefs of my realm, I have agreed only on the articles that you will see, which I judge advantageous for me and a benefit to my kingdom.

SOURCE: Charles IX to Fourquevaux, Angers, 7 February 1570, *LCM*, vol. III, pp. 294–5n.

## 19  Norris on peace talks, 9 July 1570

Touching this long lingering peace, although the sieurs de Biron and Malassise be returned from the Princes and come to court, and that it is commonly given forth, and also the aforesaid [*Spanish*] ambassador believeth no less, but that peace is concluded, yet they stay upon two points, both for the payment of the Princes' reiters and also restoring the officers to their offices and estates whereof others are now possessed. I find not how it will be brought to pass. All other points are agreed upon according to the last Edict of Pacification concluded at Chartres. . . . And notwithstanding these pourparlers of peace the armies cease not the one to molest the other what they may. . . .

The duke of Guise is lately fallen into the disgrace of the King, being broken out that he sought Madame Margaret in marriage and it is thought by some that he hath consented thereto. . . . The quarrel grown twixt the Duke Montmorency and the Marquess de Maine for the antecedence in the royal and solemn service hath been lately decided by the King's Privy Council in the favour of the said Montmorency.

SOURCE: Norris to Elizabeth I, 9 July 1570, SP70/113 no. 761.

## 20   The Edict of Saint-Germain, August 1570

1 First, that the remembrance of all things past on both parts, for and since the beginning of the troubles . . . shall remain as wholly quenched and appeased, as things that never happened [*no legal consequences to follow*].

2 Forbidding also our subjects of what estate or quality soever they be, that they renew not the memory thereof, to take hold, to revile or provoke either other, by reproaching them with things past, to dispute, to despise, to quarrel, to outrage or offend either other in word or in deed; but to keep themselves within their bounds, to live peaceably together as brethren, friends and fellow citizens, upon pain that the offenders be punished as breakers of the peace . . .

3 We ordain that the Catholic and Romish Church be set up again and established in all places and quarters of this our realm and country under our obedience, where the exercise of the same hath been left off, and that it may be freely and peaceably exercised without any trouble or let upon the pain foresaid; and that all those which during the present wars have gotten unto them any houses, goods and revenues belonging to the churchmen and other Catholics, and hold and occupy the same, shall leave unto them the full possession and peaceable enjoying.

4 And to the end that none occasion of trouble or contention be left among our said subjects, we have permitted and do permit them to live and dwell in all our towns and places of this our said realm . . . without enquiry, vexing or molesting, or constraining to anything concerning religion against their consciences, neither by reason of the same to be searched in their houses . . . so that they behave themselves according to the tenour of the present edict.

5 We have also permitted to all gentlemen as well *regnicoles* as others, having within our realm . . . high justice or full fief of *haubert* as in Normandy, whether it be in property or *usufruict* in part or in all, to have in such of their houses of the said high justice or fief as they shall name for their principal mansion to our bailiffs and seneschals . . . to exercise of the religion which they

call Reformed, so long as they shall be resident thereat. And in their absence, their wives and household, for whom they shall answer. And shall be bound to name the said houses to our said bailiffs and seneschals, before they enjoy the benefit therof; they shall also have like exercise in their other houses of high justice . . . so long as they shall be present and no longer; which shall be permitted as well to them as to their families subjects and others that will go together.

6 In the houses of fief where the said of the Religion have not the said high justice or fief of *haubert*, it is permitted them to use the said exercise for themselves and their household only. Not meaning nevertheless that if any of their friends chance to come together to the number of ten, or constrained by any christening, so that the company exceed not the said number of ten. . . .

7 And to gratify our aunt the Queen of Navarre, we permit to her, besides all that is before granted to the said lords high justices, that she may have in [*each of*] her dukedom of Albret and earldoms of Armagnac, Foix and Bigorre, in one house to her belonging, where she shall have high justice (which shall be by us chosen and named) the said exercise for all those that will come thereto, though she herself be absent.

8 And also those of the said religion may use their exercise in these places following. That is: [*in the suburbs of the following: Île-de-France: Clermont, Crépy-en-Laonnois; Champagne and Berry: Vézelay, Villenoce; Burgundy: Arnay-le-duc and Mailly; Picardy: Montdidier, Ribemont; Normandy: Pontaudemer, Carentan; Lyonnais: Charlieu, Saint-Genis-Laval; Dauphiné: Crest, Chorges; Provence: Mérindol, Forcalquier; Languedoc: Aubénas, Montaignac; Guyenne: Bergerac, Saint-Sever; Orléans, Touraine, Maine, Chartrain: Sancerre, Maillé.*]

9 And further, we have granted them to use and continue the exercise of the said religion in all such towns as it is publicly found to be used the first day of this present month of August.

10 [*No religious activity or teaching allowed anywhere else.*]

11 Also there shall be no exercise of the said Religion pretended reformed in our court, or within two leagues of the same.

12 Likewise, we mean that there shall be no exercise of the said Religion in the town, provostship and viscounty of Paris nor within ten leagues compass of the said town [*to include Senlis, Meaux, Melun, Chartres, Montléry, Dourdan, Rambouillet, Houdan, Meulan, Vigny, Méru, St. Leu-d'Esserent*] but yet without search or enquiry of the houses of those of the religion. . . .

15 There shall be no difference or distinction made for religion['s] sake in the receiving of scholars, sick or poor into the Universities, schools, hospitals, spittles or common alms houses.

16 And that the upright meaning of our said aunt the Queen of Navarre be not doubted of, or our said brother and cousin the princes of Navarre and of

Condé, both the father and the son, we have said and declared, say and declare, that we hold and esteem them our good kinsfolks, faithful subjects and servants. . . .

22 And to remove all complaints hereafter, we have declared and declare those of the said Religion capable to hold and exercise all estates, dignities and public charges, both royal, lordly and of the towns of this realm, and to be indifferently admitted and received into all councils, deliberations, assemblies, seats and functions, which depend on the things aforesaid, and not to be in any wise rejected or hindered from the enjoying thereof. . . .

23 And the said of the Religion pretended reformed shall not hereafter be overburdened or oppressed with any ordinary or extraordinary charges more than the Catholics . . . and nevertheless considering the great charges that those of the Religion have borne, they shall be discharged from all such other charges as the towns shall lay on them for expenses past, but shall contribute to all such as we shall lay upon them. . . .

26 We ordain, will and our pleasure is, that all those of the said Religion, as well generally as particularly, shall return and be conserved, maintained and kept under our protection and authority in all and every [one of] their goods, rights, actions, honours, estates, charges, pensions and dignities of what quality soever they be; excepting the bailiffs and seneschals of the long robe and their lieutenants, whose places have been by us provided for in title of office during this present war. To whom assignation shall be given to receive in just value of their said offices in the best payment that we have in our coffers. Except they had rather be councillors in our Courts of Parliament or Great Council, where they remain at our choice. In which case, they shall receive but the overplus of their said office, if it so fall out, as they shall also pay the overplus if their offices be of less value. . . .

32 And to quench and blot out as much as may be the remembrance of all troubles and divisions past, we have declared and declare all sentences, judgments, arrests and proceedings, seizures, sales and decrees made and given against the said of the Religion pretended reformed, as well living as dead, since the departure of our most honoured lord and father King Henry, by occasion of the said Religion, tumults and troubles . . . to be from henceforth broken, revoked and of none effect, which for this cause will be razed and put out of the registers of our courts, as well high as low, as also all marks, tokens and monuments of the said executions, books or defamations against their persons, memory and posterity, we ordain the whole to be taken away and defaced and the places which were upon this occasion broken down, or razed, to be yielded again to their owners to use them at their pleasure. . . .

34 We also ordain that those of the said Religion shall be subject to the politic laws of our realm; that is, they shall keep holy days and they of the said Religion

shall not work, sell or make any show on the said days with any open shop; and on fasting days, in which the use of flesh is forbidden by the Catholic and Romish Church, the butcheries shall not be used.

35 And to the end that justice be done and administered to our subjects without suspicion of any hatred or favour, we have ordained and do ordain, our will and pleasure is, that the process and difference moved or to be moved between parties of contrary religion, as well in demanding as defending . . . shall be heard at the first instance before our bailiffs, seneschals and other of our ordinary judges. . . . And where any appeal shall be made to any of our courts of Parliament, touching that of Paris, which consisteth of seven chambers, that is: the Great Chamber, the Tournelle and five Enquiries, those of the RPR may if they will for matters that they have in any of the said chambers, require that four, whether they be presidents or councillors, may be absent in the judgment of their process. . . .

36 [*Those cases in Toulouse can be sent before the masters of requests of the household.*]

37 [*In all other Parlements, Protestants can require six abstentions (three per chamber), except Bordeaux (four per chamber).*] . . .

39 And because that many particular persons have received and suffered injuries and damages in their goods and persons, as hardly they can so soon forget the remembrance thereof, as it is requisite for the execution of our intent, willing to avoid all inconvenience and to give some mean for those that might be in some fear that returning to their houses they should not be at rest, in tarrying till such rancour and enmity might be assuaged, we have given to the keeping of those of the Religion, the towns of Rochelle, Montauban, Cognac and La Charité, in which, such as mind not so soon to return to their own houses may withdraw themselves and remain. And for the safety thereof our said brother and cousin the princes of Navarre and Condé and twenty gentlemen of the said Religion which shall be by us named, shall one for all swear and promise for themselves and for the whole of their Religion to keep the said towns and at the end of the term of two years to render it again into the hands of him whom it shall please us to appoint. . . . At the end of which term, the exercise of the said Religion shall be continued as it was while they held it [*though the clergy are to be allowed to re-enter these towns*].

SOURCE: Stegman, pp. 69–81; trans. *An Edict Set Forth by the French King for Appeasing the Troubles of his Kingdome* (London: N. Bynneman, for Lucas Harrison, 1570).

# 5 The Era of the Saint Bartholomew Massacre

## From the Peace of 1570 to the Massacre

The peace was followed by a period which saw Charles IX (now aged 20) at the most independent stage of his reign, symbolised by the much delayed triumphal entry into Paris (6 March 1571) followed by that of his new Queen, Elizabeth of Austria (29 March). Though the influence of Coligny over him has been exaggerated, the policy of the crown was, for once, based on peace with the Protestants because the militant Catholic party had shown itself incapable of concluding the war and the Protestants of winning it. The finances of the state were ruined. As Henry Norris pointed out, though many welcomed the end of fighting the peace had been concluded of necessity by both sides and settled none of the antagonisms within the nobility (see Document 3). Yet again, to many Catholics it seemed as though their cause had been betrayed (see Document 1). One of the main problems here was that the peace policy was fundamentally incompatible with the interests of Catholics and of the house of Guise, which saw itself excluded from influence in the years 1570–2 (see Documents 2–4), and the King's brother Anjou, who was increasingly the figurehead of Catholic partisanship. The Guises could not be permanently ignored. Quite apart from their patronage of the Catholic cause and the backing it received in the form of Spanish cash, the house of Lorraine was of critical importance in providing avenues to credit for the monarchy via the duchy of Lorraine.

The role of Coligny is central in this period but difficult to disentangle (see Document 6–7). He was won round to Catherine's policy of a marriage alliance between her daughter Marguerite and Henry of Navarre, a marriage that plainly symbolised the irreversibility of the royal policy of conciliation, making clear that the crown, at any rate, had abandoned hope of crushing the Protestants. Coligny, having been initially hostile to it, understood, as a realist, that the Catholics could not be defeated in pitched battle and that the tide of Protestant conversions was now ebbing. An arrangement with the crown was the best policy for him. In July 1571, secret negotiations between the crown and the Protestants were reported. It is fairly clear that Coligny stood for a solution to the internal problems of France by the renewal of the old conflict with the Habsburgs in the Netherlands (see Document 9). Catherine would oppose this, but the idea that she was plotting to eliminate him because of his foreign policy does not stand up; Coligny was alone in the Council as a figure who considered war inevitable. There was therefore a degree of fluidity and flexibility possible in the formulation of policy that had not been present for some years. In 1571, moreover, the King was talking of active foreign policy moves in Flanders and Italy. On three occasions: September 1571, June 1572 and August 1572, the Council discussed the issue of war with Spain. Coligny remained in a minority of one, faced by a range of councillors who saw conflict with Philip II as potentially disastrous (see Document 9–11).

On 7 October 1571 the great naval victory at Lepanto had given the Spanish monarchy a decisive advantage in the Mediterranean. However, spring 1572 saw fair prospects for those who wished to bring France into war with Spain. On 1 April, the Sea Beggars captured Brille, on the 19th the Treaty of Blois was signed with Queen Elizabeth and on the 27th Charles IX wrote a highly encouraging letter to Louis of Nassau, later discovered by the Spaniards (see Document 8). On 24 May, the Protestant nobleman Genlis captured Mons in a semi-private enterprise but wrote immediately to Charles IX for backing. From this point, the situation became much more ominous. On 16 July, the relief column sent out from France was defeated by Alva and the Spanish position immensely strengthened. Arguing for war thus became more disruptive. Coligny could not guarantee to control the Protestants in France who wanted to go to the aid of Orange in the Netherlands and by the first days of August was already well into plans for putting together an expedition. He told the King on 6 August that, should Orange be defeated, he would enter France and bring in the duke of Alva after him. His view may have been that, in these circumstances, a renewal of civil war would be inevitable and that he considered the pacification within France was dangerously fragile. If Coligny, therefore, becomes a much more unpredictable figure for the court, it is equally possible that the true meaning of all this is that Charles IX was sensibly using Coligny in the age-old scheme of covertly undermining an enemy (Spain) while unwilling to declare open war. By early August, it is clear that the King had drawn back from foreign war (see Document 12). However, it remained the case that Catherine's policy was anchored in pacification and, on the evidence until August 1572, she had no reason to wish to kill Coligny. He was essential in making the policy that surrounded the marriage of her daughter Marguerite to Henry of Navarre work.

The years 1570–2 were also ones of adverse economic circumstances and growing political and administrative strain. One way in which this was expressed was in the increasingly acrimonious relations between the King and the Parlement both over the policy of toleration and over taxation and fiscal expedients. In October 1570, the Parlement collided with the King over the restoration of the benefices of the Protestant cardinal of Châtillon and in March 1571 the King gave a stinging admonition to the court, telling it in effect to keep its place, in a manner that echoed his speech of 1563 (see Document 5). Above all, though, it was taxes that hurt. Compared with the reign of Henry II, the 1560s were a decade of falling taxes, but the rate started to rise again in 1568 from 6 to 7.5 million *lt.* of taille and reached 9 million for 1571. The total revenues in 1572 were 14–15 million, but the accumulated debt was four times this. 2 million went on the payment of interest on *rentes* raised on the credit of the Paris municipality and another 2 million on short-term loan interest and repayments to the ever-unpopular Italian financiers. These were taxes and payments which were thought by Catholics to be going into the pockets of Huguenot lords who had gained control of royal policy, and to pay off the German reiters and Swiss brought in by Coligny and the crown in the late 1560s (to whom 7 million were owed). Such were the views of opinion in Paris conveyed in the journal of the curé Jean de la Fosse (see Document 6). The criticism of royal luxury in the midst of this calamity anticipated the more venomous attacks on Henry III in the 1580s. It is clear, though, that the more the royal coffers were empty, the more essential it was to put on a show in order to keep the crown's 'credit' intact.

Besides the taille, all sorts of other subsidies were being demanded and new offices being created in the sovereign courts; these devices were the inevitable consequence of the royal debt. Most to the point as far as Paris is concerned, is that the city collided with the crown over the levy of 1571 on the walled towns, destined to pay off military debts. In March the sum of 300,000 *lt.* was agreed and all were to pay, but in June salt was rubbed in the wounds by the King's exemption of nobles and financiers in his suite from assessment. Royal fiscal demands were thus highly controversial. The 'advis' that may have been drawn up on 22 August 1572 by Tavannes for the retrenchment of expenditure, especially on the army and the royal guards, is perfectly comprehensible in this context and may have some bearing in the relations between the King and his military household at the time of the Massacre (see Document 13).

We must also bear in mind the profound hatred felt throughout Paris, among the bourgeois and the people, for Coligny and his followers, who had briefly besieged the capital in 1567 and defeated its troops. The Edict of Saint-Germain was widely hated as a concession to him, and the Catholic fanaticism, already being built up on the basis of confraternities, preaching and secret leagues, grew stronger. In November–December 1571, the upheaval over the removal of the croix de Gastines (erected in the Summer of 1569) to another location, under clause 32 of the peace of Saint-Germain, showed the depth of antagonism. The whole city coalesced in opposition and only obeyed under the military compulsion of François de Montmorency's troops. There were, then, many reasons for royal policy to be unpopular during the apparent collaboration of Charles IX and Coligny which linked politics and religion.

## The Massacre

In the Massacre of Saint Bartholomew, we are dealing with one of the most imponderable problems of the sixteenth century. Not only is the authorship of the event still in doubt; its significance is still argued over. It is essential to distinguish between two intertwined sequences of events. The first was the assassination attempt on Coligny in the morning of Friday 22 August, followed by decisions taken at the highest levels to eliminate the Admiral's relatives and supporters on the evening of the 23rd; this began in the early hours of Sunday 24th, when the Admiral's house was stormed by Guise retainers and members of the royal guard. The second was the mass outbreak of slaughter to which the city of Paris has been occasionally prone, from the killings of the Armagnacs in 1413 and 1418 to the September Massacres of 1792 and the 1871 Commune. Unfortunately, the connections between all these events remain impossible to fix with certainty. The fundamental unreliability of the most quoted printed contemporary sources has been strongly argued by Sutherland. Protestant and Catholic accounts that blamed conspiratorial councils involving Catherine, Anjou, Retz, the Guises, or combinations of them are largely propaganda, written with a view to incriminating one or all of them. Goulart's *Mémoires de Estat de France sous Charles IX* is a Protestant account that contains some important documents but is totally partial and misleading in that it creates the impression that Coligny was dominant at court in 1571–2 and that his killing was a reaction to this. Hotman's *De Furoribus Gallicis*, widely translated in Protestant countries, was influential in its picturesque details and, above all, in pointing the finger at Catherine. Two Catholic tracts, ostensibly emanating from the circles of Henry of Anjou, are contradictory. The *Vera et brevis descriptio* (Cracow, 1573) seeks to disculpate Henry and argues that there really was a Protestant plot; the *Discours du Roy Henri III*, in any case unknown before it was published with Villeroy's *Mémoires* in 1623, firmly blames Catherine and Anjou. It is almost certainly an attempt to clear the duke of Retz, the most widely canvassed author of the anti-Coligny action at the time. All these are of value for telling us what was being thought about the Massacre at the time but not really for explaining motivation. Sutherland goes on to dismiss the accounts of foreign ambassadors because they were not in an inside position; only the Papal and Florentine envoys, she says, had much to report which might be of use to the historian; the Florentine Cavriana's was the most intelligent analysis but recounts the story of the fabricated 'plot' that the Huguenots were supposed to have mounted (see Document 18). This 'plot' was no more than a figleaf to cover the crime. As far as the Papal nuncio is concerned, to dismiss his account is to neglect one of the best informed contemporary sources and he certainly does point the finger at Catherine (see Document 22–3). The Venetian envoys hinted as early as 25 August that the plan had been long premeditated (see Document 24) and, in their famous Relazione for the period, confirmed this view.

Most modern analysis would dismiss the notion, advanced by the Protestants at the time, that the crown had been heinously plotting the Massacre for years, though Sutherland emphasises the long-smouldering feuding and enmity between the Guises and Coligny. It is possible that, whoever plotted the initial murder attempt (the Guises are most likely, given the house used by the assassin, but Alva and the duke of Savoy have also been suggested) Catherine and the courtiers were panicked into taking measures by fear of a Protestant revenge attack. Sutherland argues this, though as Elizabeth I fairly pointed out, Coligny could hardly have masterminded such a thing 'being in his bed lamed . . . being also guarded about his private house' by the royal guard (Digges, p. 248). In any case, Paris in 1572 was massively a Catholic stronghold in which the Huguenots were the isolated and beleaguered party. Bourgeon, in a series of studies that paid great tribute to Sutherland's analysis of the sources, nevertheless failed to carry through her conclusion: that the court was panicked into the Massacre. He is sceptical that such a threat was the real cause of the panic. For him, it was Catherine and Anjou's realisation that they were isolated in the middle of a full-scale Catholic insurrection in face of the threat posed to the Guises, that more or less reduced them to impotence on the 23rd (see Documents 21 and 25). In effect, then, the court was coerced into agreeing with what it could do nothing to prevent. The most recently published source, that of the Italian Sassetti, who may have been drawing on information from the ambassador Walsingham, and wrote his account by 13 September, is clear as to the central role of Catherine in the planning and accepts the idea that her resentment at Coligny's influence and her long-standing desire for revenge were central to the initial killings, though not to the general Massacre (see Document 19).

As for the Massacre's meaning, modern historians have taken a predictably wide range of views. Where Janine Garrisson argued that the event was a 'popular crime' – or 'the sword being given to the common people' in Francis Walsingham's graphic phrase (Digges, p. 239) – and the result of a movement of mass frenzy with socio-economic overtones, Natalie Davis tended to see ritualistic violence. Barbara Diefendorf has pointed out that the key to the connection between the initial killings and the 'popular' massacre is to be found in the words of Guise after Coligny's murder: 'it is the King's command'. This could have spread rapidly as authorisation for more general killing and allowed things to get out of hand. More recently Bourgeon has argued, fortified by an intriguing re-reading of the History by the Parlementaire J.-A. de Thou, that what was happening was in effect a coup mounted by the Catholic leadership; at first Charles IX denied responsibility but, faced with the shame of having to admit he was powerless, he took the full blame, though not until the 25th, by the force of a great 'lie of state' (see Document 28). This is an effective explanation for the sequence of royal documents issued through the period, which show a bewildering set of contradictions (see Documents 15 and 26). The crown's ultimate story was that it was faced with a Protestant coup on the Saturday night. The story for ambassadors abroad emphasised this, for Fénelon was to tell Elizabeth I that Charles IX faced 'imminent danger of a new civil war and, being overcome with this extremity, and having no time long to deliberate hereupon, scant the space of an hour' (Digges, pp. 246–7). The problem with this is the transition from the argument of reluctant self-defence to the positive relish subsequently taken in the extermination of the Huguenot 'vermin'.

Bourgeon's analysis of the sinister inactivity of the Parlement is suggestive. What he does not do though, as Crouzet has pointed out, is explain why, if the crown had been faced by a Guise coup, which it managed to head off, it took the monarchy until 1588 to rid itself of the threat or why, indeed, no attempt was ever made to reverse the lie. The implication, therefore, is that the royal family and the Guises were complicit in at least parts of the Massacre, a view stressed in his review of the debate by Marc Venard. By emphasising the accounts of the Papal nuncio and Thomas Sassetti, he concludes that Catherine and Anjou cannot escape responsibility. The volte-face in her policy is explained by a certain desire to revenge the indignity and treason of the Protestants' failed coup-de-main against the court in 1567. It is in any case clear that the initial Massacre of the Protestant leaders was carried out by royal guards acting with Guise, though whether this was because the royal family had lost control of its guards is not clear. Crouzet accepts that Guise is most likely as the culprit in the attempt on Coligny's life. But his explanation is at the least controversial: that Guise actions (from Vassy onwards) were meant as violent intervention in order to 'create a situation of political rupture' dragging the crown towards the policy of eradicating heresy. All this, for Crouzet, takes place in the context of a situation in which the sacral King and the city were rivals 'in the accomplishment of God's law'. Crouzet pays great attention to what he calls Charles IX's policy of restoring the kingdom to a 'golden age' in the years 1570–2, but his argument that the initial killings were a last-ditch attempt to rescue this vision from imminent disruption seems forced. It should also be remembered that by 1572 twelve years had passed since the monarchy effectively lost the ability to control Paris.

One result of the royal avowal of guilt was that the crown was able to gain the credit for it in the eyes of the Catholic populace of Paris and also, to some extent, to neutralise the Guises. The duke had in any case left the city soon after the Massacre in quest of further personal enemies, leaving in some senses a power vacuum. Assumption of responsibility also enabled the King to prevent the Montmorencys from immediately joining the Protestant camp, as they would have done had the Guises alone been held responsible.

On 28 August, the Edict of 1570 was suspended (see Document 29), and on 22 September, all Protestant office-holders were forbidden to exercise their offices, except minor functionaries who were allowed to continue if they abjured. On 30 August, Protestant nobles were required to cease holding services on the argument that the King's desire was to bring back his subjects 'to a true and perfect union' (BL, Egerton 6, Instructions to the duke of Guise). There followed a contradictory series of orders from the crown, some of which sought to rein in the massacres, while others seemed to encourage them (see Document 31–2). Usually, the evidence for the latter is contained in oblique and rather suspicious accounts.

## The Aftermath of the Massacre

Not all Catholics approved of the Massacre. From abroad, the envoy at Constantinople bemoaned the fact that it had transformed Philip II's prospects (Noailles, vol. I, p. 31), while the envoy in Venice firmly relayed the dismay there and the talk that Catherine had 'preferred to ruin the kingdom in revenging yourself on the Admiral' (La Ferrière, *Les Valois*, p. 328).

Two themes are intertwined in this period: the military operations launched by the crown against the Protestants as a result of the Massacre, and the formation of a loose combination of both Protestants and Catholic Malcontents among the high aristocracy. The duke of Alençon, Navarre and Condé were kept under close supervision at court and their attempts at regaining their independence of action were caught up in the obscure plots that came to a head at the end of February 1574, known as the 'Mardi Gras uprising'. The arrests following this plot in effect detonated a new civil war. There is no doubt that the Massacre was seen as a terrible blow by Protestants and as a test of faith which many failed (see Document 31).

The slightly farcical 'fourth civil war' was in effect an attempt on the part of the crown to force the city of La Rochelle to submit. In September 1572 it refused to accept a new royal governor, Biron, so on 6 November the King ordered a siege. Comanded by Anjou and Biron, this did not begin until

February 1573. The losses on both sides were great and the costs to the crown enormous. On 11 June, the one serious assault was beaten off. The royal army began to fall apart and the siege had to be called off. There were also signs that Languedoc, where Protestants were organising militarily as early as September 1572, was slipping out of control. The peace was signed at La Rochelle on 2 July, registered as the Edict of Bois de Boulogne. This was a travesty of toleration, in that, although it permitted freedom of conscience, only the people of La Rochelle, Nîmes and Montauban were allowed even private worship. It was a botched document, rushed through so that the negotiations for the election of Anjou as King of Poland could be concluded.

By 1573, even Blaise de Monluc, one of the staunchest defenders of the Catholic cause and always a loyal servant of the crown, was prepared to advise the King to conclude a real religious peace in order to restore French strength abroad (Monluc, vol. V, pp. 312–14). Monluc had greeted the Edict of 1570 with dismay (see Document 1) but had now seen the consequences of 1572. The Edict of July 1573 could hardly be seen as the sort of peace he recommended.

---

# THE UNEASY PEACE, 1570–72

## Charles IX and his policy

### 1   Monluc's reaction to the peace, 1570

Shortly after, the peace, which was very advantageous to our enemies, was published; we had beaten them time and time again but, despite this, they had such credit in the King's council that the edicts were always to their advantage. We won the battles but they won by those devilish writings. Ha, poor prince, so ill served, so ill-counselled! If you do not take care, your kingdom, once so flourishing, will be more miserable than ever.

SOURCE: *Monluc*, vol. III, pp. 456–7.

---

### 2   Politics in the aftermath of the peace (i)

The peace so much desired was declared and enrolled in the Parlement here in Paris the xjth of this present in the presence of the whole court, the which I send herewith to Your Highness in printing. The articles being long, it is much to be doubted by the intricateness of them how they will be observed and, besides these, are certain private articles not put in the edict, signed by the King's hand, which are sent by the deputies to the cardinal of Châtillon. . . .

   . . . Here is great talk of some enterprises to be taken in hand when all is finished and concluded, and whispered to be into Scotland. But when I consider that the chiefest about the King at these present are of the Religion and your cruel enemy the cardinal of Lorraine not admitted to the Council, nor as now any estimation had of him, the King also deeply endebted with the marvelous sums to the strangers, I judge they will rather choose to rid them first from these debts and till then live in quiet.

SOURCE: Norris to Elizabeth I, 11 August 1570, SP70/113 no. 807.

---

## 3  Politics in the aftermath of the peace (ii)

I beseech Your Majesty to weigh in what terms the peace is made, upon what occasions and to consider the two former pacifications with the present peace. And when all these circumstances are digested and one likelihood compared with the other, the very same causes yet remaining, we may presume of the like effects. For, although this peace doth procure and entertain a certain community and civil policy amongst the meaner sort, drawn partly hereunto by weariness of the wars and partly by the commodities, yet doth not the same bring any firm reconciliation betwixt the nobility, so that these being but an accident, the original cause and spring of the war still continueth. But hereunto it may be objected that time will qualify many things and that those matters which in the beginning seem hard and difficile will be by wisdom and policy modified and made easy. Whereupon I judge that this peace, being made on both sides of necessity, it cannot be but suspect, shall still nourish hatred, procuring new attempts against the chiefs of the Religion, which cannot be well eschewed except the general cause be continued and maintained by the princes of the same Religion. For otherwise, if their enemies perceive that they be abandoned of their own faction, then there is no doubt but they will seek their ruin. Some others do otherwise judge hereof, being of opinion that the King will proceed in another manner. For, by courteously entreating the gentlemen and captains of the Religion, it is not impossible to win them from bearing arms; and so, the chief conductors, being left of their companies, to fall by this means into eminent danger. . . . Divers in this Court are not otherwise to be persuaded but that cure of this commonwealth must proceed by the same means that the inconvenience grow, meaning hereby that as this civil dissension hath chiefly come from want of a foreign enemy, so in assailing some one of their neighbours to make in a case of common danger a friendly reconciliation amongst themselves. This device tendeth to Monsieur d'Anjou's advancement, divers thinking it necessary to make this enterprise upon England by the way of Scotland. [*The Queen should be on her guard, though the King of France is in debt to 37 million lt. and cannot make a sudden move*] for the cardinal of Lorraine, long since attempting to trouble your state and presently to infringe this edict, being now in disgrace and Montmorency bearing the vogue in Court, there is no doubt of good success if time and occasion be observed, in advancing the professors of the

Religion, whereby should grow a general benefit to as many as depend upon the same.

SOURCE: Norris to Elizabeth I, 31 August 1570, SP70/113 no. 831.

## 4 Politics in the aftermath of the peace (iii)

The state here (thanks be given to God) is very quiet, where all strife and old grudge seemeth utterly buried; and men live in good hope of the continuance thereof, since the occasion of all troubles in this realm [*the Cardinal of Lorraine*], yet out of credit, neither haunteth the court and council as he was wonted. Yet what underhand that he may do to cause new troubles here or elsewhere no men that knoweth him doubteth of his readiness in that behalf.

SOURCE: Norris to Cecil, 23 September 1570, SP70/114 no. 869.

## 5 Charles IX's speech to the Parlement, 12 March 1571

Wherever I look in my kingdom, I see things misdirected, out of order and confused, especially in the administration of justice, which is so ill-regulated that the old hallmarks of devotion that ought to be in it are scarcely seen.

I do not intend, by saying that, to prejudice the honour of worthy men but to declare, with regret, a truth that none can ignore.

For this reason, in so far as justice mainly depends on the prosperity of a state and the peace of its subjects, I have decided to proceed to a reformation of abuses. In this I wish that you, as the superiors of all the other judges, should do your duty first and that, having the honour to represent me in this place, premier and most ancient seat of my sovereign justice, you start by yourselves correcting the abuses which in the course of time may have crept in here. . . .

I admonish you, then, to enquire carefully whether any among you are stained with some intolerable vice and to correct it without dissimulation so that the scandal does not rebound on all. Get rid of factions and partialities, permit no intrigues or practices, vices too repugnant to justice but from which, by common opinion, this company is not exempt.

I say this unwillingly but so that you deal with it and so your good conduct in future should wipe out the blame in common opinion.

Furthermore, I command you to keep strictly my edicts and ordinances and remember that I have put you in this place to obey my laws, not to command or hold them in contempt.

If, in the verification of edicts or other letters I send you, you find problems over which you decide to make remonstrances, do it without delay. I shall always hear them willingly but I also wish that, once I have declared my intention, you obey without entering into dispute with me, your sovereign King and master who knows better than you what must be done for the good and necessity of my State, whose affairs I will not suffer that you have cognisance of and I reserve to myself alone.

So take care to remain modestly within the limits of your posts, which are established solely for the administration of justice, the correction of crimes, and to make sure my edicts and ordinances are observed.

If you obey my commands, I shall have reason to praise you and gratify you with honours and payments to suit your merits. Those who scorn them must not find it strange if I am indignant with them. . . .

SOURCE: *La harangue que feit le roy à messieurs de la Court de Parlement* (1571), fos. 3v–5v.

## 6   The supposed influence of Coligny at Court

[*September 1571*] During this month, Gaspard de Coligny, restored to the position of Admiral by the Edict of Pacification, was summoned by the King from La Rochelle to meet him at Blois. All the house of Guise withdrew from the court, so that the King was governed by the Admiral and Montmorency. . . .

[*November 1571*] At this time the kingdom of France was governed thus by the Queen Mother, the Admiral de Coligny, Montmorency and others, the house of Guise being put out. Everyone was amazed at the string of edicts which were quite to the disadvantage of the Catholics; even foreigners were astonished, so that the Spanish ambassador, seeing everything in France go ill, returned to his king without taking leave of the King of France. . . . There was much talk of witches and warlocks and it was said there were more than 30,000 at work, that the men were marked behind the ears and the women on the thighs. Many were arrested and [*it was said that*] even the king of the witches had been taken and sent to the royal court, where he performed his sorcery in the presence of the said lord.

SOURCE: La Fosse, pp. 132–3.

## 7   The Florentine ambassador on Coligny's influence

The Admiral arrived at court on the 12th with fifty gentlemen and was not greeted because he did not wish it. He quickly entered the castle accompanied by Marshal de Cossé, who had brought him. Advised that the King was with the Queen Mother because she was unwell, he went to His Majesty's chamber, where he entered alone with the marshal and, after the initial compliments, was received with reasonable cheer but not too much state. He then went to Monsieur, whom he found in bed with a fever, and was received by him fairly graciously, perhaps not to make tongues wag. Thus for three or four days the Admiral showed little satisfaction and was kept in suspense, during which time he was, it is said, greatly annoyed at some light words of the duke of Montpensier and might have left the court much earlier than he had planned without putting anything forward. But the

King, who spoke to Montpensier and prayed him not to give occasion for offence, for the kings his predecessors had made use of the Admiral's services and he too had a mind to do so, . . . placated him. Thus, in a discussion between them a short while ago, when matters past were raised, Montpensier cut him short and said: 'Let us speak no more about that, for the Edict has decided everything. Rest assured that as long as you are the King's good servant, I will do you all service.' . . . It is thought Montpensier's action was instigated by others, for he is naturally good-natured. Thus the Admiral and he are now good friends.

Some days ago, after the Admiral's show of humility towards His Majesty, his brothers and the other chief lords of the court, the King made him good cheer and the Queen Mother and Monsieur spoke freely to him. . . . Then, in a garden, his opinion was asked for on the government of the kingdom, on matters of state, of foreign powers and the administration of finance; it is now seen that many matters are submitted to him and he is often present in all the Councils. The Admiral sought to have the Edict observed, and, where all could not be accorded, he sought to have matters agreed as far as possible to the satisfaction of both sides. There was great instance to have preaching restored at Lyon but in the end this could not be obtained, though a place three leagues away has been assigned to those of the Religion. When the Admiral had dealt with matters of the Edict, he proposed certain matters of finance . . . he proposed a means to repay the King's debts in three years without touching the goods of the church or too much burdening the people. It is thought that he proposed a reform for their religion so as to unite it with our Catholic faith. . . . It is thought all these things might lead to an agreement with Germany and draw those princes into some design he has, which could in the end be an enterprise against Flanders.

SOURCE: Petrucci, 19–20 September 1571, Desjardins, vol. III, pp. 704–6.

## 8 Foreign policy

Sir, the sieur de Teligny, the bearer of this letter, has several times informed me and in great detail of the great opportunity there is at present for some good enterprise for the liberty of the Low Countries, at present oppressed by the Spaniards. We were simply asked to give them the means to tear themselves out of this oppression and we were told of the many means we could use. This is truly a matter of compassion and something in which every noble and Christian prince should employ the forces and resources that God has given him, and, as far as I am concerned, I am determined to do so as far as the disposition of my affairs permits.

SOURCE: Charles IX to Louis of Nassau, 27 April 1572, AGS Estado, leg. 551.

## Debates in the Council, June–July 1572

### 9   Coligny's memorandum on war

Sire, though the conflicting humours of the French and the long relapses of this old
malady caused by differences over religion could but indicate the likely ruin of your
state or at least the partial loss of its territory and strength, nevertheless God, the
only physician who in this desperate illness can provide a remedy, does Your
Majesty the grace to see it cured, refreshed and on its feet again. It remains to
preserve it from a relapse and maintain it in health by all means possible. For this,
there is nothing more suitable than timely exercise. . . . This is to undertake a
foreign war in order to maintain peace at home. . . .

This war must be just, easy and useful with the profit no less honourable than
the honour profitable. Such, to put it briefly, can at present only be against the
King of Spain. You can justly do so because of the injuries you received from him
in your youth, which show how little he is a friend to you. . . . [*There follows a
justification for the war.*] Need we now dispute whether it should be undertaken?
Let us think rather of how to do it. You have already begun, Sire, and whatever
outward show he makes, he would thank you no less than if you had armies in the
field against him and were commanding in person. When he sees that Your
Majesty has received and favoured count Louis of Nassau in your court as well as
other gentlemen he considers rebels; when he knows you are in touch with the sieur
de Genlis . . . what else can he think than that Your Majesty would wish to injure
him? . . . The war is not only just, it is necessary if we wish to avoid a more
dangerous one in future. . . . Next it must be shown that the war is easy for you,
both because your forces have grown since the peace with him and because his have
diminished. . . . [*The bulk of the paper concerns the general diplomatic situation,
favourable to France.*] Thus, since Your Majesty is stronger than him in terms of
soldiers and equal in revenues, there is no doubt that war with Spain will be easy to
prosecute. But where? [*The rest is an argument in favour of war in the Netherlands.*]

SOURCE: *Mornay*, vol. II, pp. 20–37.

### 10   Morvillier's opinion, 20 June 1572

[*Denies that intervention in the Low Countries is just.*] Besides the fact that he who
has right on his side is always full of hope, he pursues his claims more courageously
and surely, and risks his own position while his subjects serve and supply him as
much as they can. In short, in all events, justice is his comfort. . . . Now, leaving
this to one side, I turn to the questions of the ease or difficulty of this war, the
utility one could expect from it, the problems to be feared and means available to
prosecute it. [*Seeks to refute the argument that Flanders is ready to rebel and the King
of Spain must be pre-empted.*] It cannot be denied that the subjects of the

Netherlands feel oppressed by the harsh and rigorous treatment by the duke of Alva and the Spaniards, that they hate them and try by all the means they can to deliver themselves from this yoke. But there is great reason to doubt that they are disposed to submit themselves to the King's obedience and many reasons to think the contrary. . . . If Artois and Flanders were once subject to the crown of France, nevertheless they have always shown themselves far from willing to be obedient subjects and their character has not changed. [*The King of Spain's power is not to be forgotten and*] as for the trust that should be placed in the prince of Orange and his brothers, is it to be believed that they would rather die than live in the condition to which they have been reduced? Thus, we should not be surprised if they seek to disturb the world and they would rather turn somersaults than stay as they are. [*Thus, are they trustworthy and to be relied on? Moreover, what may result from helping the rebels? Would there not be an eternal war with Spain? We are told we have many allies, but is it wise to rely on the queen of England?*] She made the recent alliance with the King to bolster herself against the conspiracies and understandings the Queen of Scots and the duke of Alva have with her malcontent subjects. From this, it must be concluded that she has no thought for the aggrandisment of this crown but rather for her own profit and security. . . . As for the German princes, I would admit that they hate the Spaniards as being contrary to their natures and for other reasons . . . but, for all that, it should not be thought that they would make open declaration of war and that they would willingly contribute to the expense. . . . [*Nor would the Emperor join France against Spain.*] Now let us speak of the outcome or utility of the war. We call useful something that brings certain profit and no danger. Truly, it must be confessed that the conquest of the Low Countries would be the finest and most suitable that the King could accomplish. I do not say it is impossible but I cannot imagine it being done.

SOURCE: BN, fr. 3177, fos. 120–3; Baguenault, p. 268.

---

## 11   Opinion of Tavannes, 26 June 1572

[*Draws attention to the dangers that France would be in should war be declared openly and the rebels in the Netherlands be beaten by Alva,*] in which case the kingdom would totter and be wagered on the board against Flanders; especially since there are so many people in this kingdom of the old religion, mostly malcontent and likely to be made desperate since there is no money for the war and it would have to be raised from them. Thus the quarrel of a handful of rebels abroad would turn into making a greater number at home.

The Flanders rebels have paved the way for rebellion in France, saying that their cause was over taxes. On this the French people know what to blame: recent taxes raised to punish those who rose, supposedly for the cause of the Reformed Religion, and now new taxes to support it. This is dangerous for great princes, who deceive themselves if they think they can reign through force. For princes must reign as kings of their people and be obeyed and loved. Otherwise, the best they can hope for is to control religion and rebellion by force and with foreign troops, enriching them through the ruin of their kingdom and acquiring the name of tyrant in perpetual fear for their lives. Added to this, if His Majesty declares war, he will be attacked through Piedmont, Provence and Languedoc. . . . Even if the duke of Alva does lose the battle and most of the Netherlands, the reputation and power of the Huguenots will be so great, especially if the present well-intentioned leaders die or are replaced, that the King and the kingdom will always be controlled by them. It would be better to do without Flanders and other conquests than be for ever under the thumb, for that would be to lose everything by winning. . . .

I leave to one side the question of the broken word of the King, who professes honour, and, having been helped in his need, the ingratitude of his returning ill for good. . . . I also leave aside that it used to be that kings divided peoples the more easily to control them and now peoples, dividing kings, could, if they wished, do the same. All that is obvious. [*Goes on to refute the argument that, should Alva win, he would chase the rebels into France. The best way to deal with this is to reassure the King of Spain, put off intervention in Italy and maintain a guard.*]

It should be considered that henceforth the Netherlands can be of no profit to the King of Spain and that, to control them, he would have to ruin them completely and spend much money. Thus in the end one could set foot there by love and alliance, or by force when our weakness is over. In the end, it is better not to profit from this than to get it by means of those who have so many battle-hardened men within France. . . . Let us, then, leave off such an unjust and ill-founded enterprise that is so dangerous to us. Let us maintain our reputation with God and men and peace with everyone, above all with our own people, keeping our word over religion. Let us take breath and let our enemies exhaust themselves. That is what this crown and state needs above all.

SOURCE: *Tavannes*, pp. 121–3.

## 12    The King's instructions to Schomberg, 10 August 1572

The King and Queen have charged the sieur de Schomberg to tell the princes of Germany that there are two reasons which have cautioned the King against declaring openly for the prince of Orange. The first is the division of his subjects, who are not yet as united as he would wish. . . . The second is that the prince of Orange has neither before nor during his enterprise advised the King of his intentions and what he intends to do. . . . His Majesty has charged Schomberg to assure the princes that he is resolved to behave towards the prince of Orange and the Netherlands as they behave. If the princes concerned wish to declare themselves openly, His Majesty will do so; if they wish to furnish money and men underhand, he will do the same.

SOURCE: Instruction to Schomberg, 10 August 1572, Noailles, vol. III, pp. 286–7.

## 13 Tavannes's diagnosis of the ills of the realm

[*The Marshal, after repeating his warnings against war, goes on:*] To restore the King and his realm to their splendour, this habit of raising extraordinary subsidies and taxes, at which the people are already in despair, must be removed, thus allowing the King to escape the peril of his subjects' indignation. Besides the fact that this word 'subsidy' is the same as tyranny, this threatens (if it is levied) to allow any prince, lord or rebel, under the guise of the 'public weal', helped covertly by foreigners, to take arms and put the state in danger. Because this is difficult, without some extraordinary aid from his people, I would deal with this (unless there is a better way) through economies, which cannot be done to the pleasure of those who normally have large grants and pensions. But it is better to do a displeasure to a small number with equity than with iniquity discontent the greater number, the people, through these subsidies, thus putting the state in danger. . . . Thus, it would be necessary to abolish all pensions, both private and to foreigners, to princes, lords, ladies, gentlemen and all others for three years . . . except in Italy at Mirandola, where we must always keep a foothold, and to the Swiss, which cannot be touched; otherwise all those on this side of the Rhine except Sedan and maintain, nay augment, those beyond the Rhine. . . . All infantry should be paid off, except those in frontier towns. Howbeit, the gendarmerie, guards and gentlemen of the household and those on His Majesty's staff should be paid, though making some reductions. . . . May His Majesty acquit these posts and expenditure according to his revenues, which is to say spend and save of his own, without burden to his conscience, allowing the people to breathe freely now we are in peace, and to live of its own, considering the danger of rebellion and disturbance in the state.

SOURCE: *Tavannes*, pp. 456–8, originally dated 22 August 1572.

## THE MASSACRE OF SAINT BARTHOLOMEW: POLITICS AND MOTIVATION

### 14 The attempted assassination of Coligny: the city Council reacts

Friday, 22 August at about 11 in the morning, news was brought to the Provost of the Merchants and the échevins in the city office that the lord Admiral de Coligny had just been shot and wounded in the arm and two hands, returning from the Louvre and passing in front of Saint-Germain l'Auxerrois on the Louvre side. In consequence, to avoid any disturbance in the town, once the facts were ascertained, orders were issued to the quarteniers and guard.

SOURCE: *Registres, Paris*, vol. VII, p. 9, 22 August.

## 15   22 August: the official story

As my cousin, the sieur de Châtillon, Admiral of France, was presently leaving the Louvre to go and dine in his lodging, a shot was fired at him from the window of a house where lodges the sieur de Villemeur, preceptor of my cousin the duke of Guise, by which he was badly wounded in the right hand and the left arm. I am very grieved at this, having immediately taken measures to do everything possible to apprehend (as I hope he will be) the perpetrator of this act and know who is behind it, so as to see that justice is rapidly done as an example to my whole kingdom. I have also written to all the governors of the provinces and the main towns of how I deplore this wicked and unfortunate act and of my resolve to carry out exemplary justice, expressly forbidding any rising on account of this or any other motive but on the contrary that everyone keep and observe my Edict of Pacification inviolably. . . . I would not omit to tell you that this wicked act stems from the enmity between his house and those of Guise. I shall give order that they do not drag my subjects into their quarrels, for I wish that my Edict of Pacification should be observed in all points.

SOURCE: Charles IX to Fénelon, 22 August 72, *Fénelon*, vol. VII, pp. 322–3.

## 16   De Thou on events of 23 August, morning

At the same time there was arrested a certain person suspected of the murder, who admitted he was one of the duke of Guise's household servants. As soon as this was known, the dukes of Guise and Aumale and others of that house came to the King to allay all suspicion. They complained of being oppressed by the favour shown to their enemies; that the judges were listening to their enemies' calumnies; that, though they were innocent, they were openly attacked; that for a long time they had thought, without knowing why, that they were more and more unwelcome to the King; that they had, however, dissimulated this and that they hoped that time, which would show the truth, would one day make him understand. But, since they were unable to defend their innocence, they asked, against their wishes and under constraint, that they be allowed to leave in his good grace. This was said publicly and it was noticed that the King made them a cold reply. . . .

SOURCE: De Thou, 1659, vol. III, p. 657.

## 17   General uncertainty and speculation on 23rd

This business of the Admiral was planned long before. Some believe it was done on
the orders of M. de Guise; others that it emanated from the court, though without
the King's knowledge; others, and this seems likely, that neither M. d'Aumale nor
M. de Guise knew anything but that its author was the cardinal of Lorraine, in
conjunction with the duke of Savoy, and this with the count of Retz with help
from the Spanish ambassador. . . . The count of Retz is very close to the duke of
Savoy and Madame de Dampierre his mother-in-law works here for the court of
Savoy, so that messengers are frequently sent about plans against the Huguenots; it
seems that, since the Admiral married his new wife, he has been strongly disliked
by the duke of Savoy. Giuliano del Bene gives credit to this opinion, saying openly
that what happened is done and of no consequence because vengeance cannot be
got for it. . . . When it was put to him that both God and the prince of Orange
might well make some move, he replied: 'God loves Catholics.'

SOURCE: Commander Petrucci to Francesco de Medici, 23 August 1572, Desjardins, vol. III, pp. 807–8.

---

## 18   Cavriana on the supposed Huguenot 'plot'

The King, informed of everything, went to visit the Admiral after dinner, with the
Queen Mother, his brothers, sisters, relatives and friends, in short all the court,
both men and women, except Guise and his wife and Mme de Nevers with Mme
de Nemours, who alone stayed in their quarters. To honour him the more, the
King ordered his doctors and surgeons to care for him constantly, because he had
wanted none who were Catholics. They talked to him for a while and consoled him
and prayed him to come to the castle so that the King might more easily visit him;
but he, with gentle excuses, refused their offer. . . . [*The King ordered that the
Huguenot chiefs be lodged around him for his defence.*] The last words that the
Admiral spoke to the King were to demand justice for the attempted assassination
(so he put it) and to beg him strongly to believe that what he would say to him
finally did not stem from any ill will he bore to King Philip but from the King's
service and the needs of the times. And this was, that it was essential to start war
against Philip; otherwise it would not be long before he had civil war in this
kingdom more ferocious than ever, because he would no longer be able to restrain
the nobility in the business, so determined were they to fight.

Lodged as they were, as the King had commanded (though they were suspicious
of this proceeding, because of its novelty), they began to discuss the form of their
revenge. They were already talking so openly about it that Teligny several times
asked a very close friend of ours to tell the Queen that, while he had worked for
and desired the peace more than any other, he would now do all he could to break
it if justice were not done for this attempt, and swaggerlingly threatened death and

extermination to their enemies at court. He informed their churches to hold themselves ready; on the following Tuesday, which would have been the 26th, a certain number of cavalry should have arrived in Paris, which would have made 4,000 with those already there. They were intended to seize the Louvre and spill the blood . . . of all those who had counselled or been implicated in the attempted murder. The bravo Piles would seize the gate, Moneins kill Guise, Briquemault Nevers and his wife and sons; and, with these tasks allocated, would commit a Sicilian Vespers. It is likely that they would not have spared the royal blood, fearing Monsieur and the Queen greatly. The enterprise would have succeeded more easily because in the castle a good 80 valiant gentlemen were sleeping in various rooms on pretext of serving the King of Navarre, the prince of Condé and other lords, who could have striven to overcome the guards by surprise, and surely killed most of those destined to be slaughtered.

Now as things happened, either the plot was revealed to the King, as some say by Bouchavannes, governor of the prince of Condé, or their threats to kill Guise in the very arms of the King were such that, in fear of them, it seemed necessary to forestall them and serve them that death they had prepared for others. It was decided, on Saturday night, that on Sunday they would be cut down and their memory obliterated.

SOURCE: Cavriana's account, 27 August, Desjardins, vol. III, pp. 813–15; passage continued in Erlanger, *Saint Bartholomew's Night*, pp. 244–8.

## 19   Tomasso Sassetti's account (information from Walsingham?)

So thus, the Admiral, believing in his King, reassured by many and perhaps guided by his fatal destiny, returned to court. . . . Being therefore at court, where affairs were managed with feigned honesty on both sides, he daily had the ear of the King and the Queen Mother. He was given a lucrative appointment for the sieur de Teligny, his son-in-law, for Briquemault and La Noue and many others, with a gift of more than 100,000 *livres* and 40,000 to his wife, reputedly as compensation for damages to his estate at Châtillon. And thus he was often in the King's cabinet and, perhaps flattered by the supreme favours done him by the King, could not, as a great man of wisdom and affairs, remain inactive, either because he knew better than any the warlike nature of this people, or through long experience of war, which made it impatient of a prolonged peace. . . .

[*After a lengthy analysis of the Admiral's policy towards the Netherlands war, he goes on:*] From these aforementioned things, then, I believe the argument can be sustained that his death, and those of his followers, was premeditated and more than once discussed, especially in the bloodstained thoughts of His Majesty and his mother, who knew best how dangerous it was to have in their realm a subject of so elevated a spirit, prepared to carry out to the end every enterprise, however great and malevolent it might be and, as the Papists would say, of malign spirit. . . .

[*After the first attempt on the Admiral.*] The King, hearing this news while he was playing tennis, seemed to be very shaken and to be very angry with the arquebusier and his accomplices. And because the common talk was that Guise had had the shot fired out of his old enmity, His Majesty, turning round to him, because he was there present, asked him if what was being said was true. He denied knowing anything, nor did he leave the royal palace for worthy reasons and so as not to give cause, by the sight of him, to the followers of the wounded to rise up. [*There follows a description of the Huguenot demands for justice and threats of taking it into their own hands.*] . . .

The King, the Queen Mother, M. d'Anjou, the duke of Nevers and others, some of them accomplices in what had been done, and even more so in what was to follow, putting on a show, went to visit the Admiral to condole with him. . . .

[*On the morning of the 23rd, La Rochefoucauld, Piles and others went to the Louvre and told the Queen of Navarre that, if they were not to have justice, they would seek their own vengeance.*] The King, having heard these brags, called his inner council, including, other than His Majesty, the Queen Mother, Monsieur d'Anjou, Chancellor Birague, Guise, Nevers, Tavannes, Retz and a few others. They decided, having got wind how the friends of the Admiral had given the order to assemble and take him out of his house at 1 o'clock on the following Wednesday with 400 horse they had in the faubourg Saint-Germain, not to allow him to depart. And it was therefore given out that they wanted to kill Their Majesties. It is thought (by dispassionate men) that this was hit upon as a pretext for the affair. Then the Queen Mother, Monsieur d'Angoulême (the King's bastard brother) and Guise got together and decided that since the plot against the King's person and his government had been revealed by one of the accomplices, it would be best to finish the business and not lose the opportunity to avoid another civil war by slaughtering the Admiral and his followers. So the Queen Mother spoke to the King, describing the matter, how small was the risk and how great the advantage from it; first, because God and the holy Roman Catholic Church would be served by it and there would be great benefit to his kingdom, its churches and his authority, adding other clear reasons that were not to be scorned by anyone who wished to rule his people according to his will.

Now, though the King wanted to punish him by vengeance, the time did not seem opportune and the faithlessness of so many princes gave him pause and doubt and he did not know what to do. Therefore, Monsieur de Guise, Nevers, Aumale and the bastard of Angoulême, Tavannes and others sent to speak to him and reassured him, and then governed the King's mind with demonstrations which they made to him and with the weight of M. d'Anjou, which it is to be presumed was the thing that tipped the balance. . . .

Thus, they ordered the city councillors and the Provost of the Merchants and their other allies that they should quietly and adroitly assemble the officers of the guard, ready to carry out what might be ordered by His Majesty; that they should take great care with the gates so that those who came in should deposit their arms, and that none be allowed to leave without passport. These citizens obeyed only with some opposition, because they feared that this might bring some ruin on the Catholics, or some other harm, as punishment for the shot fired at the Admiral. In the end, they obeyed as faithful subjects and good Roman Catholics, occupied the gates of the city, placed good guards at the ends of the streets, forbad boats to cross the river and mounted heavy guard on the bridges. In short, they put all matters in such order as they could in the brief time available.

SOURCE: Sassetti, pp. 119–20, 128, 130–1, 133–5.

## 20    The account in the city registers for 23–4 August

Today, Saturday 23 August, lord president Le Carron, Provost of the Merchants, was summoned by the King to his castle of the Louvre very late at night. His Majesty told him in the presence of the Queen Mother and my lord the duke of Anjou his brother and other princes and lords, that he had been warned that they of the New Religion intended to mount a conspiracy against His Majesty and his state and disturb the peace of his subjects and this city of Paris. He added that this evening certain grandees of the New Religion and rebels had conspired together against his state and proffered certain hauty and threatening words to His Majesty. He told the Provost that he wished to give order for the security of the Queen his mother, my lords his brothers and the peace and tranquillity of his kingdom, the city and his subjects. To forestall these plots and their wicked plans, he enjoined the Provost to lay hands on the keys of all the gates and have them carefully guarded so none might go in or out, to draw up all the boats in the river and fix them with their chains, to forbid any to pass, and to arm all the captains and officers and bourgeois of the quarters and districts of the town capable of bearing arms to receive and carry out the orders of His Majesty as will be needed. [*These orders were diligently carried out*] from Saturday night and the following night, following His Majesty's commands [*and orders transmitted to the guard early the following morning*].

SOURCE: *Registres, Paris*, vol. VII, 23–4 August, pp. 10–11.

## 21    The powerlessness of the court, recalled by de Thou

The duke of Guise, after nightfall, summoned some Catholic captains of the Swiss guard, from the five small cantons, and some colonels of the French guard and told them . . . that the hour was come that . . . a head odious to God and men should be smashed, thus getting revenge on the whole faction of rebels; that the beast was caught in the net and that care must be taken not to let it escape; that they should not let slip such a great occasion to carry off such a glorious triumph over the enemies of the kingdom. . .; that the victory was an easy one and the booty great and assured so payment for such a great success could be got without danger. Then the Swiss were stationed around the Louvre and the French guard were brought, with the order not to allow the King of Navarre and the prince of Condé to leave. Guard of Coligny's lodging was given to Cosseins, with a troop of musketeers to occupy the surrounding houses so no one could escape. With all this done, the duke of Guise summoned Jean Le Carron, president of the Court of Aids, who, after first refusing, had been made Provost of the Merchants in place of Claude Marcel, with orders to make sure the Échevins summoned the guard, and to be at the Town Hall at midnight to hear what was to be done. He gave the same order to Marcel . . . [*who*] told the people, who were already in commotion themselves, that the duke of Guise's will was that they take up arms to exterminate Coligny and all the other rebels and that none be spared . . . that the signal would be that the Palace bell would be rung several times. . . .

SOURCE: De Thou, 1659, vol. III, pp. 658–9.

## 22   Salviati's account for Rome, 24 August

If the shot had killed the Admiral straight away, I am not prepared to believe that things would have happened in the same way, the Admiral being a man of heart and marvellous courage; although many might take issue with this, they perhaps are not aware that it was beneficial in making the King more clearly understand the perilous situation he found himself in. Monsieur and my lord duke were in the palace, armed with the guard. . . .

The city was in arms, and the houses of the Huguenots were besieged and broken into and many men slain and their houses put to the sack with an incredible avidity by the common people. . . . So that matters should not get out of hand and disorders follow by the madness of the people, an edict was issued at about three o'clock, by which it was ordered that the spoilation and killing cease, though it was not entirely obeyed. . . ..

[*The Pope is to be congratulated at having witnessed in his reign the action of divine providence and that*] the King and the Queen Mother have been able to pull up these pestiferous roots with such prudence, at a time so opportune that all their rebels were caught in a cage under lock and key.

SOURCE: Salviati, 24 August 1572, *ANG*, vol. XII, pp. 203–5.

## 23    Salviati, 2 September

While the Admiral was at court, he insinuated himself with the King with such art and authority that he effectively ruled, deciding most matters as he thought fit, to the discontent of Morvilliers, the count of Retz and others and the great jealousy of Madame the Regent, who, secretly planning with Madame de Nemours, decided to get out of the difficulty and to have him murdered. Before it was decided that the German, page to old M. de Guise, should fire the shot at him, Mme de Nemours discussed it with the young M. de Guise her son and was by him persuaded to take the shot at the Admiral while he was with the Queen, persuading her by showing her how easy it was to fire a gun at someone who was not on his guard and that his being among the women and with the Regent would reasonably dispel all suspicion. But since the shot was fired by the German with the knowledge of M. d'Anjou and not of the King, the Queen, seeing that the Admiral did not die and the danger she was exposed to, both from the suspicions arising in her own mind and from the insolent words coming from the Huguenots, who in no way could be persuaded to believe that the shot was fired by an agent of the duke of Alva, as she had wished to make them believe, turned to the King, exhorting him to the slaughter of them all that followed. The Most Christian King, in all these matters, both in judgment and in valour has shown a most Christian spirit. He would have saved none, but the other princes, who make great profession of being Catholics, and of meriting the favour of the Pope, then took great pains to save as many Huguenots as they could. Do not be surprised if I do not name them individually, because they all did the same and shamelessly.

SOURCE: Salviati, 2 September 1572, *ANG*, vol. XII, pp. 217–18.

## 24    The Venetian envoys, 25 August

All those of the Religion were very angry with M. de Guise, holding it for certain that the shot had been fired on his order. But either because these threats from the Huguenots raised fears of new uprising, or because the matter had been planned for a long time and brought to the point the King wished by the state the Admiral found himself in and by the coming together of all the leaders of the sect inside the city, or for some other reason, in the night of Saturday to Sunday, at daybreak, after secret orders issued from house to house through all the quarters to stand to arms, M. de Guise and M. d'Aumale his uncle went forth with the Marshal de Tavannes, M. de Nemours and a good troop of gentlemen and captains.

SOURCE: Michiel and Cavalli to the Council of Ten, 25 August 1572, Martin, pp. 89–90.

## 25   The reasons for the royal avowal of the Massacre

The King had consented more out of necessity than by design. In effect, after Coligny had been wounded the King had been unable to do anything. If he had acted against a suspect duke of Guise, who was as yet unconvicted, he knew that the Protestants would have acted violently. But he also knew how dangerous it was for him and his affairs to act against a man who was so loved by the people without giving him time to defend himself, especially at Paris, where everyone knows so many thousands are devoted to that house. Thus, on all sides he was reduced to extremities and knew he must expect a fourth civil war if he could not maintain Coligny and certain captains in his obedience, which was his first plan. But meanwhile, the people, with soldiers under the duke of Guise's command, alerted to the danger that threatened him, had done everything to forestall his ruin at his enemies' hands, caring nothing for the King's commands and plans, and had killed Coligny and all his supporters they could find. Thus, the thing being done, the King, who could not do otherwise, approved it as if it had been done on his orders, or at least pretended to.

SOURCE: De Thou, 1659, vol. III, p. 702, based on Monluc's account for the Poles.

---

## 26   24 August: the official story for envoys abroad

You will have heard what I wrote the day before yesterday about the wounding of my cousin the Admiral and how I did all I could to search out the truth of the matter and see speedy justice done as an example, wherein nothing was forgotten. Since then, it has happened that they of the house of Guise and other lords and gentlemen their adherents, whereof there is no small number in this city as everyone knows, when they knew for certain that the friends of the Admiral would pursue and carry out vengeance for this hurt, and because they were suspected of being the authors of it, were so stirred up this last night that a great and lamentable sedition arose between them; so that the guard that had been appointed about the Admiral's house was set upon and he himself with some other gentlemen killed, and others slain in divers places of the city. This was done with such fury that it has not been possible to remedy it as I would have wished but had much ado to employ my guards and other forces to maintain my security within my castle of the Louvre. Meanwhile, I have given orders for the general pacification of the sedition, which is still extremely grave throughout the city. All this happened through a private quarrel long fostered between these two houses. As I had always foreseen that some evil consequence would result from this, I had beforehand done all I could to pacify it, as everyone knows. The Edict of Pacification is not broken by all this and I want to maintain it more strictly than ever, as I have given to understand in all places

throughout my kingdom. . . . I have with me my brother the King of Navarre and
my cousin the prince of Condé to take such chance as myself.

SOURCE: Charles IX to Fénelon, 24 August 1572, *Fénelon*, vol. VII, pp. 323–5.

## 27    De Thou on the royal assumption of responsibility

[*Catherine and Anjou said to the King in Council:*] What would be the reputation of
the kingdom where, with the royal Majesty despised, everyone was his own judge
and gave rein to all his passions and hates? Finally, what would foreign princes
think of a king who let himself be compelled by his subjects, unable to contain
them in their duty or use the reins of sovereign power? There was no way of
forestalling such a great evil other than that the King approve by public declaration
what had been done, as if it had been done on his order. Thus he would master the
situation, disarm the house of Guise, stop the Montmorencys taking arms and
prevent the Protestants, who were already ruined, from joining the latter. For the
rest, the King should not fear blame, for there was less peril in this atrocity, that
could be softened by some excuse, than there was in a confession of weakness,
which brings in its train disdain, almost always fatal to great princes. They easily
persuaded an imperious prince who feared hatred less than disdain, to confirm by
public avowal, and in order to bring the Guises to obedience and retain the
Montmorencys in their loyalty, that all had been done on his orders.

SOURCE: De Thou, 1659, vol. III, p. 675.

## 28    The royal session of the Parlement, 26 August

Tuesday 26 August, two days after the killing started, the King went to church to
thank God. . . . After that, he went to the Palace and the gilded chamber, where the
Parlement was assembled, and, accompanied by the princes of the blood and
others, seated in his throne of justice, declared to all, with grave words, some of the
reasons which had led him to carry out such a killing of the Huguenots who were
rebels, telling them that he had dealt so rigorously with them . . . whom he had
pardoned a few months before, because they had lately been so bold as to conspire
against his person and all those of his blood and his crown, not even wishing to
spare the King of Navarre, who was of their sect and who had been recommended
to the charge of the traitor Admiral de Coligny by his mother. To better
accomplish his objective, Coligny had wanted to crown the prince of Condé, a
child, as king, so as the more easily to maintain his control and perhaps then kill
him when he thought he could become king himself. He might even have
succeeded in his aim . . . so, the King, understanding that he could not punish
them as they deserved by other means than those that were taken, he used them,
perhaps prompted by the divine majesty since he so fortunately succeeded. And so

that the lords who had been the agents and executors of his will may never be impugned as infamous for this act, he wished to make known to them that everything had been done by his express command for the above reasons. The King having concluded his speech in these words, everyone in the assembly, of both the short and long gown, agreed, approved and declared everything to have been well done and wisely executed; they praised His Majesty and thanked him for the great benefit that had been received through his counsel and diligence. In approbation and by common consent, the body of the Admiral was condemned to be dragged at the horse's tail throughout the city and then, with a calf's tail stuck up its behind, hanged by a foot as a traitor at the public gibbet of Montfaucon.

SOURCE: Capilupi, *Stratagème de Charles IX, AC*, vol. VII, pp. 440–2.

## 29 Royal declaration of 28 August avowing the Massacre and suspending the Edict of 1570

His Majesty therefore declareth, that which was done was by his express command and for no cause of religion, nor breaking his Edicts of Pacification, which he always intended and still mindeth and intendeth to observe and keep; yea, it was rather done to withstand and prevent a most detestable and cursed conspiracy begun by the said Admiral, the chief captain thereof, and his said adherents and accomplices, against the King's person, his estate, the Queen his mother and the princes, his brethren, the King of Navarre and other lords about him.

Wherefore, His Majesty, by this declaration and ordinance, giveth to understand to all gentlemen and others of the Religion which they pretend reformed, that he mindeth and purposeth that they shall live under his protection, with their wives and children in their houses, in as much safeguard as they did before; following the benefit of the former Edicts of Pacification.

Most expressly commanding and ordaining that all governors and Lieutenants-General, in every of his countries and provinces, and other justices and officers to whom it appertaineth, do not attempt, or suffer to be attempted, any thing in what sort soever, upon the persons and goods of them of the Religion. . . .

And nevertheless, to withstand the troubles, slanders, suspicions and defiances that may come by sermons and assemblies, as well in the houses of the said gentlemen as in other places, as is allowed by the said Edicts of Pacification; it is expressly forbidden and inhibited by His Majesty, to all gentlemen and others of the said Religion, to have no assemblies for any cause at all, until His Majesty hath provided and appointed otherwise, for the tranquility of his realm. . . .

SOURCE: *Déclaration du Roy de la cause et occasion de la mort de l'Admiral* (Paris: J. Dallier, 1572); Isambert, vol. XIV, pp. 257–8; trans. *Furious Outrages, Harleian Misc.*, vol. VII, pp. 362–3.

## 30    An English report of early September 1572

The King is now become so bloody that it is unpossible to stay his thirst to quench the same in innocent blood. Riding on hunting the last week, he went to Montfaucon to see the Admiral hanging by the feet, a spectacle which showeth what good nature is in the King. It is much lamented to see his cruelty even by the Papists. Many be sorry that so monstrous a murder was invented and partly they dread their own lives in so much that Monsieur de Morvilliers wished himself dead ten years ago. The duke of Guise himself is not so bloody, neither did he kill any man himself but saved divers. He spake openly that for the Admiral's death he was glad, for he knew him to be his enemy, but he thought for the rest that the King had put such to death as, if it had pleased him, might have done him very good service.

After the Admiral had been hurt, he requested of the King that he might have some armour in his house for his safeguard, which the King granted and sent his passport to Marcel for a cart load. Marcel presently advertised the Queen Mother and Monsieur and the cart was by their means taken by the way. And the Queen Mother about 11 of the clock in the night went to the King, telling him that the Admiral caused armour to be carried into his lodging. The King answered that he had granted his passport for the same, whereupon the Queen Mother with her loving and motherly persuasions began to inform the King that the Admiral did hate the King, herself, Monsieur and the rest of his house and that he would give him arms to destroy them all. She so persuaded the King that he swore they should every one die and presently Monsieur de Guise was sent for to take this execution in hand and used as a butcher to the slaughter. The inventors of this monstrous bloodshedding were the Queen Mother, Monsieur, duke Nevers and Tavannes. The revealers of this invented conspiracy were Grammont and Bouchavannes.

SOURCE: SP70/125 no. 311, September 1572.

_____

## Responsibility for transmission to the provinces

### 31    Montpensier calls for the massacre to spread to Brittany

The Admiral was such a wretch that he hatched a new plot to kill His Majesty, the Queen his mother, my lords his brothers and all the Catholic lords of his suite yesterday or today. You can well imagine that I was not forgotten in this. But God, who has always, at the hour of need, shown that he loves his own and that the cause we support for his honour is holy and just, willed that this conspiracy was discovered and has so inspired our King's heart that he immediately decided to carry out the same act against that wretch and his followers. In this he was so readily and faithfully obeyed that on that day in the morning the Admiral, with ten or twelve of his leading followers, was killed in his lodging and thrown down into the street. This execution was repeated against all the leaders of that party who could be found in the city so that there were so many dead I cannot tell you. I can say that the leaders were despatched first and hardly any escaped, except the count of Montgomery, who was lodged in the faubourg Saint-Germain. In this way, His Majesty's intention for the treatment of the Huguenots in other towns is clear enough, as also the means by which we hope our poor Catholic Church may have some peace hereafter. We cannot neglect to do what we can to carry this out after the King has made such a declaration of his devotion to it.* In this I pray Our Lord to lend a hand and ensure that he be perpetually praised.

SOURCE: letter to Nantes, 25 August 1572, *BSHPF*, 1 (1852), pp. 60–1.

* In fact Nantes refused to do this.

## 32   Auvergne, the massacre thwarted at Issoire

On Saint Bartholomew's day in the year 1572, the King had the massacres carried out at Paris in which he had the Admiral and many captains and gentlemen who had made war on him at the start of his reign killed. He then sent to all the governors of his provinces to do the same in their governorships without sparing anyone. Captain Combelle, native of Clermont, was sent by the King to M. de Saint-Herem with a packet containing the order to do the same to the Huguenots of his government. Combelle, having collected his post, met on the road a certain man of Languedoc who had escaped the massacres and who told him he was on his way to the Marshal de Damville with full commission to put all the Huguenots of his government to death. Combelle, believing what he said, told him he had the same order addressed to the sieur de Saint-Herem and became so friendly with him that they travelled several posts together. But when they had arrived at Moulins and were sharing a room, the Languedoc courier, who knew where Combelle's despatches were, got up earlier than him and took his packet, travelling with such speed that he had gone four posts before Combelle was up. Combelle, on awakening, asked where his companion was and was told he had left four hours earlier. This made him look in his bag and, not finding his packet, he began to despair, shouting and raging horribly against his host and threatening to kill him.

Meanwhile, the lad with the packet arrived at Issoire and went to find the minister, called Baduel, to whom he gave the packet saying that, unless he left very soon, he would be massacred and that he should warn the faithful of this terrible crime. The minister lost no time in quickly warning those of the Religion, took horse and got to Languedoc.

Combelle, seeing himself deceived, did not fail to go on, and having recounted the disaster to the sieur de Saint-Herem, told him at length of what had happened at Paris and of how the King had ordered him, in the despatches he had lost, to have those of the Religion in his government slaughtered, begging him to believe what he said and execute the King's order rapidly. M. de Saint-Herem, a wise man, told him he could not do such a momentous thing without the King's express orders in writing. Nevertheless, to content Combelle, he had all those of the Religion in Issoire arrested. . . . However, Combelle, on his return to the court for a second despatch, found the fury died down and instead of massacre, only brought back a commission to the sieur de Saint-Herem to administer an oath of loyalty to those of the Religion and to make them abjure heresy. On doing this, they would be set free. They did this and were thus set at liberty.

SOURCE: Julien Blauf, pp. 48–9.

## 33   The shock to Protestantism

Truly, if ever the Catholics had reason to say: 'those of the Religion are done for, we'll hear no more of them' and to ask them where their God was now, this was the time.

SOURCE: Gaches, *Mémoires*, p. 121.

At this time, there were perverse and wicked men, living without religion, who were called atheists; they tried men's consciences and sowed doubt. They asserted the obedience we owe to our kings, princes and superiors, according to God's commandment, adding the [*threat of*] loss of property, honour and life as well as the old Catholic and Roman succession; this influenced the richest. They further asserted: 'Your God sleeps!' . . . so that they caused some to turn from the Gospel, especially merchants and lawyers, for the lesser and little people stood firm without wavering. Thus some went to the vicar of the town with notarial act . . . while others informed the bishop of Rodez by notarial act that they were good Catholics, protesting that henceforth they would live and die in the King's religion, the roman, and also would hear Mass when required.

SOURCE: *Millau*, pp. 243–4, 1572.

# 6  The Accession of Henry III and the Estates-General, 1574–7

Charles IX died after a brief but agonising illness in May 1574. Much was expected by Catholics of his successor Henry III but the logic of his position forced him to disappoint them. Catherine had hoped her son's arrival would institute a new period of firm government (see Document 1) and was blamed for the confusion in the King's apparent intentions (see Document 2). From the first, the image that the King projected was confused and certainly not the martial one that many had hoped for (see Documents 4–5). Added to this, the continuing hostility between factions at court made a firm policy impossible (see Document 3). By the start of 1575, the now exiled prince of Condé was assembling German troops near the frontier and the prospect of civil war had returned.

## The Development of the 'Politique' Movement

By the mid-1570s, those we can only very loosely call 'politiques' were increasingly significant in the balance of forces. To some extent they attracted those who at least since the early 1560s had put the repose of the common weal before religious loyalty, though it should be remembered that the term 'Politique' is itself anachronistic; it was used frequently from the mid-1580s as a term of abuse to signify compromising Catholics. Nevertheless, though to talk of a *Parti des Politiques* in the mid-1570s is in some ways misleading, the idea of combinations of interests independent of or cutting across religious parties is important. A strong feature of their thinking was the defence of 'absolute' monarchical power in its time-honoured forms. In the early 1570s, there is no question of their being a single movement. The 'Malcontent' group, that had formed around Montmorency, Turenne, Biron and Cossé-Brissac in the aftermath of the Massacre, drew into itself several different interests and strands. Their figurehead became the youngest Valois brother, Alençon, around whose hostility to his elder brother (later Henry III) a polarisation of loyalties began. A man of limited abilities, his position in the succession encouraged a significant number of leading 'politique' intellectuals (Bodin, Gentillet, Plantin, Brantôme and Ronsard) to serve in his household. The range of interests involved is apparent in the Court conspiracy in March–April 1574 to free the princes. Marshal Montmorency had been sent to the Bastille and his brother Damville, governor of Languedoc, was on the point of arrest when Charles IX died. Damville was already in negotiations with the Protestants of his province assembled at Millau. He sought to reach a modus-vivendi locally by joining Catholics and Protestants who valued peace before religious purity. In April 1574 he reached an agreement with the local Huguenots. He concluded a truce with them and on 16 July the 17 articles that formed the foundation of the alliance between Protestants and the 'united' or 'associated' Catholics were agreed (see Document 6).

After Henry III's accession, relations between Navarre and Alençon deteriorated, so Alençon moved without him when he made his bid for independence in September 1575 and isssued his Declaration of Dreux, a classic manifesto of princely discontent (see Document 8). An initial consequence of the following negotiations was the release of Marshals Montmorency and Cossé from detention (2 October). In Languedoc, despite attempts by Henry III to win him over, the King had been unable to offer Damville concessions on freedom of worship. Military measures against Damville were taken, so he called on the exiled Condé for help. In November, he issued a declaration combining loyalty to the crown with the policy of joining with Protestants for the peace of the kingdom (see Document 7). This led, at an assembly held at Nîmes (January–February 1575), to the drawing up of the 'Articles of Union', which more or less created the basis for an independent government of Languedoc, shared by the Estates and Damville as representative of Condé. The Languedoc regime to some extent set it apart from the rest of the country, for Damville's followers, the 'Catholiques unis' or 'associés', chose to ally with Protestants when they thought it necessary and act with the King when they thought his policy of pacification had some hope.

The first fruit of all this was the 91 articles agreed by Condé, the gentlemen of the Reformed religion and Damville (11 April 1575, printed 1576) that prefigured the 92 articles they submitted in March 1576, including the concession of places of security and the calling of the Estates-General.

## The Experiment in Toleration, 1576

The terms of the peace of Monsieur, though concluded at Ettigny near Sens, were embodied in the Edict of Beaulieu, the secret articles also conceding a virtually independent position for Damville and Condé in the south (see Document 9). The Edict more or less embodied all the demands of the Protestant 92 articles of 19 February, with the restriction that Protestants

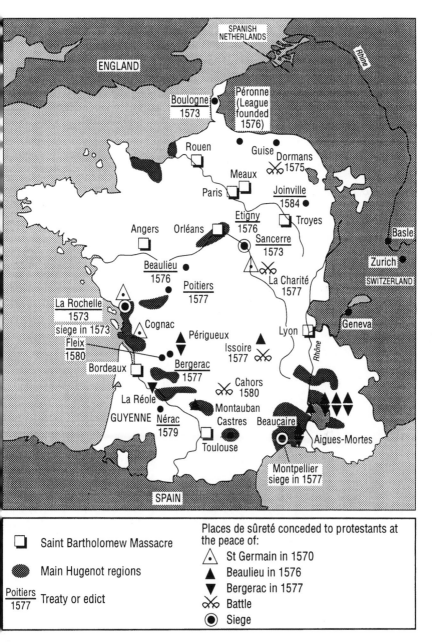

**Map 3**   The wars from 1572 to 1585

*Source:* Based on Michel Péronnet, *Le XVI Siècle, 1492–1620* (Paris: Hachette, 1995), map 10

could not worship within 2 leagues of Paris (the King had wanted 10 leagues). Resistance to the Edict was fierce and the King used *lits de justice* on 14 May to force its registration, and on 7 June of the 'chambre mi-partie' to hear mixed law cases, a key Protestant demand. In fact, the Peace of Monsieur was a stratagem forced on the King and his mother by their lack of resources and to regain some control over Anjou's movements. It seems improbable that they sincerely intended to carry it out. In addition, the Catholic popular and aristocratic response soon made it unworkable.

## The Catholic Leagues

The Catholic League is sometimes referred to in contemporary documents as though it were a monolithic organisation. As far as its origins were concerned, nothing could be further from the truth. In the 1560s, the first provincial League of Catholics had been a response to Protestant attempts to gain control of the fortress at Bordeaux in 1560. The assassination of Guise in 1563 provoked a Catholic league at Toulouse under the leadership of the local Parlement and others in Guyenne. Usually, the initial impetus for such movements came from urban confraternities and less skilled artisans. When leagues emerged again in the 1570s, noble participation was crucial to them. This was the case in the 'league of gentlemen' formed in Dauphiné early in 1574 and soon joined by the magistrates of Grenoble. In January 1576, the first secret league of Catholic aristocrats was reported between the Guise brothers, Nemours, Nevers and Chancellor Birague to oppose any further concessions to the Protestants to the point of war. The first nationally important such movement emerged in direct consequence of the 1576 Peace of Monsieur and Edict of Beaulieu. The peace had provided for the restoration of the prince of Condé to his family's governorship of Picardy and assigned him the town of Péronne for his security. As Péronne was to some extent the family fiefdom of the Catholic Humières family and the province was by this stage dominated by its catholic nobility, this produced a protest by the 'nobility and towns' of Picardy (see Document 12) and the text of a 12-article 'association' that was widely circulated throughout the country and whose origins and objectives have been much debated (see Document 13). It may be that there was Guise involvement in its inception since the Catholics of Champagne were also involved; L'Estoile certainly thought this (see Document 10). Protestants saw it as the nucleus of a vast anti-Calvinist international. The mention of the laws of Clovis also testifies to the influence of contemporary debate set on foot by works like *Franco-Gallia*. More controversial was the dimension of thought represented by the supposed discovery on the body of a Catholic envoy sent to Rome in 1576, Jean David, of an ambitious plan to depose all the descendants of Hugues Capet and place the Guises, as descendants of Charlemagne, on the throne. At most this was the dream of an extreme ultra-montanist fanatic but its publication by Protestants was a propaganda coup and would certainly have given the King pause for thought (see Documents 10–11).

## The Estates-General of Blois

Most parties were dissatisfied with the Peace of Monsieur and the German troops remained on the French frontier until cash and jewels were found to buy them off in June. For the Protestants, the Edict was seriously flawed in its implementation. The King, as specified in the Edict, issued a summons for the Estates-General on 6 August to meet on 24 November. In the circumstances of suspicion, however, the preliminary meetings and elections were unpropitious. There were virtually no Protestant deputies (see Document 15) and the mood of the assembly was at first for a renewal of war. The King had come to view the Estates as an answer to the acute financial shortage caused by years of war but many of the deputies arrived at Blois with their own agenda; they too were concerned at the financial problems but wanted to know more about the state of the treasury. The third estate was not disposed to vote new taxes for war. Henry III decided he needed the voice of the nobility behind him to sustain a renewal of war and, to do so, hit upon the idea of grasping control of the movement of Catholic leagues. On 29 November, the diarist Pierre de Blanchefort noted that he had been summoned to a meeting with some prelates and nobles where a 'certain formula of association' was proposed to break the Edict of Pacification and return to war. This was an idea close to the new draft association signed by the King on 2 December and circulated generally, rather longer than the earlier league document and couched in terms much more respectful to the monarchy (see Document 14). The King was essentially aiming to co-opt the military power of the Catholic nobility for his own uses in returning to war with the Protestants. The document was circulated and the Catholic nobles and magistrates in each local government area were required to append their signatures. In fact, as Damville pointed out to the King, the military help which might be expected from such an organisation was questionable (see Document 16) and the whole issue became overlaid with the problem that soon emerged at the Estates: the contradiction between the demand for suppression of toleration and the unwillingness to grant the means to effect this.

The royal Council decided on 22 December to promulgate the Catholic association throughout France and to order religious uniformity for a trial period of 6 months. This meeting also registered Anjou's swing against the

Protestants, whether under coercion or because he felt his demands had been satisfied is unclear. Though the majority of the nobles were for revocation of the Edict, a significant minority were opposed and signed a remonstrance to this effect on 28 February. In his speech on the same day, a prince of the blood, Montpensier, formerly among the zealous Catholics, argued passionately against war (see Document 17). When the final cahiers of all three orders were presented on 9 February 1577, all called for uniformity of religion but failed to provide the funds for the inevitable renewal of war. The problem this posed was reflected in the debates that took place in the royal council on 1 March (see Document 18).

## The Renewal of War, 1577

The sixth war of religion was the direct consequence of the revocation of the Edict of Beaulieu. Jean de Monluc warned that a war was impracticable since the King's Catholic subjects would not pay for it and it would be more destructive than ever (see Document 19). Though it is likely that Henry III would have preferred peace, war was forced on him by the general threat to his authority on all sides, not least from the Catholic leagues. The King's renewal of war was reluctant, possibly, but he had won over Damville by holding out the prospect of the north Italian marquisate of Saluzzo, to which the Montmorencys had some distant claim. Damville, who had argued strongly against the renewal of war, broke with the Protestants in March largely as a result of his local quarrels with them. The King appointed Anjou as head of the royal armies. The campaign, marked signally by the brutal sackings of La Charité (May) and Issoire (June), left the royal army shattered and without cash, as was by now the usual pattern in such campaigns. The paying off of John Casimir's army, still encamped on French soil, remained a problem. Meanwhile, as Damville had predicted, the Protestants of Condé and Navarre had seized the port of Brouage and thus acquired a port through which they could be supplied from England. The King, who had been negotiating on and off with Navarre, through the duke of Montpensier, since before the fighting began, had to come to terms at Bergerac in September.

A new edict of toleration was issued at Poitiers on 17 September 1577, Henry III's first genuine attempt to create a workable regime of toleration. While it repeated much of that of Beaulieu, it was essentially a compromise between it and the policy of total repression canvassed at the Estates-General. Widespread toleration was accorded but practice of the Reformed faith was circumscribed in detail and modifications were introduced into the vexed arrangements for bipartisan chambers. For Henry III, its great advantage was to outlaw leagues and associations and give him a freer hand in implementing pacification. In practice, the years 1578–83 were a disappointment in that the pacification failed to take hold in the face of continuing hostility concentrated in the Huguenot strongholds.

## THE IMAGE OF HENRY III AND THE COURT

### 1 Catherine's advice to her son, August 1574

Monsieur de Cheverny, tell the King my son that, since it has pleased God to call him to the government of this kingdom . . . for the love he knows I have borne him since his birth, that I have always desired, since the death of the king my lord his father, to see him great, even though this may have been by the death of the king his brother, since God willed it so. I pray him, therefore to preserve his greatness and, since he comes into the kingdom with such expectations and reputation, in view of the great experience, which by God's grace he has acquired, that a man of 50 could not have had more or have seen so many princes and lands, that this should serve him greatly in governing this kingdom; and I pray him to enter his kingdom like a prince not accustomed to see our disordered ways and our fickleness, combining the gravity God has given him with his native gentleness, to show himself the master without an equal and free from liars. Let not people think: he is young, we will make him do what we like. . . .

SOURCE: Catherine to Cheverny, 8 August 1574, *LCM*, vol. v, pp. 73–5.

### 2 The reputation of the King and Queen Mother

The Queen Mother has been blamed for having lately dissuaded the King, on his arrival from Italy at his accession, from that wise course of entering his kingdom without arms, proclaiming a general pardon, releasing all prisoners and quashing trials; in that way he would have started his reign with a new way of governing. The Queen Mother advised him, on the contrary, to come with troops so as to be not only respected but feared. Thus, when it came to pardoning and releasing prisoners, he would seem to act through greatness and magnanimity, not through cowardice and fear. This advice, carried out properly, would not have been bad and it was approved by the duke of Savoy, as he told me himself. Unfortunately, the troops who came with the King (whatever they were intended for) were unimpressive. Those who came from Turin to Lyon, rather than inspiring fear, were scarcely to be considered. Thus, the King entered his kingdom neither in arms nor in peace. This advice, the effects of which were so baneful, was, I repeat, blamed on the Queen and her councillors and was the cause of all this misfortune.

The King himself realises this, was and is in his heart very regretful about it. But such is the Queen's power over his mind that neither he nor others dare contradict her.

SOURCE: Relazione of Michel, 1575, Tommaseo, vol. II, p. 244.

## 3   Factional hatreds

The Queen Mother is so vexed with these dissensions at home that she will have peace abroad *quoi qu'il coute* and that I have heard for certain, from them which heard it of her own mouth, she beareth the Guises more in spleen than ever she did. Somewhat she is appeased with ridding of the Queen's women from her and the Queen of her side snubbed much with the matter. Notwithstanding, the King is wholly entertained by the Guises as familiar companions and not as attending upon their prince. The King of Navarre hangeth on among them. Monsieur showeth openly he cannot bear it and I believe the Queen Mother be half content privily to bear with him in that behalf. . . . It is a very hell among them, not one content or in quiet with another, nor mother with son, nor brother with brother, nor mother with daughter, in love nor any one with another. It is much to be doubted lest the Guises have won away the King of Navarre from Monsieur and now, with putting away of the Queen's women from her, there is a new revel but always the Queen Mother hath her will, though she be vexed of all sides and liketh as little of the Guises as others do. It is thought verily she can be content to make Monsieur great to keep down the Guises. The [*Protestant*] deputies cannot but make their profit of these things.

SOURCE: V. Dale to Walsingham, 23 March 1575, SP70/133 nos. 49 and 50.

## 4   The King's image

Friday 11 February, the King arrived at Rheims, where he was anointed Sunday 13th, exactly one year after his coronation in Poland. When it came to placing the crown on his head, he said quite loudly that it hurt him and it slipped twice as though it wanted to fall off, which was noted and interpreted as a bad omen.

SOURCE: L'Estoile, p. 67, February 1575.

The King stayed at Paris throughout Lent in this year 1575 and went every day to one parish church after another to hear the sermon and Mass and pay his devotions. Meanwhile, he sought out every means of finding money that his experts could devise. In fact, he levied on the good towns of his kingdom 3 million *livres* (besides the 1 million levied on the clergy), of which Paris was levied at 1 million by poll tax on the well off. . . . In short, there was no talk at court at this time but that the King had nothing for dinner and that he could only get by with loans. [*On 18 March, the King sent to the legal officers to ask how much they would be willing to lend.*] The said money was used by the King to make a present to Captain Le Guast to the value of more than 50,000 *livres.*

SOURCE: L'Estoile, March 1575, p. 69.

---

At the start of November 1575, the King restored in the churches of Paris the oratories otherwise called the 'paradises' and went every day to offer alms and prayers in great devotion. He left off his shirts with great fringed collars, to which he was before so given, and took up the reversed collar, Italian style. He goes by coach through the streets of Paris with his wife to find little lap dogs, which give both of them great pleasure; likewise to all the nunneries around Paris in quest of such little dogs, to the great regret and displeasure of the ladies to which they belonged. He has started to be taught grammar and is learning to decline [verbs]. On this word, which seemed to presage the decline of his state, considering the great affairs he had to deal with, scandalous Latin verses have been circulated.

SOURCE: L'Estoile, November 1575, p. 85.

---

The King went on foot through the streets of Paris to obtain the pardon of the jubilee sent to France by Pope Gregory XIII, accompanied by only two or three people and muttering paternosters. It was said this was done on his mother's advice to make the people of Paris believe he was devoted to the Catholic Church, and so encourage him to dig into their purses more deeply. But the people of Paris (though it is very easy take advantage of them, especially where religion is concerned) did not heed the message and verses were spread through the streets about it (the devotions of kings are found good when they are done for a good purpose, but otherwise they are mocked).

SOURCE: L'Estoile, August 1576, p. 124.

---

## 5   The 'mignons', 1576–7

The name of 'mignons' started at this time to be chattered in the mouths of the people, to whom it was most odious, both because of how they behaved, which was bantering and hauty, and because of their effeminate and immodest manners and garb, but above all because of the immense gifts that the King made them, which the people thought was the cause of their own ruin, even though, as such gifts could not remain in their pockets for a moment, they were soon passed back to the people like water through a down-pipe. These fine mignons wore their perfumed hair like whores in a brothel, curled and recurled by artifice, sticking up under their bonnets, and the ruffs of their fine linen shirts stiffened and elongated so that their heads above them looked like the head of Saint John the Baptist on a platter. The rest of their clothes were the same; their pastimes were gaming, blaspheming, jumping about, dancing and vaulting, quarrelling and whoring, and to follow the King around everywhere and say and do everything to please him. . . .

SOURCE: L'Estoile, July 1576, p. 122.

On 20 October, the King arrived at Ollainville in haste, with his young mignons frilled and curled, their hair crested like bats' wings, their manner disguised and ostentatious, well-groomed, speckled and powdered with violet scent and such odours that they sweetened streets, squares and houses that they passed.

SOURCE: L'Estoile, October 1577, p. 154.

## 6   Damville and Languedoc

[*In October 1574*] Marshal Damville adhered to the party of the *Politiques*, as it was called then but since has been called the *Union*, which is to say that those of both religions had united to bring the King to agree to a full peace. This Damville, though, had some time before declared himself secretly by letters to the Estates-General held at Millau, to which he sent a trumpet and messages for certain secret reasons not to be revealed until he had handed over certain towns to the religion. At that time he had sent 400 arquebusiers to reinforce the garrison at Livron in Dauphiné, to make it known that he was more of the Religion than Papist. In fact, he made himself protector of all the churches of Languedoc and Guyenne. He sent letters signed by his own hand to all the towns of the Religion and the nobility that he had devoted his life and property to the aid and comfort of the Religion. [*All this to the anger of Charles IX, who had dismissed him.*]

SOURCE: *Millau*, pp. 320–21.

## 7   Damville's Declaration, 1/13 November 1574

[*Having perceived the constant civil wars*] grounded upon the pretence and controversy of religion and how under this pretence hath followed the total ruin of the more part of the good towns. . . [*how the edicts of toleration since Orléans have been broken, without those in power stopping it*] even so far as that they have suffered that cruel, barbarous and unnatural murder of the more part of the nobility of France committed in the town of Paris at Saint Bartholomew's Day in the year 1572. . . [*and in Toulouse, Bordeaux, Rouen, Lyon, Orléans and other towns; and how power is held by foreigners*].

How since the decease of the good King Henry, the nobility hath been wholly defaced in France and their merits and virtues despised, how strangers have been preferred before them to the charges and estates of the crown and of the King's household, against the ancient laws of the establishment of this realm. Yea, and which more is, the same estates have been given to some that be no gentlemen, nor have showed so much as any small proof of anything near to any deserving of such charge. Whereof ensueth an extreme grief to an infinite number of old knights and captains of France in respect of their long services. . . .

. . . And since the disorder and subversion have been brought in by these new governors with their novelties, they have sought to make the King's subjects live like brute beasts, without doctrine or observing anything that they ought, depriving them of such learned men as were in the universities either by murder or banishment into strange countries, permitting that the ecclesiastical persons . . . neither study nor preach, nor be resident, nor exercising themselves in any part of their duty, that their insatiable covetise and their plurality of benefices hath freer course than it ever had. . . .

How, since that justice is administered for money and that there hath been suffered in France against our laws that the president Birague, a Milanese, hath been made Chancellor of France and all the learned and sufficient Frenchmen that might have been chosen to those charges have been rejected, we have nothing but mischief in justice and allowance of all murders, slaughters and traitorous outrages that have been executed and conspired since he hath been in charge; briefly, how all his edicts have tended only to the subversion of the nobility . . . by which means he hath done what in him lay to create a stranger the King's Lieutenant-General in his realm, disappointing my lord His Majesty's brother of the promise that was made him by the late King.

[*They have caused the murder of the count of Martinengo in Montpellier and have tried to murder or imprison Damville. The latter went to Piedmont at the new King's invitation and was assured*] of this his so sincere and laudable intention to enter with peace and to embrace the unity of his said subjects of both religions, to make them partakers of the benefit and quietness that he meant to them, in such sort that we looked for nothing but this universal good at our return from the town of Suze to this our government . . . [*to oversee pacification on the King's instructions*]. But he, being still in the power of those that had counselled the late King, to the oppression and ruin of his estates, hindering the fruit of his good purpose, they have continued as they yet daily do continue, the execution of their practices and devices, consuming wholly the finances of France in the entertaining of an army in a manner of all strangers. . . .

[*Thus, having been called on by the princes and officers of the realm,*] we . . . having well considered that the controversy which is in this realm for matter of religion neither can nor ought to be determined by arms but by a holy and free council, general or national, and likewise that it is most requisite that there be an establishment of all things in their first estate, by the advice and deliberation of an assembly of the States General. . . . We, having an extreme grief to see His Majesty possessed by persons that have small regard unto him that they publicly abuse his sacred name to cover their ungracious intention, insatiableness and ambition, have embraced the common protection, preservation and defence of the crown, and of the said good and natural subjects, as well of one religion as of another . . . and of the liberty of my lord the King's brother, the King of Navarre, my lord the prince of Condé and other princes of the blood, officers of the crown, lords and gentlemen and other captains prisoners and exiled. . . .

[*Summons all princes of Christendom to his aid and notifies those subjects who support him*] that they shall be preserved, maintained and kept in all liberties of their conscience and exercise of their religion, as well Catholics as Reformed, according as shall be particularly advised at this next assembly general by us assigned in the town of Montpellier . . . and also declare that they which shall show themselves contrary to us . . . shall be run upon as enemies of the estate and crown of France and disturbers of the unity and common peace.

SOURCE: BN, fr. 3239 fos. 69–78; printed Strasbourg, 1575; Le Laboureur, *Addn.* vol. II, p. 132 (this trans. London, 1575).

## 8  The duke of Alençon's declaration, Dreux, 17 September 1575

Francis, both son and brother of a king, duke of Alençon, first peer of France etc. To all men whom it shall appertain, greeting. Know ye that we, being truly advertised and informed that of the observation of laws dependeth the conservation of all realms and lordships and, by that means, peace groweth and is entertained among the subjects; so, when they are not kept in the purity that our ancestors have left them unto us . . . the subjects, being emboldened, do license, dispense and easily give themselves to all dissoluteness, which doth cause oftentimes civil wars . . . if in time it be not remedied by the divine goodness of God, which doth raise (when it pleaseth him) excellent and mighty persons to withstand the tyranny of those which seek not but to bring all things to confusion, only to make themselves rich (at whose cost soever it be) of the blood and sweat of the poor. . . . And for to bring their purpose to pass, do nourish and maintain the dissensions which we see at this instant, colouring their dealings with the controversy that is in religion, which they would be right sorry to see pacified . . . to the intent they may colour the better the taxes, imposts and subsidies which they do daily invent and gather in the King's name upon the poor people, the nobility and the clergy, under pretence to pay his debts; tending only to the wealth of few persons, almost all strangers, which rule the King and occupy the chief places and offices of this realm against the laws of the same. . . .

. . . But seeing the wound wax daily worse and worse and no person to be more unworthily used than we, and that so many princes, lords, gentlemen and ecclesiastical persons, citizens and burgesses had their eyes fixed on us, stretching forth their hands and imploring our aid; we, being overcome with their prayers, and partakers of their miseries, resolved (and fear of death set aside, which was near to ensue) to attempt to get out of the captivity we were in, to take the public case in hand and to withstand the wicked and pernicious counsels of the perturbators of this realm, in which attempt God hath so favoured us that the 17th day of September we arrived in this our town of Dreux, where many lords, gentlemen and others as well of the clergy as of the commons of this realm, have repaired unto us. To whom we have declared that our will and intention was not to take upon us, or to attempt in any wise upon, the authority of the King our said lord and brother, the which we desire to preserve and increase with all our power. But only to employ us with all our forces, yea not to spare our life and goods for to put out and drive away all the perturbators of the public rest; to pursue by law and justice all such spoils, thefts, murders and slaughters so abominably and against all right and reason committed in the open sight and knowledge of all men, to deliver so many lords, gentlemen and others committed prisoners or wrongly banished without cause; to restore them again (and all other honest men) to their goods and livings, estates and honours; to abolish all taxes, subsidies and imposts set upon the poor people by the malice and suggestion of strangers, against the ancient laws and statutes of this realm; to maintain the nobility and clergy in their ancient privileges, freedoms and liberties. And so to stablish in France a good, firm and stable peace. . . .

SOURCE: *The Protestation of the most high and mightie prince Frauncis* (London, 1575), *from Protestation de Monseigneur fils et frere du Roy, Duc d'Alençon* (1575) and *Brieve remonstrance à la noblesse de France sur le parct de la declaration de Monseigneur le duc d'Alençon* (Paris, 1576) by I. Gentillet, MS in BN, fr. 3342 fos. 5–6.

---

## 9   The Edict of Beaulieu, 6 May 1576

3  We ordain that the Catholic and Roman religion shall be set up and stablished again in all places and parts of this our realm and of the countries under our governance, where the exercise thereof hath been left off. That it may be freely and quietly exercised without any trouble or let. Forbidding most expressly all persons, of what state, condition or calling so ever they be, under the pain aforesaid, to trouble, vex or disquiet the ecclesiastical persons in the celebration of the divine service or in the enjoying and taking up of the tithes, fruits and revenues of their benefices and of all other rights and duties [*sic*] belonging to them. And our will is that all such as in the time of these present and former troubles have entered upon the churches, houses, lands and revenues belonging to the ecclesiastical persons, and do still hold and occupy the same, shall give up the whole possession of them and let them peaceably enjoy them with such rights, liberties and assurances as they had before they were dispossessed of them.

4  And to take away all occasion of trouble and disagreement among our subjects, we have granted and do grant free open and general exercise of the RPR, through all cities and places of our realm, and through all countries under our obedience and protection, without restraint of time, person or place, conditionally that the same places belong unto themselves, or that it be done with the good will and consent of the owners to whom they belong. In the which towns and places, the professors of the said Religion may preach, pray, sing psalms, minister baptism and the Lord's Supper, ask the bands of matrimony and solemnise marriages, publicly catechise and read lectures, use discipline acording to the said Religion and do all other things belonging to the free and full exercise of the same. Also, they may hold consistories, synods, assemblies or councils, as well provincial as general, so they make our officers privy thereunto in the places where those synods shall be called and assembled. And we enjoin our said officers or some of them to assist [*sic*: for 'be present at'] those general and provincial councils. Yet nevertheless, we will and ordain that the professors of the said Religion shall forbear the open exercise thereof in our city of Paris and in the suburbs thereof and within two leagues about the same. Which two leagues we have limited and do limit to the places following, that is to wit: Saint Denis, Saint Maur des Fossés, Pont de Charenton, le bourg La Reine and Port de Neuilly. In the which places our meaning is that there shall not be any exercise of the said Religion. Howbeit, notwithstanding that, the professors of the same Religion shall not be sought or sifted for anything that they do in their houses as concerning the said Religion, nor their children or the teachers of them be compelled to do anything contrary or prejudicial to the same. Also, they shall abstain from the said exercise of Religion in our court and within two leagues about it. And likewise in our lands and countries which are on that side the mountains, saving that in those countries they shall not be sought or sifted for aught they do in their houses concerning the said Religion. And we hope that God will grant us the grace to see all our subjects knit together again in one faith, religion and belief, by the determination of a free and holy general council, which is our desire and chief intent. . . .

16  In all public acts and actions where any speech shall be made of the said Religion, there shall be used the words: 'the pretended Reformed religion'.

17  To the end to knit the hearts of our subjects the better together according to our intent, we enable as well the Catholics confederate as the professors of the RPR to hold and execute all manner of estates, dignities, offices and charges whatsoever, whether they be of royalty and lordship, or of government of the cities of our realm and of the countries, lands and seniories under our dominion; and we will that they shall be indifferently admitted and received unto them, without being bound to take any other oath, or to be tied to any other inconvenience, than the good and faithful behaving of themselves in their

callings, dignities, charges and offices and in the keeping of the ordinances of them. In the which estates, dignities, charges and offices, whensoever they happen to be void, we, as in respect of such as shall be of our own gift or disposition, shall provide indifferently and without respect of persons, to place such as we may perceive to be able men to deal well in the service of us and of our subjects.

18 And forasmuch as the administration of justice is one of the chief means to maintain our subjects in peace and concord: we, inclining to the request that hath been made unto us as well on the behalf of the Catholics confederate, as on the behalf of the professors of the said RPR, have ordained and do ordain that, in our Court of Parlement at Paris, there shall be erected a chamber of two presidents and sixteen councillors, the one half of Catholics and the other half of the said Religion. The which officers of the Religion shall be created and erected by us to the said end, with like wages, honour, authority and prerogatives, as our other councillors of our said Court have; so as all pleas and controversies wherein the said Catholics confederate or those of the RPR shall be principal parties, either in serving or defending, in all matters as well civil as criminal, whether the said suits be made by writing or by appeal by words, if the parties think it good . . . shall be heard and judged in the same chamber. . . . And the same chamber, made and stablished as is said before, shall be appointed to our city of Poitiers, there to sit and minister justice to our subjects, the Catholics confederate and the professors of the said Religion, in our countries of Poitou, Angoulême, Aunis and La Rochelle, after the same form and fashion as is used in the sessions of the chamber in our Court of Parlement at Paris; and this to be done three months together every year, namely from the first day of August to the last day of October. . . .

22 The provosts of our right dear and well-beloved cousins the marshals of France, under-baillifs and vice-seneschals, lieutenants of the short coat and all other like officers, shall judge according to the laws and injunctions heretofore given forth for the correction of vagabonds. And as touching householders brought before the provosts and charged with matters belonging to that office, if they concern the Catholics confederate or those of the foresaid Religion, the said officers shall be bound to call an equal number of our officers, of sufficient ability, as well Catholics as those of the Religion, to the information and judgment of the said matters, from out of the next Presidial courts or from out of the royal courts in the provinces where there are no Presidial courts if there be so many of the said Religion there; or else, in their steads they shall call as many advocates of the like sort, if they be to be found there.

23 It is our ordinance, will and pleasure that our right dear and well beloved brother-in-law, the King of Navarre, our right dear and well-beloved cousin the prince of Condé, our right dear and well-beloved cousin Monsieur de

Damville, Marshal of France and likewise all other lords, knights, gentlemen and other persons, of what state or condition soever they be, as well Catholics confederate as those of the foresaid Religion, shall enter again into their governments, charges, rooms and offices royal, which they had before the xxiiij of August 1572, and be maintained in the enjoying of them, without driving of them to take new commissions or patents, notwithstanding any sentences definitive and judgments given against them, and notwithstanding the patents that have been obtained of those rooms by other men. Likewise, they shall enter again into the enjoying of all and singular their goods, rights, titles, duties and doings notwithstanding the judgments that have ensued by reason of the said troubles. Which definitive sentences, judgments, patents and all other things that might ensue thereof, we have for the same purpose denounced and do denounce to be utterly void and of no effect nor value. . . .

32 The disorders and outrages committed the xxiiij of August and days following at Paris and in other cities and places of our realm, happened to our great grief and misliking. Wherefore, to show our singular well meaning towards our subjects, be it known that the widows and children of all such as were slain the same days, in what part of our realm so ever it were, shall be exempted from contribution of any imposition that shall be made by reason of lands holden in chief or by knights' service (if the husbands or fathers of them were noble). And if the husbands and fathers were of the third estate, that is to say of the commonalty, and therefore taillable, we for the foresaid considerations do discharge their wives and children of all tallages and impositions utterly, for and during the space of six years next following, forbidding all and every of our officers to levy anything of them in prejudice of this our present will and intent.

33 Also we do it to be known that all sentences, judgments, arrests, processes, attachments, sales and decrees made, given and done against those of the RPR, as well living as dead, since the decease of the late King Henry, our most honourable lord and father, by occasion of the said Religion and the turmoils and troubles thereupon ensuing, together with the executions of the same judgments and decrees, are and shall from henceforth stand reversed, repealed and annihilated. . . . The like do we will and ordain to be done for the Catholics confederate, and namely in respect of the judgments and verdicts given against the sieurs de La Mole, Coconas and La Haye, Lieutenant-General of Poitou. . . .

34 And to the intent that by the means of our foresaid declaration and sentences and judgments given against the late sieur de Châtillon, Admiral of France, and the execution of them, may stand void and of none effect as things never done or come to pass; we, according to the same declaration, do will and ordain that all the said sentences, judgments, proceedings and acts done against the said

sieur de Châtillon be razed, defaced and put out of the registers of record, as well of our courts of Parlement as of all other courts of justice; and that as well the memorial of the said Admiral, as also his children, shall continue unappaired in their honour and lands in that respect, notwithstanding that the said sentences and decrees import reunion and incorporation of the said lands to the domain of our crown, whereof we will cause a more ample and special declaration to be made to his said children if they think good.

35 We will the like to be done on the behalf of the sieur de Montgomery, Montbrun, Briquemault and Cavaignes.

36 We forbid the making of any solemn processions, as well in respect of the death of our late cousin the prince of Condé as in respect of the journée of Saint Bartholomew and of all other doings that may renew the remembrance of troubles.

37 We protest and we take and accept again our right dear and dearly beloved brother the duke of Alençon, for our good brother; our very dear and entirely beloved brother the King of Navarre, for our brother-in-law [and good kinsman]; our right dear and well-beloved cousin the prince of Condé for our kinsman, faithful subject and servant. Likewise also we hold and repute our dear and loved cousin the Monsieur de Damville, Marshal of France and all other lords, knights, gentlemen, officers, town dwellers, commonalties, cities, boroughs and other places of our realm and of the countries under our dominion, that have followed, succoured, aided and favoured them by any manner of means, for our good and loyal subjects. And upon the hearing of the declaration made by our said brother the duke of Alençon, we hold ourselves well and sufficiently satisfied and informed of his good meaning and that neither he nor any of those that held with him, or intermeddled themselves by any other means with the matter, whether they be alive or dead, have done anything but for our service. . . .

58 And forasmuch as the grievousness and long continuance of the troubles within this our realm have put all things so far out of order that, without bringing them to a stay again, it were unpossible to hold our subjects in so good union and agreement as ought to be among them, that they may live in quietness and rest, which hath been always our chief care and endeavour; considering that to bring the same to good pass we could not tell how to do better, than to hear the advice of all the provinces of our realm: we have, ever since our coming to the crown, been minded to call a general assembly of the States, which thing (to our great grief) we could not yet do by reason of the troubles. Whereof, sith it hath pleased God to give an end, we continuing still in our good and holy purpose to the welfare of our subjects, do denounce and declare how it is our will and pleasure that the said States shall generally be summoned and called together into our city of Blois, there to make their appearance according to the

good, ancient and commendable customs of this realm, within six months next, accounting from the day of the publishing of our present Edict in our Court of Parlement at Paris. . . .

59  The said Catholics confederate and they of the foresaid Religion shall be bound to cause all garrisons to avoid and, incontinently after the publishing of this our present edict, out of the cities, towns, castles and houses which they hold, belonging either to us or to any private person, and namely to any of the clergy, and them to leave, yield up and set again freely in the same state wherein they were in the time of full peace, before the present and former troubles. Nevertheless, for certain good considerations, we have given the said Catholics confederate and those of the said Religion the keeping of these eight cities ensuing: that is to wit, Aigues Mortes and Beaucaire in Languedoc; Périgueux, le mas de Verdun in Guyenne; Noyons and Serres both the town and the castle, in Dauphiné; Issoire in Auvergne and Seine le grand'tour and the circuit about it in Provence. And our said brother the king of Navarre, the prince of Condé, the Marshal Damville and they to whom the keeping of those cities shall be committed, shall promise upon their faith and honour, to keep them well and faithfully to our use. Also, there shall no governors nor garrisons be sent by us into the other cities which they hold at this present, and are to be yielded up as is said afore, other than such as have been wont to be there at all times, yea even in the reign of the late King Henry our lord and father. . . .

SOURCE: *The Edict or Proclamation set forthe by the Frenche kinge upon the pacifying of the troubles in Fraunce,* trans. A. Golding (London: Vautrollier, 1576); Stegman, pp. 97–120.

## 10   The emergence of the Catholic Leagues, 1576

At this time, various gentlemen threw themselves into the town of Péronne, determined to guard it and not to allow the entry of the prince of Condé; and a rumour went round that there was a covert league between the King of Spain, the Pope and some French lords against the Huguenots and Catholics allied with them.

SOURCE: L'Estoile, June 1576, p. 117.

Thursday 2 August, their Majesties, warned of a secret league and confederation negotiated covertly between various lords and towns of this realm so as to use all means to prevent the implementation of the Edict of Pacification, made the dukes of Guise and Mayenne and their step-father the duke of Nemours swear to and sign the entire observation of the Edict and its maintenance, having had warning that these lords were were suspected to be the leaders of this league, which was nothing but a conspiracy against the state.

SOURCE: L'Estoile, p. 123.

At the end of this month were distributed the memoirs of master Jean David, advocate, found among his papers after his death at Rome, where he had gone on business for the holy league, founded on pretext of religion in appearance but in reality on the pretensions of the house of Lorraine, who said they were of the line of Charlemagne.

SOURCE: L'Estoile, October 1576, p. 127.

## 11  Protestant propaganda against the League, 1576

That the civil wars which have been in France have brought more hinderance than furtherance to the Apostolic See, especially for the liberty both to write books . . . as otherwise to deface the honour thereof; by the which liberty, the minds of the heretics are encouraged and hardened and most of the Catholics brought to contempt and scorn of the said Holy See.

That the end and event of all the victories which have been gotten in France have fallen out unto some peace shameful and dishonourable to the King, whereof it may be gathered that the stock of Hugh Capet, albeit it hath succeeded in the singular and only government of the kingdom of Charles the Great; yet it hath not succeeded it in enjoying of the apostolical blessing, which blessing, consecration and inauguration properly and peculiarly was bestowed upon the lineage and posterity of Charles the Great [*and the house of Capet is cursed*] in so much that it is not to be marvelled that the victories of those kings which these 16 years past have undertaken war for the Catholic Church, have had no happy success, neither at any time shall, as long as the crown shall rest in the family of Capet.

That it may seem that God, in the conclusion of the last shameful peace, hath as it were called home the rightful and lawful heirs of the crown unto their right and have offered occasion and beginning to restore the crown unto the heads of the right heirs of Charles. . . . [*The Capetians are 'heartless, witless, of no wisdom or courage', 'reprobates', ' of evil shape of body, of foul and stained blood',*] further, that in the flower of their age they die, leaving no heirs of their body to enjoy the kingdom and that there remaineth no hope of their stock and issue [*so the realm is likely to pass to heretics*].

[*The stock of Charles the Great*] are well known to be the most fittest to achieve and enterprise the greatest matters and of most account. That the late wars hath advanced them to attain honours, rules and offices. . . .

[*There follows an outline of the organisation of a holy league, with a plan to provoke general disorder to force the King to appoint Guise to command of an army. The Estates-General is to be summoned and the Parlements to meet in formal session, the King's brother and Navarre to be entrapped and arrested.*]

[*After the victory of the duke of Guise over all opposition, he*] at the last by the licence and counsel of His Holiness shall thrust the King and the Queen into a monastery, following the example of his great-grandfather King Pepin, who drave Childeric the king, entrapped by like means, into a monastery; and by this device the secular inheritance of the crown of France, together with the apostolical blessing, being recovered, he shall restore without exception and restraint unto the Holy See the ancient dignity, power and authority; and shall repeal and revoke the privileges of the Church of France, as they are commonly called. . . .

SOURCE: *Summa legationis Guysianicae* (1577), trans. as a *Summe of the Guisian Ambasage to the Bishop of Rome, found lately amongst the writinges of one David, an Advocate of Paris* (London, 1579).

## 12    Protestation of the nobility of Picardy, June 1576

We will all remain in the obedience of God and of his Catholic Church, in the fidelity and service we owe the King and the Lieutenants and governors he has appointed and ordained in this country; we will live, also, in obedience to his edicts and ordinances. We will ensure that the officers of justice appointed by His Majesty in the towns and provinces of their jurisdictions will punish the wicked and reward the good and virtuous, preserving and securing them in their houses and lands. We will honour, follow and serve the chief leader of this confederation in all, everywhere and against all those who may attack his person. We will guard from violence both the clergy and the poor people. . . .

SOURCE: La Popelinière, vol. II, fos. 319v–20r.

## 13    The formula of the general League, 1576

In the name of God, of the Holy Trinity, Father, Son and Holy Spirit, our one and only true God, to whom be all glory and honour.

1   The association between the Catholic princes, lords and gentlemen should and will be made to re-establish the law of God in its entirety, restore and maintain its holy service in the form and manner of the Holy Catholic Church, abjuring and renouncing all errors to the contrary.

2   To preserve King Henry III of this name, by the grace of God King of France, and his successors, Most Christian Kings, in the estate, splendour, authority, duty, service and obedience which are due to him from his subjects, as is contained in the articles that will be proposed to him at the Estates, to which he will take an oath as guarantee of his coronation oath, with assurance nothing will be done against what will be ordained.

3   To restore to the provinces of this kingdom and their estates the rights, pre-eminences, franchises and liberties as they were under King Clovis, first Christian King, and others even better and more profitable if they can be found, except concerning the above assurance.

4   Should there be impediment to or rebellion against the above, by whom and

wheresoever it may be, the said associates will be obliged to employ all their goods and means, even their own lives, to punish, chastise and crush those who wished to counter and impede it, and to act so that everything is carried out effectively.

5 Should any of the said associates, their subjects, friends and allies be oppressed, molested, impeded or sought out for the above matters by whomsover it be, the associates will be obliged to employ their lives, goods and means to have vengeance of those committing the oppressions and molestations, either by justice or by arms, without any exceptions.

6 Should any of the associates, having taken the oath to the association, wish to withdraw from it, on whatever pretext, which God forfend, such renegades to their oaths will be attacked in lives, goods and all other ways that may be, as enemies of God, rebels and disturbers of the public peace, without any question of the associates being held to account, in public or in private.

7 The associates will swear prompt obedience and service to the commander-in-chief who will be appointed to accompany or give advice, comfort and aid to the association, either in its maintenance or in attacking its opponents, without exception of any; and the defaulters or delayers will be punished by the chief's authority, following his orders, which the associates will obey.

8 All Catholics of town and country will be warned and summoned secretly by the local governors to enter into the association, and to provide money, arms, horses and men for its implementation, according to the ability of each.

9 Those unwilling to enter the association will be reputed its enemies and will be hunted down in all ways possible.

10 All associates will be forbidden to enter into any quarrel or dispute against each other without the chief's permission, and at his discretion all those contravening this will be punished in matters of honour and all other sureties.

11 If for matters of fortification and the greater security of the associates there should be held conventions between provinces of this kingdom, they will be held in the abovesaid form and under the same conditions, whether the association be sought with the towns or by them requested, unless the chief provides otherwise.

12 The form of the oath of the said association: I swear by God on this gospel and on pain of anathematisation and perpetual damnation that I enter this Holy and Catholic association according to the form of the treaty that has presently been read to me, justly, loyally and sincerely, to command, to obey or to serve, and promise on my life to conform to it until the last drop of my blood without contravention or withdrawing, on whatever order, excuse or reason there might be.

SOURCE: BN, fr. 15591; pr. Loutchitksy, pp. 39–42; La Popelinière, vol. II, fos. 320v–21r; faulty copy, Palma Cayet, ed. Buchon, pp. 8–9.

## 14   The League of Péronne, as revised by the King and by the League in Picardy, December 1576

Firstly, the great practices and conspiracies against the honour of God, the Holy Catholic Church, the State and monarchy of this realm of France [and house of Valois], both by certain of its subjects and by foreigners, being generally known; as well as that the long and continuous wars and civil strife have so weakened our kings and reduced them to such need they of themselves can no longer sustain the expenditure that is suitable and expedient for the preservation of our religion, nor that they will hereafter be able to maintain us in their protection in security of their lives, families and goods, in which hitherto we have suffered such loss and damage.

We have considered it most necessary [and to the point] firstly to render the honour we owe to God, to the maintenance of our Catholic religion, and to show ourselves more devoted to its preservation than those who have strayed from true religion are to the advancement of their new [and false] opinion.

To this purpose, we swear and promise to employ all our powers in restoring and maintaining the practice of our Catholic religion, in which we and our predecessors have been raised and we wish to live and die.

We also swear and promise all obedience, honour and most humble service to king Henry, now reigning, given us by God as our sovereign lord and king, legitimately called by the laws of the realm to the succession, and after him to the descendants of the house of Valois [and others after the said house of Valois who are called by the law of the realm to the crown].

We promise, on the obedience and service we owe to our King Henry now reigning, to employ our lives and goods for the preservation of his authority and the execution of the commands that he, his Lieutenants-General and others having power under him will make to us, [both for the maintenance of the exclusive practice of the Catholic religion in France and to bring his rebel subjects to order under his obedience,] without recognising the authority of any but him and those appointed by him.

In so much as it has pleased the king our sovereign lord, of his goodness and prudence, to do his subjects the signal act of summoning a general assembly of all the orders and estates of the kingdom, to hear the complaints and grievances of his subjects and undertake a good and holy reformation of the abuses and disorders which have long continued in this kingdom; and hoping God will give us some good resolution for them, we promise and swear to employ our lives and goods for the entire implementation of the resolutions of the Estates, [notably in what concerns the maintenance of our Catholic religion, the preservation of the King's greatness and authority, the good and quiet of our fatherland, all, however, without prejudice to our age-old liberties and franchises, in which we expect to be for ever fully maintained and preserved].

[*Undertaking to provide troops.*]

[Without it being permitted to gentlemen to take a post under other cornets than those of the chief or of the bailliages in which they are resident, except with the permission of the King or his lieutenant or the chief of the association, who is M. de Humières, to whom we promise all honour and obedience, to whose council six of the principal gentlemen of the province and others of quality and fidelity will be summoned to provide, with their advice, for the implementation of the above, the expense, upkeep and other costs necessary for it, so far as the country can bear and supply.]

[*Offer to raise four cornets of horse and eleven ensigns of foot for Picardy, the nobility not to contribute financially as it will serve in person.*]

If any of the Catholics of the province, having been required to enter the present association, show reluctance or delay, and considering this is for the honour of God, the King's service, the good and quiet of the fatherland, he will be reputed the enemy of the whole country, enemy of God, deserter of his religion, rebel against the King, traitor to and betrayer of his fatherland and, by the general agreement and consent of all upright men shunned by all and exposed to all injuries and oppressions that may happen to him, without ever again being received in society, friendship or alliance with the said associates and confederates who have promised friendship and understanding among themselves for the maintenance of their religion, the King's service and the preservation of the fatherland, their persons, goods and families.

[*Any disputes between them to be settled by the King's Lieutenant-General or those appointed by him. Neighbouring provinces to be helped if necessary, the clergy protected.*]

Also, since it is not our intention in any way to travail those of the new opinion who would content themselves with undertaking nothing against God's honour, the King's service and the good and quiet of his subjects, we promise to preserve them without disturbing them in their consciences or injuring their persons, provided that they in no way contravene what His Majesty will ordain after the conclusion of the Estates-General or, in any way, the Catholic religion.

In so far as this cause should be common, without distinction, to all persons who make profession of living in the Catholic faith, we the undersigned admit and receive in the present union all persons called to authority in matters of justice, corporations of towns and communities and generally all others of the third estate living as Catholics, as it is said, promising likewise to maintain, preserve and guard them from all violence and oppression in their persons and goods, each in his estate and calling.

We have promised and sworn to keep the said articles and observe them in all points without contravention and without regard to any kinship and alliance we might have for any persons, of whatever quality of religion they be, who would contravene the commands and ordonnances of the King, the good and quiet of the kingdom, likewise to keep the present association secret, without transmitting knowledge of it to anyone except those of the present association. This we swear and affirm again on our conscience and honour and on the abovesaid penalties, all under the King's authority, renouncing all other associations if any have been made before.

[Having heard the contents of the above articles, we have promised our subjects of the country of [    ] to execute what is contained in them and granted the power to raise the necessary funds. Blois, 2 December 1576.]

*[194 signatures of gentlemen and ten for the corporation of Péronne, dated 13 February 1577]*

SOURCE: BN, fr. 3323 fo. 140, *LH3*, vol. III, pp. 85–8; passages in brackets added to the final version published in Maimbourg, *Histoire de la Ligue* (1684), pp. 527–40, from the original.

---

## ESTATES-GENERAL OF BLOIS

### 15   The Protestants and their Catholic allies protest against the legitimacy of the Estates-General, December 1576

[*They praise the peace that had been brought by the Edict of Pacification.*] However, the common rumour runs throughout your kingdom, and is held for certain, that the deputies to the Estates are demanding its breaking. On this, your most humble servants and subjects, united Catholics and those of the RPR, because of the natural obligations they owe you and in the lively apprehension of the past ruin and calamities of the last 17 years that have overwhelmed this kingdom and whose ashes are all too warm, have confidently sent to Your Majesty and throw themselves at your feet to beg you most humbly to remember that the Edict is the only means to recall your subjects to complete union and concord and remove all causes of trouble and dispute between them. They ask you to command the deputies to refrain entirely from discussing it and cancel out anything that may have been said. Otherwise, since the Edict is a body whose limbs are inseparable from it, it can only happen, should it be impuned in any one respect, that the rest will be altered. In consequence the memory of past injuries would be revived and the wounds refreshed. . . . [*The Edict had been concluded on the assumption that matters of religion would be remitted to a free and general council*] and since the Estates were summoned only for the re-establishment of matters not dealt with by the Edict, as your commissions show, the Estates in the several provinces were not to discuss matters other than those for which they were summoned, nor could the Estates, when discussing such matters, call themselves such. [*They thus challenge the legitimacy of the provincial Estates and ask the King to preserve the Edict.*] The petitioners protest that the articles and remonstrances to the contrary cannot be said to have been done by the Estates but were done by purely private persons, since the united Catholics and those of the Religion were not summoned and heard but were rather excluded by intimidation and the continuation of violence and overt threats. Nor have they been restored to their homes and positions. . . . Also the articles are contrary to the views of the Estates of Orléans and Pontoise and contrary to the edicts issued in those Estates during time of peace and by the advice of the princes and officers of the crown; they are contrary to the authority of the sovereign courts, . . . to the public peace of your kingdom, to your state and crown, and likely to bring back civil war to this kingdom and multiply taxes and levies, ruin trade, bring agriculture to a stop and finally bring everything to confusion and extreme desolation. [*They offer their lives and goods for the King's support and for the maintenance of the Edict.*]

SOURCE: SP70/141 no. 961.

---

## 16   Damville's memorandum to the King, early 1577

Sire, it would be desirable for there to be only one religion among your subjects, to keep them in one opinion with good justice and without mistrust between them, but past events have made it plain that in their split there was something other than the work of men involved and that all the miseries we have suffered have stemmed from the will of God to punish our sins. It must be admitted, however late, that it is impossible to go on or to restore ourselves to our original state without the intervention of His grace and goodness, . . . there being great likelihood if we return to war either that the great towns, with the authority they have seized and knowing their power, will revolt and form republics, of which there is already sign, or that victory will go to a third party which, after we have ruined each other, will with time force us to agree, to our own loss, and will control your kingdom. . . .

[*Defence of the role of the nobility.*] . . .

Sire, the way of force we have tried for 16 years now, the great battles, with endless sieges, storming of towns and slaughters perpetrated in your kingdom on both sides have served for nothing but mutual destruction. Now your subjects find themselves in as great a conflict as ever, should they not conclude that it is with God we have to deal and not men?

Whatever Leagues or conspiracies may be made or renewed, can they bring to bear any more force or effectiveness than those used in the past? Looked at more closely, are they not the same as the forces seen in your kingdom for making war against those of the RPR at the start of the first troubles . . . the same in every province of your kingdom?

The forces of this League consist for the most part of a numerous recruited infantry, mostly inexperienced and knowing nothing of military discipline, and daily deserting because unused to the rigours of service or to leaving their homes.

[*The League army is doubtful and impossible to pay for more than two months*], neither in which time nor in twenty years would they be able to bring to heel those of the RPR in the 1,200 towns they have in their control, the least of them able to hold up an army for two or three months; also they are widely scattered in so many different provinces that, while armies might be able to lay siege to three or four at a time, those of the Religion would be able to take others in other provinces. . . .

And if, by chance, they ignore the forces of those of the Religion, they may be assured they will have to deal with closely allied princes and lords and 500,000 openly declared families of the Religion as well as another 500,000 covert, besides the Catholics associated with them to the number, if need be, of 50,000 fighting men who will fight on to the end to defend themselves, well understanding that they are not dealing with you, Sire, but that with the said League they lose their honours and lands; while, fighting on the defensive, they have the advantage that one man equals four.

[*Further likelihood that foreigners will take advantage and overcome the kingdom.*]

Sire, whatever is said to Your Majesty to the contrary, your Edict of Pacification is not at all to your disadvantage and you have gained more by it over those of the Religion than your predecessors did, for they submit their Religion to the judgment of a free, general and national Council, a thing they never did before; since this has been done, is this not the right way to reunite your subjects, not only in religion but in all other matters?

As for matters of justice, in what you have granted them you have provided as the times require. This is the greatest reassurance they could have that they would not be judged by their enemies.

[*They will accept the King's ordinances for the restoration of the State; the guarantee towns are no danger since the Protestants consider him their true prince and most are in provinces governed by Damville and Navarre, who will know how to control them.*]

[*Call for a general Council to reform the church*] and let Your Majesty effect a good and general reformation of all Estates, restoring each to its order, rank, estates and dignities, and have entire faith in each to efface jealousies, pretexts, suspicions, mistrust and ambition, rejecting all false reports and calumnies that a heap of little galants sow constantly in Your Majesty's ears to obtain grants, offices and other things far beyond their merits.

[*Bishops should be sent to preach in their dioceses, scholars and theologians sent out to correct bad doctrine, and the avarice and negligence of the clergy generally corrected. Corruption in the appointment of judges should be ended.*]

Meanwhile, to avoid a renewal of war and to begin this good work, should the assembly of the Estates-General of your kingdom want to raise problems to do with the implementation of certain matters related to your Edict of Pacification, those of your subjects who wish only the peace of your kingdom would desire that, to avoid the Edict's alteration without the consent of those of the Religion and their Catholic allies . . . it please you to deal promptly with the petitions and remonstrances of the Estates and as soon as possible send some of your councillors to those of the Religion and their Catholic allies to confer with them in a general assembly that you will authorise and which can be quickly summoned; and those you will send, Sire, can report back what they have negotiated before the dissolution of the Estates-General so that a decision can be taken with common consent. For otherwise, the Estates cannot alter the Edict in any way since it is an ancient and inviolable law issued on your faith, Sire, from which those of the League, whatever they say, cannot absolve you. . . .

Meanwhile, the assembly of the Estates-General will continue to discuss affairs of state in all matters lawful for the restoration of your kingdom to its original splendour, for the success of your affairs and the ruin of all conspirators, rebels, thieves and others who can only live by trouble and divisions.

SOURCE: BN, fr. 4047 fos. 75–6; Loutchitsky, pp. 46–56.

## 17 Montpensier's speech to the Chamber of the Clergy, 28 February 1577

[*Having outlined his negotiations with Navarre at Agen, holding out some hope of agreement, he adds:*] I think no one here will doubt my zeal and devotion to the advancement of God's honour and the support of the Roman Catholic Church. . . . Nevertheless, when I consider the ills that past wars have brought us and how much this division is leading to the ruin and desolation of this poor kingdom, how much our neighbours profit from our misfortunes and seek to foster them so as to break up our once flourishing state. . . . When, also, I think of the shortage of means Their Majesties have for waging war, through lack of experienced or devoted men or for lack of money and supplies; the forces of our enemies . . . the King's great debts and the absolute impossibility of repaying them in the event of war; the fact that the battles we have fought for 15 years have neither quelled the troubles nor brought back to our Catholic faith those who had wandered from it. . . . Futhermore, when I think of the calamities I saw the poor immersed in myself on my journey, without hope of getting out of them except by means of peace. . . . Finally, remembering the war waged by the Emperor Charles V against the potentates of Germany for the same reason as this, and that he had his chief enemies at his mercy and was still reduced to letting them have free exercise of their religion [*and also the difficulties since of king Philip in the Netherlands*]; all these considerations . . . constrain me to advise Their Majesties to make peace and soften the strict terms of the declaration on religion . . . [*and to try to bring the Protestants to a compromise on the modification of the last edict; toleration to be conceded temporarily until a general council or another meeting of the Estates can effect an agreement and we can have one religion again. Calls on the clergy to join in pressing the King for this. They refuse.*]

SOURCE: Lalourcé and Duval, vol. II, pp. 210–13.

## 18   Meeting of an expanded royal Council, 1 March 1577

[*In the course of this meeting the cahiers of the Estates were discussed.*]

[*On the article that the King will seek by all the best means to bring his subjects to one religion with the peace of his realm, Marshals de Cossé and Biron held to their opinion, arguing from what the Emperor Charles V had done concerning the Interim and that for 25 years now the King had been unable to establish religion as he desired by force of arms. . . .*]

M. de Montpensier said he was a Catholic and he was minded to die in that religion but that he advised making peace because there was no money and no men; that it was expedient to satisfy the Huguenots somehow, as there were no means to do otherwise. . . .

[*The duke of Nevers argued that the King should hold to his initial determination on war.*] 'If the Huguenots cannot be satisfied, you will be forced to carry out your resolution by force of arms, using the resources God has given you. If you are now seen to change your mind, what will all Christendom say? . . . I am thus of the opinion you should hold firm to your initial decision. . . .'

The Queen Mother, having listened to me quite impatiently, opposed my opinion and said the execution of what had been decided must be delayed until she saw more certainty for the King's power in the matter. [*She said she was a good Catholic and had advised the King to maintain only one religion in the kingdom, but*] there are few resources for making war and scarcely enough to live; that the prince of Condé would take the towns and hold the countryside and, until now, no means had been found of resisting him; that, for her part, she had no wish to see the state put at risk. . . .

Then the King spoke: 'Gentlemen, you have all seen how I have striven to embrace everything that was for the honour of God and how much I have desired to have only one religion in my kingdom. In view of this, it has to be said I even canvassed the deputies of the three estates, who had to be pushed, to demand religious uniformity, in the belief that they would help me carry out this holy resolution. But, seeing what little money they have given me, I now understand what little hope there is of executing my initial intentions, which I want everyone to understand had been such. However, as M. de Nevers said, opinions can be changed when necessary. I do not consider myself to have failed if, for the present, I do not declare for permitting only one religion in my kingdom, because I do not have the means to do so. I want my intentions known so that, outside this Council, I am not slandered and libelled. As for me, I am more devoted to my religion than anyone. There are those who, to be called pillars of the church, say what first comes into their mouths. I want this article, therefore, to be shelved.'

The Queen Mother, very relieved, got up to go for a walk. She said to me, laughing, 'Well, cousin, so you wanted us all to set off for Constantinople?'

SOURCE: Nevers, vol. I, pp. 176–7, Journal of the Estates.

## 19   Jean de Monluc's analysis of the renewed conflict, 1577

The words and devices of the enemy make me fear that this war will be the most dangerous ever in this kingdom, for it is no longer a question of Catholics or Huguenots, since even the Catholics are divided and some of them linked with the Huguenots. We daily hear said that some of them have sworn union, some because they are filled with avarice or ambition, others because they are discontented with their lot and think that by changing their master they can improve it. But most revolt because of the hope of peace which is held out to them. It seems plausible when they are told: this is not against the King or his crown but against those who have infringed the Edict of Peace, with the added point that those who have called for the Edict's revocation have neither the power nor the means to bring this about and still less to offer funds. Rather they were sent to remonstrate over the people's poverty and are troublesome men who will not dip into their pockets, and have made a good bargain with the blood of the King's subjects, knowing that they will be disavowed. For them it is all one, since once the King has started the war, he will be abandoned by most of the Catholics, considering it is an inopportune and unneeded war. If the Estates had been called to hear the complaints of the poor people and deal with the reform of the abuses that war has brought, that should have been the priority and reforming religion could come last. But the King's Council has shown that they only wanted to return to war, not being satisfied with so much blood spilt and lands ruined. As for [the Protestants], they have taken arms to defend themselves, having heard that the Estates were discussing only war and removing from them the liberty of their Religion, for which they have been fighting for sixteen years. Though they have been defeated several times, they have still not given up the pursuit of their Religion. Thus, having gained a hundred stout cities (the least of which would take a royal army to reduce), they will not give up what they have won with so much blood and the death of friends and family;

should the princes abandon their cause they still have leaders enough. They protest that the King sends against them four regiments, which have wrought such murder, pillage and rape in Auvergne and along the Loire that its memory alone will be enough to bring down the wrath of God on all those of the Catholic party. They protest too that in the areas they hold, they simply raise enough funds to support their men and for the rest the peasants are secure in their persons and goods; on the other hand, our peasants are burdened daily with new taxes and are still beaten, their lives and the chastity of their women in constant danger. The worst is that when peace comes, their followers are declared free of levies for the period of the war while ours are forced to pay their arrears. . . . Such is what I have been able to gather from their remonstrances and I have been promised them in writing; with them they win many Catholics to their party while others cast aside the mask and say that this crown is finished and it is every man for himself and for what he can get. Such people are willingly heard in Languedoc and Dauphiné. . . .

SOURCE: Early 1577; SP70/147, fo. 527; La Ferrière, *Les Valois*, p. 220 (misdated 1568); *LCM*, vol. III, appendix.

# 7 The League and the Collapse of Royal Authority, 1584–8

The death of the duke of Anjou, of chronic tuberculosis, on 10 June 1584 was a major turning point. Though the country had remained disordered, Henry III had been able to hope for an eventual pacification. The duke's death opened up the devastating problem of the royal succession, since it was generally believed, and sometimes openly stated, that the royal couple would remain childless. The house of Valois was bound to end, therefore, in the male line and the question of which branch of the house of France would succeed to the crown became entangled with the religious and political problems that already existed. By the normal rules of male primogeniture, the next in line was plainly Henry of Navarre, but his Calvinism was enough to rule him out for Catholic enthusiasts and their champions in the house of Lorraine. Henry III would have recognised his right had he been prepared to reconvert but Navarre had his own problems, being at this stage unable to risk the loss of his base of support among the Huguenot churches of the south and west. Navarre's cousin, Henri prince of Condé, was also ruled out by his solid Protestantism (he was to die in March 1588, thus simplifying Bourbon family politics). Navarre's uncle, Charles de Bourbon, now emerged as the Catholic choice for the succession but, as an elderly cardinal, Bourbon could not be expected to found a dynasty, so discussion of alternatives to his family became more serious. The Navarre cousins Conti and Soissons were Catholics but ruled out for various personal reasons and, for some, as sons of the heretical first prince of Condé. Montpensier, of another branch of the Bourbons, had some supporters but few serious backers (see Document 7). After that, the issue broadened into whether the Salic law might be set aside (thus opening the way for Philip II's daughter Isabella as the senior granddaugher of Henry II) and, beyond that, the claims, canvassed by some since the 1560s, of the house of Lorraine, represented in France by the Guises, to be senior descendants of Charlemagne.

The prospect of a Navarre succession led very rapidly in 1584–5 to the refoundation of the League movement, this time anchored in an uneasy alliance between the Catholic princes (including the duke of Lorraine) and Philip II negotiated between September 1584 and March 1585 by Philip's envoys Tassis and Moreo. First came the the Treaty of Joinville, (31 December 1584) (see

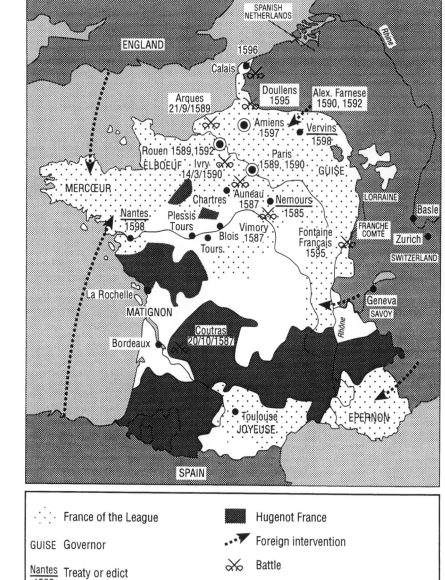

**Map 4**   The last wars, 1585–98

*Source:* Based on Michel Péronnet, *Le XVI<sup>e</sup> Siècle, 1492–1620* (Paris: Hachette, 1995), map 11

Document 2). In March 1585, the League's manifesto was issued at Péronne in the name of the old cardinal of Bourbon as a comprehensive critique of royal secular and religious policy and with the programme of excluding a heretic succession (see Document 4). Guise and allied aristocrats controlled large areas of Champagne (the duke), Burgundy (Mayenne), Brittany (Mercoeur), Normandy (Elboeuf) and Picardy (Aumale). In addition the dukes of Nemours and Nevers were sympathetic. Guise sought to draw Spain into French politics but the main objectives were to exclude Navarre, champion true religion and drive the King's mignons, Épernon and Joyeuse, from power. This was one of the reasons why the King's contradictory personality became such a major issue (see Documents 1 and 3).

Guise seized Bourges, Toul and Verdun but was resisted by Épernon's forces at Metz and by Montpensier's at Orléans. Marguerite de Valois raised Catholic forces in Agen. In the south, Navarre, Condé, Turenne and the Catholic Damville met at Castres but could not agree on what to do. The King demanded the disbandment of the League (see Document 5). As so often in the past, Catherine's diplomacy patched up an agreement in the Treaty of Nemours (see Document 8), embodied in an edict in July 1585 by which Henry III was forced to abandon his policy of pacification and revoke religious toleration (see Document 6). In September, Navarre and Condé were excommunicated by the Pope, to which they replied by a new manifesto. In fact, Henry III had no intention of fighting a war for the League and did little to prosecute it, retiring strategically into his religious devotions while small-scale campaigning during 1586 in the west and south failed to defeat the Huguenots and the war began to degenerate into brigandage. In the winter of 1585–6 there were rumours reported by the Spanish envoy Mendoza that Henry III was trying to win over Navarre by promising him the succession if he became a Catholic. Nothing conclusive was decided but a truce brought an end to the 'campaigning' between Navarre and the royal Marshal, Biron, in August 1586. Over the winter and until March 1587, Navarre negotiated fruitlessly for peace with Catherine, who tentatively agreed to his divorce from her daughter but could not break his obduracy over religion. By the summer of 1587, German mercenaries financed by the English agent Horatio Palavicino became available. This altered the military balance.

From the Treaty of Joinville in late 1584, most witnesses accept that connections later known as the 'Sixteen' in Paris were beginning to emerge (see Document 3). During 1587, the original large council of the Sixteen was transformed into a small inner command committee and established informal domination of all the organs of municipal life as well as links with Catholic partisans in other towns. By now the pamphlet war was approaching its peak and the King's reputation in Paris was being seriously undermined by vilification and satire. The King's attempts to control this were in vain (see Document 8). Early in 1587, pulpit denunciations of the heretic queen of England for the execution of Mary Stuart were accompanied by denunciations of the mignons. Louis Dorléans's *Advertissment des Catholiques anglois* violently called on the French to avoid the fate of their co-religionists in England by exterminating all heretics.

Henry III felt that he had to make his own military effort to regain control and formed armies under his two favourites, Joyeuse against Navarre, Épernon in reserve and Guise deputed to face up to the Germans under duke Casimir's deputy, von Dohna. Thus was set the stage for the aptly-named 'War of the Three Henries'. However, the King's schemes were devastated by military reality. In October 1587, Joyeuse's army was annihilated by Navarre at Coutras and the duke killed. When Guise was able to beat the Germans at Vimory and Auneau, Épernon did what he could to minimise the éclat by escorting them back to the frontier.

The impression that the King wished to minimise a Catholic victory was disastrous for his reputation in Paris, where writers like Boucher were pouring out venomous libels against Épernon and indirectly against the King. In January 1588, the League leadership met at Nancy to draw up the Eleven Articles, demanding that the King dismiss any servants they disapproved of, accept Guise command in a war against heresy and publish the decrees of the Council of Trent (see Document 9). The King, incredibly, seemed to acquiesce in what was an effective abdication of his powers, but only to gain time. Spanish money was offered to Guise at Soissons in April as part of a general plan to neutralise Henry III during the period of the Armada. The King had forbidden Guise to come to Paris, but already an effective revolution in the control of the city had taken place over the previous months, with power increasingly in the hands of the Sixteen. Henry III was indecisive at this point, even though he was warned that a rising was on foot (see Document 10); in Paris, rumours went the other way, that Henry had deputed Epernon to raise troops in Normandy to attack the city. It has been argued, perhaps too easily, that the Spanish envoy Mendoza was the prime orchestrator of these events. He was certainly *au courant* and rejoiced at the outcome but large popular movements are never likely to be entirely planned. The duke was invited to Paris and arrived on 9 May, in defiance of the King, to a hero's welcome, probably with the intention of imposing his will on the King's Council. The King was subjected to the humiliation of meeting him at the Louvre but on the 12th moved to control the city by his Swiss guards, provoking what was in part at least a reaction of popular fury. The outcome was a fiasco and all pretence of royal power in the capital collapsed in the Day of the Barricades, the King slipping quietly out of the city.

Paris now became the centre of revolutionary movement with Guise as its military chief. Several major towns joined in and Guise sought to win wider support. Henry III had few resources, was gradually worn down and had to allow his mother and Villeroy to negotiate an agreement which was virtually a capitulation. The Edict of Union was promulgated, incorporated into the Treaty of Rouen, and signed by the King (see Document 13). Epernon, already under threat in late May, was disgraced (see Document 11), the cardinal of Bourbon recognised as heir, and Guise made Lieutenant-General. Guise went to meet the King at Chartres on 3 August in a meeting that had sinister undertones (see Document 15); the duke had been advised by his counsellors to establish his control of the court through keeping the King suspended between love and fear (see Document 14).

In fact, the King was burning for revenge in secret and partly blamed his mother for his predicament (see Document 12). The Day of the Barricades also brought an end to the collaboration of moderate Catholics in the 1585 Treaty of Nemours. A new political alignment could therefore now emerge. The defeat of the Armada in August was another sign of change. In September, the King moved decisively to remodel his council and the personnel of the administration, dismissing among others Villeroy, intermediary in the treaty with Guise, in an act which aroused widespread amazed speculation (see Documents 16–17).

Part of the agreement had involved the King's promise to summon the Estates-General. The meeting was bound to be risky for the King, whose experience of the assembly in 1576 had not been happy. It may be that he intended his former ministers to be scapegoats. However, the signs were not promising when the Estates actually met at Blois on 16 October. The assembly was controlled by League supporters, with 380 deputies out of 505 and all of the presidents of the chambers. However much they were divided on specific issues, it was not possible for the King to exploit the divisions of the Estates as he had done in 1576. He tried to claim, in his eloquent opening speech, that the Edict of Union had rendered all associations treasonable without his authority, but was obliged to excise this from his printed speech (see Document 18). The King was forced to accept the declaration of the edict of Union as fundamental law. After that, as the weeks went on, he was forced to concede one demand after another. Criticisms of him were routine and he was denounced viciously from the pulpit. In his own justification, he claimed that he had been reduced to the position in which the Estates were subordinating his authority to theirs (see Document 21). At all events, the perception of a break in the ranks of the Guise family, notably the possibility that the King had been warned by Mayenne against Guise's intentions, as well as a fear that the duke was aiming at the office of Constable, may have prompted him to act on 23

December and carry out the extra-judicial execution of the duke and cardinal of Guise and the arrest of several members of their family, as well as of the cardinal of Bourbon (see Document 19). There is no doubt that the King thought he had cut the gordian knot. Catherine de Medici, who had spent the previous few years trying to negotiate her son's way out of the problem, seems to have responded to the event with resignation (she died early in the new year) (see Document 20). The Estates-General went on meeting, now cowed, until 16 January. It seemed briefly that the King had wrongfooted his enemies (see Document 22). But in Paris, things were very different. The King may have had the theoretical power to decree summary judgment but the act could not fail to be regarded as one of the most monumental tyranny. The stage was now set for the final phase of the reign. While Henry III spent time penning justifications for his actions (see Document 21), he lost the golden opportunity to crush the League while it was in shock.

---

## 1   The personality of Henry III: a pro-League account

The King is about 36 years old, though either through ill health or through anger at the difficulties of the affairs he is confronted with now, he is grey before his time and nearly white-haired, so he looks older than he actually is. I leave aside the actions in his youth. When he came of age, he attracted to him many gentlemen of different kinds and manners. Among those who were closest to him was the sr de Villequier, a great mocker, a bon viveur without scruples about religion, who has no other aim or God but the vanity of the court, a disposition that easily slips into atheism. Of him one could say the same as what one hears about Alexander the Great and Leonidas, his tutor, from whom he learned drunkenness: for he was introduced by him to the vice that nature detests, which he has never been able to unlearn. I will not write further all that I know in detail, for, beyond blushing at the mere thought of it, I would not, by such a filthy tale, offend the chaste ears of Your Highness nor sully my paper with it. I will only say that the cabinet is a veritable seraglio of every lubricity and lewdness, a school of sodomy, where there are accomplished all the filthy sports that everyone has learned of. The King, however, feels great remorse of conscience so that he has frequently detested his disordered manner of life, to the point of one day complaining to one of his intimates after having observed Easter, saying: 'all my life I have feared that, on coming to the crown, I would have some sins in me that would make my people detest me: God has punished me in this more than I had feared. But the worst misfortune happened to me by Villequier's doings. Would to God that I had never known him. It seems that, for my greater affliction, these infamous games of my youth have become a habit from which I cannot now shake myself free. But I will do my best, with the grace of His Divine Majesty, to get away from it and quit this bad life.' I heard this from one who was present and who was afterwards rebuffed because he had then wanted to exaggerate – seeing the king in this good humour – the indignity of such detestable acts. I will say no more and keep silent on this and go on with the other manners and public actions of the King.

Before he became King, while he was Monsieur, he commanded in the field auspiciously in the post given him. . . . As soon as he was anointed King, suddenly this martial humour left him and little by little he came to want to live in peace the rest of his days, with the result that now, having stagnated so long in idleness, he is believed pusilanimous and worthless. In truth, I think that when he was the king's brother and had no other means, he had to engage in war and thus his better martial side was forced out. We also know that the late King Charles almost put a dagger to his throat to force him to go to Poland. Now he hates nothing so much as war and seeks only repose and the private life. As for matters of the soul, he has the capacity to speak well and succeeds in it, and a great liveliness of mind. He has his work hours in the morning when he diligently despatches many secret affairs without communicating them to anyone, especially since these latest activities of the League, which horrify him and he hates vastly. From time to time, he takes up his devotions, to follow which he withdraws from public view. But then he will suddenly return to his vomit without for all that being able to break from his unworthy ways. Presently he takes pleasure in the hunt. He is devoted to little dogs; then he wants some from Flanders, even though he has three hundred. He does all he can in the matter of distributive justice and the settlement of requests. He handles the affairs of his state very secretly. He is a prince who can marvellously conceal his passions, feign and dissimulate. He is brave in speech but lacking in action. He threatens but without effect. He can be vindictive if difficulties in carrying out his vengeance do not stop him. He is changeable and inconstant in all his actions. His life is moderate as to food and, though he is well, he tries to avoid illness by remedies, which he often makes use of. He greatly fears the pain of gallstones, for he has been told that he is likely to be subject to it; it was that which led him to take the spring waters of Pougues. His own people, who depend most on him, judge that he cannot live long. Every day he has the sound of his death in his ears, either from his friends in letters or from his most cherished subjects in person. For everyone comes to the same point regarding the affairs of France after his death: 'If your Majesty dies, such and such a thing will happen; if you die without children, such and such'; and most often he learns that his enemies plan to kill him. In short, in all their words there is nothing but the King's death and the desolation of France after him. He still suffers from inadequate sperm flow and the problems of his ulcer which grow worse as a result of his disorders with women and other dissipations. He has a singular devotion to Saint Francis, because he hopes, through the intercession of this saint, to have issue. For this reason he often dresses in grey and of a simple and cheap cloth. He is also devoted to Saint Francis de Paule, which sometimes leads him to wear a hair shirt.

SOURCE: Lucinge, *Miroir*, pp. 104–7.

## 2　The Treaty of Joinville, January 1585

Firstly, that the said contracting French princes will declare as successor to the crown of France the said lord cardinal of Bourbon . . . as a Catholic prince, nearest to the royal blood and to whom the succession comes by right, excluding for ever all princes of the blood of France at present heretics or relapsed, from among others of that house, only those who are notorious heretics and no others, so that no one will reign who is a heretic or who, being king, would permit heresy to be publicly unpunished; the pretensions of which heretic princes they will always oppose by all means possible, including arms if need be.

[*Continuation of the Treaty of Cateau-Cambrésis between Philip II and cardinal de Bourbon should he come to the throne.*]

All practice of heresy will be banished in the kingdom of France by public edict and all other means, with no exceptions, so that no other but the Catholic religion will be permitted; nor will any town or fortress be left in the hands of heretics or sectaries; and those who do not reconcile themselves to the obedience of the Catholic religion will be pursued to the end until they are destroyed.

[*The decrees of the Council of Trent to be enforced in France; French alliances with the Turks, and piracy and intervention in the Indies will be renounced.*]

His Catholic Majesty, notwithstanding the heavy costs he finds himself burdened with for the long and continuous war he has waged in the Low Countries for the reduction of the heretics, will provide for the contracting French princes, for the period they need to maintain their armies for the restoration of the Catholic religion in France, or to oppose the designs of those Frenchmen in favour of the heretics and sectaries of the Low Countries, the sum of 50,000 *écus pistolets* per month, to be employed in war, to begin on the day arms shall be openly taken up.

But since, to ensure the success of such a holy enterprise, it is necessary to begin it with great forces, His Catholic Majesty will pay in advance the ordinary sum for the first year, amounting to 600,000 *écus*, in the first six months beginning tomorrow, 1 January of the year 1585 and this in two terms, 1 March and the last day of June following.

And so that for the following six months they do not fall short of funds to pursue their holy enterprise, he will at the end of the year 1585 advance a further 400,000 *écus pistolets* out of the funds of the second year and will see that my lord duke of Lorraine will assure and promise them that this sum of 400,000 will be paid without fail. . . .

[*To recompense him, the French princes will restore to him the town of Cateau-Cambrésis as it was before its occupation as well as all other places the heretics of the Low Countries might have placed in French hands. All aid to the rebels in the Low Countries will cease. On the cardinal's accession, the French princes will repay all they have been given and Philip II will reimburse all expenditure in his cause.*]

This holy offensive and defensive League made for the safeguard, defence and preservation of the Catholic religion, its restoration and the entire extirpation of all heresies from France and the Low Countries, will be maintained inviolably on both sides, His Catholic Majesty and his heirs remaining for ever the true friends and allies of the contracting French princes and their heirs. . . .

SOURCE: Dumont, vol. V, pp. 441–3.

## 3   Nicolas Poulain on the origins of the League at Paris, 1585–6

In 1585 . . . on 3 January at 8 a.m., I went to the house of [*Jean*] Leclerc [*procureur in the Parlement*] where there were several inhabitants of their party, with a gentleman called the sieur de Maineville who was (so they said) sent by the duke of Guise to discuss their enterprises with them. In their presence, Leclerc said to me that the Catholic religion was lost unless prompt action were taken to prevent it and that there were more than 10,000 Huguenots in the Saint-Germain suburb ready to cut the Catholics' throats and crown the King of Navarre, that there were many titled persons in the city and suburbs of his party, some Huguenots some Politiques . . . but that they had in their support some good princes and lords, including the dukes of Guise, Mayenne and Aumale and all the house of Lorraine. The Pope and all the clergy were in their favour, along with the Sorbonne, and they had the support of the King of Spain, the prince of Parma and the duke of Savoy . . . there were already many in Paris secretly sworn not to endure it. Their task was easy because they had only to break the King's forces in Paris, which were but weak, namely the 200–300 men of the guard at the Louvre, the provost of the royal household, and Hardy, provost of the Île-de-France. . . . During the period arms were being assembled, I entered more fully into knowledge of their affairs. Every day, they were suborning persons to their side in the same way: those of the Chamber of Accounts by La Chapelle Marteau; those of the Parlement by president Lemaistre; its procureurs by Leclerc and Michel, the clerks of the Court by Senaut, the ushers by Leleu; the Court of Aids by president Nully, the clerks by Choulier; the generals of the Court of the Mint by Rolland; the commissioners of the Châtelet by Bart and Louchart. . . . Bart and Michelet also suborned all the boatmen and boys on this side of the river (more than 500). Toussaint Poccart, tinsmith, and Gilbert, pork-butcher, suborned all the butchers of the city and suburbs, more than 1,500 men; Louchart, commissaire, the more than 600 horse dealers. All of them were told that the Huguenots intended to cut the throats of the Catholics. . . .

Meanwhile, the mass of lesser people, who were impatient and eager to start pillaging under this pretext, were grumbling. It was necessary to go into the districts and tell them to have patience, otherwise all would be lost, that the leaders were not ready yet, that this was an enterprise of great consequence. Despite these reasons, which they took little account of, they said they were afraid of being discovered unless the matter were hastened, that the King would hang them all (so they told me) and that he was in league with the Huguenots. So they started their own plans to get rid of the King, without talking to any prince, chief or Council other than themselves. Some said they must attack him and kill him, others that he just had to be captured and put in a monastery. One day, they were planning to surprise him in the rue Saint-Antoine, when he was coming back from Vincennes with an escort of only a couple of horsemen and four lackeys. . . . But they were told by one of the wiser sort that a King was not to be taken in that way, that it could not be done without disgruntlement and, were it to be done, the lead must be taken by some prince of note. . . .

After having thought long over this damnable and wicked enterprise (I speak now for myself) and that it was nothing but robbery; also that the princes were playing this game through the little people to deprive the King of his crown and invest those of Lorraine with it after cutting the throats of the true heirs and chief officers of the crown, the horror of it all overcame me, and, constantly thinking about the blood that would be spilt . . . I then determined to withdraw from the League and its sworn company of wickedness and to do what I could, with God's grace, to prevent such great carnage among men of honour. . . .

SOURCE: Procès-verbal by Nicolas Poulain, lieutenant of Hardy, provost of the Île-de-France, drawn up after the Barricades in 1588, *AC*, vol. XI, pp. 289–91.

## 4   Declaration of the League, Péronne, 31 March 1585

In the name of almighty God, the King of Kings: it is clear to all that, while France has been for 24 years tormented with the plague of rebellion moved to undermine the religion of our fathers (which is the strongest bond of the state), remedies have been tried which, against the expectation of Their Majesties, have nourished rather than extinguished the evil, and given peace only in name while leaving untouched those who disturbed it, much to the scandal of decent men in their morale and damage to their property.

In place of a remedy that might with time have been expected for these evils, God has allowed the previous kings to die young without heirs able to succeed to the crown, nor has it pleased Him to give any to our King, to the great regret of men of honour, who have not failed nor will fail to supplicate divine goodness in this matter. So that, remaining alone of all the children given by God to the late King Henry, it is all too much to be feared that this house will pass away, to our misfortune, extinguished and without hope of descendants, and that, in the setting up of a successor in the royal State, great troubles will result for the whole of Christendom and perhaps for the subversion of the Catholic religion, since the reign of a heretic could never be accepted, considering subjects are not bound to recognise the rule of a prince who has so many times broken with the Catholic religion and that the first oath our kings make when they are crowned is to maintain the Catholic religion, in return for which oath they receive the fidelity of their subjects and not otherwise.

[*There follows a description of the dangers since the death of the duke of Anjou.*]

A ray of hope appeared when, after frequent complaints and clamours from the entire kingdom, the Estates-General were summoned to Blois, the ancient remedy for domestic wounds and a conference between the prince and his subjects, to agree together on due obedience and due preservation, both sworn to and born to, of the royal name and the fundamental rules of the French State. But from this expensive and painful enterprise nothing resulted except through the evil counsel of some who, feigning themselves good Politiques, were in effect most ill inclined to the service of God and the good of the State. They [*the Politiques*] were not content with diverting the King (who by nature is well inclined to piety) from his holy and most useful intention, undertaken at the humble request of all his Estates, to reunite all his subjects to a sole Catholic religion, so as to make them live in the age-old piety with which the kingdom was established, preserved and since extended until it was the most powerful in Christendom, all of which could have been done without peril and almost without resistance. On the contrary, they persuaded him that it was necessary for his service to weaken the authority of the Catholic princes and lords, who with such great zeal had often risked their lives fighting under his banners for the defence of the Catholic religion, as though the reputation they had acquired by their virtue and fidelity had made them suspect instead of to be honoured. . . .

For these just causes and considerations, we, Charles de Bourbon, first prince of the blood, cardinal of the Catholic Church . . . assisted by various princes, cardinals, peers, prelates, officers of the crown, provincial governors, chief lords, gentlemen, many towns and communities and a great number of good and loyal subjects, being the better and sounder part of this kingdom, having wisely weighed the objects of this enterprise . . . declare we have all sworn and religiously promised to take arms

‑so that the Holy Church of God should be restored to its place as the true and only religion, that the nobility enjoy, as it should, its entire liberties, and that the people be alleviated, new taxes abolished, all increases since the reign of King Charles IX (whom God pardon) removed, the Parlements restored to the plenitude of their competence and sovereignty in judgment, each in their jurisdiction, and all subjects of the realm maintained in their governments, charges and offices without being deprived, except in the three established circumstances and by judgment of their ordinary judges with appeal to the Parlements. All money levied on the people should be employed for the defence of the kingdom and for the purposes raised, and henceforth, the Estates-General, free and without management, should be held frequently and as the needs of the kingdom demand, with full liberty to all to make complaints, which will be duly provided for.

[*Loyalty to the King protested.*]

And though His Majesty may justly be required, for the well-being of his subjects and to prevent factions and divisions in the future on the question of the succession should he (which God forfend) die without male children, to declare him whom the laws nominate and call to be true successor to the crown, we refrain from this, for fear that wicked men blame our actions, as though we, in our old age, were thinking of another kingdom than the one whose enjoyment is most assured, desirable and long-lasting, having no other desire than the conservation of the Catholic religion and the State and that the King may have descendants to reign happily after him.

[*Hostility intended only to those in arms against them and calls for all Catholics to reform their lives in order to appease God's anger.*]

Signed: Charles, cardinal de Bourbon.

SOURCE: AC, vol. XI, pp. 7–19.

---

## 5  Henry III's declaration calling for the disbandment of the League, April 1585

But as the iniquity of the time hath emboldened some to burden His Majesty with other faults and that corruption and malice are so replenished with boldness and impudency that many have even taken pleasure in defacing his most holy and best actions, whereby to cause his subjects to mislike of them and so to get themselves their good wills with the expense of his reputation; yea, so far as sometimes to dare interpret the most commendable zeal that he hath to cause the decrees and sentences of the said Chambers [*in the Parlement*] against evil doers to be executed, unto over great rigour and severity.

His said Majesty, had therefore begun by the means aforesaid to provide for the creating of these two pillars [*piety and justice*], the only foundations and preservation of every monarchy and had conceived some assurance wholly to set them up and restore them to their perfection through the continuation of the peace, if it had pleased God to have given His grace to make his realm and subjects worthy thereof. This also it seemeth these men which seek to move the subjects to take arms and yet under colour of providing for both the one and the other, did as soon fear and foresee.

They did also give out that they take arms to the end to withstand the troubles which they say they fear should happen after His Majesty's decease in the establishing of a royal successor to the disadvantage of the said Catholic . . . religion; being persuaded, or at least giving forth, that His said Majesty, or they that are about him, do favour the pretences of those that have showed themselves persecutors of the said religion. A matter whereat His Majesty desireth and warneth his subjects to believe that he never thought, as being, thanks to God, in the flower of his age and likewise the Queen his wife, and so hopeth that God will grant them issue to the general contentation of his good and loyal subjects; besides it seemeth to him that they seek to force both nature and time and withall do too much mistrust the favour and goodness of God, the health and life of His Majesty and the faithfulness of the said Lady Queen his wife in motioning at this time any such question, but much more in prosecuting the decision thereof by force of arms. . . .

His Majesty therefore warneth and exhorteth his subjects in this case to look about them and not to persuade themselves that this war can be finished so soon and easily as is given out; but rather to weigh and deeply consider the event and inevitable consequence thereof; and not to suffer their reputations to be stained and their weapons to seem as an instrument to the destruction of their country and to the increase of the power of the enemies thereof, who only will triumph and reap benefit by the miseries and calamities of the same. For, while we, blinded in our own benefit, shall war one upon another and be succoured in outward appearance but in effect fed on by their assistance, they should reign prosperously and establish their power.

They complain also of the division of the offices and houses of this said realm, saying that such are put from them as have better deserved of the estate and His Majesty's service. A weak foundation and of no great honour to build the ruin and salvation of so flourishing a realm whose kings were never bound to use the service of one more than another. For there is no law that bindeth him thereto except as the benefit of his service requireth. Nevertheless, His said Majesty hath of all times greatly honoured and cherished the princes of his blood as much as any of his predecessors and hath shown a will to prefer others to credit, honour and reputation by using their service; for oft as His said Majesty hath levied any power or army, he hath still, by preferring them, committed the charge and conduct of the same to them. [*Namely the authors of the present complaints.*] But say they, they have but the name and in effect are deprived of the prerogatives depending upon the said offices, which other men do usurp. Before we judge of the merit of such complainant, it were good to see and deeply look into the rights and pre-eminences of every office attributed and then to consider how and by whom they have been administered in the time of the King's predecessors. A matter which His Majesty hath often propounded, when he hath endeavoured to set order to every man's office, and had long since been determined and decided if those that have interest therein had according to their duties aided and assisted him as they ought. But shall it therefore be now said and so left to posterity that private interests and discontentations should be the cause of troubling a whole estate, and replenishing the same with blood and desolation? . . .

In consideration hereof, his said Majesty desireth and exhorteth the captains of the said risings speedily to disperse their bands, countermand the strangers and depart from all factions and, as his kinsmen and servants, to repose assured confidence in his love and good will, which in so doing he offereth to continue to them, by honouring them with his favour and making them partakers of such honours as he is accustomed to bestow upon men of their calling. . . . He also warneth all ecclesiastical persons and gentlemen his subjects well to weigh the consequence of these stirs, sincerely to embrace his intent and to believe that his mind always hath and still shall tend to do good to all and displeasure to none.

He doth therefore most straightly command them and all other his subjects to depart and withdraw themselves from all leagues and associations and to reunite themselves unto him, as nature, duty and their own wealth and health doth bind them, to the end that if these commotions do proceed any further (which he beseeched the goodness of Almighty God not to permit) he may have assistance and succour in their counsel, weapons and commodities to the preservation of the realm, whereunto is linked the Catholic. . . Church therein, their honour, reputation, persons, families and goods.

SOURCE: Goulart, *Ligue*, vol. I, pp. 63–73; *A Declaration set forth by the Frenche King . . . concerning the new troubles in his realm . . .*, trans. E. A. (London: John Wolfe, 1585).

---

## 6   Royal Edict revoking religious toleration, 15 July 1585

Firstly, in this our kingdom, land and territories of our obedience there will be no practice of the new RPR but only that of the Catholic religion. This we forbid to all our subjects of whatever quality and condition that they be, on pain of arrest and confiscation of goods, notwithstanding the permission granted by our previous

Edicts of Pacification, which we have revoked and revoke by these presents, by which we will and ordain, on the same pains, that all ministers of the said new Religion shall leave our kingdom and lands of our obedience one month after its publication by our court of Parlement. And the better to reduce the opportunities for great ills and calamities that tolerance of differences of opinion in religion has hitherto brought into our kingdom, and to restore an assured peace and tranquillity between our subjects, we have ordained and ordain, on the same pains, that all our subjects will have henceforth to live in the Catholic religion and those of the new Religion to leave it and conform to the Catholic religion and make profession of it six months after publication of these presents; and where they do not wish to do so, we will that they leave our kingdom and lands; in doing which, we have permitted and permit them nevertheless to sell or otherwise dispose of their goods, movable or immovable, as they think fit. For the same causes and considerations, we have also declared and declare by these presents that all of our subjects, of whatever quality and condition they be, attainted of heresy, shall be incapable of holding and exercising any public charges, estates, offices and dignities in our kingdom and lands; and to extinguish the memory of troubles past and the disputes between our subjects over religion, we henceforth revoke the bipartite and tripartite chambers and others established in our courts of Parlement by virtue of our Edicts of Pacification. . . .

We also will and ordain that the towns heretofore handed over to the guard of those of the said new Religion as surety, should be left by them and the garrisons depart and be put out as soon as these presents are published by our courts of Parlement in the jurisdictions they find themselves. . . .

[*forbids all private vengeance.*]

Since what has been done [*by the League*] has been for the zeal and affection they have had for the maintenance and preservation of the Catholic religion, we have declared and declare by these same presents that we hold it as agreeable, approve it and will that they remain discharged in and for all without being pursued in the future in any way. . . .

SOURCE: Goulart, *Ligue*, vol. I, pp. 178–82.

---

## 7 The succession problem, early 1586

Sir, the chief cause of my dispatch at this time is to advertise your honour of a dangerous practice of *the Queen Mother* to sow a great sedition considering *the duke of Montpensier* between him and the rest of that house. The dispatch is kept very secret and yet I have found means to have warning of it. *The Queen Mother* meaneth to send presently *the abbot of Gadaine* to him to put him in remembrance what danger *the King of Navarre* hath put himself into by taking arms against the French King, what a spectative he hath himself who, if he look well into it hath as much and more interest in *France, the cardinal of Bourbon dying*, than *the King of Navarre*; and putteth him in remembrance of a thing as I have heard long talked of [?concerning] the stirps of *Saint Louis* to them he is nearer. What effect this may work on *Montpensier*, considering his little judgment and that those men want that have ordinarily ambition without any discretion the wiser in their heads, besides that he hath men about him fitter for that humour than for anything else, by whom he is commonly governed, I leave to wiser than myself to judge; besides that his trusty servant *du Perron*, that he sendeth hither, whom I have been somewhat curious to seek after his manner of proceeding here, I find hath held two or three sundry and very dangerous kinds of speeches, the one speaking to . . . that *the King of Navarre* undid himself with being so obstinate in religion, held speech that *Montpensier* if it came to the election of the people was very like to carry it away for being *Catholic* and when it was said to him that [?*Conty and Soissons*] were Catholic and afore him, he answered they were sons to an *heretic* and therefore not that assurance to be had of them as of *Montpensier*, who had never had any kind of suspect, besides some nearer interest; having these speeches together and the *Queen Mother's* dispatch to *Montpensier* maketh me to fear that *Perron* may be here corrupted and that he may be made an instrument to put bees in *Montpensier's* head, adding another thing to it that, speaking to one of *Navarre's* folks, who speaking of these matters cast out a word that *the King of Navarre* might perchance be brought, if he had some fair colour, to alter, he told him that, if *the King of Navarre* did it he ruined his affairs and reputation for ever. Which contrary speeches well marked make me very suspicious. I have given . . . warning to look well to him and to prevent it with *Montpensier*, who indeed he is governed by more than any and by *the count of Soissons*, but he is not now in the town, gone under colour of making merry this caresme prenant with *Madame Lonbevye* to have further conference of some of his *party*, whereas I have also dealt with some others that have interest both in the cause and *Montpensier* to look to it. Truly, Sir, in mine opinion the best way is to engage him all that can be presently, for when he is once in he cannot get out again.

SOURCE: Stafford to Walsingham, 10 February 1586, BL, Harl. 288, fo. 159, passages in cipher in italics.

# HENRY III AND THE PARISIAN LEAGUE

## 8    Henry III's reply to the preacher Jean Boucher at the Louvre, 5 June 1587

[*Boucher had incurred the King's indignation by criticising a book that urged compromise in the course of a Pentecost sermon. Henry III summoned him to his cabinet and listened to a long and boring rant:*] Doctor Boucher having finished, the King, as a prince who spoke well and fluently, spoke at no less length. . . . For the first point, he took up what Boucher had said about His Majesty's honour and the zeal he had always shown for the Catholic religion, referring to what he had done during the reign of the late King Charles IX in the wars from 1567. He referred to his decision, after his accession, to allow the exercise of only the Catholic religion; that his first action after his return to Lyon from Poland had been to decide on war against the Huguenots; that he had founded and authorised the League for religion at the Estates of 1576; that he had signed it (and complained of being ill served by it); that it would be wrong to accuse him of favouring the Huguenots . . . adding that his extraordinary devotions justified the contrary; that he would not have such views spread among the people and would hold those who did so responsible; that he would be content to have all his actions, not only public but private at night and in the secrecy of his cabinet, observed; that his recent decision to make war on the Huguenots should stand as witness to his intentions over religion; that he had the honour to be the Most Christian King and would take care not to sully the title his predecessors had acquired.

But he could not approve (this was his second point) the enterprises of those who seemed to encroach on the inheritance that was his by right of succession, which was the crown of France, nor speeches against him. . . .

For his last point, His Majesty insisted on his complaint that preachers were meddling in matters that did not concern them, which was to speak of matters of state. He would not endure it, adding in justification: 'that, if those who have been brought up to it could not easily take up where they leave off after two or three days' absence, how will it be with those who speak of things they have never understood and in which they have never been employed? It is not their calling. He would resent and could never tolerate it.'

SOURCE: Valois, pp. 151–71.

---

## 9    The Eleven Articles of Nancy, January 1588

1   The King will be called on to adhere more openly and with a will to the League. And to remove from his entourage and from important offices those who will be named to him.

2   To have the Council of Trent published in all his lands, except with a pause in

its execution for a certain time, in matters concerning the revocation of the exemptions of some chapters, abbeys and other churches from episcopal authority, as will be advised.

3 To establish the Holy Inquisition, at least in the walled towns, which is the best way to defeat the heretics and suspects, provided the Inquisitors are outsiders, or at least not natives of those places, with relatives and friends there.

4 To accord to the clergy the power to repurchase in perpetuity the alienated property of their churches or those hereafter so alienated, whatever the quality of the said goods or those who have purchased them; nevertheless, to constrain the beneficed to repurchase quickly (within a certain stated time) what has been or will be sold from their benefices, according to their available means, by those who will be appointed to investigate their revenues.

5 He will be asked to place in the hands of certain chiefs some strongholds of importance which will be named to him, where they will be able to make fortresses and establish garrisons, as they decide, at the expense of the towns and the countryside, as also in those they already hold.

6 To pay the wages of the soldiers that must be kept in Lorraine and nearby to prevent an invasion by foreign troops. And to this end, to continue the war already begun, to sell as soon as possible and without more ado, all the goods of the heretics and those allied with them.

7 Furthermore, that those who have been heretics, or reputed such since the year 1560, of whatever quality or condition they be, be assessed at a third or at least a quarter of their property while the war lasts.

8 And the Catholics at one-tenth of their revenue per annum only, to be repaid afterwards, according to the receipt and expenditure made. And that commissioners be appointed to make the sales and assessments, both of clergy and lay people and of officers of the sovereign courts, and that promplty and with the least cost.

9 That the relatives of heretics or their allies will be forced by all means to buy their property, remitting the fifth part of the just price. Where it is sold to others, if they refuse, they will have no right to plead lineage right or other claim.

10 That the first money to be raised in this way will be employed in paying the most pressing debts that the chiefs have hitherto incurred. The rest will be then placed in the hands of those appointed and is not to be used for anything else.

11 That mercy will not be shown any enemy prisoner unless he gives assurance of living as a Catholic and paying the value of his property in cash, if it has not already been sold; if it has, renouncing all right he can claim and agreeing to serve for three years and more wherever it is deemed necessary, without pay.

Source: Goulart, *Ligue*, vol. II, pp. 269–79.

## 10    The Barricades, 9–12 May 1588, and its aftermath: the King's account

My cousin, I was in Paris . . . when my cousin the duke of Guise arrived, to my dismay, on the 9th of this month. His coming in this way so added to suspicions that I was in great anxiety, because I had been informed beforehand from many quarters that he was going to come and was awaited by certain inhabitants of the town suspected of causing mistrust. I had told him beforehand because of this that I did not wish him to come. . . . However, considering he had come with only 14 or 15 gentlemen, I did not wish to avoid seeing him. . . . While I did nothing for two or three days, my city filled hourly with gentlemen and other strangers who rallied to the suite of the duke, and the searches I had ordered the magistrates to carry out were done only half-heartedly, for the fear they were in, and also the hearts and minds of some of the people were everyday getting more bitter. Added to which, I received warnings every day that some great trouble was being hatched in the town. So I decided to order stricter searches through the districts to learn for certain the state of the town and expel the strangers who had no business there. To do this, I decided to reinforce in four or five places certain bourgeois guards companies with Swiss companies and those of my guards regiments who were billetted in the suburbs [*and gave warning to Guise and others to avoid alarm*]. However, matters were exacerbated by the inducement of some people, who went about spreading and imprinting in the hearts of the inhabitants that I had brought in these forces to establish foreign garrisons in the town and do even worse. So, they were so worked up against them that, if I had not expressly ordered their commanders to do nothing against the people and to endure all the disasters in the world rather than that, I believe for certain that it would have been impossible to avoid a general sack with great loss of life. So, I decided not to continue with the searches and to withdraw the forces I had sent in, on this occasion only. It is clear that, had I intended otherwise, I would have tried it and probably carried it out before the uprising of the inhabitants and before they had raised the chains and built the barricades in the streets. They started to do this soon after mid-day, egged on by certain gentlemen, captains and strangers sent by the duke of Guise. [*Next day the King sent troops out of the town to calm the situation and countermanded the regiment of Picardy, then a few leagues off.*] However, instead of the result I expected . . . they continued to raise their barricades and reinforce their guards day and night and bring them closer to my castle of the Louvre, almost up to the watch-posts of my ordinary guards. They even seized the Town Hall and the keys to the Saint-Antoine gate and others. Things had reached such a point on the 13th that it seemed beyond anyone's ability to control a more violent uprising, even against my castle. So, not wishing to use my forces against the inhabitants . . . I decided to leave that day and rather get away from a place I so loved, as I still do, than see them at greater risk . . . having prayed my mother the Queen to stay to see whether by prudence and authority she might quieten the tumult . . . and I came to this town of Chartres. . . . [*He is to make this known to those in his government of Guyenne*] what great confidence they should have in me, their true King and prince, both for what concerns the advancement of God's honour against the heretics as well as for their own well-being and preservation. . . .

SOURCE: Henry III to Matignon, 17 May 1588, Callières, pp. 231–3.

## 11   The disgrace of Épernon

Sire, I had a great struggle in my soul and great trouble in my decision, having received Your Majesty's command not to approach you. . . . I beg Your Majesty very humbly to pardon me this disobedience in consideration that I committed it out of fear of having disobeyed you, as is shown by a devotion to your service which is greater than that of all other men. I see well, Sire, that I am the target at which all the envy and calumny of France are going to shoot the sharpest arrows and shots of their harshness. I must prepare myself to face my enemies . . . and hope that God will give me the grace not only to repulse them but also to diminish them in the sole light of your favour. . . . For I do not rate as transient the friendship with which Your Majesty, with such affection, has honoured me for so long, that you have maintained without interval with such a will, and sustained such attacks that I do not fear a new one will annihilate it . . . that the reply you made to one of those close to you who said you made me too great: 'I would not, to make him so great', replied Your Majesty, 'that it be not in my power to defend him when envy attacks him.' These are the words with which Your Majesty rejected the violence of those who envy me, words truly worthy of the greatest, most magnanimous monarch in the world and that I have engraved in my soul with an immortal desire to make myself worthy of them. You have raised me from the dust to the highest honour of your state and from the unworthy younger son that I was you made me a great duke. I am of Your Majesty's making; you will not let your work remain unfinished, and having raised me to the heaven of your greatness, you will not have given me wings of wax so poor as to melt in the violent storm and rage of my enemies and allow me to fall in the impetuous flood of their desires. On the contrary, may you protect me and take pleasure in seeing the power you have given me repulse the designs of your enemies, if Your Majesty wishes the repose of your people.

SOURCE: Épernon to Henry III, July 1588, copies, SP78/18 no. 188; BL, Cotton, Caligula, E XII, fos. 129–32.

## 12   The King and his mother, July 1588

The Queen Mother, what show soever she maketh, is marvellously jealous of the

King and feareth this peace, that I can upon my credit assure you, and that being apart the Queen Mother doth nothing but sigh and weep and the duke of Guise himself is in the like taking and marvellously feareth the King will serve him some evil part and so do all his followers and I hope I dare warrant you he shall not be deceived. I hope we shall see some great handiwork of God.

SOURCE: Stafford to Walsingham, 6 July 1588, BL, Harl. 288, fo. 214.

---

It is a strange thing but upon my credit I assure it to be very certain that the League was never so hated as it is of everybody in the court openly and the King himself never spake so well of the duke of Guise as he doth. When that La Châtre and the bishop of Lyons were at Rouen, the King asked his privatest friends if he had not made them good cheer enough, but I can assure you it was so much that they came home afraid and are yet; and yet they be gone with Guise but with an evil will. The King is not in perfect love with the Queen Mother nor never was since his going away, even though he serve his turn of her in these things. And the Queen Mother at her last being at Mantes hath found it and I know is marvellously perplexed at it. One thing did shrewdly trouble her: that the King, when she, thinking to govern him, told the King that it were good for him to send his companies now to pass over the Loire, he answered that he meant so but that, when that were done, if they did enterprise here to take his towns and perchance his own person, how he should then do that it were good to find a way to assure that first. Whereat the Queen Mother remained greatly amazed without answering. One of the principalest of my friends and near about him was with me the last day that told me that the King has a hard conceipt of her and with all that he thought we should see some great matter the King had in his head but that he would discover to nobody but himself. And withall told me that, if Épernon had not been so much hated and that they fear his tyranny, for that was the word he used to me, the duke of Guise had now been rotten, for that never was the duke hated about the King as he was. I hope ere long you shall hear some great matter.

SOURCE: Stafford, 20 July 1588, BL, Harl. 288, fo. 222.

---

## 13    The Royal Edict of Union, Rouen, July 1588

1  Firstly, we swear and renew the oath we made at our coronation to live and die in the Catholic religion, to promote its advance and preservation, to employ in all good faith all the forces at our disposal, without sparing our own life, to extirpate from our kingdom, lands and territories in our obedience all schisms and heresies condemned by the holy Councils and chiefly by that of Trent, without ever making peace or truce with the heretics or any edict in their favour.

2 We will and ordain that all our subjects, princes, lords, clerical, noble, townsmen, country people and others of whatever sort and condition they be, should unite and join with us in this cause and take a similar oath to use all their powers with us, including their own lives, for the extermination of those heretics.

3 We swear and also promise not to favour or advance them in our lifetime; we ordain and will that all our subjects thus united swear and promise henceforth and for ever, should it please God to call us to him without giving us children, not to accept as king or swear obedience to any prince who was a heretic or abettor of heresy.

4 We declare and promise only ever to promote to military charges in our kingdom Catholics and persons who make public profession of the Catholic religion: and we forbid most expressly that any should be received in any office of judicature and finance in this our kingdom before his Catholic faith be attested by the bishop or his vicars, or at least the curés and their vicars accompanied by the deposition of ten witnesses who would be persons thus qualified and not suspect. And we will that this ordinance should be inviolably observed by all our officials to whom such receptions of officers may be addressed on pain of deprivation of their positions.

5 We swear and promise also to all our subjects thus united and conjoined with us, following the order to them made by us, to preserve and treat them as a good king should his good and loyal subjects, to defend and protect with all our power all those who have followed and served us and have risked their lives and goods at our command against the said heretics and their adherents; similarly, others who before now have joined in association together against them, whom we have at this time united with us, and promise to defend both of these against all violence and oppression that the heretics, their abettors and adherents would wish to use against them for having opposed their plans as they have done.

6 We also will that all our subjects thus united should promise and swear to defend each other against the violence of the heretics and their adherents.

7 Similarly, all our subjects will swear to live and die in the fidelity they owe us, and fully risk their lives and goods for preservation of us, of our authority and that of the children that it may please God to give us, against all with no exceptions.

8 Our subjects, of whatever dignity, quality or condition they be, will also swear to leave all unions, practices, understandings, leagues and associations, both within and without this our kingdom, contrary to the present union and to our person and royal authority and similarly to that of the children that it may please God to give us, on pain, under our laws, to be held as breakers of their oaths.

9 We declare rebels and disobedient to our commands and criminals guilty of treason those who refuse to sign the present union or who, after having signed it, may depart from or contravene the oath they have made to God and to us; and the towns who disobey the present ordinance will be deprived of all privileges, acts of grace and *octrois* granted to them by us and the kings our predecessors; and should they have sovereign courts or established seats of officers in judicature or finance, they will be transferred to obedient towns, as shall be by us considered for the good and comfort of our subjects.

10 And to render the present union permanent and lasting, since we intend for ever to bury the memory of past troubles and divisions among our Catholic subjects and snuff out all the sparks which could rekindle the fire, we have, to promote peace and the advance of the Catholic religion said and declared, say and declare by these presents signed by our hand, that there will be no enquiry concerning understandings, associations and other things that our said Catholic subjects may have done together, both within and without our kingdom, considering that they have given us to understand and informed us that what they have done has only been for the zeal they bore to the preservation and maintenance of the Catholic religion. All which matters will remain extinguished, asleep, and as if they had never happened, as in fact we extinguish, allay and declare them so by these presents and similarly all that happened on 12 and 13 May last and since in consequence, until the publication of these presents by our court of the Parlement of Paris, both in our town of Paris and in other towns and places of our kingdom, as also all acts of hostility that might have been committed, seizures of our moneys in our general or local receipts or elsewhere, victuals, artillery, munitions, bearing arms, levy of men and generally all other things done and carried out in that period and have since followed because of these troubles, without our said subjects being pursued, disturbed or sought directly or indirectly in any way it might be. All which matters we have once more made to slumber and declared not to have happened, excepting none, without need to specify them further: adding that our receivers, general and local, farmers and other accounting officers, will remain entirely discharged of the moneys in their receipts and farms which have been stayed and taken for the abovesaid causes since 12 May, once they return the mandates, orders and receipts which have been drawn up for their discharge; without those who may have taken the said moneys being held in any way accountable to us and whom we have in doing this discharged and discharge by these presents, of which a list is presently given to serve as check for those who claim the said discharges.

Thus we give order etc.    Registered 21 July.

SOURCE: Isambert, vol. XIV, no. 320; Griffiths, pp. 166–9.

# THE 'RECONCILIATION' OF THE KING AND GUISE

## 14  Espinac's advice to Guise on his return to court, July 1588

You must first move back to court, where you will find it easy to place and install your servants as you think fit and order business to the good of this state and your establishment.

To be well placed at court, three things are necessary: the King's favour, a command and the third, which stems from those two, that is to say, that all the other courtiers should depend on the affection you bear them or on their fear of your authority and greatness. By courtiers, I mean those whom the King favours extraordinarily or are those appointed to estates and charges necessary in the government of this state.

The King's favour will be continued towards you and even grow day by day if you are able to maintain him between a state of love and fear, that is, if he always remains convinced as he is now that you have such power in his state that he has no power to rid himself of you and also that by your words and actions you let him know that you are far from wishing to abuse your power and that, on the contary, you would employ it all in his service.

You will keep the King in his view that you are invincible if you maintain well those of your party and do not allow them to become fickle, like men and like Frenchmen too, and if you restrain them all by the ties that hold back the most savage and discontented men, that is, by the liberality and benefits they will receive at your hands. Spare nothing, then, at this start, either in credit, means, favour, posts, estates, in short everything you could to gratify your own and those you would win over, so as not to fail in this matter, in this place and time when many men strive by all means and artifices to acquire and assure themselves of servants.

The King will be more and more convinced that you do not wish to abuse your power if you frequently tell him that such is your intention and you repeat it often, and if he sees actions follow from words. For this, you must keep an eye on what is happening throughout the provinces and make clear to all my lords your relatives, of your party, that, whatever their plans are, they do nothing that would prevent you from taking root at court, where you must strengthen yourself so you can then help yourself and their affairs.

As for the post you shall have, it would be best to get the most ample power you can obtain for it and the sooner the better. The good will of the secretary who will make out this power will serve you well, for one or two things added to it are very important, both for the execution of the said power and for your reputation, as it will be viewed by the Parlements and published everywhere. If it is not Villeroy who has the charge of drawing it up, he should know, both to serve in this matter and to remain in your favour, that the Treaty of Peace he lately negotiated has provoked against him such envy on one side and such hatred on the other that, since by his work you have been able to return to court, he must do even more and be the cause of your remaining there with dignity. He should consider that the peace that has driven out Épernon, which he so desired, will be maintained for as long as you remain at court and no longer, and he so much more praised for what he has done and the more assured for your being there; and if the power has already been sealed, the declarations and additions above mentioned will not be omitted.

The same reasons that will serve for Villeroy will serve all the more with regard to the Queen Mother and the King himself, in so far as he desires peace, provided that those reasons are said, well expressed and repeated. Sometimes, this office will be better done by your followers than by you in person.

But the most singular fruit you will receive from this position will stem from yourself, such is the King, so is his state, and as a man is established in dignity, so is also the dignity he obtains. So, whatever powers you are given, do not measure them by the contents of the letters but enlarge them to the furthest extent of your power and favour. . . .

This is why you should pursue underhand, by the powers the King will give you now, the office of Constable, even though you are given another title for the moment. . . .

Having the estate and favour you do, or at least its appearance, it only remains that the whole court should depend on you. . . .

SOURCE: Villeroy (1622), vol. II, pp. 166–74; partial version in Loutchitsky, pp. 225–7, after BN, Colbert, 30, fo. 177.

## 15   The meeting of Henry III and Guise at Chartres, 2 August 1588

The duke of Guise, with a large suite, had come to meet the King at Chartres. His Majesty, speaking to the duke at dinner, proposed a toast, then, laughing, asked to whom they should drink. 'To whom you please, Sire,' replied the duke, 'it is for Your Majesty to propose.' 'My cousin, said the King, let us drink to our good friends the Huguenots.' 'Well said, Sire,' replied Monsieur de Guise – 'and to our good barricaders of Paris,' the King quickly went on to add, 'let's drink to them and not forget them!' At which the duke of Guise started to smile (but with a smile that scarcely passed his throat) then retired soon after very thoughtful and angry, ill-content at this new link the King wanted to make between the Huguenots and the barricaders.

Source: L'Estoile, p. 569.

## 16   The dismissal of the ministers, September 1588 (i)

Strange news was brought that a great sudden change was at the court, that the Chancellor, Villeroy, Brulart, Pinart, Bellièvre, Chenailles, his first physician's brother, Le Roy treasurer of Épargne were all *chassés* and that one Montholon, an advocate which is counted the honestest and consciencest man in France is sent for to take the seals, that one Revol that was commis to Monsieur de Sauve and since Monsieur d'Épernon's factotum, a very sufficient man, is secretary. They give out at Paris that they be *chassés* because the King hath found them halt and to look upon other favours than his, but for my part I dare not think it to be so but that they be men that have managed the state and that they give up their offices at this time that they may become private men at the Estates to answer to any that shall demand account of them; and that it is the King's meaning to make them in that predicament first to bring others into that he meaneth to make to give an account to. This is a thing I have heard to be in the King's mind a great while and which carrieth likelihood.

SOURCE: Stafford to Walsingham, 1/11 September 1588, SP 78/18, fo. 326.

## 17 The dismissal of the ministers, September 1588 (ii)

Some said that the King had been persuaded that I had too much power and influence in my office; others that he had taken against his secretaries opening his post other than in his presence or that they should write to the provincial governors and ambassadors and his other servants as well as receive despatches from them about his business; others that His Majesty had discovered that some of my men . . . were passing on information about His Majesty's affairs to the League and even that I had some understanding with them. . . . Some taxed me with the powers drawn up for M. de Guise and the negotiation of peace with him, even that the Queen Mother had become jealous of me because of this. Those thinking themselves perceptive said that the King had also thrust his old ministers and servants from him for their excessive closeness to the Queen Mother.

SOURCE: Villeroy, M&P, p. 130.

## THE ESTATES-GENERAL OF BLOIS

## 18 The King's speech from the throne at the Estates-General, 16 October 1588

. . . Lend favour to my upright motives, which are only to cause the glory of God and of our holy Catholic faith to shine forth more brightly, to extirpate heresy from the provinces of this kingdom, to re-establish good order, to relieve the poor people who are so greatly oppressed, and to raise up my own authority, which is now so unjustly abased. . . .

This assembly of the Estates is a remedy for curing, with the good counsel of the subjects and the holy resolve of the prince, the maladies that time and the negligent observation of the ordinances of the kingdom have allowed to take root, and to reaffirm the legitimate authority of the sovereign, rather than to unsettle or diminish it, as some ill-advised persons or those full of ill will would make believe. . . .

It is most necessary to regulate evocations, letters of grace, remissions and abolitions and that justice be speedier and less expensive for the people, and that crimes be exactly punished.

You will not forget either the enrichment of the arts and sciences, the embellishment of the towns of my kingdom, the regulation of commerce on both sea and land, the retrenchment of luxury and unnecessaries and the limitation of high prices.

The renewal of the old ordinances concerning the authority and dignity of the sovereign prince and the reverence due to him and his magistrates will be embraced by you, as reason wills.

The just fear you have of falling, after my death, under the domination of a heretic king, should it happen that God leaves us in such misfortune that I have no descendants, is no more deeply in your hearts than in mine; that is why I first made my holy Edict of Union, to abolish this damnable heresy, which I have earlier sworn most piously and solemnly . . . to hold irrevocable by good and holy oaths. I am of the view that, to make it more stable, we should make it one of the fundamental laws of the kingdom, and that this coming Tuesday, in this same place and assembly of all my Estates, we all swear it so that none can ever pretend cause of ignorance. . . .

By my Edict of Holy Union, no other leagues are to be tolerated under my authority and even when it is not clearly enough stated, neither God nor duty permit it and they are formally contrary to it; for all leagues, associations, practices, intrigues, plots, levies of men and money and reception of it are acts for the King, and in all well-ordered monarchies, crimes of treason when lacking the sovereign's permission.

Some grandees of my kingdom have made such leagues and associations, but, with my accustomed goodness, I wish to put the past behind me; but since I am obliged, as you are, to preserve the royal dignity, I declare that from now on, after the promulgation of the laws that I shall have decided in my Estates, those of my subjects who do not leave them or who get involved in them without my consent will be tainted and convicted of the crime of treason.

Source: Mayer, vol. XV, pp. 350–1.

---

## 19   Stafford's report of the execution of the duke of Guise, 25 December 1588

On Friday morning between 8 and 9 of the clock, the duke of Guise being at counsel with the rest in the Council chamber, was sent for to come to speak with the King in the cabinet, between which and the said Council chamber there was an ante-chamber where he was slain by 8 of the quarante-cinq, who were there appointed for the same purpose, who executed their charge so promptly he was entered into the said ante-chamber he never spake word until he was dead.

The King, being assured that he was dead and having seen him on the ground, he went to his mother and told her: Madame, I am now come to tell you that I am King without companion and that the duke of Guise, the enemy of all my proceedings, is dispatched. Whereunto, she answered that he had given a great blow, so all the rest might succeed accordingly.

The same day and time, the cardinal his brother was taken prisoner by Monsieur Larchant captain of the guard; the cardinal of Bourbon commanded to his chamber and certain guards appointed for him; Madame de Nemours in like manner and so the duke of Nemours.

SOURCE: News from Sir Edward Stafford, 25 December 1589, BL, Cotton, Caligula D III, fo. 321.

---

## 20   The King's words to his mother

'Good morning, Madame, please excuse me. M. de Guise is dead and will no more be mentioned. I have had him killed, only anticipating the same plan he had formed against me. I could no longer tolerate his insolence. I had tried hard to bear it so as not to stain my hands with his blood; I had forgotten the injury to me on Friday 13 May, the day he forced me to flee Paris; I had even forgotten that he had wanted to take my life, my honour and my power. But knowing, and with proof, that he was again undermining my authority, my life and my state, I resolved on this execution, which I have long turned over in my mind, wondering whether I should do it or not. However, seeing that my patience brought me into dishonour and shame and that his offences and perfidies redoubled daily, I was at last inspired and helped by God, to whom I am now going to give thanks in the church at Mass. To those of the League who talk to me of what has happened, I will do the same as to M. de Guise. I wish to help my people and hold the Estates but I wish that the latter speak as subjects, not as sovereigns. I wish no ill to the family and house of M. de Guise; I will aid and favour the dukes of Lorraine, Nemours and Elboeuf and Mme. de Nemours, whom I know to be faithful to me. But I intend now to be King and no longer captive and slave, as I have been since 13 May until this moment, when I start again to be King and master. I have placed the prince of Joinville and the dukes of Nemours, Elboeuf and Mme de Nemours under guard, not to harm them but for their own security. I have done the same for the cardinal of Guise and the archbishop of Lyon, and the cardinal of Bourbon, my uncle. I wish no ill to the latter but I will put him somewhere he cannot harm me. I will pursue the war against the Huguenots with ardour, for I wish to extirpate heresy from my kingdom.'

Without weakening and with the same firm tone, the King left, seeming untroubled either in his face or in his mind. To me, who was present, this seemed truly remarkable. And I fell to thinking how sweet must be vengeance, so to revive the spirits and clear the face.

SOURCE: F. Cavriana to sec. of Grand Duke of Tuscany, 24 December 1588, Desjardins, vol. IV, pp. 842–3.

## 21   Henry III's justification for his liquidation of the Guises

The duke had reduced His Majesty and his affairs to such a state that he no longer had the power to punish rebellion or any other crime. Most of the towns were seduced and withdrawn from him, the rest divided by constant plots. Those who held firm in their loyalty and devotion were mistreated and persecuted, denounced from the pulpit as heretics or worse than heretics. So that the worst thing you could be was the King's servant, and the rest, whatever vices they might be stained by, were held in good repute. His Majesty's rights were denied in various matters, his officers prevented from exploiting them, his authority was vilified, his person in such disdain that everyone thought he was finished; His Majesty realised that those who wronged him within his kingdom were doing the same by stratagems among foreigners: so that there remained nothing more for the last act of this tragedy but to seize his person so they could better order things at their pleasure. . . .

But this was not just a matter of suspicions; various warnings were given him from several sources. He knew that arms and a number of men had been brought from Paris into this town and its environs. The deputies of Paris declared that after the Estates he would go to Paris, which they could not have learned from him; this must have been part of their plan. For the greater elucidation of the latter, it should here be noted that more than six weeks before the death of the duke of Guise, the duchess of Aumale, having warned him that she had something of importance to tell him, told his Majesty in the Queen's chamber that her husband the duke of Aumale had written that he had been at a council in Paris where it had been decided to arrest His Majesty, bring him to Paris and seize his authority and that, to do this, 3,000–4,000 men would be brought to Blois so that they would have the upper hand in case of resistance. Her husband, unable to approve this, told her to warn His Majesty about it. . . .

. . .Furthermore, three or four days before the death of the duke and cardinal of Guise, the lord Alfonse d'Ornano came to him in haste with credence from Monsieur de Mayenne that he should be on his guard because there was a plot against him, of which the execution was so close that he told the said lord Alfonse when he left that he knew not if he would arrive in time before the blow was struck

. . . in which may be seen the great goodness and power of God to preserve those in his protection, as he has always held His Majesty, to have touched the hearts of the nearest relatives of the duke and cardinal of Guise. . . .

What is more, it was sometimes reported to His Majesty that the cardinal had often said, and this recently, to his intimates that he did not want to die before holding the head of His Majesty in order to shave it and make him monk. Added to which, the dowager duchess of Montpensier, in her violent way, had not refrained from saying that she carried the scissors with which His Majesty would be tonsured.

By all the abovesaid things and other likelihoods that were so great as to be obvious, everyone thought His Majesty could not escape, the evil had come to such extremes that he no longer had the means to save his life or his state other than by ending the life of those who had built their greatness on such wicked and iniquitous foundations. So that God, nature, reason, justice, his concern for the dissolution and ruin of his state, which would inevitably follow their objective, had they carried it out, forced him to decide to punish them as they merited, following the legitimate power that God has given him over all his subjects when they commit and undertake that which they should not do.

And in so much as they had so stripped His Majesty of his authority and the obedience of his subjects that, if he had wished to undertake the said punishment by the ordinary rules of justice, not only could he not have done it but he considered his ruin and destruction would have been quite certain, he had chosen the surest means to put him to death; having by the same means placed under guard Monsieur the cardinal of Bourbon, Monsieur de Nemours, the prince of Joinville, the duke of Elboeuf and the archbishop of Lyon. . . .

SOURCE: Instructions to Angennes, ambassador in Rome, early 1589, *Recueil de mémoires et instructions servans à l'histoire de France*, 1626, pp. 568–622.

## 22    The shock to the League

So the duke of Guise is dead and, unless God gives the duke of Mayenne and M. de La Châtre the means of escaping, there is no more reliance to be placed on the League. In effect, the duke of Aumale, who is at present in Paris, is a young man of little experience. He will have much ado to be able to withdraw to some place in Picardy. . . . I am of the view that, should MM. de Mayenne and La Châtre have been killed, and the plan of massacring the Huguenots threatened at Orléans not be effected, not a single town will be able to defy the King.

SOURCE: Mendoza to Philip II, 27 December 1588, AGS, K 1567, fo. 190; Croze, vol. II, pp. 381–4.

# 8  Henry IV and the League, 1589–95

Henry III's decision to eliminate the Guises marked the effective end of his authority. The news of the events at Blois immediately sparked off a frenzy of venomous attacks against him at Paris that sealed the destruction of his reputation among Catholic enthusiasts and opened the way for the emergence of an alternative Catholic regime that built on the League and the Sixteen of the previous years and the federal structure of Catholic towns that had formed after the Day of the Barricades.

On 7 January 1589, the Sorbonne released the King's subjects from their obligation of obedience (see Document 1). Necessity forced the leaders in Paris to put together a new government, which on 18 February 1589 took the form of the General Council of the Union, of about 40 members elected by committees of the 16 quartiers, which appointed Mayenne as Lieutenant-General on 13 March. It was the Council that co-ordinated relations between the cities and looked after public order. The experience of Paris was a slide towards radicalism. Other cities were different. In Picardy, Amiens moved quickly to join the League but its efforts to create a provincial government in the form of the 'Chambre du conseil' were overcome by local particularism (see Document 2). At Toulouse (see Document 3), polarity between radical and moderate wings was avoided by the relative isolation of the city and the ability of Mayenne's representative, Joyeuse, to gain control in September 1589. Burgundy, though it was the base for Mayenne's power (see Document 4), was a divided province; the majority of the nobles were against him and many of the rest out for themselves. The towns here and in Champagne were divided against each other. In Dijon the Parlement was divided and the city council under Jacques La Verne formed the backbone of the League. Thus, Dijon and Burgundy were Mayenne's fiefdom, yet he could not entirely control the city as he would have wished. In Rouen, the city elite was for the King but the militia and popular unrest ensured a League takeover in February. There were widespread peasant movements – the *Gaultiers* – in favour of the League in Normandy but these were put down.

The King maintained a following but his supporters were increasingly beleaguered (see Document 5). He had little alternative but to come to terms with Navarre and recognise him as his successor (see Document 7). This only added to the conviction of the League that the King was a heretic, and to the general vilification now directed against him (see Document 6). However, the joint royal and Protestant armies began what looked like an increasingly successful campaign for the conquest of Paris. This was effectively broken up by the King's assassination on 1 August by Jacques Clément, a Jacobin friar. The origins of his act have long been debated. Mme de Montpensier liked to claim she had arranged it but Clément was probably acting from genuine religious passion and a desire for 'martyrdom'. At any rate, he was killed before he could explain his motives (see Document 8).

The succession dispute now came fully into play. Navarre was the technical successor if his religion were not held against him. On 4 August he issued a declaration guaranteeing to uphold the Catholic religion (see Document 10). Many of Henry III's attendants and advisers rallied to him, including, among the most prominent, Montpensier and Biron. Épernon and Nevers, though, retired into neutrality (see Document 9) and Villeroy was being wooed by Mayenne. Doubts were too widespread and the determination of the League too intransigent for Navarre to be other than one claimant to a disputed throne. He was forced to abandon the siege of Paris, while Mayenne sought to bring in Spanish troops.

The insuperable problem for the League was that its claimant, the cardinal of Bourbon, proclaimed at Paris as 'Charles X' (see Document 11), was an octogenarian of no discernible ability, firmly imprisoned by his nephew Navarre. He could never be more than an image on coins and medals and died quietly in May 1591. Navarre sought to win the military initiative and gained the victory of Arques, near the Norman coast, in September 1589 and a more decisive defeat of Mayenne at Ivry in March 1590. He was now in a position to besiege Paris closely between April and August 1590. Only the intervention of Parma with Spanish troops at the behest of Mayenne saved the city and forced Navarre to retire, though without much positive advantage to Mayenne.

The siege had been devastating to the population and speeded up the radicalisation of the Sixteen (see Document 12). Originally drawn from a wide range of influential social groups, as the League went on it was increasingly dominated by poorer lawyers and represented a more popular or radical social attitude that was able even to contemplate the formation of a Catholic republic. Radicalism was enforced by a reign of terror in the form of purges and executions that became more frenetic after the entry of Parma's Spanish troops and culminated in the slaughter of Barnabé Brisson and two other Parlement magistrates in November 1591. Mayenne, as representative of the more conservative and aristocratic wing, could tolerate this no longer and on 18 November entered the city and hanged the leaders of the radical movement and expelled the rest.

Navarre's position evolved gradually during 1591; the main pressure was the need to win over more moderate Catholic support without alienating too many of his Protestant followers. In this, he was faced by the covert discontents of the 'Third Party', who sought in the aftermath of the failure before Paris another possibility in the person of 'Charles X''s nephew, the cardinal of Vendôme. In July, the King issued the Edict of Mantes, consisting of two documents. The first reiterated his declaration of August 1589 on his willingness to maintain the Catholic religion and accept instruction from a duly constituted National Council (see Document 13). The second, though, repealed Henry III's Edicts of Union of 1585 and 1588, thereby reinstalling the toleration regime of 1577 and, crucially, allowing Protestants to hold public office (see Document 14). This remained unregistered by the Parlements. Militarily, Navarre decided in November to move onto the offensive again and started a siege of Rouen with English help (providing an odd symmetry with their intervention in 1562–3). Again, Parma's intervention saved the day for the League and the siege was broken in April 1592.

Mayenne's party were as yet only prepared to deal with Navarre on impossible terms. The negotiations conducted for him by Villeroy during the siege of Rouen in the spring of 1592 show this only too well. Mayenne may have been prepared to recognise Henry IV after his conversion but was severely limited by his dependence on Spanish support. He could thus not negotiate seriously. Mayenne also faced the inordinate problem of how to set up a legitimate regime. He had already agreed to a meeting of the Estates and in Autumn 1592 authorised the election of deputies from the League cities, who assembled in January 1593. With only 128 deputies, as a result of much of the country being under the domination of the royal army, the Estates could scarcely be called 'general' but, on the other hand, that they were able to meet at all was something of a triumph. It posed a direct challenge to the royalist party which had to be replied to. The result was the conference held at Suresnes in May between the Catholic royalists and the moderates. Much of this served only to exchange positions but it also had the effect of pushing the King finally into deciding, around 10 May, to accept instruction (see Document 19). On the surface, the League remained obdurate that it could not recognise a heretic king.

However, the issue of the succession predictably tore the League apart, while public opinion in Paris and elsewhere was moving towards an acceptance of a converted Navarre despite the trumpeting of die-hard preachers. Mayenne, in his dependence on Spain, had committed himself, in return for subsidies, to the Infanta Isabella (see Document 15) but could not carry her marriage to the Habsburg Archduke Ernest. He was also unenthusiastic about a marriage between her and his nephew Guise, the more 'French' alternative. In the end, the intervention by Guillaume du Vair on 20 June against any immediate election (see Document 16), and that of the Parlement in issuing the famous *arrêt Lemaître*, restating the principal of the Salic Law, proved decisive (see Document 17). The Estates were unable to proceed further with an election (see Document 18). This, coupled with the effect of Henry IV's abjuration at Saint-Denis on 25 July 1593 (see Document 20) and his coronation at Chartres on 27 February 1594 gave a death blow to the political justification of the League, which immediately began to suffer a fatal haemorrhage of support. The Estates effectively disbanded in August. Radical League leaders did not take all this lying down. The abjuration was accompanied by the last great wave of propaganda, arguing this time that the conversion was a sham and that time would reveal this. Time to prove their case, however, was something they did not have, as support for them ebbed away. The abjuration also marked a shift in the King's policy towards conciliation, symbolised by the three months' truce he concluded with Mayenne on 1 August. This was badly observed on both sides but it was a major propaganda coup for the King; its terms were often to be repeated in individual or local agreements during the following year.

The year 1594 was therefore set for the inexorable winning over by the royalist camp of the various groups opposing them, both urban and aristocratic. All the pressures went the same way: the justification for opposition had been cut away; the countryside was in a turmoil of revolt against the continued demands of war (see Documents 22–4). Villeroy's advice to Mayenne in January 1594 was to seek genuine talks (see Document 21). He left him in no doubt as to the fragility of his position. The King, no longer prepared to prolong the truce, was eager to win the towns and leaders of the League with generous terms, though he was determined to negotiate separately, not with the League as a whole (see Document 25). In the event, the King's entry into Paris on 22 March 1594 was remarkably smoothe (see Document 26) and led in turn to a rapid coming to terms on the part of other cities (see Documents 27–9) and of individual aristocrats (see Document 30).

After the loss of Laon in August 1594, Mayenne was faced with the disintegration of his party and desperate to avoid precisely the outcome envisaged by the King – separate treaties (see Document 31). His authority was confined to Burgundy and increasingly precarious there. The declaration of war against Spain in January 1595 put him in a more difficult position. Dijon was slipping out of his control (it opened its gates to Biron on 28 May) and his position collapsed when Henry IV won the cavalry battle against the Spaniards, who had entered Burgundy, at Fontaine-Française on 5 June. From his final refuge at Chalon, he began negotiating for terms, helped by the publication of the Papal absolution of the King on 17 September. The process is an interesting further example of Henry IV's kid-glove treatment of his former enemies. Incredibly, Mayenne still demanded the governorship of Burgundy, and, though he was forced to abandon this claim, was able to prolong the talks. A truce was signed on 23 September that enabled him eventually to come to court. Agreement was sealed in a royal edict at Folembray on 31 January 1596 which took the form of a general peace with the remaining aristocratic leaguers but, in its 31 secret articles, dealt alone with Mayenne's personal needs (see Document 32). Though his cousin Mercoeur held out in Brittany until early 1598, this was really the end.

Mayenne signalled his conversion by joining the royal army facing the Spaniards in Picardy. The declaration of war, which Admiral Coligny had pressed for so disastrously, may have been encouraged by the current Protestant military chief, Turenne, for similar reasons and against the King's better judgment. At any rate, it posed a massive military burden with the invasion of Picardy. Cambrai had already fallen and Calais was to do so in 1596. Then in spring 1597, Amiens was taken and required a massive siege operation for its recapture in September. Only then could a definitive peace at home and abroad be considered.

Internal and external threats had continued to be interwined, and above all, the problems of Huguenot disgruntlement remained to be settled, but by the end of 1594 the fatal link between religion and politics had been severed for the first time and a real and lasting settlement could be contemplated.

---

# 1  The repudiation of Henry III at Paris, 7 January 1589

The year 1589, 7 January, the most holy Theology Faculty of Paris assembled at the College of the Sorbonne, after the petition of all the orders of the Faculty and the celebration of the Mass of the Holy Spirit there (required by the most illustrious lords the provosts of the merchants, aldermen, consuls and Catholic citizens of the dear city of Paris, both in person and by written acts signed and sealed by the public registrar of the town) to deliberate on the following articles contained in the request of those citizens:

Whether the people of the kingdom of France may be delivered and released from the oath of fidelity and obedience made to Henry III.

Whether, in conscience, the same people may be armed, unite, raise money and contribute to the Catholic religion against the King's wicked devices and efforts and those of his adherents and against the violation of the public oath he made at

Blois to the harm of the said Catholic religion and the Edict of the Holy Union
and the natural liberty of convocation of the Three Estates of the realm.

The mature, careful and free deliberation of all the masters (to the number of 70)
on these articles having been heard, also various reasons advanced for the most part
in very eloquent words, based not only on sacred scripture but also on canons and
papal decrees, it was concluded by the Dean of the Faculty, *nem. con.*, by manner
of council, to free the consciences of the people:

1 That the people of this realm are released and delivered from the oath of loyalty
  and obedience made to King Henry abovesaid.
2 That this same people may legally and with a safe conscience be armed and
  united, gather funds and contribute for the defence of the Apostolic and Roman
  Church against the wicked devices and efforts of the said King and his adherents,
  whoever they be, since he has violated his public oath to the Edict of Holy
  Union, to the harm of the Catholic religion and the natural freedom of
  convocation of the Three Estates of this realm.

Which conclusions it has seemed good and profitable to the said Faculty of Paris to
send to the Pope, our most holy lord, so that he might confirm them by the
authority of the Holy Apostolic See and give aid and comfort to the Gallican
Church, which is grievously travailed.

SOURCE: Stegman, pp. 216–17.

## REACTION IN THE PROVINCES

### 2   The League at Amiens

[*Word arrived from Paris of the events at Blois on 26 December and measures were
immediately taken to arrest royalist suspects. On 29 December*] it was proposed that
the poor people of this province are so tormented with great and unbearable tailles
that, in consideration of what has happened, which will cause various troubles, they
will find it impossible to pay the taille as decided by the King. They had hoped
they would be reduced in their assessment to the same level as 1576, as had been
agreed in the Estates at Blois, for which there had been bonfires in all the towns.
Thus it is to be feared that if there is no reduction, the peasants will be ill-disposed
to the party of men of honour. After the assembly carefully debated all this, it was
decided that only two-thirds of the taille in the King's letters patent to the *élus*
would be levied; the *élus* will be informed. To avoid any royal revenues, of whatever
kind, even the *décimes* and alienations of clerical property, getting into the hands of
those who might be opposed to the Union, it was decided that they be detained
and employed as shall hereafter be decided. . . .

[*Assembly of 31 December*] After careful consideration of the great matters that arise from hour to hour [for the conservation of the Catholic Church], for which the city council alone cannot provide, because it is preoccupied both with the security of the city and the administration of royal and municipal justice as well as with other routine affairs, it was thought expedient to create a Council Chamber composed partly of the clergy, partly of the nobility and partly of the third estate with two échevins of the city, which will consider and decide on the general affairs of the province. The decisions of this Chamber will be reported to the mayor and échevins for implemention, if they think fit. . . . It was unanimously decided that all the Catholic and confederate towns of this province would be written to, to invite them to send deputies to this Chamber and to add their voice to decisions and avoid confusion.

[*City proclamation of 2 January:*] The King, by his letters of 23 December, has informed us that he had put to death my lord duke of Guise. . . . The inhabitants of the city of Amiens have resolved to take up arms for the maintenance of the Catholic religion, determined to risk their lives and property. In this they exhort each and every good gentleman to assist them and, to this end, make their way quickly to this city to give their advice on what is necessary for the preservation of God's honour, religion, and the security of the province. They declare those who take the opposite party enemies and traitors to God and the fatherland, forbidding, on pain of death, all persons, of whatever quality or condition, to make disturbance without power and mandate signed by the mayor, provost and échevins of the city.

SOURCE: *IS, Amiens*, vol. II, pp. 150–1.

## 3   The League at Toulouse:

Council of 7 January 1589

[*On the refusal of entry to the town for the royal seneschal, Astourgy, capitoul, reported that*] on 23 December last, the most illustrious prince my lord duke of Guise as also my lord cardinal his brother were killed in the town of Blois, and that if the news were true it would be a most deplorable event and by it each and every one may know how God is angered against us, the thing proceeding only from our sins. However, we must humble ourselves before God more than ever and rise up and take courage to preserve our Catholic faith and religion and unite together to prevent the heretics, our enemies, from attemping anything against this town.

[*Daffis, for the clergy, talked of*] the deplorable act and slaughter of my lords the duke of Guise and the cardinal his brother at Blois, who were protectors and pillars of our holy Catholic faith and religion in this kingdom, as the lord duke showed in effect last year by combatting and defeating the foreign heretics on the field of battle. It is sure that for his merits he is of the number of the saints and martyrs before God, as is the late lord cardinal. This has caused the chapter and clergy to assemble to take measures for our security, for it is to be feared that there are plots in all the chief towns of the kingdom to exterminate the good Catholics. . . .

8 January 1589

Ruling drawn up for the conservation of the Catholic religion:
All the inhabitants of this town will address prayers to God that it please his divine goodness to appease his anger against us.

That all be united in the support of the Catholic faith and religion.

That the rulings for the guard and administration of this town will be maintained and carried out in all points. . . .

Furthermore, and following the request of the clergy, there will be established a committee of eighteen persons, that is, six from the counsellors of the Court, six from the clergy and six bourgeois including two of the *capitouls*, who will be hereafter named at the good pleasure of the Court, to deliberate on affairs of state and the measures necessary for the preservation of the country and towns of this province and the maintenance of the Catholic religion.

That sixteen bourgeois named today to the general Council will assist the capitouls in discussing business as it arises.

Source: Loutchitsky, pp. 245–6.

---

## 4   The League at Dijon

The Union of the Inhabitants of Dijon
I. We swear and promise to God and all the celestial court to live and die in the Catholic religion, employ our lives and goods for its conservation against all those who openly or covertly attempt, now or hereafter, anything to its prejudice.
II. We swear to maintain this town in repose and tranquillity, to hunt down all those who cause any trouble and to have them punished by justice or otherwise.
III. We will employ all our forces and means to preserve the province and this town of Dijon in full, to make it peaceful and guarantee it against all oppression, as well as all other cities and towns of the kingdom united for the good and augmentation of the Catholic religion, and to make open war against the heretics, their abettors and adherents.
IV. We swear to assist all the princes, prelates, lords and gentlemen, cities and towns united in this holy resolve and all others who will join hereafter, and not to suffer any outrage against their persons, honour and goods either in effect or in words by whomsoever it be.

V. We will take great care that commerce and traffic be free and to remove all impediments that might be made, as also to ensure that the roads stay open and assured for the communication one to another of the business of this Holy Union and everything concerning its administration and good.

VI. We will not suffer any alteration or diminution of the authority and privileges belonging to the three orders and estates of this province, to the town and to all others united, which we will observe inviolably.

VII. We swear to maintain the Court of Parlement in this town of Dijon in its ancient splendour, as also the Chamber of Accounts according to the agreement made between former kings and the Estates. . . .

XII. We hold as heretics and disturbers of the public weal all those who refuse to join and subscribe in effect and without dissimulation to the present Union. . . .

XIII. We swear to obey the commands of my lord the duke of Mayenne, governor of this province and in his absence M. de Fervacques, his Lieutenant-General, from whom we will never break, whatever orders and commands arrive to the contrary. . . .

SOURCE: Loutchitsky, pp. 229–32.

## 5   The King's supporters in extremes

Sir, the pitiful tragedy of this kingdom started to be played out long ago and you have seen events that show that the last act of all, which is coming soon, must be the ruin of the state and of us all. Our divisions are the argument, our passions the speeches, our wars the scenery and France the stage, foreigners the audience and the end our end. [*There are two causes of all this.*] The first is the bad advice that the King has hitherto received and acted on, the greed of his counsellors, which he has encouraged by his huge gifts, the lack of care and fidelity in his affairs, the secret contacts some have had with his enemies, that have led to leagues and factions, the sale of offices of judicature and the corruption of them, justice ill administered, tyrannical exactions on the people, new edicts and cursed parties built for his ruin, the impunity of conspirators, the all too filthy and general lewdness, the poor organisation of the finances and many other things to our misfortune we have witnessed.

All these have been followed by others that have brought the state to desolation and to the edge of overthrow, such as the universal outpouring of hatred for the King, the disdain for his name and authority, the freedom to rebel against him, the inaction and the pleasures some have thrown themselves into, the baneful names of League and Huguenot which have created two parties set against the state and the princes. . . .

The fever of sedition and rebellion is so widespread that most of the towns of France have risen against the King in vengeance for the death of M. de Guise, as if he had been their King and father; such was the way this prince had charmed the people into thinking that without him their religion was finished, that Paris, the leader of the other towns, which has always violently followed the factions opposed to the King, as well as the rich, the grandees, the officers and followers of the King, are all in the power of the people. . . . Now brigandage rules and the fire of all impieties burns under cover of zeal for the Catholic religion, unworthy of our pure and true faith. Preachers from the pulpit pour out nothing but lies, set the gospels aside and conjure rebellion out of the pure word of God and cruelty out of his precious blood. They would spill the blood of worthy men. Their tongues, like bellows, fan the flames of crime and disobedience. Amiens does the same. Orléans holds out against the King's forces and waits for M. de Mayenne. . . . The King, too, arms with all diligence. . . . Campaign must be started to defend the King's life with just force and Orléans must be captured if possible, as an example, Mayenne fought and Paris reached. But money is necessary for war; this is what is important yet difficult to find. The provinces of Champagne, Picardy, Burgundy, Provence, Languedoc, Guyenne, Poitou, Paris and its region give nothing and all that are left to contribute are the little provinces of the centre, a poor resource. . . .

Nothing is said of this in the closing speeches of the Estates, nor of the duke of Guise. He brought us many troubles in life and in death gives us more. That shows the favour which, to the King's prejudice, he had acquired in this kingdom. The Estates, who wanted to make him equal with or superior to the King, or King himself, by their wicked advice and plans, forged the daggers that killed him and drowned his life and objectives in his blood, and made of this fair body, of this great prince and captain, a sacrament and victim sacrificed to his unbridled ambition. . . . He believed that the King did not have the courage to stand up to him, an idea that brought his death, the ruin of his house, his cause, his relatives and friends, the imprisonment of his supporters, his goods seized for his debts and France in rebellion and general uproar. The few hearts who remain to the King, outside the two opposed parties of the League and the Huguenots, are not very enthusiastic for him. But he tries in every way suitable to win friendship and good opinions. But misfortunes conspire against us. . . .

SOURCE: Letter to Marshal Biron, from Blois, 26 January 1589, *Biron*, vol. II, pp. 457–63.

## 6  Anti-monarchical propaganda of the League

Parisians, alerted to the alliance between the two Kings, spread the word throughout the kingdom and especially in Paris, through their usual vehicles of sedition. Mme de Montpensier, through her paid preachers, had it declared everywhere that the mask was off and the tyrant had removed the veil of his hypocrisy in declaring himself openly the abettor of the heretic with whom he had allied himself . . . the pulpits resounded with insults to the King, whom they called a dog, tiger, heretic, tyrant, making the people abhor him as much as they could, neither wishing nor allowing him to be called anything else. The puniest preacher found place in his sermons for a flow of insults against the King and there was not a vulgar pedant who failed to pen sonnets on the subject. Not even the poorest printer failed to find means to keep his presses rolling daily with some foolish new discourse or defamatory libel against His Majesty, stuffed with the most atrocious insults that even the old ruffians, bawds and trollopes of the Petit-Pont could think up. I was curious enough to collect more than three hundred of them, all different, all printed at Paris and hawked through the streets, making up four large volumes that I have had bound in parchment and annotated in my hand, not to mention a large folio full of pictures and defamatory posters of all sorts, that I would have consigned to the flames, which is all they are worth, did they not serve to reveal the abuses, impostures, vanities and furies of this great monster of the League. . . .

SOURCE: L'Estoile, April 1589, pp. 625–6.

## 7  The one-year truce between Henry III and Henry of Navarre, 3 April 1589

The King of Navarre will serve the King with all fidelity and affection, with all his forces and means, both private and those of his party, against those who violate His Majesty's authority and trouble his state; and will not use them elsewhere, at home or abroad, without His Majesty's command and consent.

To allow him to assemble the greatest force possible and so that His Majesty may also more easily prevail in this war with all his own, a general truce is concluded throughout the whole kingdom of France between His Majesty and the lord King of Navarre . . . for one entire year, to start from the date of this agreement . . . during which time all things will remain on each side as they are at present.

The states of Avignon and Comtat Venaissin, belonging to our Holy Father the Pope, will also enjoy this truce as being under His Majesty's protection.

The lord King of Navarre will cease all hostilities from this time in the province where he is, ordering all those under his command in other provinces immediately to do the same, namely to cease all enterprises. [*As will the King.*]

[*Agreement in the provinces on the raising of money and restoration of all places taken after the truce.*]

So that the lord King of Navarre may more easily carry out the service he has promised His Majesty, the latter will, the day after Low Monday, 10 April, hand over to him or his men Ponts de Cé, so as to use the crossing of the river Loire.

The lord King of Navarre, having control of this crossing, will immediately march with his forces . . . straight to where the duke of Mayenne is, to oppose his designs, and will only wage war against the duke and those of his faction, without allowing any attempts against the places where His Majesty's authority is recognised, nor in any place through which he passes will he change or permit to be changed anything concerning the Catholic religion; nor allow any offence or displeasure to the Catholics. . . .

[*Any conquests by the King of Navarre are to be placed in the King's hands, while the King will appoint governors agreeable to Navarre. Navarre may retain one place per conquered bailliage as gage for his expenses and to provide for his wounded. At Ponts de Cé, Navarre will be able to raise 20,000 écus p.a. on the King's dues. Dues in the generality of Tours held by Navarre will be left to the King.*]

The lord King of Navarre, outside the territories at present in his obedience, will not divert or touch His Majesty's revenues and will not impose his own in any manner, nor in the towns he retains. But he will only take from His Majesty's officers and receivers what he shall be assigned for the pay of the garrisons that he needs to keep in those places, which shall be allocated as their quality demand.

In consequence of the above, His Majesty accords restoration of goods to the lord King of Navarre and those of his party and will expedite all necessary documents, to enjoy them as long as the truce lasts; as also reciprocally they will allow the Catholics, both clergy and His Majesty's loyal servants, to do of their goods and revenues in the lands of their obedience.

SOURCE: *Mornay*, vol. IV, pp. 351–5.

---

## 8  The assassination of Henry III

On the last day of July, returning with one of my friends from Paris to the town of Saint-Cloud where the King was staying, I met a Jacobin aged, to judge by his appearance, 27 or 28, who was between two soldiers of Comblanc's regiment. Thinking they were holding him prisoner and knowing the King's intention was for such persons to be unharmed, though most were sowers of this bloody rebellion, I asked if he were their prisoner. They said no but that he was a monk who was bringing letters and news to His Majesty from some of his servants in Paris and that they were thus taking him to his lodging. Having met me by good fortune, they asked me to take him, which I did, thinking it was some news useful to the King.

Once at my lodging, I questioned him closely about his mission and, after some obstruction, as though he could declare it only to His Majesty, he told me he came from the First President to tell him that all His Majesty's servants in Paris were highly concerned at having no news of his army, though they knew he was close. Those of his servants who had stayed in the city were under threat, since 1,000 or 1,200 had been imprisoned the day before . . . and that the First President, though he was a prisoner, was working to discover their aims and the means of serving him and had sent him to His Majesty to tell him they were ready to seize a gate to give him entry into the city. . . . I asked him if he had a letter from the First President or some other evidence by which he could be believed, at which he showed me a letter in Italian which he said was in the hand of the First President, and in fact it seemed most likely, Italian writing being easy to imitate. . . . We had a long discussion, as I tried by all means I could to discover who he was, fearing he was a spy . . . but I found him firm and resolute in what he had first told me. . . . Then, unable to get anything else from him, I left him with my men and went to seek the King, who had not yet returned from near Paris. I waited in a lodging of one of my friends near his. Having supped and heard that His Majesty had returned, I told him all the above. He was very pleased at this, seeing the way open to him, without further ruin to his subjects to rescue his servants in the city from the cruel tryanny in which they languished, commanding me to bring him the next morning early at 6 or 7 o'clock. . . . Next morning, 1 August, for ever a lamentable day for France, having risen to attend His Majesty as he had commanded, I woke him up, he having spent a peaceful night, and before entering the King's lodging, I had him speak to Portail, to whom he gave some private news of his wife, his son and his household. Once in the lodging and called by du Halde, who also ushered in the wretch by the King's command, I found him seated unbuttoned in his chair. For this reason, I made him stay at the door and took his note of credence to present it to His Majesty, who, having read it and deceived by the likeliness of the letter, thought it was from the First President. Because it was only a credence, he called the monk to him to hear what he had to say. He approached, with me between him and the King and on the other side my lord Master of the Horse who was then in the room. He told the King that he had come from the president and others of His Majesty's servants in Paris to tell him matters of great importance for his service, which he could only say to him alone. At this, I know not whether moved by some spirit of love for France, I spoke, saying that he should speak up and that there were only the King's faithful servants in the room. He still insisted in speaking in secret and I said again to the King that he need not come so close. But then, the misfortune of France being too great, and in his usually welcoming way, he had him stand in the Master of the Horse's place, enclining his ear, we two apart, when we were astonished to hear him cry out: 'Ah! wretch, what have I done to you for you to kill me?' and getting up, with blood spurting form his stomach, from which he pulled the knife, followed by the bowels, and with it struck the wretch on the face. He, standing firm, I feared he had further aims to attack His Majesty, so I pushed him onto the floor beside the bed with my sword hilt. At the noise, the ordinary guards rushed in, and while one held him the others killed him, though I shouted to them several times not to. . . . You can imagine the pitiful and miserable spectacle: on the one side the King covered in blood, holding his bowels in his hands, on the other his servants filing in, weeping and crying. . . . .

SOURCE: Evidence of La Guesle, *AC*, pp. 376–9.

## HENRY OF NAVARRE AND THE SUCCESSION

### 9   De Thou on reactions in the royal camp

[*On the day of the assassination, first the Swiss troops were assured and it was decided to continue the siege of Paris. Navarre then went to Saint-Cloud to meet the officers of the army.*] There were murmurs in the camp about the new King's religion. However, in fact everyone agreed that in the present circumstances when the strongest supports of the throne had been rocked, it was only a blow from heaven that had, in giving France a prince endowed with such virtues and who was renowned for his successes, assured the succession to the Crown. But this was not found sufficient to guarantee religion. Thus in the afternoon, the lords and councillors of state in the camp, almost all men of the sword, assembled at the Gondy mansion. There it was debated whether to recognise the King of Navarre and opinions were divided. There were some who claimed the decision must be taken by the Estates, which would be summoned for this purpose, and that meanwhile no decision should be taken which would prejudice the outcome. These, when they referred to the new King, called him the Navarrese, adding that he was too remote in degree from the crown to be declared for. . . . Others, not disagreeing with this idea, were of the opinion that it was proper to place the decision before the Estates. But, so as not to place Henry's rights entirely in doubt, they thought that he should still be recognised as generalissimo of the army. In that name they would take the oath to him. The greater number held, on the contrary, that there was no time to be lost and that he must be immediately recognised as King without limits to the obedience they owed and should swear. The least delay would bring massive dangers. To leave the rights of this prince under a cloud would give time for the different parties that had formed in the kingdom to coalesce and this would make them more difficult to destroy afterwards. This opinion won the day in the end and it was decided that, after taking all precautions, the oath would be taken to Henry of Bourbon as legitimate heir to the crown. [*Henry then swore to preserve the Catholic religion and the princes, peers and officers of the crown took the oath to him on 4 August.*]

Among the lords then in the camp, there were some who, though they approved this move and had been among the first to press forward the decision just taken, refused to subscribe to this act so as not to prejudice their rank. Among these was Jean Louis de Nogaret, duke of Épernon. As his rank as duke and peer placed him above the Marshals d'Aumont and Biron, he refused to sign after them. . . . Soon after, on pretext of his private affairs, for which he said he had already obtained leave from the late King, he left with his troops and some others who were only looking for an excuse to leave.

SOURCE: De Thou, vol. XI, pp.1–11.

## 10  Henry of Navarre's declaration, 4 August 1589

We Henry, by the grace of God King of France and of Navarre, promise and swear on the word of a king by these presents signed by our hand, to all our good and faithful subjects, to maintain and preserve the Catholic religion in our kingdom in its entirety without any innovation in either its form or practice or to the persons and property of the clergy and the provision to them of capable Catholics according to established custom. Also that, following the open declaration made by us before our accession to the crown, we are entirely ready and desire nothing more than to be instructed by a good, legitimate and free general and national Council and to follow what will be decided by it, which we shall summon for this purpose within six months or earlier if possible.

Meanwhile, there will be no exercise of any religion other than the Catholic except in the towns and places where it happens at present, according to the articles agreed in April last between the late King Henry III of good memory, our most honoured lord and brother, and us until otherwise has been decided by a general peace in our kingdom or by the Estates-General, which will likewise be summoned within six months.

We promise in addition that the towns and fortresses taken from our rebels and reduced by force to our obedience will be committed by us to the charge of our good subjects and no others, except those which were reserved under the said articles for those of the Reformed Religion in each bailliage and seneschalcy. . . .

We also promise that all offices and governorships, when they fall vacant, other than in those towns and fortresses in the power of those of the Reformed Religion, will during the same time of six months be filled by us by capable Catholics who are our good subjects.

Furthermore, we promise to preserve, keep and maintain the princes, dukes, peers, officers of the crown, lords and gentlemen and all our good and faithful subjects equally in their property, charges, dignities, estates, offices, privileges, pre-eminences, prerogatives and accustomed rights and especially to recognise, as far as we can, the good and faithful servants of the late lord King.

Finally to devote our person and means, at need, with the help of all our good subjects, to punish with exemplary justice the murder, wickedness, felony and disloyalty committed against the person of the late lord King.   (Signed, crs Ruzé)

SOURCE: Isambert, vol. XV, pp. 3–4.

## 11  Mayenne's declaration, 5 August 1589

. . . While awaiting the liberation and presence of the King our sovereign lord ['*Charles X*'], we admonish, exhort, pray and request all princes, prelates, officers of the crown, lords and gentlemen . . . both on the obedience they owe to God, the lover of peace and union, and to their Catholic, natural and legitimate King, the love of their country and for the public weal of the state in which we all have an interest in joining, to rally to us either to bear arms against the heretics or to return to their homes, in which we permit them to live as long as they swear before the baillis and seneschals in their place of residence to live and die in the Catholic religion and employ all their means with us in its defence, preservation and advancement and not to favour, help or assist in any way the heretics, their aiders and abettors; of which a transcript will be give them.

SOURCE: Isambert, vol. XV, p. 7.

## 12   Paris under siege, 1590

The people, seeing the small effect of this furious battery, just laughed at it. However, it prompted a renewal of courage and reason to inflame their hatred all the more against the enemy, as well as encouraging their hope in God, in whose goodness, their only refuge, they had never ceased to trust. There was seen an increase in solemn processions in the places designated for the stations of the cross. The citizens reported that these lost nothing in comparison with the year of the great jubilee. Sermons that were full of piety, doctrine and zeal were preached in the usual places to great crowds. These were all the greater since employment for those who lived by manual work was slumping and as a result the number of beggars was growing daily; the charity of decent people helping to feed them as much as possible increased.

SOURCE: Franklin, *Journal*, pp. 160–3.

Paris was so burdened by hunger that those accustomed to delicate meats could only have rye bread while even donkeys and horses were rare and expensive. The poor lived on gruel made from bran. . . . The preachers of the League faction . . . omitted nothing to encourage them to endure *pro aris et focis*, for God, their religion and their country. These are specious pretexts. . . . Doctor Boucher and the other preachers of the faction of the Sixteen, with Panigarola and other Italian preachers of the legate's household, then showed how eloquence, in conjunction with the pretext of religion, can move the people. In short, they were able skilfully, by processions and weekly prayers and ceremonies held as they thought appropriate, to contain the Parisians so that some compared this siege of Paris to that of Jerusalem. . . . Meanwhile, hunger and need grew. Dogs, cats, rats, mice, old tallow and bread baked with grass were the meat for people who had no money for oat bread and bran gruel. Some died of hunger; many went up to five days without food and then died. Nothing more deplorable was ever seen.

SOURCE: Palma Cayet, vol. I, pp. 260 and 262.

## 13   Letters-patent of Mantes, 4 July 1591

It was our first act as sovereign to declare solemnly that we desired nothing so much as the convocation of a holy and free Council by which the differences in the matter of religion might be so well clarified and settled that there could never again be any dispute or uncertainty and that, for ourselves, we bore no stubborn opinion or presumption of knowledge in doctrine; and that our intention was to receive as willingly as ever all good instruction that could be given. . . . We meanwhile promised that we would not change or allow to be changed anything in the exercise of the Catholic religion, which we wish to preserve and maintain; and those who profess it in all their authorities and liberties as is more specifically set down by the act signed by us, viewed and registered by all our courts of Parlement. [*However, those who wished to conceal their previous crimes and ambition, rebelled in the name of religion.*] The leagues and associations they made for the invasion of this kingdom with the King of Spain, the dukes of Savoy and Lorraine, and their agreement for division and usurpation, show clearly that this trouble is none other than a faction of state and that they hold this war to be but a matter of trade. . . . [*In this they have practised deception, tried to claim that the King does not wish to take instruction, and induced the Pope to send a nuncio who issued declarations in all their towns against the King's faithful servants.*]

We now declare by these presents, and in conformity with our previous declaration, we protest before the living God, that we desire nothing so much as the convocation of a holy and free council or some notable assembly sufficient to decide the differences over religion, for which we will receive personal instruction, calling only for divine grace, if we are in error, to make us understand it in order to bring us to the best way as quickly as possible. We have no greater ambition than that, in our reign, God should be worshipped uniformly by all our subjects according to his commands. . . . We promise meanwhile and swear to preserve the Catholic religion . . . as is more amply declared in our previous declaration, which we have confirmed anew. . . . [*Orders to the Parlements to proceed against the Papal Nuncio and his actions in the kingdom.*]

[*Order for registration by the royalist Parlement, 5 August; for annulment of the Papal bulls, to declare Pope Gregory XIV enemy of the peace, of the Roman religion and of the King, and for the arrest of the Nuncio.*]

SOURCE: Isambert, vol. XV, pp. 28–31.

## 14   Edict revoking the anti-toleration edicts of 1585 and 1588, July 1591

1   We . . . by our present perpetual and irrevocable edict . . . quash, revoke and annul by our full power and authority royal the edicts issued in July 1585 and

1588 which revoked the previous edicts issued by the kings our predecessors on the pacification of the troubles of this kingdom and all that followed from them; together with all judgments, sentences and orders given by virtue of them, suppressing all execution of them whatsoever for the future.

2  We will and are pleased that the last edicts of pacification should hereafter be maintained, executed, kept and observed inviolably in all our lands and territories in our obedience as they were in the lifetime of our late lord and brother and before their revocation. The which edicts we have, in so far as they need to be confirmed and authorised, confirmed and authorised by our most ample power by these presents. All this provisionally until it please God to give us the grace to reunite our subjects by the establishment of a good peace in our kingdom and to provide for religion, as we promised at our accession to the crown. . . .

SOURCE: Isambert, vol. XV, p. 30

## THE ESTATES-GENERAL OF THE LEAGUE

### 15  Mayenne's engagements with Spain, 23 February 1593

We Charles de Lorraine, duke of Mayenne, Lieutenant General of the crown and state of France, promise in good faith and on the word of a prince, to do all things necessary and employ all honest means in our power so that the princes, prelates lords and deputies at the Estates of this realm of France, at present assembled in Paris, should nominate as Queen of France the most serene Infanta doña Isabella. We recognise this, in effect, to be the shortest way and the most effective means to accomplish the extirpation of heresy, to the preservation of our holy Catholic faith of the Roman Church and the re-establishment of the kingdom in its integrity and pristine state. In return, His Majesty, whose works have hitherto been an assured guarantee of his good and loyal intentions, will willingly assist this cause in the manner that will seem to him most appropriate, with his royal armies and all means indispensable for achieving the ruin of the enemies of our holy religion, to the satisfaction of the said prelates, lords and deputies. His Majesty will furthermore undertake to have this election approved by His Holiness.

SOURCE: 25 February 1593, Croze, vol. II, p. 412

### The Election

### 16  Guillaume du Vair's speech, 20 June 1593

[*Opposing the election of a sovereign, saying that the deputies had no powers to do so from their constituents.*] However, they were approached at 5 or 6 o'clock with th greatest and most difficult proposal which could ever be discussed in this assembly, by means of which everything that had been treated concerning the reconciliation of the Catholics and the opposing party was tacitly set aside and all hope of reunion among Frenchmen is removed. There is a great difference between what is proposed now and what was last decided, that is to know from the King of Spain's envoys if they could and would give the Infanta of Spain to a French prince. That request committed us to nothing and kept open our freedom to decide what was most useful for the public good. But the proposal that is made to them now binds us to what we propose to them and obliges us, when they receive it, though they may have no intention to carry it out, to cease all other means of dealing with the desolate state of this kingdom. It would give means to foreigners, by delays and tricks, to reduce this state to such extremity that it would remain a prey to those who wished to seize it. Though he doubts not the prudence of my lord of Mayenne and my lords the princes, nor their affection for the good of religion and the state, nevertheless (not privy to the reasons that have moved my lords the princes to pass over the many difficulties that can be seen by anyone who examines the matters carefully), seeing that the security or ruin of religion depend on the decision that is taken, not only in this kingdom but throughout Christendom, as do the preservation of the greatest and most noble kingdom in the world, the good or ill of posterity, he is compelled to ask the company to excuse him but he cannot decide on the matter without time for thought and to sound the opinions of those who elected him.

[*The session ended with most of the other deputies agreeing to Mayenne's proposal, which was then put to Feria, namely to refuse the Archduke Ernest but ask for the Infanta to be married to a French prince.*]

SOURCE: Bernard, pp. 283–4.

---

## 17   The decree of the Parlement of Paris on the succession, 28 July 1593

On the remonstrance heretofore made by the King's procurator and the matter having been debated, the Court, having assembled in all its chambers, with the sole intention, as it always has, to maintain the Catholic religion in the State and crown of France under the protection of a Most Christian King, Catholic and French, has ordained and ordains that remonstrances will be made this afternoon by my lord president Lemaître, accompanied by a good number of the Court, to M. de Mayenne, Lieutenant-General of the State and crown of France, in the presence of the princes and officers of the crown at present in this city: that no treaty be made to transfer the crown to foreign princes or princesses; that the Fundamental Laws of this realm shall be kept; that the decrees of the Court for the declaration of a Catholic and French King be executed; that he employ the authority committed to him to prevent, on pretext of religion, the crown being transferred to a foreigner contrary to the laws of the realm; to work as promptly as possible for the peace of the people, because of the extreme necessity they are in; and nevertheless henceforth has declared and does declare all acts past or to come for the establishment of a foreign prince or princess null, void and of no effect, as done to the prejudice of the Salic Law and other Fundamental Laws of the realm of France.

SOURCE: 28 June 1593, Goulart, *Ligue*, vol. V, pp. 377–8; Bernard, pp. 547–8.

## 18    Session of the Estates, 22 July 1593

My lord of Mayenne, after having risen and greeted the company, said that it had pleased the Catholic King to give his daughter to my lord of Guise, his nephew, provided he was elected King by the Estates. However, it was not at present appropriate to proceed to an election since we had no forces and the [*renewal of*] truce was asked for by the enemy. We should not refuse this, considering the necessity of the people, especially here in Paris, and the Estates must accord it for the greater good.

SOURCE: Bernard, p. 666.

## THE ABJURATION

## 19    Henry IV's declaration of intent on religion, April 1593

[*Speaking to François d'O.*] No one can doubt that, even had I become a Catholic at my accession to this crown, my people would not for that have had peace. Those of the Religion would have sought their own protector and there would have been danger in that in view of what happened in the past and the writings then published in fear of my conversion. The leaders of the League had too much force at hand to obey me as they should. People demanded war and had not yet felt its effects. Now we are not in that position, for I have taken steps to have with me all those of the Religion who might stir. As for the leaders of the League, they no longer have the troops to resist me without Spanish help. As for the people of that party, I know that the effects of war they have felt make them desire peace. Assured, then, of those of the Religion who could cause trouble in my kingdom, I am resolved entirely to finish the Third Party by my conversion to the Roman Catholic religion, which I hope to do through instruction by French prelates, whom I shall assemble in three months at the latest.

SOURCE: Palma Cayet, vol. I, pp. 489–90.

## 20   The King's abjuration, 23 July 1593

[*Entering the lodging of the cardinal-archbishop of Bourges at Saint-Denis, between 7 and 8 on the morning of 23 July, the King said:*] that from his accession to the crown he had, at the request of the princes and officers of the crown, all his nobility and generally all his loyal Catholic subjects of all orders, promised to receive instruction to adhere to the Catholic Church. He had been unable to do this earlier because of the continual wars and the obstructions of his enemies. Knowing ever more the extreme desire of his subjects and touched with compassion at the misery and calamity of his people; knowing also that many persons of outstanding doctrine and piety contradicted the opinions that separated him from the church, and inspired by the spirit of God, he desired in all conscience to be able to content his people. To this end, he had discussed on several occasions with several learned Catholics and by them had been assured that the Catholic was the true church to which the interpretation of scripture belonged. He had been brought up in the opinion that there were many abuses in it but had learned that these were rather matters of usage and practice than of doctrine. He had thus decided to adhere to that church. . . .

SOURCE: Procès-verbal . . . *AC*, vol. XIII, p. 345.

## PEACE NEGOTIATIONS, 1593–4

### 21   Villeroy's warning to Mayenne, 2 January 1594

[*Urging him to negotiate seriously.*] You have always rejected this for various reasons more concerning private interests than the public good. This has led to your policies and those you have employed in the matter to be blamed and slandered and this has lost you the good will of the people, which was the chief foundation of your authority. In the end it will destroy your party, at the expense of religion and the state. You feared to offend the foreigners who are helping you. These, though, have not been grateful nor have they been eager to help and strengthen you, as was needed, in order, by the conjunction of your reputation and armies, to deal with these secret discontents and the public despair which are likely to result from the renewal of war. The enemy think you only want to continue the truce while awaiting your forces and strengthening your position at Rome and in Spain; the people that you wish to prolong the war to your private advantage. That being the case, how do you hope, from weakness, to persuade the first that you are negotiating in good faith and the latter that you wish to save them by a public and genuine negotiation, of the sort I have described to you, which makes your intentions clear to all? . . . You think this course too dangerous and shameful. I for my part think it not only most sure and useful for the general good, and also most honourable for your private interest; but it is also the only way to stop the ills that crowd in on us. My lord, I tell you this frankly, as a lover of my country, careful of the preservation of our religion and of your reputation and following. In the end, everyone is sick of war. In future it will be a matter not only of religion but also of your ability to defend yourself, nor for you to act alone. . . . There are few men who take pleasure in losing joy and embracing despair for the rest of their lives and those of their children. The cities and communities are the most wrought up over this, being the most disappointed in the hopes they conceived of this war and who suffer more torment than others. Do not, then, wait for the effects of their despair. . . .

SOURCE: Villeroy to Mayenne, 2 January 1594, Villeroy, pp. 254–5.

## 22    Rural disorder in Champagne, 1593–4

*[Jacques Carorguy, royalist registrar of Bar-sur-Seine, was living under the control of the League, after the conclusion of the three months' truce on 30 July 1593.]* Our garrison, knowing of it, did many ills to the poor villages, from whom in these last days they took what remained to them, their horses, cattle and pigs. . . . At Villemorien, they rebelled and some retreated to the church tower and killed some soldiers on the spot . . . and in fact today, 8 August, they sold some animals in front of the market hall to the sound of the drum while the bells for Mass were ringing. Everyone was scandalised, particularly with our Spaniards, who now swagger around and marry our widows and daughters. . . . They want to eat up the people and master them, since they have control of the castle under captain Verdun, a Gascon.

*[November 1593]* What makes us almost despair, in the absence of justice during these troubles, is that the most unimportant people dictate to the great. We have seen Dandenot occupy the priory of Viviers by force and take its revenues like the lord; also cobblers, vine-growers and tin-smiths occupy manors, having chased away the true owners, who had nothing from them except for the truce, which restored everyone to his property. . . . Honourable men should really desire this peace so as to live under a king who restores his subjects to their own and governs them henceforth under better laws. . . . In a word, the subjects of the Turks are not in such servitude as the inhabitants of Bar-sur-Seine. No one dares speak freely without being imprisoned by the Spaniards, who do as they please and daily oppress the poor villagers. Today, 13 November, when they came to the village of Arrelles to force them to pay for the fortifications of the castle, the inhabitants rebelled and, from the church, greeted them with gun fire, so that two were killed there and as many wounded. But they could not defend the church, which was taken, and 15 prisoners taken to the castle and garrotted like convicts and all their goods pillaged.

Around 27 April [*1594*] there happened a great and unexpected misfortune for this country because of the *douzains* counterfeited at Troyes in the name of Charles de Bourbon, which the villagers refused point blank to accept. The result was that there were no sales at the market that day and thus great confusion and disorder. The bakers, salt merchants, taverns and butchers were closed and the poor village people returned lamenting the disaster because that was the only coin they had. In short, there was such misery that some people were wounded as a result. Losses followed for there was no regulation or edict to cry down these *sols*, which were refused until 6 May, when an order from the court of the mint arrived from Paris. The *sols* then ran as before since it was forbidden to refuse them, at Troyes as well, on pain of death.

. . . On 3 May . . . a great scandal occurred at the Seine gate between the gatekeepers and a soldier of the garrison of Bar, Lenfant [*who wanted to arrest some villagers for their contribution to artillery costs. When he was stabbed*] more than 20 other soldiers rushed up sword in hand into the guard house and wounded three of the keepers. The inhabitants, alerted to this, wanted to assemble and fall on the soldiers, aiming also to recover our ancient liberty. However, the garrison's control held them back, for without that they would have been in great danger.

SOURCE: *Carorguy*, pp. 136–7, 160–1 and 180–1.

---

## 23   Troubles in Burgundy, early 1594

News that the communes of the villages of Pommard, Volnay, Meursault, Auscey, Fontenay, Saint-Aulbin, Gamay and others have summoned M. de Corrabeuf to be their leader, and that when they see any gens d'armes they ring the tocsin; that when one of those villages starts the rest follow, so that they all go to each others' help; that some time ago they slaughtered thirty gens d'armes of M. de Thianges's company who were out seeking clothing. The castle of Montsaujon is under siege and those without have placed four cannons from the town of Langres on a platform where the church used to be and three others on the windmill side. It is said that there are more than 2,000 peasants from Rivières and other villages around who are set on taking it because of the extortions they have suffered, and demand first place in the assault. . . . News came that Montsaujon has still not been fired on, though mines are being built. At this same time, there is news that the communes of Guyenne, Xaintonge, Périgueux and Limousin were in arms up to 15,000 men, making war on the nobility. They had issued a cry that soldiers of both sides should join them within 8 days otherwise their homes would be burned.

SOURCE: *Breunot*, vol. II, pp.19–20.

## 24   Peasant troubles in the south-west, 1594

[*April 1594*] While many of the great lords and cities of France had their representatives at Paris in the King's court to make an agreement, there was a great stirring of peoples in the regions of Limousin, Périgord, Agenais, Quercy and thereabout, through a general uprising of a great number of people. Their pretext was that they were too burdened with taxes and pillaged by the nobility, chiefly by some gentlemen of the party of the Union, who withdrew to their castles and pillaged the poor peasants. At the start, these rebels were called *tard avisés*, because it was said they decided to take up arms too late, since everyone wanted peace. These people called the nobility *croquants*, saying they only wished to chew up the people. But the nobles turned this nickname of *croquants* against the rebels, on whom it stuck.

There are various reports of how these people rose up. First a mass of them rose in Limousin in great disorder. Among other things, they scoured up vines, cut down trees and burned the houses and barns of those who would not join them. After they had roamed the land for some time, the sieur de Chambaret, King's governor, assembled the nobility, rode them down and defeated them. The news of the uprising came to Angoumois, where several communes rose [*but were quickly put down*]. It was in Périgord where the uprising was greatest, for they united with the other communes of Gascony and Quercy and assembled several times in force, though the viscount of Bourdeille, King's governor in Périgord, attacked and defeated several of their troops. [*Narration of an assembly of 120 deputies of the communes on 22 April, which was persuaded by Porquery, lawyer in the Parlement of Bordeaux, to send a petition to the King, which was discussed in the Council.*] The conclusion of this request was a pardon for those who had assembled in arms without permission, the suppression of a number of superfluous offices especially in finance, the reduction of the tailles, and permission to elect a syndic from the inhabitants of the country to ride out and force His Majesty's enemies to obey him As far as the pardon was concerned, this was granted.

SOURCE: Palma Cayet, vol. I, pp. 635–7

---

## THE WINNING OVER OF THE TOWNS OF THE LEAGUE, 1594

### 25   Negotiations with Villars for the reduction of Normandy

[*Villars was making trouble about accepting the authority of Montpensier as governor over him and over the office he held from the League as Admiral, now granted to Biron and wanted some abbeys that the King had given his servants. Henry wrote to Sully:* My friend, you are a beast of burden in so many matters and bear so many difficulties and problems in an affair whose conclusion is so important for the establishment of my authority and the alleviation of my peoples. Have you forgotten the advice you have given me so often, illustrating it with that of a certain duke of Milan to King Louis XI at the time of the War of the Public Weal, which was to divide by private interests all those who had leagued against him under general pretexts? This is what I want to do now. I would much rather it cost me twice as much in dealing separately with each individual than to achieve the same result through a general treaty with a single head (as you know many people wanted me to do). This could further prolong a party formed inside my state. So, don't go on bothering to be so respectful to those in question, whom we will otherwise content, or worry about money, for we shall pay for everything we receive, which would cost us ten times as much if we had to do it by force. So, as I trust you entirely and love you as a good servant, do not shrink from using your powers boldly, which I confirm by these letters as necessary, and conclude as quickly as you can with M. de Villars. But so arrange matters that there can then be no change. Then send me news of it for I am in constant doubt and impatience until I hear. Then, when I am reigning in peace, we can make the economies you have so often spoken to me about and you can rest assured that I shall neither spare travail nor fear peril to raise my glory and my State to their greatest splendour.

SOURCE: Henry IV to Sully, 6 March 1594, Sully, vol. I, pp. 420–1; BN, fr. 13665, fo .6.

[*After some bluster, Villars accepted the terms but this still left Montpensier and Biron to be contented. On the evening of his entry into Paris, Henry said to Sully:*] 'It will be easiest to content them in a way I have thought of. This is, that I shall pretend when they are here to call you to know the news you bring from Rouen as though you had not already told me. . . . You will say that you would have easily been able to come to an agreement but that the two articles concerning them prevented you from concluding it. You knew well that I would rather lose Villars and Rouen than them. But you think them so devoted to me and so full of prudence that they would never agree that, for some little private interest . . . they should be the cause of losing me the opportunity of getting such an important province as Normandy into my obedience.' This invention succeeded so well . . . that both of them had nothing to say, rather they were ashamed to see the King saying that he would rather lose Normandy than annoy them. [*Biron was given the office of marshal and 27,000 écus in place of that of Admiral.*]

SOURCE: Sully, vol. I, pp. 436–7.

## 26  The fall of Paris

God, by continuing the holy grace and goodness with which he has aided me during these troubles, to the preservation of this State and the confusion of those who wished to thrust out the true and legitimate heirs in order to seize it, has so favoured my wishes and good intentions towards the people of this my good city of Paris that, through the great and signal services of the count of Brissac, I today entered peacefully and without any spilling of blood or any incovenience in persons or property to a single bourgeois. Only two or three got themselves killed, by their obstinacy and disdain for the pardon I had given them, while opposing my troops and also the desires of nearly all their fellow citizens to recognise me. This they showed by coming to meet me, arms outstretched with joy and acclamations, crying 'God save the King!' The foreign troops in the town withdrew to their quarters and laid down their arms, on condition that I granted them their equipment on leaving. This they did this afternoon. The Bastille still holds out, but with so few men and supplies that I expect to take it in a few days. . . . At 8 o'clock with the town in order, I went to offer thanks to God in the cathedral of Notre-Dame, where I heard Mass. I wish that, by processions and other solemnities, you render like thanks, with bonfires, as this success warrants, which can lead on to others through its example.

SOURCE: Henry IV, circular letter, 22 March 1594, *LMH4*, vol. IV, p. 120

---

## 27   The reduction of Champagne

Those of Troyes wanted to follow this route, and when their envoys returned from His Majesty, today Tuesday 5 April, they made a full and voluntary declaration without any disturbance. The people, before so rebellious, all took up the white sash willingly. In fact, the next day my lords Admiral de Biron, de Dinteville Pralain and Preipape, who had earlier taken the King's side, entered Troyes and were warmly welcomed. Women and children cried: 'Long live the King!', a remarkable thing and truly amazing for there had been no more seditious a town in France and full of vengeance against the King. Even a month earlier they had administered a new oath even to children and domestics never to leave the League. But as the wise man said, the people that revolts quickly is still quicker to give up and return to its duty. . . . What can I conclude when so many towns come over Vézelay surrendered with Auxerre, fully and with the same humane conditions a the others received . . . those who cursed [*the King*] are those who now pray God for him to reign in peace. . . .

At last came the happy day of 10 May in our good year. Fortune, joy and happiness are granted us all together, since this good work of reconciliation with our King happened through the declaration made by the sieur de Grammont, declaration that is full of good will, piously made with a firm voice in the general assembly of that day . . . when with eloquence and vivacity he said that he would henceforth serve none other than Henry IV his legitimate King and sovereign lord

As witness, he intended that the royal symbols be set up and the white sash cover the green and red.

SOURCE: *Carorguy*, pp. 181–3.

## 28   Picardy: Henry IV and Abbeville

Since it has pleased God to call us to the government of this French monarchy, for which he has ever had a particular care, His divine goodness has clearly revealed, through the happy success He has conferred on all our plans and enterprises, His approval of our legitimate establishment therein. This grace has been still more fully shown when our enemies, omitting nothing to thwart us and willing to try their last throw to achieve the usurpation of our crown, no longer able to conceal the ambition they had until then hidden behind the pretext of religion, tried to persuade our subjects that the disposition of our crown belonged to them, hoping to obtain the election of a Spaniard or one of themselves. Good Frenchmen have found this so little to their taste that those who heard the proposition as deputies of our provinces, having shown their fellow citizens the pernicious intentions of our enemies, entirely abhorred and disapproved of their effects. So, turning to us as their prince and natural lord, they have entirely resolved to enter our obedience, from which they expected, and some have already felt, as much benefit and relief as their rebellion had brought them ruin, loss and need. Our towns of Paris, Meaux, Orléans, Rouen, Bourges, Lyon, Verneuil have one after the other submitted to their duty and have since been followed by Troyes, Sens and Auxerre. These examples and the favours and benefits you may still feel at the hands of our house, and in particular the honour done you by our lord and father, whom God pardon, when he was your governor, make us hope that you will not be the last to obey us. Nothing can now excuse you, God commands you, nature obliges you, the Spaniards who are at your gates, brought into our other towns by those who think they have much power over you, to the prejudice of your liberties and franchises, force you to. Have no doubt about our religion, for the defence and preservation of which we have given a solemn oath at our conversion, repeated at our coronation and since confirmed at the summons of the Orders. Nor let you fear the pursuit of past faults. The promise we make you now to pardon you, and knowledge of the gentleness and mercy that the most seditious rebels of this town have felt, should make you forget such fear. Fail not, then to come to us, for we are ready to receive you and embrace you with a paternal benevolence and royal good nature. We want from you only a pure and frank will to serve us and build in your hearts the firmest and most stable foundations and defences of our authority, under which you will be maintained in the free, peaceable and entire enjoyment of all your goods and rights and all the fine and ample privileges that your fathers obtained from our predecessors for their signal loyalty. We assure you we will do more for your satisfaction if, by your services and merits, you give us occasion to.

SOURCE: Henri IV to Abbeville, Paris, 11 April 1594, Prarond, vol. III, pp. 115–17.

## 29   Picardy: Amiens, August 1594

[*On 4 and 8 August, the council debated requests to Mayenne for help and letters from the city council and Parlement in Paris to come over. On 9 August, 2 hours after midnight, some councillors met in the absence of others held up by insurrection in the streets, along with officials, the bishop and lords.*] The Lieutenant-General said that the war had begun for the preservation of religion. At present the King had become a Catholic and promised to preserve the Catholic religion, so the reason for war was over. This is why the people had today risen in arms to recognise the King. For fear that this rising might happen before getting some articles granted by the King, he had, with certain clergy, lords and chief inhabitants, agreed several good articles with His Majesty, which he placed on the table. After the reading of these articles, hereafter transcribed, it was reported by some *échevins* and the registrar that, on the mayor's instructions, they had visited all quarters of the city in which the people are in arms demanding peace with the King, and were not prepared to lay them down until the King was ackowledged and obeyed in this city. The meeting decided, on the request of the procurator fiscal, that the King be acknowledged and obeyed in this city and that proclamation of this be immediately made at the crossroads. His Majesty and M. d'Humières, the King's Lieutenant-General in Picardy, will be informed. For the safety of the city, the duke of Aumale will immediately be asked to leave.

SOURCE: *IS, Amiens*, vol. II, pp. 247–8.

## THE NOBILITY

### 30   The agreement between Sully and the duke of Guise, 15 July 1594

1. M. de Rosny is asked to obtain from the King the restitution of the governorship of Champagne and Brie, which the late duke of Guise held at the time of his death.

Reply: [*In view of the fact that Nevers and Rethel hold these positions and it would be unjust to remove them, to show his esteem, the King agrees to gratify him with some other governorship.*]

2. M. de Rosny is asked further to agree to the restitution of the estate of Grand Master of France for the same reason.

Reply: [*The office is held now by the count of Soissons. Compensation is offered.*]

3. Further, the provision of all the benefices held by the cardinal of Guise for my lords the two younger brothers of my lord duke of Guise destined for the church.

Reply: [*Sully asks Guise to be satisfied with the abbeys of Saint-Denis, Ourscamp and Corbie and the promise of gratification when other benefices fall vacant.*]

4. M. de Guise asks the King to discharge all the debts of the late duke of Guise and the cardinals of Guise his brother and uncle, of whom he is the heir, and all the property mortgaged for this reason.

Reply: [*The King cannot take on unlimited debts but offers 1,200,000 lt. over several years to discharge valid debts.*] Futhermore, according as M. de Guise and my lords his brothers show their loyalty and service to His Majesty, he will willingly gratify them with good sums from time to time to this effect. Meanwhile, in order to allow MM. de Guise and Joinville to attend his person, he accords them an annual pension of 30,000 *lt.* to M. de Guise and 12,000 to the prince of Joinville.

As a result of these articles . . . he came to meet His Majesty with all the friends he could muster and was received most favourably and with such smiling caresses, familiarity, priviness and freedom of speech as if he had been raised with him from his earliest years and had only ever rendered him faithful service and entire obedience. . . .

SOURCE: Sully, vol. I, pp. 548–51.

## 31    The remains of the League, 1594–5

On Leaving Laon, the King of Navarre spoke to President Jeannin, who had been inside the city during the siege, and offered a conference to explore ways of negotiating peace. He replied that he thought I would not agree unless His Holiness and you, Sire, approved, as well as the remains of the party. He has since returned to me in this city . . . and told me the reasons he thought this conference was necessary. . . . I advanced the reasons for its usefulness [*to the Archduke Ernest*]. These are: that all over the kingdom deputies are flocking to the King of Navarre to negotiate with him; this conference would hold them back from concluding anything. Moreoover, war is so universally rejected that it must definitely be justified. If it is continued, it can be done best through a conference in which the King of Navarre makes difficulties about giving the necessary assurances concerning religion. If there is agreement with Your Majesty's approval . . . it will be received as a great blessing from God. . . . As for me, Sire, I judge it well to consider, in view of the state our affairs are reduced to, that it would be most useful, provided Your Majesty were included and you give your consent. Without that, I see no security for religion or for the Catholics. . . . Such a conference will also serve to bring together the remains of the party, which cannot be done otherwise. If it is concluded that war must be continued, all of them can take the decision together without giving their opinion separately. Their despair and suspicion will make them conclude for particular sureties and advantages and thus in the end religion will be lost.

SOURCE: Mayenne to Philip II, Brussels, 6 September 1594, BL, Vesp. F V, fo. 393–4, copy.

---

## 32   Edict of Folembray, dealing with Mayenne, 26 January 1596

[*Despite the blessings of the King's conversion for the peace*] this work would not have been complete had not our right dear and well-beloved cousin the duke of Mayenne, head of his party, followed the same route, as he resolved to do as soon as he saw that our holy father had approved our adhesion [*to the church*]. All this has made us accept in good part what he has told us of his zeal for religion and praise his desire to see the kingdom preserved in its entirety, nor allow its dismemberment when, in his prosperity, he could have done so. Nor did he do so after his power began to weaken but preferred rather to throw himself into our arms and show us the obedience that God, nature and the laws commanded than try other remedies which might have prolonged the war to the great harm of our subjects. This makes us wish to recognise his good will, to love and treat him in future as our good kinsman and faithful subject; so that he and all the good Catholics who follow his example in this duty should be ever more confirmed and others encouraged to follow this salutary course; also so that none hereafter can pretend to doubt the sincerity of our adherence to the Catholic Church and on pretext of this scatter fresh seeds of dissension to seduce our subjects and bring them to ruin. [*Renews his profession of the Catholic faith.*]

[*There follow 31 articles concerning Mayenne and his followers.*]

SOURCE: Palma Cayet, vol. II, pp. 85–90.

# Epilogue: Henry IV and the Protestants

The events of 1594–6 solved one major problem: the objections of Catholics to a Bourbon succession. They did not solve the problem of the Huguenots, who continued to depend on their collective military strength to maintain their security. From August 1589, Henry had been anxious to avoid losing his basis of support in the Huguenot provinces and may have taken some time fully to realise that his rule could only be established by his conversion. Nevertheless, Mornay was aware almost immediately that the King would be under pressure to convert. His policy was one of conciliation of the Catholics but cast-iron guarantees for Protestants (see Document 1). As late as 1591, the Edicts of Mantes seemed to indicate Henry's determination to protect Protestant gains (see Chapter 8, Documents 13–14). However, Henry recognised the logic of the situation by 1593. Early in May of that year, the Protestant leaders complained to Henry about his proposed conversion and the King told them: 'If I followed your advice, in a short time there would be neither King nor kingdom in France. I desire to give peace to my subjects and repose to my soul. Decide among you what is needed for your security; I shall always be ready to satisfy you' (Palma Cayet, vol 1, p. 249). At the time of his decision to convert, Henry took care to insist that his Catholic councillors formally promise to maintain the Edicts of Toleration (see Document 2). Once the King had converted, the emergence of Protestant alienation was rapid. The assembly of the Religion that had been called to Mantes under Mornay's direction was overtaken by the event and he left the court, having to be cajoled by his master to return (see Document 3–5). When the Mantes Assembly did meet in November 1593, its cahiers demanded guarantees, paid garrisons and full access to royal office, covered in the Edict of Mantes but not implemented. It formalised a Union of the churches for mutual aid (see Document 6). However, Henry IV was most concerned at this time to win over the Catholic cities, and ignored the demands.

The Protestants took two courses: one, which did not succeed, was to seek a foreign 'protector'. The other, much more effective, saw the creation of a military protection network at the series of Assemblies that took up the themes of the Mantes meeting. They began at Sainte-Foy in May 1594 (see Document 7) and continued at Saumur in 1595. The assemblies of 1596 and

1597 were increasingly dominated by disgruntled noble clients of men such as Turenne and La Trémoille, an ominous sign. Though Henry IV was determined not to make concessions as a result of his weakness during the war with Spain, the pressures from the Huguenots of threatening to withhold their taxes forced the King's negotiators, such as Schomberg, to consider terms (see Document 8). The King was highly disgruntled at the terms, and negotiations dragged on over the winter of 1597–8. The final compromise was agreed in April 1598 when Henry, after the recapture of Amiens and the start of peace negotiations with Spain at Vervins (the treaty was concluded in June), had brought his army to the west to deal with Mercoeur in Brittany, thus bringing some intimidation to bear (see Document 9). The next phase was for the King to pressure the Catholic Parlements into accepting the Edict (see Document 10).

The Edict of Nantes was one more in the long series of attempts to codify the position of the Protestant minority. It shared many of the provisions of previous edicts but with the crucial difference of security guarantees that had a realistic hope of working. The bulk of the edict survived the cancellation of those guarantees between 1620 and 1629 and lasted until 1685. In 1598, though, it may have seemed very temporary. That the country did not return to civil war, despite the growing fears of the Protestants, and as so many times in the past, is a complex problem. 'War weariness' is too simple an explanation, while the argument that a neo-stoic concept of tranquil obedience to the state was spreading, in itself explains little beyond the realm of ideas. Perhaps only Henry IV could have balanced the interests in a way needed to avoid a fresh declaration of hostilities and convince all parties that there was something to be gained by compromise. However, it was a close-run thing.

---

## 1  Mornay's view in 1589

The Catholics are alarmed about their religion. There must be a declaration to reassure them. The terms can be: to innovate nothing in the Catholic religion and meanwhile to seek, by all legitimate means, with the advice of the princes of the blood, officers of the crown and qualified persons of the realm, the reunion of all his subjects.

Because, on the other hand, those of the Religion must not be offended, the terms in which they are mentioned in all public acts must be agreed. The most suitable are: *the Religion that we call Reformed* or *called Reformed*.

If those of the Religion need to ask His Majesty for greater liberty, as is reasonable it seems the most suitable way is for it to be by a request of the leaders in each province, founded on the previous edicts, which have only been broken through the violence of the League, whose actions should all be detested, as they have caused the ruin of this kingdom. No one in the Council will dissent from such a reasonable thing. It could be modified in regard to justice. As for sureties, His Majesty is their best surety.

It is needful to write to the churches and the governors of places where the Religion is practised that they comport themselves more modestly in word and deed than ever, suppressing the insolence of the people, and live in peace and unity with the Catholics. . . . Rulings for the preservation of churches, relics, maintenance of services, should be repeated and more closely observed than ever. His Majesty may be requested to restore the mass at Niort and other places. This will give reason to accept the request of those of the Religion when they require their exercise.

The people have for some time longed for some relief and the times in which God has called His Majesty to the throne are inopportune. This demands a declaration of intent to provide such relief and of regret that God has called him to the throne at such a difficult time. . . .

SOURCE: Mornay's Memoir for Henri IV, *c*.10 August 1589, *Mornay*, vol. IV, pp. 393–8.

## 2  Declaration of the Council on the Protestants

We, the princes and officers of the crown and other lords of the King's Council undersigned, wish to remove from those of the Religion called Reformed all occasion of doubt that at the talks which are being held, with permission, at Suresnes between the deputies of the Catholic princes and officers of the crown who recognise His Majesty, and the deputies of the Paris assembly, there should be any agreement to the prejudice of that Religion concerning what was accorded them by the Edicts of the late kings, until measures for the re-establishment and maintenance of the peace of the realm are taken, with the advice of the princes, lords and other notable persons of both religions whom His Majesty has decided to assemble in this town of Mantes on 20 July next. We all promise, with His Majesty's permission, that, until such resolution, nothing will be done in that assembly by our deputies to the prejudice of the good union and friendship between the Catholics who recognise His Majesty and those of the Religion, or of the Edicts. We also promise to advise our deputies at Suresnes of our present promise that it is necessary to avoid any ill-feeling between His Majesty's good subjects, so that they may for their part conform to it.

SOURCE: 16 May 1593, Palma Cayet, vol. I, pp. 514–15.

## 3   Mornay's view of the Abjuration

[*Advice on whether to send ministers to Mantes in July 1593 on the King's summons:*]
He does not think it is His Majesty's intention that the ministers confer with the
bishops and less so that the bishops would enter discussions with them, either for
fear of the force of truth or so as not to displease the Pope, by whom they would
certainly be excommunicated. Besides this, it would be too dangerous to enter into
a conference before the King had decided to attend.

M. du Plessis judges that His Majesty wants the ministers of each province to
come in order to assure them of his desire to continue to preserve the churches so
they can take back some assurance to the people.

His opinion is thus that they should go, because their presence would doubtless
move His Majesty's soul, if not to restrain him from changing his religion, at least
to accord them what is needed for their security and preservation. . . .

As for the lords, gentlemen and notable persons called by His Majesty, the sieur
du Plessis thinks likewise that much good could come for the churches if the affair
is well handled. His opinion is that in each Colloquy there be a small meeting of
the most notable persons of the Religion of all Estates, in which, to avoid discord,
those who would attend His Majesty would be chosen. [*They would remonstrate the
following:*] For more ample [*liberty of*] religion, they should remonstrate that, by the
rigour of the troubles, the countryside is these days closed to us; thus we must
exercise our Religion, if not in the towns, at least in the suburbs. To request to have
it at court and in His Majesty's armies. In default of this, they are clearly closed to
those of the Religion and His Majesty deprived of their service. It is unacceptable
that until now burial has been refused to those killed in battle in His Majesty's
presence.

As for justice, the Parlements will never accept the Chambers included in the
Edict. Instead, it is needed that in each Parlement or Presidial Court a certain
number of those of the Religion should be appointed. . . .

For sureties, it must above all be determined that the important fortresses be
well maintained, because it is intended that they be whittled away by lack of
payment. . . .

SOURCE: Memoir of Mornay, 9 June 1593, *Mornay*, vol. V, pp. 450–3

## 4   Henry IV and Mornay (i)

Monsieur du Plessis, I find most strange that, as some have reported, you of all
people complain about me. For besides the fact that I have given you no reason and
have loved you more than any gentleman of my kingdom, I have always spoken to
you so openly that, if you had subject for grievance, you should have informed or
told me of it yourself and not to another. I have written to you to join me several

times, but in vain. I see clearly what is the matter; you love the cause rather than me. However, I shall always be your good master and king. Give me the pleasure of seeing you, either post-haste or otherwise, and leave excuses aside. For, besides the fact I have things to tell you which cannot be written, I want to consult with you over my domain of Navarre. My sister complains that at Saumur she is not prayed for. Let me know what this is about, for I cannot believe it.

SOURCE: Henry IV to Mornay, 7 August 1593, *LMH4*, vol. IV, pp. 5–6.

## 5   Henry IV and Mornay (ii)

I deplore and weep at His Majesty's torment, of which I am fully aware. I pray you to tell him that, should he ever desire to escape this temporal and spiritual captivity, my fidelity in his service can only increase; indeed, I will double my courage for the just grief that I feel. They do not give him peace in the state and rob him of peace in his conscience. They do not reconcile the rebels to him and alienate his most faithful followers. They do not restore his kingdom to him, for it is for God not the devil to do that, and they rob him as far as they can of his heavenly kingdom. . . .

SOURCE: Mornay to Lomenie, 11 August 1593, *Mornay*, vol. V, p. 511.

## 6   Assembly of Mantes, December 1593

We, the deputies of the Reformed Churches of this realm . . . have heretofore learned by most evident proofs how far union and concord is needful [*for the preservation of the churches*] and that they cannot last long without a good and close conjunction and mutual understanding one with another, better kept than in the past. For this reason, we desire to remove all seeds of division and subjects of conflict between the churches and prevent all pretence, calumny and manoeuvres by which those ill-disposed to our Religion try to ruin and divide them. We foresee also that the league of rebels against His Majesty and their abettors is entirely bent on the ruin of this state and extermination of the churches; that it is more than ever needed that by common consent they seek the means of their just, legitimate and necessary defence and preservation, to oppose (when necessary), under the King's authority and protection, the violent efforts of our enemies. We have thus, in the name of the Reformed Churches, for their security and preservation and for His Majesty's service, the good of the state and re-establishment of the public peace of this realm, continuing the treaties of Union hitherto made by the deputies of the churches . . . renewed and confirmed . . . by these presents that Union between the churches and we protest and swear piously before God . . . to remain inseparably united under our humble obedience to the King, whom we acknowledge to have been given us by heaven as our sovereign lord. . . . This not only in the church discipline and doctrine of our general confession long ago published, following the declaration and protestation we made in the    first articles of our cahier of remonstrances, but also in all offices and duties of public and private charity and in all that stems from mutual preservation, aid and assistance.

Followed by signatures for each province

SOURCE: 9 December 1593, SP78/32, fo. 343, copy.

## 7   Assembly of Sainte-Foy, May 1594

Meanwhile, the Reformed, with the King's general though not express permission, summoned a general assembly for their affairs at Sainte-Foy in mid-May 1594. They had received complaints enough on all sides to dare this innovation.

At Sainte-Foy there were thirty deputies from every region assembled on return from the Synod of Montauban. To begin with, various letters and complaints from the lords, governors and communities were read. Then three memoranda were tabled by persons who had been accustomed to have a hand in the party's affairs, concerning the means to revive and preserve them. The most important will show the state of anxiety the Reformed were reduced to. It was by one of their oldest and most renowned captains who had several times incurred the King of Navarre's wrath because of his great zeal for the party's affairs. This is what in summary it said: First . . . he was of the view that, for the direction of affairs, a notable person from Languedoc and Dauphiné, one from Guyenne, one from the Loire region and another for the rest of France be maintained at court to liaise with a secretary of state, then to be Reformed, to deliver necessary complaints and hear the King's will; that in the course of events they assemble as a Council the ministers of the church of Paris, the lords at court for their affairs, and some royal valet de chambre; that money be levied in the provinces for a pension of 4,000 or 5,000 écus to be paid to the secretary. A bolder move would be to give a pension of 10,000 to the duchess of Beaufort, the King's friend, who was in spirit with the Religion, as was shown by the fact that she confided in none of her servants who did not profess the Religion. [*The assembly approved the following articles:*]

1    That there be a General Assembly of the Reformed Churches of ten persons at most once or twice a year according to need and in a secure place. At the end of each meeting, the place and time of the next will be agreed. The first is convoked to Saumur when the deputies who will go to court shall have returned, with power to decide for the general good what the times require.

2    [*The provinces from which the deputies are to come.*]

3    There will be ten regional Councils for each deputy to the General Assembly. If some, for their commodity and greater union, wish to join together in sending to the General Assembly or if some provinces find difficulty in the

grouping, they can agree together and report the matter to the General Assembly at Saumur so it can be approved.

4    For the ten deputies to the General Assembly, there will be four gentlemen, two ministers and four of the third estate. The province which choses a minister one year will elect the following year a gentleman or one of the third estate.

5–18  [*The conduct of the national and regional assemblies.*]

19    [*Provisions for the maintenance of military governments in Protestant hands.*]

20    Governors and captains commanding in places held by those of the Religion under the King's obedience will be warned not to allow any of their garrisons or enlist any soldier who is not of the Religion properly certified. If there be any others, they will be promptly dismissed. Should it happen that the garrisons be reduced without the consent of the churches before the conclusion of a peace, governors and captains will pursue their payment in the following ways under the garrison list of January 1594.

21    As for payment of the garrisons needed for the defence of fortresses held by those of the Religion, article 98 of the Mantes cahier will be pressed for and scrupuloulsy observed. Thus, the governors and captains may seize moneys of the election or receipt they are in, up to the sum required by the establishment of the garrison.

22–8  [*Other regulations concerning payment.*]

Secret articles:

1  [*The King will be petitioned*] that it please His Majesty to grant those of the Religion bipartisan chambers in all the Parlements except in Dauphiné, with prohibition of hearing cases involving the Reformed until their estabishment. . . .

2  In view of the extreme affliction of the Reformed Chuches of this kingdom, it was decided to petition Her Majesty the Queen of England and the lords of the Estates of the Netherlands to favour, by their intercession with the King our lord, the most humble requests that we present to him. . . .

3  Letters will be written to all the grandees and notables who profess the Religion in this kingdom to confirm them in true piety and exhort them to observe the union of the churches and that the freedom of pure Religion be preserved in France.

Source: Aubigné, vol. IX, pp. 85–97.

## 8 Articles negotiated between Schomberg and the deputies of the Reformed Churches in July 1597

The exercise of the Reformed Religion will continue in all towns and places where it was done publicly in 1570 and also in those places where it is at present. It remains to agree terms to remove all ambiguity.

As for the places in each bailliage, there is agreement to the King's replies, provided there is no clause by which they of the Religion are seen to approve the treaties with those of the League and that the suburbs chosen in each bailliage are convenient for those of the Religion, to be agreed at the conclusion of the treaty.

To settle the matter of the great cities in whose suburbs it is impossible at present to establish exercise of the Religion without tumult, as at Rouen, Dijon, Orléans, Angers, Poitiers, Bordeaux, Bourges, Lyon, Rennes, Beziers, Vienne and others, they shall be given a place for public worship as near as possible according to the quality of the city. This will not, however, abridge the privileges conceded for worship in hauberk fiefs, those of high justice, and minor fiefs. As far as possible, places will be chosen which belong to the King or those of the Religion, or in default of this, Roman Catholics.

As for Paris, on the issue that public worship be established in a place no more than four French leagues away, the sieur de Schomberg has agreed on five and promised to write to the King to obtain four, as he was asked.

As for Blois, Châlons-sur-Marne, Dieppe and other places, exercise of the Religion is on tolerance. It will be continued by His Majesty's authority at least under a secret article; at least the suburbs will be conceded as bailliage centres.

In small fiefs, the restriction on attendance of friends and on baptisms will be removed and the number of 30 plus the family agreed. Where it has been asked that the number be raised to 50, the sieur de Schomberg will write to H.M.; as well as that, on the issue of accommodating the countryside and townships far from a city and where there is no high justice fief belonging to those of the Religion, a small fief be accorded in each bailliage where public worship may take place.

It has been asked that the restriction on preaching within two leagues of the court be removed as well as that worship should not cease in places where the court be established; also that when the court is in places where worship is not permitted, it be lawful for lords to worship in their lodging without investigation. The sieur de Schomberg will write to H.M.

For the upkeep of pastors and schools of the Religion, the said lord has offered the sum of 43,000 *écus* p.a. in perpetuity.

Besides the bipartisan chambers of Languedoc, Guyenne and Dauphiné already agreed, the sieur de Schomberg has agreed a Chamber of Justice at Paris made up of seven Roman Catholic councillors and a president and six councillors of the Religion, to judge the cases of those of the Religion in the jurisdiction of the Parlements of Paris, Rouen and Rennes. As for Dijon, those of Burgundy may chose whether to go to Paris or to the bipartisan Chamber of Dauphiné.

[*Arrangements for the nomination of the councillors.*]

That those of the Religion have the choice of the President and two of the Catholic councillors in the Chamber of Paris at each replacement. The sieur de Schomberg has promised to write to H.M. but has promised absolutely the choice of three councillors, and that, as for the other Catholics, H.M. will choose the most moderate.

[*Five further articles on details of the Chamber.*]

That the strongholds held by those of the Religion will be left in their control at least for eight years, that is: two years under the Edict and six by secret article. After that, they will be listened to concerning changes to be made.

For the necessary payment of the garrisons, H.M. has offered those of the Religion 180,000 *écus* p.a. during that period, to be made from reliable receipts.

In this sum will not be included the garrisons of Dauphiné, which will be provided for by a memoir to this effect handed to the sieur de Schomberg.

That on vacancies of governorships and captaincies in those places, His Majesty will appoint on the nomination of those of the Religion while they are in their control. The sieur de Schomberg has agreed that those of the Religion will nominate three and the King choose one of them.

That the commissioners for the execution of the Edict will be equally divided between both religions.

The officers of the crown and all others will swear to the observation of the Edict as in articles 63 and 64 of the edict of 1577. As for His Majesty, they will accept his word alone.

Source: Drawn up in the General Assembly at Châtellerault, 20 August 1597, BL, Cotton, Vesp. F V, fos. 395–6.

---

## 9  Aubigné on the negotiation of the Edict of Nantes

The treaties were further delayed during the siege of Amiens because the duke of Mercoeur, in new hope of the King's affairs being diverted, put off the agreement he had embarked on. The treaty with the Reformed was condemned to follow in its train, so the talks at Châtellerault cooled off. When the King, after taking Amiens, marched on Brittany . . . the deputies of the Reformed feared that the King, by caprice, would come unexpectedly to Châtellerault. The alarm in their assembly was unbelievable. The King's men were ordered to press matters forward and concluded a peace. But it was still necessary to get the agreement of the King, then at Nantes in triumph at seeing himself without enemies. There, the articles concluded were reviewed and diminished by the King's authority. This was not all, for the Parlements joined together against its registration, whatever the wiser senators said, notably those who had been fugitives at Tours and said they had seen the loyalty of the Reformed at close hand.

SOURCE: Aubigné, vol. IX, pp. 280–1.

## 10  Henry IV's admonition to the Presidents of the Parlement, January 1599, on the registration of the Edict of Nantes

You see me in my closet, where I come to speak with you not in royal habiliments, with my rapier and my helmet, as my predecessors, nor like a prince who intendeth to speak to foreign ambassadors; but apparelled like a father to a family in a doublet, to speak familiarly to his children. That which I have to say is to pray you to verify the Edict which I have granted unto those of the Religion. That which I have done is for the good of the peace, which I have concluded without and I will now have it within my realm. You ought to obey me, although there were no other consideration but my quality and the obligation of all my subjects and especially you of my Parlement. Some I have replaced in their houses, from which they were banished, and other some in the faith which otherwise they would not have had. If the obedience was done to my predecessors, as much and more is due to me, because I have re-established the estate, God having chosen me to set me in my kingdom, which is due to me by inheritance and purchase. The lords of my Parlement should not be in their seats without me. I will not vaunt or boast, but this much will I say: that I have no other example to imitate but myself. I know full well that there hath been a great bribery and that seditious preachings have been raised up. But I will set good order for those men and will not refer the same to you. It is even the way which was taken to make the barricadoes and to come by degrees to the murder of the late King. Nay, I will look into all that, I will cut the root of all those factions and of all factious sermons and will shorten all those which shall raise them. I have leapt upon the walls of cities; I shall also be able to leap upon your barricadoes, which are not so high. Allege not unto me the Catholic religion; I love it better than you. I am more Catholic than you; I am the eldest son of the Church. . . . You may do enough; I shall know what every one of you say. I know what is in your houses; I know all what you do and say. I have a little demon, who revealeth all to me. Those which will not have my Edict to pass seek wars. I will declare them tomorrow to those of the Religion but I will not make the wars. You yourselves shall go, together with your gowns, and gather again the procession of the Capuchins, which shall carry their muskets upon their garments. It will be a goodly sight to see you. If you will not pass my Edict, you will make me go to the Parlement. You shall be unkind, when you shall have engendered in me this ennui. . . . Necessity constrained me to make this Edict.

Through the same necessity, I have at other times played the soldier. It is spoken of and yet I have not made any semblance thereof. I am King now and speak like a King. I will be obeyed.

SOURCE: *The speeche which the French King made to the Lords of the Parliament on the 5 Januarie 1599*, trans. H. W. (London: John Wolfe, 1599).

# Suggested Further Reading

## Abbreviations for Journals

| | |
|---|---|
| Am. HR | *American Historical Review* |
| ARG | *Archiv für Reformationsgeschichte* |
| BHR | *Bibliothèque d'Humanisme et Renaissance* |
| BIHR | *Bulletin of the Institute of Historical Research* |
| CJH | *Canadian Journal of History* |
| EHQ | *European History Quarterly* |
| EHR | *English Historical Review* |
| ESR | *European Studies Review* (continued as *EHQ*) |
| FH | *French History* |
| FHS | *French Historical Studies* |
| HJ | *Historical Journal* |
| J.Eccl.Hist | *Journal of Ecclesiastical History* |
| JES | *Journal of European Studies* |
| JIH | *Journal of Interdisciplinary History* |
| JMH | *Journal of Modern History* |
| JRH | *Journal of Religious History* |
| PAPS | *Proceedings of the American Philosophical Society* |
| PER | *Parliaments, Estates and Representation* |
| P&P | *Past and Present* |
| PWSFH | *Proceedings of the Western Society for French History* |
| SCJ | *Sixeenth-Century Journal* |
| SFS | *Seventeenth-Century French Studies* |
| TAPS | *Transactions of the American Philosophical Society* |

The sixteenth century in France is now amply supplied with general surveys. These include:

F. J. Baumgartner, *France in the Sixteenth Century* (London: Macmillan, 1996); J. Garrisson, *A History of Sixteenth-Century France, 1483–1598* (London: Macmillan, 1995); R. J. Knecht, *The Rise and Fall of Renaissance France, 1483–1610* (London: Fontana, 1996); E. Le Roy Ladurie, *The French Royal State, 1460–1610* (Oxford

Blackwell, 1993); H. A. Lloyd, *The State, France and the Sixteenth Century* (London: Unwin, 1983); D. Potter, *A History of France, 1460–1560: The Emergence of a Nation State* (London: Macmillan, 1995).

For the period of the Wars of Religion specifically see J. H. Salmon, *Society in Crisis* (London: Benn, 1975). M. P. Holt, *The French Wars of Religion, 1562–1629* (Cambridge: Cambridge University Press, 1995) is the most recent survey and concentrates on the theme of the interweaving of politics and religion. R. J. Knecht, *The French Wars of Religion, 1562–1598* (London: Longman, rev. edn. 1996) gives a brief overview with some documents. A clear and well-researched narrative of an older, kind is to be found in J. W. Thompson, *The French Wars of Religion* (Chicago: Chicago University Press, 1909) but unfortunately concludes in 1576. R. Briggs, *Early Modern France, 1560–1715* (London: Oxford University Press, 1977) has some useful indications.

## Studies of wider themes

N. Sutherland, *The Huguenot Struggle for Recognition* (New Haven, Conn.: Yale University Press, 1980) deals with the various plans for religious toleration and their outcome; Sutherland's *The Massacre of Saint Bartholomew and the European Conflict* (London: Macmillan, 1973) concentrates on the political and diplomatic context, and discusses the sources for the actual event in some detail. On the course of the fighting and the military imperatives we now have J. B. Wood, *The King's Army: Warfare, Soldiers and Society during the Wars of Religion, 1562–1576* (Cambridge: Cambridge University Press, 1996) and his 'The Royal Army during the Early Wars of Religion', in M. P. Holt (ed.), *Society and Institutions in Early Modern France* (Athens: Georgia University Press, 1991). On the effects of the fighting, see J. B. Wood, 'The Impact of the Wars of Religion: a View of France in 1581', *SCJ*, 15, II (1984). The final stage of military operations is covered in H. A. Lloyd, *The Rouen Campaign* (Oxford: Clarendon Press, 1973).

## Biographical Studies

There are biographies of Catherine de Medici by Paul van Dyke (New York: Scribner's, 1922) – which contains many extracts from her letters (not always accurately translated) – and by J. Héritier (London: Unwin, 1963). N. M. Sutherland, *Princes, Politics and Religion* (Hambledon, 1984) contains 'Catherine de Medici and the Ancien Regime' as well as essays on 'Antoine de Bourbon, King of Navarre and the French Crisis, 1559–62' and 'The Role of Coligny in the French Civil Wars'. See also N. L. Roelker, *Queen of Navarre: Jeanne d'Albret, 1528–72* (Cambridge, Mass.: Belknap, 1968). On Condé, there is Henri d'Orléans, duc d'Aumale, *History of the Princes of Condé in the 16th and 17th*

*Centuries,* trans. R. B. Borthwick (London, 1872), esp. vol. l. On Coligny, see J. Shimizu, *Conflict of Loyalties: Politics and Religion in the Career of Gaspard de Coligny* (Geneva: Droz, 1970); A. W. Whitehead, *Gaspard de Coligny Admiral of France* (London: Methuen, 1904), and M. P. Holt, *The Duke of Anjou and the Politique Struggle during the Wars of Religion* (Cambridge: University Press, 1986). The important figure of Henri de Montmorency-Damville is covered by a now dated biography by F. C. Palm, *Politics and Religion in the XVIth Century: Henry of Montmorency-Damville, Uncrowned King of the South* (Boston, Mass.: 1927). This can now be supplemented by M. Greengrass, 'Noble Affinities in Early Modern France: the Case of Henri I de Montmorency', *EHQ,* 16 (1986), and J. Davies, 'The Duc de Montmorency, Philip II and the House of Savoy', *EHR,* 417 (1990), 'Neither Politique Nor Patriot? Henri duc de Montmorency and Philip II, 1582–89', *HJ,* 34 (1991), and 'The Politics of the Marriage Bed: Matrimony and the Montmorency Family, 1527–1612', *FH,* 6 (1992), pp. 63–93.

## On Politics and Religion in the Initial Stages of the Conflict

See N. M. Sutherland, 'Queen Elizabeth and the Conspiracy of Amboise', *EHR,* 81 (1966), pp. 474–89, and her *Princes, Politics and Religion,* pp. 97–112; B. C. Weber, 'The Council of Fontainebleau (1560)', *ARG,* 45 (1954); J. G. Gray, 'The Origin of the Word "Huguenot" ' *SCJ,* 14 (1983); N. M. Sutherland, 'The Cardinal of Lorraine and the Colloquy of Poissy', *J.Eccl.Hist.* (1977); D. Nugent, *Ecumenism in the Age of the Reformation: The Colloquy of Poissy* (Cambridge, Mass.: Harvard, 1974); A. E. Shaw, *Michel de L'Hopital and His Policy* (Oxford, 1905); A. C. Keller, 'Michel de l'Hospital and the Edict of Toleration of 1562', *BHR,* 14 (1952), pp. 301–10; S. Neely, 'Michel de L'Hospital and the *Traité sur la Réformation de la Justice*: a Case of Misattribution', *FHS,* 14 (1986) pp. 339–66; S. -H. Kim, 'Michel de l'Hopital Revisited', *PWSFH,* 17 (1990), pp. 106–12, 'The Chancellor's Crusade: Michel de l'Hôpital and the Parlement of Paris', *FH,* 7 (1993), pp. 1–29, 'Dieu nous garde de la messe du chancelier: the Religious Belief and Political Opinions of Michel de L'Hopital', *SCJ,* 24, III (1993); P. van Dyke, 'The Estates of Pontoise' *EHR,* 27 (1913); N. M. Sutherland, 'The Assassination of François Duc de Guise', *HJ,* (1981) and in her *Princes, Politics and Religion,* pp.139–56.

## The Role of the Parlements

There is now an overview in the form of N. L. Roelker, *One King, One Faith: The Parlement of Paris and the Religious Reformations of the Sixteenth Century* (Berkeley: California University Press, 1996), but see also C. Stocker, 'The Parlement of Paris and Confessional Politics in the 1560s', *PWSFH*, 15 (1987), pp. 38–47; L. L. Taber, 'Religious Dissent within the Parlement of Paris in the Mid-16th century: a Reassessment', *FHS*, 16 (1990), pp. 684–99; F. J. Baumgartner, 'Party Alignment in the Parlement of Paris, 1589–94', *PWSFH*, I6 (1978), pp. 34–43.

The literature on the *Lit de justice* is now extensive. S. Hanley, *The* Lit de Justice *of the Kings of France* (Princeton University Press, 1983), is a provocative thesis now corrected by E. A. R. Brown and R. Famiglietti, *The* Lit de Justice: *Semantics, Ceremonial and the Parlement of Paris, 1300–1600* (Sigmaringen: Thorbecke, 1994) and the critical review of Hanley's thesis in M. P. Holt, 'The King in Parlement: the Problem of the *lit de justice* in Sixteenth-Century France', *HJ*, 31 (1988), pp. 507–23. On the Parlements and Gallicanism, see J. Powis, 'Gallican Liberties and the Politics of Later Sixteenth-Century France', *HJ* (1983) pp. 515–30.

## The Image of Kingship and Politics in the 1570s and 1580s

See J. R. Smither, 'The Saint Bartholomew's Day Massacre and Images of Kingship in France, 1572–74', *SCJ*, 22 (1991); A. Lynn Martin, *Henry III and the Jesuit Politicians* (Geneva: Droz, 1973); K. Cameron, *Henri III: Maligned or Malignant King?* (Exeter University Press, 1978); N. M. Sutherland, 'Henri III, the Guises and the Huguenots' in K. Cameron (ed.), *From Valois to Bourbon* (Exeter University Press, 1989); D. A. Bell, 'Unmasking a King: the Political Uses of Popular Literature under the Catholic League, 1588–89', *SCJ*, 20 (1989), pp. 371–86; D. Potter, 'Kingship in the Wars of Religion: the Reputation of Henri III of France', *EHQ*, 25 (1995), pp. 485–528. On the course of the wars in the period, see M. Greengrass, 'Dissension in the Provinces under Henri III, 1574–85' in J. Highfield and R. Jeffs (eds), *The Crown and Local Communities* (Gloucester: Sutton, 1981), pp. 162–82.

## The Reign of Henry IV

The most accessible recent work is M. Greengrass, *France in the Age of Henri IV* (London: Longman, rev. edn., 1995), which concentrates on the King's compromises with the great interest groups. D. Buisseret, *Henri IV* (London: Unwin, 1984) is a narrative which tends to concentrate on the military history of the period but his *Sully and the Growth of Centralised Government in France* (London: Eyre & Spottiswoode, 1968) is essential reading on the King's minister. In financial matters, it can be checked by R. Bonney, *The King's Debts* (Oxford: Oxford University Press, 1981). On the sources, see E. H. Dickerman, 'Man and Myth in Sully's Economies Royales', *FHS*, VII, 3 (1972). Sully's rival is studied in

R. F. Kierstead, *Pomponne de Bellièvre* (Evanston, Ill.: Northwestern University Press, 1968) and E. H. Dickerman, *Bellièvre and Villeroy: Power in France under Henri III and Henri IV* (Providence, RI: Brown University Press, 1971); see also J. Russell Major, 'Bellièvre, Sully and the Assembly of Notables of 1596', *TAPS*, 64:2 (1974), pp. 1–34. R. Mousnier, *The Assassination of Henri IV* (London: Faber, 1973) is more than a study of tyrannicide; rather it is a survey of the general instability of Henri IV's religious settlement. The King's conversion is studied in depth by M. Wolfe, *The Conversion of Henri IV: Politics, Power and Religious Belief in Early Modern France* (Cambridge, Mass.: Harvard, 1993). K. Cameron (ed.), *From Valois to Bourbon* has some useful articles on the period, including D. Crouzet, 'Henri IV, King of Reason?' and M. Greengrass, 'The Public Context of the Abjuration of Henri IV'. On the Edict of Nantes, see F. Baumgartner, 'The Catholic Opposition to the Edict of Nantes', *BHR*, 40:III (1978); D. C. Margolf, 'The Edict of Nantes' Amnesty: Appeals to the *Chambre de l'édit*, 1600–1610', *PWSFH*, 16 (1989), pp. 49–55. On the provinces in the 1590s, see M. Greengrass, 'The Later Wars of Religion in the French Midi' in P. Clark (ed.), *The European Crisis of the 1590s* (London: Unwin, 1985) and L. Simpson, 'The Struggle for Provence, 1593–99: A Sidelight on the Internal Policy of Henry IV', *University of California Publications in History*, 17 (1942), pp. 1–23; S. Kettering, 'Political Parties at Aix en Provence in 1589', *EHQ*, 24:II (1994).

## Government and the Court Centre and Province

On the royal secretariat, see N. M. Sutherland, *The French Secretaries of State in the Age of Catherine de Medici* (London: Athlone, 1962). For the court in the period, see R. J. Knecht, 'The Court of France, 1550–1650', *SFS*, 10 (1988); D. Potter and P. Roberts, 'An Englishman's View of the Court of Henri III', *FH*, 2 (1988), pp. 312–44. On the provincial Estates in the period, see J. R. Major, *Representative Government in Early Modern France* (New Haven, Conn.: Yale University Press, 1980), *The Monarchy, Estates and the Aristocracy in Renaissance France* (London: Variorum, 1988), and his *From Renaissance Monarchy to Absolute Monarchy: French Kings, Nobles and Estates* (Baltimore: Johns Hopkins University Press, 1994)

## The Reformation

For a general introduction see M. Greengrass, *The French Reformation* (Oxford: Blackwell, 1987). On the historiography, H. Hauser, 'The French Reformation and the French People in the Sixteenth Century', *Am.HR* (1899) pp. 217–27, is a convenient statement of his classic argument that religious choice was shaped by social movements. L. Febvre, 'The French Reformation: a Badly Put Question' in P. Burke (ed.), *A New Kind of History* (London: Routledge & Kegan Paul, 1973) is an important point of departure for the study of both Protestantism and Catholicism in a period of renewal. H. Heller, *The Conquest of Poverty: The Calvinist Revolt in Sixteenth-Century France* (Leiden: Brill, 1986) and *Iron and Blood: Civil Wars in Sixteenth-Century France* (Montreal: McGill-Queen's University Press, 1991), esp. chs. 1 and 2, are both studies of the subject from a class-conflict perspective. On religious choices, see J. H. Salmon, 'Religion and Economic Motivation: Some Insights into an Old Controversy', *JRH*, 2:iii (1963); R. M. Kingdon, 'Problems of Religious Choice for Sixteenth-Century Frenchmen', *JRH*, 4 (1966).

## The Structure of the Church

See R. J. Knecht, 'The Concordat of 1516: A Reassessment', in H. Cohn (ed.), *Government in Reformation Europe* (London: Macmillan, 1971). The hierarchy is covered in M. M. Edelstein, 'The Social Origins of the Episcopacy in the Reign of Francis I', *FHS*, 8 (1973–4); F. J. Baumgartner, *Change and Continuity in the French Episcopate: The Bishops and the Wars of Religion, 1547–1610* (Durham, NC: Duke University Press, 1988) and 'Henri II's Italian Bishops: a Study in the Use and Abuse of the Concordat of Bologna', *SCJ*, 11 (1980), pp. 49–58.

## The Social Dimension of Religious Change

N. Z. Davis, 'The Rites of Violence', 'Strikes and Salvation at Lyon' and other essays in *Society and Culture in Early Modern France* (London: Duckworth, 1975) cover the interplay of social and cultural influences in religious allegiance. See also N. L. Roelker, 'The Appeal of Calvinism to French Noblewomen in the Sixteenth Century', *JIH*, 2 (1972), 'The Role of Noblewomen in the French Reformation', *ARG*, 6 (1972); D. Potter, 'Marriage and Cruelty among the Protestant Nobility in Sixteenth-Century France', *EHQ*, 20 (1990); D. Nicholls, 'The Social History of the French Reformation', *Social History*, 9:1 (1984); E. Le Roy Ladurie, *The Peasants of Languedoc* (Urbana, Ill.: Illinois University Press, 1977), part 2; M. S. Lamet, 'French Protestants in a Position of Strength: the Early Years of the Reformation at Caen, 1558–68', *SCJ*, 9 (1978); J. R. Farr, 'Popular Religious Solidarity in Sixteenth-Century Dijon', *FHS*, 14 (1985).

## The Revival of Traditional Piety

B. Diefendorf, *Beneath the Cross: Catholics and Huguenots in Sixteenth-Century Paris* (Oxford, 1991); A. N. Galpern, *The Religions of the People in Sixteenth-Century Champagne* (Cambridge, Mass.: Harvard University Press, 1976); D. Nicholls, 'Inertia and Reform in the pre-Tridentine French Church: Rouen, 1520–62',

*J.Eccl.Hist.*, 32 (1981); R. Harding, 'The Mobilization of the Confraternities against the Reformation in France', *SCJ*, 11:II (1980); R. A. Schneider, *Public Life in Toulouse, 1463–1789* (Ithaca, NY: Cornell University Press, 1989), pt. 3; A. Lynne Martin, *The Jesuit Mind: The Mentality of an Elite in Early Modern France* (Ithaca, NY: Cornell University Press, 1988).

## Religious and Communal Violence

See several useful essays in N. Z. Davis, *Society and Culture in Early Modern France*; P. Benedict, *Rouen during the Wars of Religion* (Cambridge: Cambridge University Press, 1981); P. Roberts, *A City in Conflict: Troyes during the Wars of Religion* (Manchester University Press, 1996); P. Roberts, 'Religious Conflict in an Urban Setting: Troyes during the French Wars of Religion', *FH*, 6:III (1992); J. Davies, 'Persecution and Protestantism: Toulouse, 1562–75', *HJ*, 22 (1979); M. Greengrass, 'The Anatomy of a Religious Riot in Toulouse in May 1562', *J.Eccl.Hist*, 34 (1983). On Paris, above all see B. Diefendorf, 'Prologue to a Massacre: Popular Unrest in Paris, 1557–72', *Am.HR*, 90 (1985) pp. 1067–91, and her *Beneath the Cross: Catholics and Huguenots in Sixteenth-Century Paris* (Oxford, 1991). See also R. Descimon, 'Paris on the Eve of Saint Bartholomew', in P. Benedict (ed.), *Cities and Social Change in Early Modern France* (London: Unwin, 1983). For the diplomatic background and historiography, see N. M. Sutherland, *The Massacre of Saint-Bartholomew* (especially the chapter on sources) and for a review of it: G. Griffiths, 'Saint Bartholomew Reappraised', *JMH* (1976) pp. 499–500; R. M. Kingdon, *Myths about the Saint Bartholomew's Day Massacre* (Cambridge, Mass.: Harvard University Press, 1988); A. Soman (ed.), *The Massacre of Saint Bartholomew* (The Hague: Nijhoff, 1974); P. Benedict, 'The Saint Bartholomew's Massacre in the Provinces', *HJ*, 21 (1978). [The Massacre of Bartholomew is the subject of a major current debate between the French historians D. Crouzet (*La nuit de la Saint-Barthélemy*) and J. Bourgeon (*L'assassinat de Coligny*). For a review see M. Greengrass, 'The Psychology of Religious Violence' (review of D. Crouzet's *Les guerriers de Dieu*) in *FH*, 5 (1991), pp. 467–74.] For other areas: M. Konnert, 'A Tolerant City Council? Châlons-sur-Marne during the Wars of Religion', *PWSFH*, 16 (1989), pp. 40–7; E. Le Roy Ladurie, *Carnival: A People's Uprising at Romans, 1579–80* (London: Scholar, 1986). On peasant revolts see J. H. Salmon, 'Peasant Revolt in the Vivarais, 1575–80', *FHS*, 11 (1979).

## Calvinism

R. M. Kingdon, *Geneva and the Coming of the Wars of Religion in France* (Geneva: Droz, 1956) deals with the role of Calvinist pastors sent out from Geneva in the 1550s and this theme is continued in his *Geneva and the Consolidation of the French*

*Protestant Movement* (Geneva: Droz, 1967). On the early self-perception of Calvinists, see C. H. Parker, 'French Calvinists as the Children of Israel', *SCJ*, 24:II (1993); H. Koenigsberger, 'The Organization of Revolutionary Parties in France and the Netherlands during the Sixteenth century', *JMH*, 27 (1955); M. Prestwich, 'Calvinism in France, 1555–1629', in M. Prestwich (ed.), *International Calvinism* (Oxford: Clarendon, 1985). For regional examples see P. Roberts, 'Calvinists in Troyes, 1562–72: the Legacy of Vassy and the Background to Saint Bartholomew', and M. Greengrass, 'The Calvinist Experiment in Bearn', both in A. Pettegree, A. Duke and C. Lewis (eds), *Calvinism in Europe, 1540–1620* (Cambridge University Press, 1994); J. P. Meyer, 'La Rochelle and the Failure of the French Reformation', *SCJ*, 15 (1984); G. S. Sunshine, 'French Protestantism on the Eve of Saint Bartholomew', *FH*, 4:III (1990); C. Stocker, 'The Calvinist *Officiers* of Orléans, 1560–72', *PWSFH*, 6 (1979); A. H. Guggenheim, 'The Calvinist Notables of Nîmes during the Era of the Religious Wars', *SCJ*, 3 (1972).

## Catholicism and the League

See A. N. Galpern, *The Religions of the People in Sixteenth-Century Champagne*; M. P. Holt, 'Wine, Community and Reformation in Sixteenth-Century Burgundy', *P&P*, 138 (1993); C. W. Stocker, 'Orléans and the Catholic League', *PWSFH*, 16 (1989), pp. 12–21; A. Ramsey, 'Towards a Definition of League Piety and its Relationship to Seventeenth-Century Catholic Reform in Paris', *PWSFH*, 16 (1989), pp. 23–36; M. Wilkinson, *A History of the League or Saint Union, 1576–1595* (Glasgow: Jackson, Wylie, 1929); M. Greengrass, 'The *Sainte Union* in the Provinces', *SCJ*, 14 (1983); J. Bossy, 'Leagues and Associations in Sixteenth-Century French Catholicism', *Studies in Church History* (1986); S. Carroll, 'The Guise Affinity and Popular Protest during the Wars of Religion', *FH*, 9 (1995); N. Le Roux, 'The Catholic Nobility and Political Choice during the League, 1584–94', *FH*, 8 (1994) pp. 34–50. On the social context, see D. Richet, 'The Socio Cultural Aspects of Religious Conflicts in Paris during the Second Half of the Sixteenth Century', in R. Forster and O. Ranum (eds), *Ritual, Religion and the Sacred: Selection from Annales* (Baltimore, 1982). See also B. Diefendorf, 'The Catholic League: Social Crisis or Apocalypse Now?' (review article) *FHS*, 15:II (1987), pp. 332–44. On the 'Sixteen' specifically, see J. H. Salmon, 'The Paris Sixteen, 1584–1594: the Social Analysis of a Revolutionary Movement', *JMH*, 44 (1972), pp. 540–76, and in his *Renaissance and Revolt* (Cambridge: Cambridge University Press, 1987); M. Greengrass, 'The Sixteen: Radical Politics during the League', *History*, 69 (1984), pp. 432–9. On Spanish connections, see De Lamar Jensen, *Diplomacy and Dogmatism: Bernardino de Mendoza and the French Catholic League* (Cambridge, Mass.: Harvard University Press, 1964).

## Noble Status and Clientage

See R. Harding, *Anatomy of a Power Elite: The Provincial Governors of Early Modern France* (New Haven, Conn.: Yale University Press, 1978); J. Dewald, *Aristocratic Experience and the Origins of Modern Culture: France, 1570–1715*, 9 (1993); D. Potter, *France, 1460–1560*, Ch. 6; D. Bitton, *The French Nobility in Crisis* (Stanford University Press, 1986), E. Schalk, *From Valor to Pedigree* (Princeton University Press, 1986); E. Schalk, 'The Appearance and Reality of Nobility in France during the Wars of Religion. An Example of How Collective Attitudes can Change', *JMH*, 48:I (1976), pp. 19–31; E. Schalk, 'Ennoblement in France from 1350 to 1660', *Journal of Social History*, 16 (1982).

On Clientage: see M. P. Holt, 'Patterns of Clientele and Economic Opportunities at Court during the Wars of Religion: the Household of François Duke of Anjou', *FHS*, 13:III (1984); M. P. Holt, 'Attitudes of the French Nobility at the Estates-general of 1576', *SCJ*, (1987); J. Russell Major, 'Bastard Feudalism and the Kiss: Changing Social Mores in Late Medieval and Early Modern France', *JIH*, 17 (1987), pp. 509–37 and in his *Monarchy, Estates and Aristocracy* (London: Variorum, 1988); K. B. Neuschel, *Word of Honor: Interpreting Noble Culture in Sixteenth-Century France* (Ithaca, New York: Cornell University Press, 1989); S. Kettering: 'Clientage during the Wars of Religion', *SCJ*, 20 (1989), pp. 221–39, 'Patronage and Kinship in Early Modern France', *FHS*, 16 (1989), pp. 408–35, 'Friendship and Clientage in Early Modern France', *FH*, 6:II (1992), 'Patronage in Early Modem France', *FHS*, 17 (1992); M. Greengrass, 'Noble Affinities in Early Modern France: the Case of Henri de Montmorency', *EHQ*, 18 (1986); S. A. Eurich, 'The Economy of Patronage: The Household and Entourage of Henri de Navarre (1572–87)', *PWSFH*, 14 (1987); M. Konnert, 'Provincial Governors and their Regimes during the French Wars of Religion: the Duc de Guise and the City Council of Chalons-sur-Marne', *SCJ*, 24:IV (1994).

Noblewomen: N. L. Roelker, *Queen of Navarre: Jeanne d'Albret, 1528–70* (1968); S. Eurich, 'Women, Brokerage and Aristocratic Service: the Case of Marguerite de Selve', *PWSFH*, 15 (1988); S. Kettering, 'The Patronage Power of Early Modern French Noblewomen', *HJ*,1 (1989); S. Hanley, 'Engendering the State: Family Formation and State Building in Early Modern France', *FHS*, 16 (1989); J. Munns and P. Richards, 'Exploiting and Destabilising Gender Roles: Anne d'Este', *FH*, 6:II (1992); R. J. Kalas, 'The Noble Widow's Place in the Patriarchal Household: the Life and Career of Jeanne de Gontaut', *SCJ*, 24:III (1993).

On the lesser nobility: See G. Huppert, *Les bourgeois gentilshommes* (Chicago University Press, 1977); on Gouberville, see K. Fedden, *Manor Life in Old France from the Journals of the Sire de Gouberville* (New York: Columbia University Press,

1933) and E. S. Teall, 'The Myth of Royal Centralisation and the Reality of the Neighbourhood: the Journals of the Sire de Gouberville, 1549–6', in M. U. Chrisman and O. Grundler (eds), *Social Groups and Religious Ideas in the 16th Century* (Kalamazoo, 1978). On the nobility of Normandy: see J. B. Wood, *The Nobility of the Election of Bayeux* (Princeton University Press, 1980); J. Dewald, *The Formation of a Provincial Nobility* (Princeton University Press, 1980); and on another area R. J. Kalas, 'The Selve Family of Limousin: Members of a New Elite in Early Modern France', *SCJ*, 18 (1987), pp. 147–72.

**On the greater nobility:** see R. A. Jackson, 'The Peers of France and Princes of the Blood', *FHS*, 7 (1971), pp. 27–46; R. Harding, *Anatomy of a Power Elite*; D. Potter, *War and Government in the French Provinces: Picardy, 1470–1560* (Cambridge University Press, 1993), Chs 2–4, and 'The Luxembourg Inheritance: the House of Bourbon and its Lands in Northern France during the Sixteenth Century', *FH*, 6 (March 1992); J. Russell Major, 'Noble Income, Inflation and the Wars of Religion in France', *Am.HR*, 86 (1981), and 'The Crown and Aristocracy in Renaissance France', *Am.HR*, (1964); M. Greengrass, 'Property and Politics in Sixteenth-Century France the Landed Fortune of Constable Anne de Montmorency', *FH*, 2 (1988).

**On noble ways of life:** see K. Fedden, *Manor Life in Old France* (on Gouberville); K. Neuschel, 'Noble Households in the Sixteenth Century: Material Settings and Human Communitie', *FHS*, 5 (1988), pp. 595–622; F. Billacois, *The Duel: Its Rise in Early Modern France* (trans., 1990)

## Political Thought

J. W. Allen, *A History of Political Thought in the 16th Century* (London: Methuen, 1928); W. F. Church, *Constitutional Thought in 16th Century France* (Cambridge, Mass.: Harvard University Press, 1941); N. O. Keohane, *Philosophy and the State in France* (Princeton University Press, 1980); B. Reynolds, *Proponents of Limited Monarchy in Sixteenth-Century France: Francis Hotman and Jean Bodin* (New York: Columbia University Press, 1931). D. R. Kelley, *François Hotman: A Revolutionary's Ordeal* (Princeton University Press, 1973) updates much of this and is supplemented by his *The Beginnings of Ideology: Consciousness and Society in the French Reformation*, (Cambridge University Press, 1981), useful for the early stages of the Wars. On *Ligueur* thought, see F. Baumgartner, *Radical Reactionaries: The Political Thought of the French Catholic League* (Geneva: Droz, 1976). J. H. Salmon, *Renaissance and Revolt: Essays in the Intellectual and Social History of Early Modern France* (Cambridge University Press, 1987), is a collection of his essays, many of which deal with political and social thought in this period. See also R. A. Jackson, 'Elective Kingship and *Consensus populi* in Sixteenth-Century France', *JMH*,

(1972); R. Bonney, 'Bodin and the Development of the French Monarchy', *TRHS*, 40 (1990); H. A. Lloyd, 'Constitutional Thought in Sixteenth-Century France: the Case of Pierre Rebuffi', *FH*, 8:III (1994). On one of the leading figures of historical writing in the period, see D. Thickett, *Estienne Pasquier: The Versatile Barrister of Sixteenth-Century France (1529–1615)* (London: Regency, 1979) and on historical scholarship in general, G. Huppert, *The Idea of Perfect History* (Urbana: Illinois University Press, 1970) and D. R. Kelley, *The Foundations of Modern Historical Scholarship* (New York: Columbia University Press, 1970).

# Index

Bold numbers indicate a major reference to the subject or a document emanating from the person. Sovereigns are listed by christian name, nobles by their main fiefs, seigneuries or titles, cross-referenced to avoid confusion. Only smaller places have been given regional locations (by ancient provinces and modern *départements*).

**Abbreviations:**

| | |
|---|---|
| AF | Admiral of France |
| b. | baron |
| bp. | bishop |
| c. | count (comte) |
| CF | Chancellor of France |
| CG | *Colonel-général de l'infanterie française* |
| *d.* | died |
| d. | duke (duc) |
| G. | Governor (of province) |
| KS | Keeper of the Seals (garde des sceaux) |
| *k.* | killed |
| LG | Lieutenant General (deputy governor of province) |
| m. | marquess (*marquis*) |
| MF | Marshal of France |
| sr. | seigneur/ sieur/ sire |
| v. | viscount (*vicomte*) |

263